Advance praise for

Tejano and Regional Mexican Music

A valuable and culturally important educational guide to one of the most influential regional music forms of Latin America. At a time when the whole world seems to be discovering and rediscovering the exciting Latin music forms, this guide to Tejano and regional Mexican music comes not a minute too soon.

—MICHAEL GREENE, President, National Academy of Recording Arts and Sciences, presenters of the Grammy Awards

Finally a guide to Mexican American music—one of America's long neglected (and to Anglos, largely unknown), yet delightfully rhythmic, emotional, powerful, poetic, narrative, and danceable musical genres.

—CHRIS STRACHWITZ, owner of Arhoolie Records and producer of the Tex-Mex music documentary *Chulas Fronteras*

An important and essential guide to a largely underappreciated music. Ramiro Burr has explained, anthologized, and compiled an authoritative and entertaining guide.

—GARY GRAFF, award-winning music journalist and editor of *Musichound Rock: The Essential Album Guide*

Written in elegant, no-frills prose [that is] easily accessible to the lay reader.

—MANUEL H. PEÑA, author of *The Texas-Mexican Conjunto: History of a Working-Class Music*

An in-depth, accurate, and sometimes controversial journey into what is Tejano music.

—GILBERT VELÁSQUEZ, record producer and Latin Breed guitarist

If you love Tex-Mex music and roots music, this book is extremely informative. And it's a must for all musicians and music lovers as well.

—CÉSAR ROSAS, guitarist for Grammy-winning groups Los Lobos and Los Super Seven

A wonderful resource [for] lay persons, specialists in the field, and music lovers in general.

—GUADALUPE SAN MIGUEL, history professor, University of Houston

The first important book of Tejano and Mexican music history. It's a good read and very well documented.

—GILBERTO PUENTE, requinto player of the trío Los Tres Reyes

Discloses the musical aspect of our Hispanic culture by providing biographies of regional Mexican as well as Tejano artists and [describes] how they have kept this important part of our culture alive.

—MARGARITA, EMI Latin recording artist

By placing a dynamic and unruly musical legacy in its concise historical context, Ramiro Burr has created an American treasury that is instantly indispensable.

—CAMERON RANDLE, Senior Vice President, A&R/Latin, Hollywood Records

Provocative and insightful... A must-read for anyone interested or involved in the music industry.

—JERRE HALL, Executive Vice President, Barb Wire Productions

Indispensable for anyone who wants to learn [about] and understand Latin culture in the United States.

—FERNANDO GONZÁLEZ, Arts Writer, *Miami Herald*

The most comprehensive book of this genre ever written.

—JOSÉ BEHAR, President/CEO, EMI Latin

This book will help ensure that no one [will] again be surprised by a phenomenon such as Selena.

—OSCAR GARZA, Daily Calendar Editor, *Los Angeles Times*

THE BILLBOARD GUIDE TO

Tejano and Regional Mexican Music

RAMIRO BURR

BILLBOARD BOOKS

An imprint of Watson-Guptill Publications
New York

Senior Editor: Bob Nirkind
Associate Editor: Alison Hagge
Production Manager: Hector Campbell
Cover and interior design: Farenga Design Group

First published in 1999 by Billboard Books
an imprint of Watson-Guptill Publications
a division of BPI Communications, Inc.
1515 Broadway, New York, NY 10036

Library of Congress Cataloging-in-Publication Data
Burr, Ramiro.
The Billboard guide to Tejano and regional Mexican music / Ramiro Burr.
p. cm.
Includes discographies and index.
ISBN 0-8230-7691-1
1. Tejano music—United States—Bio-bibliography—Dictionaries.
2. Popular music—United States—Bio-bibliography—Dictionaries.
3. Mexican Americans—Music—Bio-bibliography—Dictionaries.
I. Title.
ML102.T45B87 1999
781.64'089'68720764—dc21 98-51910
CIP
MN

Manufactured in the United States of America
First printing, 1999
2 3 4 5 6 7 8 9 / 07 06 05 04 03 02 01 00 99

Table of Contents

Acknowledgements

As a newspaper reporter, freelance music journalist, and syndicated columnist, I've had the privilege of working through the years with some of the best editors any writer could ask for. While all have been supportive and thorough professionals, there were a few individuals who went beyond the reporter-editor relationship and provided direction and inspiration to help me become a better reporter and a more insightful writer. For that I would like to thank John Lannert and Marilyn Gillen at *Billboard;* Melissa Aguilar and Rebecca MacInnis at the *Houston Chronicle;* David Okamoto at the *Dallas Morning News;* Louis Black at the *Austin Chronicle;* Simon Broughton at the *Rough Guides;* and Larry Birnbaum at *Rhythm Music.*

I am also indebted to Jim Kiest, Robert Johnson, and Kristina Paledes at the *San Antonio Express-News;* Cristina del Sesto at Amazon.com; Rudy Treviño, my producer at the *Tejano Gold* syndicated radio show; Lilliam Rivera at *Latina;* Antonio Mejias-Renta at *La Opinión;* and Hector Cantú at *Hispanic Business.*

For their constant and tireless support, encouragement, and indispensable advice, a big thank you to my colleagues at the *Express-News:* editors Carmina Danini and Dee Dee Fuentes, and Robert Rivard, Executive Editor.

A very special personal gratitude and big hug goes out to Jewels Rio, my loyal companion who, through thick and thin, stood by me and provided a sounding board, a sympathetic ear, and endless assistance and support.

To those music writers and critics whose work has guided and inspired me: first and foremost, the writer-philosopher Marty Racine of the *Houston Chronicle;* Mary Campbell of the Associated Press; Jon Pareles of the *New York Times;* Gary Graff of the *Detroit Free Press;* Thor Christensen of the *Dallas Morning News;* Robert Hilburn of the *Los Angeles Times;* Robert Christgau of the *Village Voice;* Cary Darling of the *Orange County Register*; and Rene Cabrera of the *Corpus Christi Caller-Times.*

A book of this magnitude would have been impossible without dozens of veteran industry men and women who enthusiastically shared their encyclopedic knowledge of music and musical history. These include Manolo González at EMI

Latin; Chris Strachwitz at Arhoolie; "Bird" Rodríguez and Lee Woods at KRIO/KLEY-FM; Emilio Garza, Margo Morones's veteran band manager, at Ramex; Rene Cabrera at the *Corpus Christi Caller-Times;* Rubén Cubillos of the Big Chihuahua; Gilbert Velasquez at Velasquez Studios; Janie Esparza at Janie's Record Shop; Ramon Hernández, founder of Hispanic Entertainment Archives; Guadalupe San Miguel and Tatcho Mendiola in the History Department at the University of Houston; José Macias and Pilar Oates at the University of Texas, San Antonio; history professor Armando Hinojosa at the University of the Incarnate Word; mariachi instructor Dahlia Guerra at the University of Texas at Pan American; mariachi historian Jonathan Clark at San Jose State University; Juan Tejeda of the Guadalupe Cultural Arts Center; Sam Zuñiga at the Tejano Music Awards; concert promoter Raúl Resendez; and CARA Records founder Bob Grever.

For the hundreds of biographical documents, photographs, and other material, I would like to thank the publicity and promotion departments at Arhoolie, EMI Latin, Sony Discos, PolyGram Latino, BMG/U.S. Latin, WEA Latina, Arista/Texas, Tejas, Sound Mex, Ramex, Freddie, Hacienda, and Joey International; SERCA Promotions and the Apodaca agency. And while everyone was cooperative, a few individuals went out of their way to help, including Jesse Rodríguez at Voltage Discos, Rafael Montiel at DISA in Mexico City, and José Rosario at Sony Discos in Los Angeles. In Austin, major gratitude for the courtesy and assistance from Casey Monahan and Deb Freeman of the Texas Music Office; Carlyn Majer of the Texas chapter of the National Academy of Recording Arts and Sciences; and Roland Swenson, Bret Grulke, Rob Peterson, and Jeff McCord at SXSW.

Special thanks to Margo Guzmán of the San Antonio Public Library and Carmen Magallon of the Asociación Nacional de Actores (ANSA) in Mexico City.

At Billboard Books, my endless gratitude to Senior Editor Bob Nirkind for his guidance and especially Associate Editor Alison Hagge, whose sharp eyes and critical mind kept this music book in focus and on track.

I also want to thank a super crew of loyal, dedicated, and tireless interns, transcribers, researchers, and editorial assistants: Lucy Cavazos, Alex García, Michelle Ozuna, and Monica Guerra from the University of Incarnate Word; Jo Anne Reyes, Terry Alfaro, and Erica Rodríguez from the University of Texas, San Antonio; Marie Ortiz, Angie Andrade, and Manuel Carranza from St. Mary's University; Sophie Reynoso from Texas Lutheran College; Roxanne Arandas and Courtney Davila from Our Lady of the Lake University; Steven Lam from Trinity University; and Doug Shannon from Central Missouri State University.

Introduction

From Carlos Gardel's elegant tangos and Perez Prado's whirling mambos to Carlos Santana's searing Latin-rock fusion and Grammy-winner Flaco Jiménez's cool, percolating accordion rhythms, Latin music has always embraced and influenced American music.

Consider for a minute the music of Tito Puente, Mario Bauza, Stan Kenton, Ritchie Valens, Sam the Sham, Freddy Fender, Miami Sound Machine, Julio Iglesias, Linda Ronstadt, Los Lobos, Poncho Sánchez, the Texas Tornados, Rick Trevino, and Selena.

The world of Latin music includes a wide variety of genres—from the vibrant energy of rock, dance, and reggae, which are covered under the term "Latin pop," to the rhythms of merengue, *son, bachata,* and other Afro-Caribbean grooves, which are covered by the general term "tropical/salsa." The purpose of this book is to introduce, explain, and contextualize one third of that music—the rich heritage of Mexican music within the United States. Generally, the many substyles of Mexican music are categorized by the mainstream media in the U.S. as "regional Mexican."

In the early '90s Tejano music basked in the media spotlight and enjoyed unprecedented growth and record revenues. Driven by young heroes and inspired by new exciting music, Tejano took off as one of the fastest growing subgenres in American music. The songs climbed radio charts and packed modern nightclubs with fresh-faced, young audiences. Tejano, however, is only a slice of the regional Mexican field, a catch-all term used by mainstream publications such as *Billboard* in its national charts to refer to a wide variety of Mexican American music styles. *The Billboard Guide to Tejano and Regional Mexican Music* focuses on nine distinct subgenres within the regional Mexican field: Tejano, norteño, conjunto, grupo, mariachi, trio, tropical/cumbia, vallenato, and banda.

This book is divided into five major sections: a history of Tejano/conjunto music; the cultural impact of Tejano's rapid rise in the 1990s; an extensive A–Z encyclopedia; a chronology of regional Mexican music events in the nineteenth and twentieth centuries; a glossary of music terms; and, finally, my personal lists of the Top 10 albums and songs from the five most extensive genres: Tejano, norteño, conjunto, mariachi/ranchera, and trio.

The A–Z entries—nearly 300 in all—provide brief biographical summaries of the artists and groups as well as analyses and/or descriptions of their musical specialties, sounds, or contributions in the larger context. The encyclopedia section also includes essays with detailed definitions and historical backgrounds of the nine distinct musical subgenres.

SCOPE AND CONTENT

There are more than 1,800 bands and artists that play Latino or Spanish-language music in the United States and Mexico. We can readily divide those bands into the three main categories long identified by *Billboard* and the Grammy folks: Latin pop, tropical/salsa, and regional Mexican. Of the roughly 600 bands that potentially fall within the regional Mexican field, we narrowed down the list to approximately 300 groups.

The driving forces that determined the length of a band's entry were impact and influence. So whether an artist had a three-year or a thirty-year career mattered little compared to how his or her music impacted or influenced others. Of course, the level of critical or commercial success—measured in terms of chart singles, best-selling records, and/or awards—also came into play, but these factors were secondary to impact and influence. These latter two criteria were gauged by how many other artists cited the group or tried to emulate its sound and style.

In some cases we consolidated individual artists who had solo careers into their original groups—Joe Martínez into the Hometown Boys and Gavino into La Sombra, for example. However, individuals who had significant solo careers before joining a group deserved their own entry—Marco Antonio Solis of Los Bukis and José Guadalupe Esparza of Bronco fall into this category. Individual musicians and musical groups that have their own entries are cross-referenced (with boldface type) the first time that they are mentioned in an entry to ensure that readers will be able to find all the appropriate information. Similarly, if a group had numerous names during the course of its existence, those names have been added as cross-references.

The overriding goal of this book was essentially to catalogue—for the first time in history—all of the important and critically successful bands in the numerous genres that fall within the regional Mexican field.

SOURCES AND INFORMATION

Only in the '90s did Latin music in the United States begin to gain even the most minimal of mainstream coverage. The successes of artists such as Tito Puente, Los Lobos, the Texas Tornados, Gloria Estefan, Little Joe, Julio Iglesias, and Selena, have helped drive that (albeit still relatively small) increase in press coverage. But therein lies part of the problem of trying to document this genre. Only those artists who have been successful in the American mainstream have enjoyed coverage. This means that even major groups, such as Bronco, Los Bukis, Trio Los Panchos, Los Temerarios, and Los Tucanes, have received little or no fanfare in the U.S.

Additionally, Latin music documentation in public libraries is almost nonexistent. The few notable exceptions include John Storm Roberts's insightful *The Latin Tinge: The Impact of Latin American Music on the United States* (originally published in 1979; reissued by Oxford University Press in 1998); the invaluable *Rough Guide to World Music* (Rough Guides, 1999); and Manuel Peña's *The Texas-Mexican Conjunto* (University of Texas, 1985).

As a result, most of the information in this book was gathered from my music files, material that I've collected over fourteen years on the hundreds of Latino groups touring the U.S. and Mexico. This material included books (precious few), daily newspaper accounts, music and celebrity magazines, and record label as well as fan club newsletters. Of course there were also the individual biographies and discographies provided by the record labels.

There were also the hundreds of interviews, features, and concert and CD reviews that I have conducted, written, and produced over those fourteen years.

Beyond my resources, though, I have also used the same vast network of music experts that I have relied on through the years as a newspaper reporter, freelance journalist, and syndicated columnist. These include, but are not limited to, ethnomusicologists, sociologists, historians, fellow journalists and critics, knowledgeable DJs, music collectors, and veteran record store owners—all of whom have helped to fill in the gaps where needed or help verify/confirm certain facts. A short list of those invaluable individuals appears on the acknowledgements page.

Music, of course, is part of the entertainment business and as such it is riddled with exaggerations, hype, and—in some cases—outright lies. Numerous artists listed Grammys or No. 1 *Billboard* chart positions in their biographies when, in fact, there were none. We only mentioned or listed such honors that we could independently verify. It is worth noting that in the music industry the Recording Industry Associations of America is the one trade association that certifies gold or platinum records (sales of more than 500,000 or one million respectively) in the United States. In the Latin music industry, however, gold is considered sales of more than 50,000, while platinum is sales of more than 100,000. Those designations in the Latin music world, though, are generally never independently certified. For those reasons, such sales designations are rarely mentioned in the entries.

In terms of organization, we arranged the A–Z entries in alphabetical order. But in Latin music, especially the regional Mexican field, groups sometimes have long names—such as David Lee Garza y Los Musicales or Aniceto Molina y La Luz Roja de San Marcos. So, in the case of Little Joe y La Familia, would the band be filed under "L" for Little, "J" for Joe, or "F" for Familia? Then there were dozens of bands whose names are preceded by "Grupo," "Banda," or "Trío."

To simplify the task, we used two basic rules: all bands were filed under the first letter of the band's name; individual artists were filed uder the artist's last name. There were exceptions, though, and in these instances we followed common usage already established in the industry. Grupo Límite was filed under "L" for Límite because that's how the band is generally filed in record stores and in catalogs. Grupo Vida, however, was filed under "G" for Grupo for the same reason. Generally, we followed the order established already by the catalogs of the record distributor Southwest Wholesale, the major record labels, and on-line web sites such as All Music Guide, Amazon.com, and Tower Records.

Capitalization of song and album titles was another problem. In Mexico, proper Spanish dictates that all titles have only the first word capitalized. However, because this book is being published in the United States, we opted to observe standard American English rules, even for the punctuation of Spanish titles.

DISCOGRAPHIES

The main goal of compiling selective discographies was to provide recommendations of what we considered to be the artists' best work and/or a good representation of it. However, because the Latin music industry's sales are small in comparison to the mainstream American market, Latin CD titles, even best-sellers, are frequently out of circulation, out of print, or have limited distribution.

Instead, the Latin music industry relies heavily on recompilations. In the cases of such venerable groups as Los Tigres and Ramón Ayala, the Southwest Wholesale 1998 catalog listed more than 100 titles for each. Almost one third of those titles were generic "greatest hits" collections.

The central consideration as to which CDs are listed in the discographies, however, was current availability. That is, we felt it was not useful to recommend a solid album if it was no longer in print. With that in mind, for artists who recorded for multiple labels, we often favored releases by major record labels over smaller indies. The majors tend to carry titles much longer, while the indies tend to release "new compilations"—essentially the same material in new packages, which explains the overabundance of such titles as *15 Éxitos...*, *16 Éxitos...*, *Grandes Éxitos...*, *Éxitos Calientes...*, and on and on. (*Éxitos* is Spanish for "hits.") We opted not to include dates in the discography section for several reasons.

The date that a compilation album was released does not reflect when the material was originally created. Likewise, non-compilation albums are often associated with their most recent release dates. Therefore, since the dates often do not add historical accuracy, and are, in fact, even misleading as to when material was originally created, we decided not to include dates in this section. Another point of confusion in the Latin music world is record labels. Given the frequency with which the record labels either changed names or distribution arrangements with smaller indies, the same album was oftentimes reissued under different label names (i.e., Little Joe's *25th Silver Anniversary* album was variously released under CBS, Tejano Discos, and EMI/U.S. Latin). For the discographies, we have listed the most current information.

We used the latest catalogs from all the Latin labels—from EMI Latin and Sony Discos, to WEA Latina, BMG/U.S. Latin, and FonoVisa. We also surveyed the catalogs of the smaller indies, including Joey International, Hacienda, Freddie, Arhoolie, and Tejas records.

We also used on-line databases to help determine the best available albums/CDs. These included Tower Records, All Music Guide, Amazon.com, Music Boulevard, CD Now, the Ultimate Band List, and CD Universe. In some ways, these on-line databases worked out the best, as they were fluid and continually updated.

FINAL NOTES

Because a project of this nature and magnitude is so dynamic, we face the challenge of constantly changing or updating information. That, in effect, makes *The Billboard Guide to Tejano and Regional Mexican Music* a work in progress.

With this in mind, we welcome any and all questions, comments, complaints, suggestions, updates, and/or corrections. Please send correspondences to: Ramiro Burr, *The Billboard Guide to Tejano and Regional Mexican Music*, P.O. Box 15747, San Antonio, TX 78212-8947.

The New Tejano Music Nation

Led by a new generation of heroes and fueled by a massive, youthful audience, Tejano music gained international attention in the early 1990s as one of the fastest-growing segments of Latin music in the United States.

At the zenith of its phenomenal rise, Tejano was as fresh and exciting as early '90s new country music and as street-relevant and youth-driven as alternative rock.

For five consecutive years, from 1990 to 1995, Tejano posted impressive sales records and concert attendance figures. The music swamped the charts, drove radio formats, and even earned its own Grammy category. By the mid-1990s it had received its fair share of considerable, if slightly belated, mainstream music press hyping its furious growth. At that point only a few astute industry insiders had realized, quietly, that the Tejano explosion had mushroomed to its maximum capacity. Soon the market, like a punctured hot air balloon, would naturally, inevitably, begin to deflate.

On the surface though, it was a bull market with fresh copycats and carpetbaggers, and Johnny-come-lately labels bottomfishing for talent.

It was against this "good times" backdrop that the shocking news of Selena's death on March 31, 1995 stunned the Tejano world. That Selena, who was one of the hottest stars of the burgeoning Tejano music scene had been shot by the ex-president of her own fan club was too incredible to believe. The news of Selena's death reached far beyond Tejano's base in the American Southwest. It received mainstream media coverage in Los Angeles, New York City, Miami—and even in Mexico City, where Tejano was rarely played.

This media blitz would have been impressive enough. But in reality it was the second wave of the media storm that had the most profound effect on American pop culture. In the weeks and months following Selena's death, the media continuously covered the unimaginable responses of millions of U.S. Latinos nationwide. This phenomenal response opened many eyes. While Latinos' political and economic power had been documented before in periodic census reports and business stories, Latinos were now flexing their collective muscles in new and impressive ways that surprised even veteran analysts.

Within weeks, a rushed biography of Selena sold more than 200,000 copies and made it to No. 1 on the *New York Times* nonfiction bestseller list. *People* magazine created its first split cover regular issue—half the country got Selena, half got *Friends.* The edition with Selena on the cover sold out its normal 133,000-issue run in Texas, as did an additional 143,000 run. Almost a month after Selena's death, *People* published an initial 600,000 copies of its commemorative tribute issue on Selena, which also sold out. A dozen Texas newspapers, and magazines like *Texas Monthly,* followed with special tributes with Selena on the cover—all of which sold out the day they hit newsstands.

In *Billboard*'s April 22 issue, Selena had five CDs on The Billboard 200 chart—an accomplishment previously only achieved by superstars like Garth Brooks, Elvis Presley, and the Beatles. Selena's posthumous crossover CD, *Dreaming of You,* debuted at No. 1 on The Billboard 200 chart in July of 1995 and eventually sold more than three million copies. Since 1995 there have been at least four more unauthorized Selena books, three more CDs, and two video specials. The 1997 Warner Brothers movie *Selena* was an unprecedented box office success for a Latino film—making more than $100 million.

While these milestones may say more about the "Selena phenomenon" than the popularity of Tejano music, they still underscore the importance of understanding the music and the culture that produced an artist like Selena.

Before Selena's death, the modern Tejano genre was the most vibrant it had ever been in its forty-five-year history. However, the '90s were actually Tejano's *second* golden age, a period that saw the music reach unheard of commercial heights. But while there were many who cheered the new glories, there were just as many who questioned whether Tejano had ventured too far from its earthy folk roots into the pop field.

Like country or rock, today's Tejano music has evolved through the years, splintering and transmuting itself, generating a fresh look and sound that is very different than its original form. Many outside factors—from world wars and international politics to economic depressions and oil booms—have impacted the music's historic development. Tejano's '90s rise came about through a strange mix of timing, economics, and opportunity that was fueled by a renaissance of cultural and political identity.

Modern Tejano is driven by youthful strains that range from Tejano-pop and Tejano-country to Tejano-R&B and even the roots-based, neo-traditional Tejano-norteño form. Contemporary Tejano, like country music in the '90s, has its own audience; the music relates to, is informed and created by its own culture. Its rural folksy origins may go all the way back to the turn of the century in America. Yet in its most modern pop-leaning form, Tejano is as engaging and youth-driven as any dance or hip-hop music.

In order to understand Tejano music and culture, it is necessary to study the past; to comprehend the political and cultural setting of the American Southwest and northern Mexico in the latter half of the nineteenth century; to see how the music took shape in a confluence of cultures along the Texas-Mexico border—how it was forged in Texas as a unique American art form, and how it was, and still is, influenced by people from both the U.S. and Mexico.

THE ROOTS

As with most musical genres, it is impossible to pinpoint the precise moment or place where Tejano—or its predecessor, conjunto—started. What is certain is that Tejano/conjunto history is replete with many elements of intrigue—from stylistic convolutions and reformations to cultural collisions and racial politics. In the twentieth century Tejano has seen discrimination and tolerance, affluence and poverty, transience and illiteracy.

Most historians agree that sometime around the early 1930s, conjunto began coalescing as a discernible style. In Spanish the word "conjunto" has several meanings, including "combined," "a group," or "an ensemble." "Conjunto" also refers to the music, the basic accordion-driven polka genre that began taking shape in the Southwest before the turn of the century.

When the U.S.-Mexico War (1846–1848) came to an end with the Treaty of Guadalupe Hidalgo in 1848, the fertile, cultural backdrop for the creation of the conjunto style was in place between two distinct countries. There was an acceleration in the exchange of customs and traditions between the native Mexicans and Indians and the immigrant settlers coming into the great expanse between central Texas and northern Mexico. There were hundreds of thousands of Europeans in the area—including the French, Spanish, Italians, Germans, Swedes, and Norwegians—who were involved in trade and industry and who were seeking opportunity and fortune.

Most scholars believe that the German, Czech, and Polish immigrants who were building the exploding railroad lines from central Texas to northern Mexico introduced the accordion and polka to the area as early as the 1860s. European customs, especially German customs, made a major impact on Mexican American culture throughout the late nineteenth century. European settlers brought industrial skills, including steelmaking and mining, as well as cultural traditions, including beer brewing and stately dancing (polkas, waltzes). They also brought their accordions, harmonicas, and brass bands. The former two had been invented in Berlin by musician Friedrich Buschmann in 1822 and 1829 respectively.

Mexican string bands, *orquestas típicas*, and early forms of mariachi combos known as *conjuntos de arpa,* were already in existence along the border. Their staple songs were folksy in nature and included rancheras and corridos. Historians believe that, because the accordion was a simple bellows-and-reeds instrument, string bands appreciated its versatility and portability.

Simple one- and two-row button accordions were commonly used in Mexican wedding dances along the border during the 1890s, sometimes accompanied by the Mexican *bajo sexto,* the twelve-string bass guitar, which was another instrument destined to be part of the conjunto lineup. Musicians also sometimes used the *tambora de rancho,* or ranch drum, a homemade instrument made from stretched goat skin.

Though these accordions were simple and played a limited range of notes (the equivalent of a small keyboard without the black keys) they were as versatile as today's synthesizer. They could hold down the bass line or play the melody.

During the Mexican Revolution (1910–1920), while early mariachi ensembles were taking shape in Mexico, two major players in the history of norteño/conjunto music were born in northern Mexico: Narciso Martínez (born October 29, 1911, in Reynosa, Tamaulipas) and Pedro Ayala (born June 29, 1911, in General Terán, Nuevo León). Reynosa and General Terán would become important cities in music history. The seminal norteño duo Los Alegres de Terán originated in General Terán in 1948 while norteño legends Los Relampagos del Norte (which was comprised of the legendary duo Ramón Ayala and Cornelio Reyna) originated in Reynosa in 1961.

By the 1930s, Martínez and Ayala had become the first giants, giving the primordial conjunto genre shape and vitality and creating the template that many others would follow. The essentials were few but critical: the accordion was the lead instrument, and the *bajo sexto* supplied the rhythm and bass. This basic setup remained intact through the '50s, when electric amplification (bass) and drums were incorporated.

Although Bruno "El Azote" Villarreal is credited with being the first artist to record conjunto music in 1928, scholars consider Martínez to be the father of conjunto music, and for practical purposes, of norteño music, too. Beyond the singers' tonal qualities, pronounced Mexican accent, and increased emphasis on corridos in norteño, there is no significant difference between the conjunto that is practiced in the American Southwest and the norteño music that is prevalent in northern Mexico.

Martínez was the first to combine the diatonic two-row accordion with the *bajo sexto* and he popularized the accordion by backing popular vocal duos, such as Carmen y Laura. In 1935 Martínez recorded his first hit—the polka "La Chicharronera." That same year another patriarch, Don Santiago Jiménez of San Antonio, recorded his first side "Dices Pescao."

By the late 1920s, while the record business was still in its infancy, the major American labels like Decca and Bluebird began an intense search to find black and Mexican American artists to record ethnic or "race" records. In these early recording sessions, record reps would travel to major cities across the Southwest with portable recording equipment that usually consisted of one large microphone and a primitive reel-to-reel console.

It was in these sessions that Martínez and Jiménez recorded their first hits. Martínez, who was then going by the nickname of "El Huracán del Valle" for his rapid-fire accordion runs, later recorded the hits "Florecita" and "La Polvadera," both instrumental *polkitas,* little polkas. Interestingly, while Martínez's first recordings were sold under his own name in Chicano areas, he was known as "Louisiana Pete" in Cajun areas and as "Polski Kwartet" in Polish areas.

Don Santiago Jiménez—who, like his son Leonardo Jiménez, was known as "Flaco"—was also influential because of his songwriting prowess. He recorded some of the classic polkas that would become part of the conjunto canon, including "Margarita," "Viva Seguin," and "La Piedrera." He was also recognized by scholars for introducing the *tololoche,* the upright or double bass, into the conjunto ensemble.

THE RISE OF CONJUNTO

It was during the genre's infancy that pioneers like Martínez and Jiménez, who had already married the accordion with the *bajo sexto,* now created the unique conjunto repertoire, which mixed the folksy, storytelling traditions of Mexican corridos, the dance form *huapangos,* and rancheras with European music/dance forms such as the polka, mazurka, and waltz. But the music and the lyrics retained a deep folk-roots focus, reflecting the rural, agrarian southwestern landscape with songs about hard work, class struggles, and longing. Perhaps because of its happy dance rhythms, the German instrumental polka emerged as the most popular form, as showcased on Martínez's instrumental "La Chulada" and "Vidita Mía." During the 1930s and 1940s, in keeping with the German tradition, few polkas had lyrics.

But while Martínez and Jiménez were considered trailblazers in conjunto, neither man was able to make a living on his music alone. Typically, the men would get anywhere from thirty to fifty dollars per 78, which usually included ten to fifteen sides or songs. There were no royalties. For live performances at *campesinos,* the labor camps of farmworkers in the rural outback, the men played *sol a sol*—sundown-to-sunup dances for which they were paid ten dollars apiece. To survive, Martínez worked a variety of jobs through the years, including stints as a truck driver and an animal feeder at the Gladys

Porter Zoo in Brownsville, Texas. Jiménez worked as a school janitor.

Although World War II caused rationing and shortages—including shortages of plastics and vinyl, which pretty much froze the recording industry—both men renewed their careers in the late '40s when the industry saw the rise of independent labels like Discos Falcon and Discos Ideal in the Texas Rio Grande Valley.

The 1940s also saw the appearance of the first key female artists in Tex-Mex music, including Chelo Silva of Brownsville, Rosita Fernández of San Antonio, and Lydia Mendoza of Houston. By this time the second wave of conjunto pioneers had arrived, men like Tony De La Rosa and Valerio Longoria injected their contributions in the evolution of conjunto. In particular, Longoria was credited by historians for, among other things, using modern drums in conjunto and for introducing boleros into the repertoire.

In time, De La Rosa gained a reputation as one of the most prolific and superb accordionists of the genre. His lineup—the two-row accordion, *bajo sexto,* electric bass (instead of the *tololoche,* which Jiménez had used) and dance-band drum set—became the basic setup for conjuntos from the '50s to the present. De La Rosa was inspired by the western swing/country music he heard while growing up, and it came through in his music. Among his best-known polkas were "El Circo," his cover of country singer Clyde "Red" Foley's "Alabama Jubilee"; "El Sube y Baja," one of Los Donnenos's first hits; and "Atotonilco," his interpretation of an old Mexican classic. All of these—and other conjunto hits—were heard in juke joints and icehouses across South Texas. De La Rosa played in a staccato style that slowed the polka tempo slightly and coincided with the introduction of a novel dance, the *tacuachito,* or possum dance, which was marked by exaggerated swaying and gliding steps.

By the early '50s events on the Mexican side of the border were almost in synch with developments in Texas conjunto. Seminal groups Montaneses del Alamo and Los Alegres de Terán were popularizing the same type of music, but they were calling it norteño. Both groups, though, were influential and they helped popularize the use of vocal harmonies with the tandem accompaniment of the accordion/*bajo sexto.*

The '50s saw the rise of another brilliant group—El Conjunto Bernal, which was led by accordionist Paulino Bernal and *bajo sexto* player Eloy Bernal. Paulino impressed with his ability to use the accordion's full range, and he also used four- and five-row chromatic models. El Conjunto Bernal is credited with finessing the use of polka as the rhythm for songs with ranchera lyrics and melody, a practice that was still common in the late 1990s. Perhaps the group's most distinctive contribution was the use of two- and three-part vocal harmonies, which was first introduced on the elemental song "Mi Único

Camino." The group's later hits included "Buena Suerte," "Me Regale Contigo," "Punto Final," and "Por Amor de Dinero."

Although Paulino Bernal retired from the band in the late '60s, El Conjunto Bernal continued as a performing unit, running through a series of lead singers (Rúben Pérez, Manuel Solis, Cha Cha Jiménez) and accordionists (Oscar Hernández). El Conjunto Bernal was known for using two accordionists and for dressing in matching suits and ties, a move that helped elevate the image of conjunto music, which had long been relegated to cantinas, outdoor dances, and parties. By the late '50s, conjunto musicians had made ballrooms part of their touring circuit. The large, paying crowds helped the best artists make the transition to becoming full-time musicians.

TWO MUSICS, ONE CULTURE

Developing on a parallel, and later intersecting, course with conjunto in South Texas was the Orquesta Tejana, or big band, movement. Like the early conjunto acts, Orquestas Tejanas were influenced by country music. They also patterned themselves after the big bands of the age—Glenn Miller, Tommy Dorsey, and others. Orquesta Tejanas and conjunto were different in several ways. While conjuntos appealed to the working classes, *orquestas* were considered *jaiton,* or high-toned, music for the upper classes. With the exception of El Conjunto Bernal, conjunto musicians dressed in everyday clothes, played nightclubs and dance halls, and learned music by ear. Conversely, *orquesta* members wore tuxedos, played in elegant ballrooms at social functions, and could read music.

Lifestyles and philosophies were at odds, too, and stereotypes were abundant. Conjunto fans were seen as country bumpkins who were unable or unwilling (read: poor or uneducated) to enjoy "good music" and who stubbornly wanted to hold on to their Mexican folk roots. *Orquesta* followers were seen as uppity Mexican Americans desperate to find middle-class status and assimilate into the Anglo culture.

From the half-dozen major *orquestas* working in South Texas, including Balde González, Eugenio Gutiérrez, Chris Sandoval, and Juan Colorado, Beto Villa became the most popular and prolific bandleader. His father, Alberto Villa Sr., had been a bandleader of a small *orquesta típica* in Monterrey, Nuevo León, but the family fled Mexico during the Mexican Revolution.

Villa's orchestra had been popular before World War II, but when the conflict broke out, he entered the U.S. Navy. After he was discharged Villa returned to the music scene, this time opening two dance halls, the Pan American and La Plaza, which consisted of raised platforms for the band and small dance areas. This was the type of setup where the traditional *bailes de plataforma* (platform dances) had been held for years.

After a few rejections, Villa eventually convinced Armando Marroquín to allow him to record for Marroquín's Alice, Texas–based Discos Ideal. It was 1946, a time in post-war America when the Mexican Americans living in the Southwest were hungry for their own homegrown music. Villa's first recordings were "Las Delicias," a polka, and "¿Por Qué Te Ríes?" a waltz. Initial success inspired Marroquín to suggest that Villa team up with accordionist Narciso Martínez on the next records. They did, producing two polkas directly to acetate, "Madre Mía" and "Monterrey," as well as two waltzes, "Rosita" and "Morir Soñando." All four became popular, but "Rosita" became Villa's signature song.

The combination of conjunto's folksy accordion with the *orquesta* in the recording studio had now been introduced. The groundwork had been laid for the creation of a distinct musical hybrid. But the next phase in the evolution that would eventually lead to the birth of modern Tejano was still one step away. And it would come in the form of singer/songwriter/bandleader Isidro "El Indio" López.

THE FORK IN THE ROAD

Although the conjunto and Orquesta Tejana movements began in the 1930s, they did not reach their maximum polar-opposite positions until the early '50s. By then, post–World War II America was flourishing. The economy was booming, as the country's massive labor and industrial complex had switched from producing war materials to producing an array of domestic goods. There were fancy new cars, commercial jet planes, modern homes, and an emerging bustling suburban culture. Color televisions, transistor radios, toasters, and TV dinners were only a fraction of the inventions being created for the first American generation to have considerable leisure time.

It was against this prosperous backdrop that country western music began to outgrow its rural origins as a regional genre that had previously been limited to Texas, Tennessee, and the South. Developing its base in the young recording capital of Nashville, country western mushroomed as a new and viable art form. The '50s also saw, for the first time in America, the nation's teens demand their own music and culture, a movement that would lead eventually to the birth of rock 'n' roll. While that history is another story, it is important to remember that Mexican American youths in the '50s were also looking for their own heroes.

Within the burgeoning world of Tex-Mex, the young Tejano sound would arrive as the rock 'n' roll for a generation of Mexican American teens who wanted to escape the ordinary and find something that challenged established norms.

While conjunto and *orquesta* styles were both thriving in the '50s, the former enjoyed the biggest recording and touring revenues. Perhaps this disparity was because the size of the working classes dwarfed the upper classes, or the proximity to Mexico made folksy conjunto more popular, or a combination of the two.

Whatever the reason, it is important to remember that Beto Villa had to insist that Discos Ideal officials record his big band music at a time when the label was enjoying solid sales of Narciso Martínez's conjunto music. Villa had recorded a few sides with accordion music and even taken Narciso Martínez out with him on a few short tours. But Isidro López would be the one to complete the sequence of events that led to the birth of Tejano.

Villa elevated the sophistication of the *orquesta,* taking the form to its maximum expression. He expanded the *orquesta,* insisted that his band members be able to read music, and incorporated other complex music styles into the basic polka/ranchera repertoire—including big band jazz, swing, and even the mambo. By the early '50s, Villa had became the hottest Tex-Mex *orquesta* all along the Southwest, a position he enjoyed until the end of the decade.

But the hybrid of musical experimentation that Villa had started was taken up by the younger López, who eventually found the right mix that would propel him to the top.

Isidro López, who was born in Bishop, Texas, was half Apache. His father, Pedro G. López, was a full-blooded Apache Mescalero from Riodoso, New Mexico. Like other conjunto pioneers, López grew up in a family of farmworkers, and he was influenced by the music he heard on the radio while working the fields. He became a fan of the seminal Mexican group Los Madrugadores as well as of country heroes like Eddie Arnold and Hank Williams.

López was already a well-known saxophonist by the time he was seventeen. By the late '40s he was securing stints with a series of top bandleaders, including the Eugenio Gutiérrez and Juan Colorado orchestras. He also recorded with noted accordionists such as Narciso Martínez and Tony De La Rosa. A developing songwriter, he became a singer by accident. During a 1954 recording session with the Juan Colorado Orchestra at Marroquín's Discos Ideal studio, the scheduled singer did not show up. López was quickly drafted on Marroquín's logic that since López had written the song that was to be recorded, "Díganle," he should sing it. He did, impressing Marroquín enough that he got the regular studio singer position.

By 1956 the twenty-seven-year-old López had formed his own Isidro López Orchestra and had begun recording for himself. He had also recorded with conjuntos, and a mariachi, creating what he called "Texachi." Then he incorporated two accordions into his orchestra, which was unheard of at that time. In later recordings like "Mala Cara" and "Marcho Rock 'n' Roll," López fused the rhythms of early rock into his Tex-Mex blend.

The final step was taking all these influences out on the road. Using some of the best musicians of the time—including accordionist Amadeo Flores, who would go on to join Tony De La Rosa—López became a solid player on the circuit. Other star players in López's group included Henry Cuesta, who later played reeds in the Lawrence Welk Band, trombonist Joe Gallardo, saxophonist Max Bernal, and trumpeter Lee Martínez Jr., brother of future Tejano legend Freddie Martínez.

THE SPIRIT OF TEJANO

By utilizing a fresh, exciting mix that included both *orquesta* and conjunto music, López was able to capture audiences for both styles. And when he added the accordions to his big-band instrumentation and included mariachi and rock 'n' roll into his repertoire of jazzy boleros, big-band polkas, and rancheras, López had finally forged Tejano music.

The nascent Tejano sound had now crystallized into a recognizable shape.

At this critical crossroads in the American Southwest of the late '50s the urbane Orquesta Tejana intersected with the rural conjunto, creating a third distinct genre—Tejano. Tejano was not strictly the former, because the accordion was not considered a classy instrument. And it could never be the latter, because the sophistication of the big-band arrangement was at odds with the music's folk roots. Instead, it was a brand-new hybrid.

This spirit of fusing styles from two cultures, of mixing country, rock, or pop songs and/or reinventing them, of adding or changing instrumentation—all this created the vital force that made Tejano distinct. And it is this template, this artistic concept, that has remained unchanged in the forty years since its creation. The music has deviated, convoluted, splintered into subgenres, and reformed through the years, but it has never changed its basic blueprint.

At the time of its creation, no one recognized this new music as Tejano. The music was variously called Mexican music, *música de orquesta,* or *música alegre.* Later terms would include *la Onda Chicana,* Tex-Mex funk, brown soul, and many more. It would not be until the early '80s that "Tejano" would become the widely accepted term.

When the '60s arrived, the first-tier Orquesta Tejanas were fading, but a new generation of smaller groups with strong horn sections arrived, including Alfonso Ramos (brother of Rubén Ramos), Roy Montelongo, Freddie Martínez, and Little Joe and the Latinaires.

The act making the biggest noise in San Antonio, though, was a small combo singing English pop hits. The lead singer was Sunny Ozuna and his group was the Sunglows. In 1963 their big hit was "Talk to Me," a remake of Little Willie John's old hit.

That Mexican Americans would try to score with English-language pop hits was no surprise. Ritchie Valens had done it in the late '50s with "Come On, Let's Go," "Donna," and "La Bamba." Later Mexican American acts that emulated American pop genres included Sam the Sham and the Pharaohs, ? and the Mysterians, and Cannibal and the Headhunters.

Within six years Ozuna would switch from English to Spanish Chicano tunes and he would enjoy a second gold rush of hits, including "Reina de Mi Amor," "Cariñito," "Árbol Seco," and "Mi Chulita."

GOLDEN AGE

By 1969 Ozuna had run out of steam in the pop field and practical economics dictated a change in artistic direction. The rush and excitement of early rock 'n' roll swept the country and influenced emerging Tejano groups, who at the very least played top pop hit covers. For Ozuna, "Talk to Me" went to No. 11 on the Billboard Hot 100 chart, and the song landed the diminutive singer on *Dick Clark's American Bandstand.* Ozuna's subsequent English hits included "Rags to Riches," "Smile Now, Cry Later," "Out of Sight, Out of Mind," and "Peanuts." More importantly, Ozuna was not alone. The first heroes to have bonafide Tejano songs as hits arrived: Freddie Martínez, with "Te Traigo Estas Flores"; Augustin Ramírez, with "Sangre de Indio"; Joe Bravo, with "Patita de Conejo"; Latin Breed, with perhaps the first Tejano anthem, "El Tejano Enamorado"; and Roberto Pulido, with "Señorita Cantinera." The young Tejano culture entered its first golden age in the early '70s.

With the exception of Pulido, most of the artists employed the classic Tejano setup—medium-sized bands with big horn sections. Pulido developed an instrumental mix that helped bridge the then-widening gap between big city Tejano and rural conjunto. He employed two saxophones to complement his basic accordion/*bajo sexto* tandem.

Interestingly, while Tejano was exploding, conjunto was falling out of favor, relegated to small bars and ramshackle dance halls. Only a few conjunto heroes were impacting on the charts, including Tony De La Rosa and El Conjunto Bernal, while the norteño flag was still bravely being carried by newcomers Ramón Ayala and Los Tigres del Norte. The negative stereotypes had resurfaced—conjunto and accordion music was considered *música de cantinas* or *música de los pobres,* "music of the bars," or "music of the poor."

La Onda Chicana, as tejano was called in this tumultuous era, however, was experiencing good days. The abundance and diversity of talent as well as the expansion of the music industry allowed tejano to become a viable, growing, and well-defined genre. It was being played on more radio stations and recorded by more independent labels such as Zarape, Sombrero, Discos Falcon, Norteño, and the newly established Freddie Records.

In the mid-1970s, a new prince would surface to elevate the music another step. But first, events far beyond Texas would impact and influence the scene.

The decade of the '70s in America was turbulent, both politically and culturally. The Vietnam War had bitterly divided the country. Anti-war protesters marched on Washington as the Chicano and civil rights movements were peaking on major university campuses. The words "Watergate" and "OPEC" had entered the national vocabulary, feeding the sense of disillusion and alienation.

Rock music, which had splintered into psychedelic and pop rock in the late '60s, splintered even further. There were soft rock/folk groups (Carole King, James Taylor); progressive art rock bands (Emerson, Lake, and Palmer, Genesis, Rush); glitter/theatrical groups (David Bowie, Alice Cooper, Kiss); the southern sound (Allman Brothers, Lynyrd Skynyrd); California rock (Eagles, Doobie Brothers); and blues-based precursors to modern hard rock/heavy metal (Led Zeppelin, Black Sabbath).

This was the bubbling cultural cauldron in which Little Joe would rise and become the top Tejano act of the decade.

Little Joe started out in his hometown of Temple, Texas, as Little Joe and the Latinaires. Like other young Mexican American band members of the late '50s, Little Joe wanted to join the young rock 'n' roll revolution. As a teenager, he had watched bandleaders Chris Sandoval and Isidro López at the top of their game. And, like them, Little Joe was inspired by what he heard on radio—from early country blues to pop and soul.

In the early '70s Little Joe moved out to California with the band, where, influenced by the power and magic of Latin rock outfits Santana and Malo as well as jazz and blues groups, he updated his music, expanding his band to include up to twelve players with percussions and horns. Ultimately, it was the radical and liberating political influences that had the biggest impact. He jettisoned the Latinaires tag and renamed the group José María DeLeón Hernández y La Familia.

Eschewing the idea of pop covers, DeLeón Hernández studied the songs of the Mexican great songwriter José Alfredo Jiménez, and rediscovered the blues and soulful sentiment of Jiménez's rancheras. In 1976 he took an old Wally Armendariz cover of a Mexican standard, "Las Nubes," and reinvented it with his now patented ranchera-based, horn-driven approach.

"Las Nubes" became a big hit, another Tejano anthem and cemented Little Joe's standing as more than just a popular performer. "Las Nubes" is very much like Bruce Springsteen's "Born in the U.S.A." Both have infectious sing-along choruses that soar over stark lyrics of reflection, despair, and disillusionment. The same period also saw Jimmy Edward explode with the monster hit

"Memories," a bilingual version of "Diez y Seis Años," and Latin Breed scoring again with the rhythmic "Qué Chulos Ojos."

ENTERING TWILIGHT

But the glory days were coming to an end. Tejano's first golden age had run its natural course, wearing out its novelty and excitement as it entered a sunset phase.

The disco movement was the rage in late '70s America—with superstars KC and the Sunshine Band, the Bee Gees, and a ton of others. Meanwhile, the main rock establishment was displaced by the growing punk rock generation, which was led by the Sex Pistols, the Ramones, and the Clash. Also making serious inroads in recruiting the country's increasingly alienated youth, including Mexican American teens, were the rising subgenres of outlaw country, country rock, and the massive "Urban Cowboy" craze.

La Onda Chicana was entering a period of darkness. With so many new, exciting sounds on radio, it is no surprise that the genre began to sound stale and dated. More importantly, though, the music was being displaced along the border by Mexican music. Young pop artists like Juan Gabriel, Yordano, and Raphael; ranchera singers Vicente Fernández, Antonio Aguilar, and Yolanda Del Río; and norteño groups Los Tigres del Norte, Ramón Ayala, and Los Cadetes de Linares were the emerging superstars.

Of fundamental importance, though, were the changes in the infrastructure of the Latin recording industry that made it all possible.

Just like the first Tejano wave, which had been possible because of the formation of the emerging indie labels, the major Mexican wave of the late '70s was realized because of the arrangements of new labels. A few American record labels had newly created Latin divisions and major Mexican labels struck distribution deals in the U.S. Critically, though, record label execs felt a better return would be realized if they released the music of proven Mexican superstars in the U.S. rather than if they released music by, or developing acts in, *la Onda Chicana,* which had always been considered a regional genre with limited sales.

Further compounding the natural cycles of music tastes and trends were economic setbacks, again far beyond the American Southwest. The late '70s were marked by tough economic times. Under the Carter administration domestic inflation reached an all-time high of fifteen percent in 1978. The monetary crisis of 1979 further exacerbated conditions. During the same period Mexico underwent its own severe economic crisis, as a series of peso devaluations further crippled the local economies up and down the U.S.-Mexico border. This region was the very heart of the Tejano market. Veteran industry observers knew that worse things were coming. Conventional wisdom dictates that when times are tight, people hold on to the basics, and nonessential expenditures—like music and entertainment—are the first to be cut. Hundreds of businesses shuttered when the '70s came to an end, and the future of *la Onda Chicana* did not seem promising.

THE NEW AGE

The dawn of the '80s marked another dramatic turning point for the music. With the advent of MTV and competition from cable and home videos, the music industry faced an all-time low. Younger audiences strayed as *Onda Chicana* groups reached a creative lull. Unless groups adapted to the changing times, it seemed certain that *la Onda Chicana* would be history.

Like early nascent rock 'n' roll in the late '50s, the new wave of groups that were mixing pop/dance and punk rock dominated the early '80s, influencing not only music, but fashion and teen politics. The Cars, the Pretenders, Blondie, Men at Work, the Police, and a host of other groups made up this exciting breed. With the extraordinary success of MTV and the music video concept, the message was powerful and clear: in the new age, just performing on stage was not enough.

Audiences, especially the youth, now wanted and expected a performance, a "show."

The '80s generation Tejano bands accepted this and began incorporating computerized spotlights, towering speaker banks, fog, and other arena concert theatrics. Their outfits, too, reflected the youthful rock age—sequinned costumes, black leather jackets, ripped jeans, big hair, and, for some male members, even eyeliner and mascara.

These new groups included La Sombra, Mazz, Pío Trevino & Magic, Patsy Torres, and, perhaps the leader of the bunch, La Mafia. The latter, which was led by brothers Oscar and Leonard Gonzáles, went the farthest to employ bigger light and sound systems and wilder outfits. The fresh look and the new music worked. By the mid-1980s *Onda Chicana*/Tejano bands began to attract large audiences again.

But before Tejano would rise to match the success of the early '70s, it had to overcome the obstacles that were being created by continuing economic derailments along the border. Many analysts suggest that the '90s Tejano explosion would likely have happened by the mid-1980s had it not been for those reversals that stemmed from events far removed from the border.

The first major blow came when President Reagan took office in 1981. It was a time of high inflation and slow economic growth. In an effort to balance the federal budget, Reagan initiated an economic recovery program that included downsizing government, especially social services. Those reductions impacted heavily on the welfare rolls, particularly those in the South. Exacerbating the situation was the country's continuing transition from a manufacture-based to a service-based economy. Global competition increased and rapidly changing technologies, which demanded higher-skilled workers, challenged the country's ability to keep up, producing dislocated and displaced workers.

A much bigger wallop followed when a worldwide oversupply of oil severely deflated the Texas oil and gas industries. Agricultural prices also declined. More ominous, however, was the fact that the same oversupply of oil, that had caused world petroleum prices to fall, completely derailed Mexico's state-owned oil industry. In early 1986 Mexico, which was already staggering under massive foreign debt, announced another of a series of steep peso devaluations that sent the southwestern economy into a tailspin.

Border businesses, which were mostly reliant on Mexico, closed by the hundreds. Texas's unemployment rate climbed to ten-and-one-half percent in June 1986, the highest since the Great Depression and three-and-one-half points above the U.S. average. The state began to lose population to other states for the first time since it had gained independence from Mexico.

But while the economic blows landed hard, they did not stop the revolution. Slowly, *la Onda Chicana* pressed forward. With the birth of two major organizations in San Antonio the name "Tejano" became widely accepted. The Tejano Music Awards were founded in 1980 by art teacher Rudy Trevino and Latin Breed saxophonist Gilbert Escobedo to recognize the best songs and artists in a People's Choice–type ceremony. In 1982 Juan Tejeda, who was the music director at San Antonio's Guadalupe Cultural Arts Center, established the Tejano Conjunto Festival to showcase the music's pioneers and young turks. Both organizations also founded halls of fame to induct the pioneers of modern Tejano and its precursor, the folksy conjunto art form.

The first TMAs were held on March 1, 1981 at the Henry B. González Convention Center and drew an estimated 1,500 fans. The awards grew each year. By 1986 the TMAs moved to the 16,000-capacity Convention Center Arena. In 1994 the TMAs moved to the Alamodome where attendance peaked at 35,000-plus in 1995.

But before the gold rush of the '90s, Tejano had to survive the '80s.

In the fall of 1986, there was a glimmer of hope when CBS Discos executive José Behar signed to its rosters Little Joe y La Familia—the first bonafide Tejano act signed to a major label. CBS then raised the stakes when it signed a promotion/distribution agreement with Cara Records, then the most powerful Tejano indie. It was owned by Bob Grever, the grandson of famed Mexican songwriter María Grever. Grever and his father, Charlie, had also administered a song-publishing concern, Golden Sands, which had accumulated thousands of songs.

When the New York–born, New Jersey–raised Grever started the Cara label in 1977, he was actually only looking for bands to record his music in order to generate publishing royalties. But Grever met with good timing and opportunity. He signed the young, then-unknown bands Mazz and La Mafia in the late 1970s. He later signed David Marez, Patsy Torres, David Lee Garza, Ramiro Herrera, and a few other Texan artists who rose to become some of the hottest names in mid-1980s Tejano. Grever also teamed up with Manny Guerra, who produced the acts, and Luis Silva, a songwriter who worked as a record promoter for the label. Cara was like the Motown of Tejano music. When CBS partnered with Grever, Cara artists benefited from increased distribution and major label promotions. Records sales began shooting upward.

That same fall, RCA announced a similar deal with Corpus Christi–based Hacienda Records. The pieces were in place, but before things got really going, unfortunately Mexico sprang the major peso devaluation of early 1986 and momentum was stalled. The RCA/Hacienda deal disappeared, but CBS honored its five-year commitment to Cara.

The gold rush had been delayed. But it was still coming. Only no one knew it at the time.

As the new wave of Tejano acts polished its songcraft and stage delivery, the market began to heat up. There were new dance halls sprouting around the state and new radio stations. In early 1985 Flexx became one of the first modern multi-million dollar nightclubs to play live Tejano music in San Antonio's affluent north side. This was significant because previously in San Antonio, as in many major cities, Tejano had been relegated to second-tier and often ramshackle clubs in the depressed sides of town. Flexx's move was soon duplicated in Houston, Dallas, and the Rio Grande Valley.

As events unfolded, there were key undercurrents sweeping the country.

For years there had been newspaper stories and recurrent census reports documenting the growing political and economic power of Latinos. Latinos were reported to have the youngest demographic in the U.S. and the fastest growing minority—with projections that they would reach almost thirty million by the millennium. Early on trend spotters were proclaiming the '80s as the Decade of the Hispanic. By the mid-1980s it was clear that that prediction was a joke. It was already evident that Hispanics would flex their muscles far beyond the decade.

In 1987 two major entertainment successes signaled the new political correctness in the country that not only tolerated but celebrated cultural diversity.

Los Lobos impacted first in the early summer with *La Bamba,* the sensational biopic about '50s rocker Ritchie Valens, and their hit remake of the song by the same name. The movie was a top draw in theaters. The single reached No. 1 on the Billboard Hot Singles Sales chart on July 17 and would win an MTV Video Music Award for best video from a film. The song received three Grammy nominations, including song of the year. The CD soundtrack reached No. 1 on The Billboard 200 chart.

That fall, pop singer Linda Ronstadt released her ranchera roots CD, *Canciones de Mi Padre,* featuring accompaniment by the world's best—Mexico's Mariachi Vargas de Tecalitlán. Ronstadt then launched a subsequent tour that drew packed houses across the U.S. In 1988 she won a Grammy for *Canciones*.

The wild, unprecedented success of these two artists ignited a growing ethnic pride in Mexican Americans and Hispanics everywhere. That two artists of Mexican heritage (Ronstadt is half Mexican, half German) could achieve the ultimate mainstream success in America seemed like a validation of their culture. All of a sudden it seemed to be cool for Latinos to bring their ethnicity out of the closet and put it on display—to admit they listened to Mexican, salsa, or Tejano music or ate beans and rice in the melting pot of America, the most powerful country in the world.

That beaming, bubbling pride, coupled with the emerging political and economic power of Hispanics, laid the potentially explosive backdrop for the '90s.

In 1989 the last critically significant development unfolded when CBS Discos executive José Behar left the company to head the upstart Capitol/EMI Latin in Los Angeles. Smartly, Behar recruited another CBS man, promoter Manolo González, to run the EMI office in San Antonio—ground zero for the coming Tejano explosion. Since the mid-1980s, Behar and González had personally surveyed the growing Tejano market and, as veteran music industry soldiers, they recognized the untapped potential that lay waiting on the horizon.

THE GOLD RUSH

When the 1990s unfolded, the stage was set for an unprecedented revolution, a musical movement that would parallel the infinitely larger country music and grunge rock movements in America. Just like country and grunge had become the media darlings in the mainstream music press in the early '90s, Tejano became the new buzz word in music circles. But before the Tejano revolution unfolded, a few key developments needed to fall into place. The significance of each individual step never became newsworthy in the national press. Nor was the larger impact analyzed by any players on the ground. The steps were simple and unadorned, but, like building blocks, they established a foundation upon which the new Tejano nation would be built.

On the morning of January 10, 1990, the *San Antonio Light* broke the story that Capitol/EMI Latin was buying the Tejano indie label Cara Records for an undisclosed sum—estimated by insiders as at least in the five-million-dollar range. The news was shocking to the regional Tex-Mex music industry, but the magnitude of what had transpired in this singular event would not be understood or felt until years later. While major record labels routinely signed promotion/distribution deals with small independents, it was not commonplace for a major to buy an independent lock, stock, and barrel. Yet here was an unknown player in the Latin music scene that was not content to simply test the waters, but instead took the big plunge. It was an enormous risk, a risk tantamount to a gambler in a Las Vegas casino putting up the entire ante in a last bid to win it all.

Complicating the matter was the fact that CBS still had a year to go on its distribution agreement with Cara, which meant that all label artists—from David Marez to La Mafia—would continue to be distributed under the CBS Discos logo, which became Sony Discos later that year.

The gamble for EMI Latin, a young untested label, was in recouping its massive investment in the Cara purchase. The question: Could EMI generate enough sales with Cara catalog artists to not only match the steep-but-undisclosed purchase price, but also achieve a sizable return on its investment?

Under the guidance of Behar and González, EMI not only recouped its investment, but, eventually the young label succeeded far beyond anyone's expectations. EMI ignited the careers of a cadre of young stars, including Emilio and Selena. The label laid the foundation and provided the laboratory where young creative minds forged wondrous new melodies and magnetic rhythms that fueled the new Tejano wildfire. However, at the start of the '90s, no one could foresee what was ahead. The only thing that was obvious in those early days was that, in construction parlance, "dirt was flying everywhere."

Signing bonuses for artists shot up, budgets for album recordings ballooned, promotional and marketing campaigns increased. Tejano stations multiplied as more live music clubs opened. Money was flowing. Big money.

After EMI stunned the industry, CBS slowly realized that overnight the upstart had taken over an estimated sixty-five percent of the Tejano business. EMI not only had the Cara artists, they owned the Cara catalog, a pristine decade's worth of hit records by those top-tier artists that had not yet been milked in greatest hits compilations. One of the reasons hit collections and compilations are so lucrative, is that they cost nothing beyond manufacturing to produce. There are no incentive bonuses for artists, nor recording studio costs. Essentially, the Cara catalog was a gold mine that was just waiting to be excavated.

While CBS's initial reaction to EMI's arrival was blasé, within weeks it initiated a series of strategic countermeasures to try to balance the scales. It signed up La Mafia,

Ramiro Herrera, and David Marez, even though each artist still owed two albums to Cara/EMI Latin. This was unprecedented. CBS also signed on producer Manny Guerra and record promoter Luis Silva.

ALL-OUT WAR

All of a sudden, EMI and CBS, two major international players, had dug in for what was quickly unraveling as a protracted record war—all this in a regional music genre that had previously been thought of by the major labels as too small-time to bother. Benefiting the most from these astounding turn of events were the artists, who previously had no choice but to deal with the smaller indie labels. They had never enjoyed decent recording budgets or national marketing campaigns. Now, instead of just having their cassettes in mom-and-pop stores, their CDs were stocked in big retail chains like Target, Wal-Mart, Blockbuster, and Tower Records.

As EMI and CBS battled for market supremacy, Texas became a wild frontier. Soon, six other major record labels—including WEA Latina, BMG/U.S. Latin, PolyGram Latino, and FonoVisa—swooped in to get a piece of the action, opening offices and signing up artists. Later, newcomers Arista/Texas and indies Barb Wire and Tejas Records opened shop to see what they could scavenge in the raging free-for-all.

Just before the purchase of Cara Records, EMI had signed six artists, including the heavyweights Mazz, a young Emilio Navaira, who had just left David Lee Garza y Los Musicales, and a promising young group led by a seventeen-year-old singer named Selena.

The arrival of the majors at the start of the decade fortuitously coincided with an unusual coalescence of high-caliber musical creativity, vitality, and diversity that had never been seen before in Tejano. Thanks to the adventurous spirit and enthusiasm of fresh, talented groups, the genre splintered into new sound fusions that included, but were not limited to: Tejano/pop (Selena), Tejano/rap (La Sombra, Tierra Tejana), Tejano/R&B (Jay Pérez, David Marez), Tejano/country (Emilio), and Tejano/jazz (Joe Posada). The depth of artistic inspiration and the breadth of the variety from 1990 to 1993 was completely unparalleled. And it would never be duplicated again.

Each subgenre leader had taken the bare essentials of the polka/ranchera repertoire and injected mainstream influences into his or her recorded music and live performances. Selena, for example, fused the tropical/cumbia rhythms with pop/reggae dance sensibilities, scoring with such hits as "Baila Esta Cumbia," "La Carcacha," and "Como la Flor." Emilio focused on torchy cumbia/rancheras such as "Y Se Pasan los Años" and country ballads like "We Had It Made in Mexico." La Sombra scored with rap cumbias "El Sapo" and "El Sancho," while La Fiebre rocked with its bluesy ranchera "Borrachos de Besos."

Meanwhile, La Mafia and Mazz made concentrated tours of Mexico in an effort to increase sales. Substantially buttressed by label promotional support, they were successful, and enjoyed top draw status in Mexico within the year. And with Mexican immigration into the U.S. continuing unabated, despite periodic clampdown efforts by the federal government, both groups began enjoying increased airplay on the West Coast, a traditional destination for immigrants.

While Mazz reinvented the classic trio and mariachi/ranchera genres in medleys like "Canciones del Corazón" and "Canciones de Amor," La Mafia made a left turn musically, switching from Tex-Mex polkas to rhythmic pop ballads in the vein of Los Bukis. La Mafia's series of early hits in the '90s included "Me Duele Estar Solo" and "Yo Quiero Ser."

The appearance of so many young artists and the avalanche of so much new music was critical because these were the core attractions for a new younger Latino audience—an audience still radiant and giddy from the cultural renaissance that had started in the late '80s with the remarkable success of Los Lobos's *La Bamba* and Linda Ronstadt's *Canciones de Mi Padre*. Unlike so many previous generations where youth had sought a cultural identity distinctly separate from their parents or grandparents, the youth of the '90s revealed an unusually high unity. In a rare period of appreciation for their culture and roots, the youth began to appreciate the classic Tejano music of their grandparents' era.

Before, Mexican American kids spoke only English and listened to pop stars Michael Jackson or Madonna at school, and never admitted that at home they spoke Spanish, ate beans, and listened to their parents' Tejano music. But now kids were blasting Tejano stars Emilio and Mazz out of radios on the streets, at schools, and in the malls.

Before, college teens were rarely found at dance halls that featured Tejano bands. Now even preteens were at festivals, standing stage front, and, even more fascinating, singing along with the lyrics. This was critical because it demonstrated that Tejano would be more than just the trendy fad predicted by many early cynics. In music industry philosophy, not to mention corporate marketing mentality, youth drives everything. If you could get the kids hooked on the music early, the business theory went, then you would have loyal fans for years.

For corporate companies like Pepsi and Coca-Cola, the idea was to get Emilio or Selena to proclaim a love for their soft drinks, and, by doing do, they would have a new generation of Pepsi or Coca-Cola drinkers. At least that was their thinking and motivation in the '90s, when they and other companies began signing up spokespeople. Budweiser, Miller Lite, Southwest Airlines, AT&T, Paul Mitchell, and a host of others entered the scene, further heating up the rise of the Tejano nation.

BOOMTOWN FEVER

The Tejano Music Awards and Tejano Conjunto Festival began attracting record-breaking crowds at their annual events. Influenced by the Country Music Award's Fanfair, the TMAs instituted their own Tejano Fanfair in 1994. It was so wildly successful, attracting nearly 5,000 fans to San Antonio's convention center, that the fanfair became a regular component.

As audiences grew, Tejano on FM radio became a reality. Before 1990, a Tejano FM station was a rarity. But from 1990 through 1995 more than 150 Tejano FM stations were broadcasting—from Brownsville to Los Angeles, including more than a dozen on the Mexican side of the border. Some were new, but most had converted from regional Mexican formats to full- or part-time Tejano. The movement peaked in November 1994, when San Antonio's KXTN-FM, employing a slick Top 40 delivery, made history when it achieved the No. 1 ranking in the city. This was not just among Latino stations. This was the number one station in the general market. KXTN had edged out traditional powerhouses like rock classic KZEP, pop/R&B KTFM, and country monster KCYY.

FM stations and huge nightclubs, major label distribution and retail chains, these were all part of the new vast infrastructure that helped Tejano expand at a fast clip. The superheated growth led to the first ever release of "classic" Tejano records from the '70s as well as club and radio remixed versions of top hits. The massive popularity of the music overflowed into conjunto as appreciation for the original Tejano music blossomed. A new wave of groups played in the neo-traditional vein (accordion and *bajo sexto*), including Jaime y Los Chamacos, the Hometown Boys, Los Palominos, and Los Desperadoz.

By 1992 EMI's aggressive approach and superior talent roster helped the label dominate the TMAs, winning twenty-three out of twenty-five awards in the previous two-year period. EMI may have been too efficient. Sony Discos, Freddie, TH-Rodven, and FonoVisa teamed up to cry foul, alleging, but never substantiating, "improprieties in the ballot process," at the TMAs. The labels launched a boycott of the TMAs and did not return until 1994. The controversy hardly mattered in the marketplace, however, as Tejano's growth continued like wildfire. Before 1990 big sales by an artist meant moving 50,000 copies of an album. By 1995 Selena, La Mafia, Mazz, and Emilio were surpassing the 300,000 unit mark.

By the mid-1990s Tejano had grown so popular that music festivals were being played at arenas and even stadiums in Dallas, Houston, and San Antonio. From 1992 onward, the Go Tejano Day at the Astrodome for the Houston Rodeo posted record-breaking attendance figures on par with superstars like George Strait and Garth Brooks. The three cities also saw the rise of monster clubs in the Fort Worth's Billy Bobs vein—warehouse size clubs with capacities of up to 2,000 people. At the peak of the genre in 1994, each city had two or three such clubs. Even in northern Mexico, Tejano fever caught on, transforming radio stations to the format. In Monterrey, dance clubs like Far West and Midnight Rodeo played the latest in Tejano and were packed each weekend.

Having already become saturated in Texas, it was only natural for the market to flow elsewhere. Mazz and La Mafia had mined Mexico with great success. In 1994 Emilio signed on with Liberty Records in Nashville to pursue a parallel country career and Selena was signed by SBK Records to record an English pop album.

By early 1995, Tejano had peaked.

The genre, expanding far beyond the market's natural ability to sustain it, had enjoyed an unimaginable five years of growth, much more than even the most experienced observers would have guessed. Already there were small signs that the movement was coming to its natural end. There was complacency and conceitedness. Fewer bands were playing new or original variations. A host of new acts seemed like clones, content to merely duplicate the sound on radio stations, which were increasingly using national consultants to dictate playlists.

The music had changed fundamentally from a dynamic and vibrant youth-propelled movement that came from the streets, to a prepackaged product developed and mass-marketed by record label executives. The rootsy approach that featured the accordion had been pushed aside by a trend toward overproduction in the studio, a movement that included overuse of keyboards, synthesizers, and drum machines. Like Nashville, albeit on a smaller scale, Tejano labels had switched to the mass-production approach. They utilized the same recording studios and session musicians in an effort to become more efficient and, incongruously, produce a better produc—as if making music was tantamount to making shoes.

Other elements for a downfall were already in place.

By 1995 Tejano did not have the inspirational magic, or the astonishing diversity, that had miraculously arrived in the early '90s. And there was not anything anyone could do about this more serious problem. Call it fate, luck, or timing. The confluence of so many innovative ideas and so much creative talent in such a short period was rare. It could not be duplicated.

ON THE EDGE OF DARKNESS

Before the collapse of the Tejano nation became evident to more than a handful of astute players, the market was distracted by incredible and shocking news.

On March 31, 1995, twenty-three-year-old Selena was shot and killed in a Corpus Christi motel by Yolanda Saldivar, a former Selena fan-club president. After an eight-hour standoff with police, Saldivar was arrested and charged with murder. Selena's death was at the top of TV newscasts that night and on the front page news all over the Southwest the next day.

First emotional shock, then stunning disbelief, and, ultimately, sadness swept the Tejano nation. Here was a dynamic, incredibly talented young woman who was about to record her crossover dream, an English-language pop album, cut down in the prime of her life. When Tejano had grown by leaps and bounds, Selena had matured with it. As a top artist Selena had provided inspiration and direction during those heady days of incredible growth.

The fans' response started naturally—but it spread quickly, becoming unbelievably massive and seemingly unending. Cars with colored ribbons and blazing headlights streamed on Texas highways. Tributes and vigils broke out in many cities. Tejano stations played her music nonstop, while TV programs aired her videos. Crowds gathered at the motel, at Selena's house, her boutiques, and at Corpus Christi's Q Production studios.

According to authorities, more than 30,000 mourners filed past her coffin at the Bayfront Plaza Convention Center the day before her funeral. And for the next days and weeks a constant line of cars and visitors passed by the key places that were part of her exciting life—her home, her boutique, her studio/office, and her final resting place at the Seaside Memorial Cemetery.

The avalanche of subsequent retrospectives in newspapers and magazines called her a Texas music legend and Tejano hero, a wonderful role model who cared about children and the elderly. The tributes continued for weeks, each issue selling out instantly. From the major dailies in Texas to two *People* magazine special issues to the first paperback bio, which reached No. 1 on the *New York Times* nonfiction bestseller list, all the Selena specials broke sales records. It was the same story in Mexico.

By late April, Selena had five CDs on The Billboard 200 chart, an accomplishment previously only achieved by superstars like Garth Brooks, Elvis Presley, and the Beatles. Her posthumous crossover project, *Dreaming of You,* debuted at No. 1 on The Billboard 200 chart in July and eventually sold more than three million copies. Then came four more unauthorized Selena books, three more CDs, and two video specials. In 1997 there was the *Selena* movie and soundtrack.

The unexpected media blitz and sales blowout on Selena helped prop up the Tejano industry for the next eighteen months. Everyone, especially the artists and the labels, benefited from the resulting national media exposure and increased public attention. The record labels intensified the hunt for the "next Selena," a young artist with crossover potential.

The phenomenon surrounding Selena's death, while limited to the Southwest, was on a scale with John Lennon or Elvis Presley. It symbolized Selena's standing—not only as a beloved hero, but as the great Tejano hope of fans everywhere. Like Ritchie Valens in early rock 'n' roll or Gloria Estefan in '90s salsa/pop, Selena was going to be the next big pop success story, bringing glory to her Tejano roots.

But for the industry, the unbelievable response to Selena's death masked the market's true condition. In mid-1997, after two years of Selenamania, it became clear label execs that sales from 1995 to 1997, which though on par with Tejano's growth since 1990, were actually mostly sales of Selena product. Beyond a few talented newcomers mining new ground—like Michael Salgado, Intocable, and Bobby Pulido—the market had started to flatten.

Worse, new regional Mexican norteño groups—like Los Tucanes de Tijuana and Grupo Límite, as well as veterans like Alejandro Fernández, Los Tigres del Norte, and Los Temerarios—had swooped in with a vengeance, taking over the charts and selling huge numbers. They all had one thing in common: fresh, compelling music with arresting melodies and rhythmic dance grooves.

Already bereft of ideas and creativity, the Tejano market was beginning to deflate faster than most officials either realized or cared to admit. The groups that had provided the spark and ingenuity at the start of the explosion—La Fiebre, Mazz, Xelencia, Tierra Tejana, and La Sombra—had all disappeared, retired, broken up, or faded. Selena was dead. Emilio had been distracted by his country career. And the new surge of Tejano acts were mostly copycat bands that were trying desperately to emulate the "new sound" of Michael Salgado or Grupo Límite.

Other acts with potential had various problems. The fourteen-year-old Jennifer Peña was still trying to outgrow the Selena tag. Bands like Fama and Eddie González y Grupo Vida lost serious momentum because of internal conflicts. Other young, exciting bands became nonstarters because of disorganization or lack of competent management.

The industry scrambled to react, but the downhill slide had started. Tejano radio stations began switching back to the larger regional Mexican format. The remaining stations became conservative with playlists, which further aggravated the situation. Live music clubs were closing or switching formats and record labels began trimming rosters. Major and indie labels quietly slipped away or dramatically reduced their Tex-Mex presence. KXTN-FM, the proud flagship of the genre, began slipping downward, dropping to No. 5 in 1998—behind classic rock station KZEP and pop/R&B station KTFM.

THE NEXT GENERATION

In some ways Tejano had become a victim of its own unparalleled success. Its rapid growth in the early years set off a chain reaction. The creation of exhilarating and relevant music by young talented artists attracted a wider audience, which in turn heated radio's growth. The music expanded, pulling in more labels, which chased other creative acts, who drew new younger fans. The cycle repeated until the genre's growth had outstripped its native pool of truly talented superstars.

The other shoe dropped when the proliferation of secondary artists and other backbenchers outpaced the market's growth. By that time, record labels were not creating new music as much as they were trying to run factories as efficiently as possible.

That the fantastic '90s Tejano story would come around full cycle to its humble beginning is not surprising. Like the new country, alternative, and grunge movements of the decade, the Tejano explosion had to have a start, a middle, and an end. Whether you call it a downturn, a correction, or right-sizing, the late '90s slowdown, no matter how serious it would play out, would not cause the end of a unique, original American genre. Tejano had survived through wars, hyper-inflation, economic downturns, incendiary politics, and the passing of fashion styles and cultural trends.

Even after the slowdown, Tejano, by any measure, was in a robust state many times above pre-1990 conditions. The market still had major record labels, FM stations, major clubs, and healthy representation on the charts; none of which had existed prior to 1990.

The long-term perspective was that Tejano would complete its shakeout period and return stronger than ever. With the industry infrastructure still in place, Tejano has all the tools and hardware to begin another amazing run.

If it is indeed true that—like business, politics, and consumer trends—music comes in cycles, then it is simply a matter of time before Tejano will rise again and make national headlines as one of the coolest music genres on the American landscape.

The Cultural Impact of Tejano

The rapid ascension of Tejano music in the early '90s may have been made viable because the music industry infrastructure—recording studios, major record labels, mainstream retailing—was already in place. Ultimately, though, it reached its maximum expression as a cultural movement because of a swiftly expanding U.S. Hispanic population that was hungry for heroes and icons.

Through fresh and dynamic rhythms, the music ignited the excitement and imagination of a mushrooming Tejano nation. The early '90s produced a musical revolution that not only changed radio formats, retailing practices, and the live music scene, but also impacted on fashion, style, and politics. The revolution also produced new young heroes to lead the way.

The biggest heroes were Emilio and Selena, but there was also Mazz, La Mafia, La Sombra, La Fiebre, Xelencia, and others. These were the artists who sparked Tejano's renaissance. And Tejano's rise was definitely a renewal, because it was not entirely new.

As a cultural movement, Tejano's rise in the '90s may have more in common with other short-lived phenomena—like grunge, alternative rock, and even modern country's brilliant rise in the '90s. These movements arose quickly, expanded in a super-heated atmosphere until they saturated their original environments, and then, as soon as they were consumed by the mass market, flickered out.

However as a distinct genre, Tejano has much in common with another original American form—country music. Both are urban genres that matured from rural, folk-based roots in the South and both appropriated the cowboy icon.

The new generation of Tejano music leaders provided tangible evidence that Mexican American culture in general, and Tejano music specifically, was something to be proud of. When Emilio and Selena achieved their crossover success, they became many things to many people. They were role models, young Mexican Americans who spoke English but sang Tejano in Spanish and achieved recognition in America—the land of possibilities.

For many people, Tejano's musical dominance in the '90s was not only a commercial success, but also a redemption—making up for all the years when Tejano was considered old hat, backward music that was only for people who did not, or would not, fit in.

Until idols like Emilio and Selena came along, there were only country, rap, and pop superstars on radio and mainstream TV. Beyond Gloria Estefan, Santana, or Los Lobos, Hispanic or Latino icons were few and far between.

For years Tejano had been relegated to AM radio and/or played only at home by those who feared being typecast. Bands that played Tejano were seen only in ramshackle clubs or rundown dance halls, further reinforcing negative stereotypes.

But at the peak of the renaissance, Tejano was on the streets, on radio, and on television. It was blasting out of car radios, and it was played in the biggest arenas and stadiums of the Southwest. The movement and its leading stars were covered in mainstream media. Tejano was selling big numbers and landing high on the charts in *Billboard,* reportedly the world's No. 1 music magazine.

And even within the Latino world, Tejano music sent out positive vibes.

For years, Latin pop was considered king, with the tropical/salsa genre a strong second. Tejano, and other forms of regional Mexican music—like norteño, conjunto, banda, and mariachi—were considered lowly and unsophisticated. It was music that did not sell very well and that mostly appealed to the recent immigrants from Mexico (read: uneducated, unskilled, and poor people).

When Tejano exploded, it began to change a lot of things.

It proved that Tejano as a genre had come of age, that there was a large enough constituency of young Tejanos who were economically and politically powerful enough not only to sustain the movement, but to challenge pop supremacy. Record sales figures proved that.

Another critical breakthrough was the success of the bilingual radio format. That was proven in 1994 when the Tejano flagship station KTXN-FM reached No. 1 in San Antonio, and not just within the Latin stations, but in the entire general market. To many it proved that the heart and soul of Tejano, of speaking in two languages and enjoying two cultures, could work. For years, the conventional wisdom in Latino radio was that one could not talk in two languages, or speak the inferior "Tex-Mex" of border people. "Tex-Mex" was not correct, and it was not the proper Mexican language.

Of course it wasn't. But then, this wasn't Mexico.

This was Texas, and the new Tejano country.

One could now have it both ways in the New Tejano Music Nation. One could assimilate and speak English and listen to

Madonna or Michael Jackson, and also jam down to Little Joe y La Familia or dance to the latest cumbia by Selena.

Just like the hip-hop nation, Mexican Americans in the Southwest had evolved a unique style with enough of a following and an identity to emerge as not only a musical form but as a distinct culture. Tejano in the '90s was not just about the music, it was about the lifestyle and the attitude of young and hip Mexican Americans.

On the larger cultural canvas, Emilio and Selena had shrewdly tapped into young Mexican Americans' desire to assimilate into a mainstream that included their own cool subculture, a place where they could be American and still hold on to their Mexican roots.

Emilio was heralded as one of the few rising Hispanics who succeeded in the country music scene in Nashville, a cultural conclave that to some is still one of the last bastions of racial exclusion. It was not too long ago that one could easily find evidence of this racial supremacy in the South—when rest rooms and schools were segregated, when black- and brown-skinned folks were refused service at restaurants, or when signs like "No Mexicans, Indians, or Dogs" were commonplace.

Of course, Emilio and Selena have not been alone in helping break the stereotypes.

Other heroes—from boxer Oscar de la Hoya and golfer Tiger Woods to film director Robert Rodríguez and actor Edward James Olmos—have helped ethnic and racial groups feel good about and proud of themselves.

Indirectly, the success of Emilio and Selena helped close a cultural gap that was felt by many Mexican Americans, a gap that made them feel inadequate and inferior in "the land of milk and honey."

American history is replete with examples of blatant discrimination and racial injustice. And yes, we have come a long way as a nation in embracing our cultural differences as individuals. But there have also been, and still are, subtle messages that Mexican American culture is not equal to Anglo culture. Some felt the English-as-the-official-language movement implied that Spanish was inferior. Others viewed American political policies as hypocritical—with an insistence on immigration control, but a simultaneous willingness to exploit undocumented immigrants as low-paid farmworkers and other less-skilled posts. And why does it seem that the Hispanic or Latino constituency is considered important by mainstream politicians only in the months leading up to the elections?

Through the decades the message has been: In order to assimilate, to be a "proper American," you had to blend in, become part of the program. Some saw that as a message that one needed to lose or bury one's ethnicity, one's accent, or else risk seeming different or standing out from the homogeneity.

In the late '90s a new trend began to take hold. It was the reverse message—that it is OK, that it is uniquely American, to celebrate one's own culture, and that of our neighbors as well. The brilliant arrival of Tejano served as a catharsis for the years of self-doubt and cultural inferiority felt by generations of Mexican Americans.

Ultimately, the struggle to fit in, to belong, and to become successful is part of American folklore that dates back to the first European immigrants in this country—the Irish and the Italians, the Germans and the French.

For Mexican Americans, the struggle began after the U.S.-Mexico War (1846–1848), which led to the Treaty of Guadalupe Hidalgo. Overnight, millions of Mexicans had a new choice—become an American citizen or remain a Mexican citizen in an environment that would soon turn hostile.

From that historical fork in the road, generations of Mexican Americans have felt confusion and ambivalence toward their heritage—the epic struggle to assimilate and yet to retain one's roots. Each choice offered its own reward and extracted its own price.

If you held on to your roots, your *Méxicanidad,* you risked being laughed at as a "Mexican beaner" and stereotyped as a backward, illiterate Mexican.

After all, the prevailing images of Latinos in America for decades were not very complimentary. The few times Latinos were covered in the media it was usually as an "illegal alien" or an "undocumented worker" who was uneducated and whose only skills were fit for agricultural tasks. Other prevalent media images were the shootings, stabbings, and other seemingly routine violence in the Latino barrio that always made the 5 and 10 P.M. newscasts.

On another level, to hang on to your own culture and language was a subtle signal that you did not want to fit in. You did not want to speak the international language of business (English), or be a part of the "superior" Anglo culture.

For youth, the choice was often to go to the other extreme—to blend in as much as possible to American norms, to drop your accent, to Anglicize your last name (or, as in Emilio's case, drop the last name altogether)—in a desperate attempt to fit in. This choice offered the possibility of material rewards and success in American society.

The downside was that your own people often abandoned you, claiming that you had purposely or ignorantly lost your own mother tongue, your sense of your roots. Nowhere did that chasm become more obvious or elicit such vitriol as when visiting your mother country, Mexico, where your lack of proper Spanish was immediately evident. Mexican citizens derided you as a *pocho,* a derogatory term for one who had lost his or her culture.

Many tried to assimilate completely, but few succeeded. It was fairly impossible. Those born with fair skin considered themselves lucky. Others could lose their accents or change their last name, but could not lighten their skin. And yet when those trying to assimilate succeeded to a degree, they were often criticized. They were considered disloyal or just plain ignorant of their own identity by trying to "act white."

And generations of Mexican Americans continued through this third world—one foot in Mexican, another in American culture.

But with every Mexican American success story, that sense of emptiness and dislocation was healed a little. For every Ritchie Valens or Carlos Santana, for every Selena or Los Super Seven, shared values were reaffirmed. In the overall Latino experience, the success of Tejano was just one more validation of Latino culture. Many consider music the chief currency by which racial and ethnic identities are perpetuated and reaffirmed.

And music, like fashion and politics, is cyclical. Tejano's flickering phase after its brilliant flame only means that the pendulum is swinging toward the other side. But it will surely return in time. And it will find the market with major components in place that previous generations did not have: major record labels, modern nightclubs, FM stations, and young successful crossover heroes.

In the new millennia, there will be new political forces at play.

According to recent studies, the children of recent U.S. immigrants from Mexico, Asia, and the Caribbean are not as anxious to blend into mainstream America as were previous European generations. Instead, new immigrants are finding the middle path. While they are learning English and other skills that will help them become successful in society, they are also holding on to their own cultural traditions and customs.

For these generations, assimilation may be more of a direction than a destination.

For others, there is a new interpretation of the idea of assimilating into the mainstream, or majority culture. With the rapidly changing demographics in the U.S., it is becoming evident that the Hispanic minority will be the majority minority, and perhaps also the dominant culture, within fifty years. Unquestionably, by the mid-twenty-first century, America will be a multi-racial, multi-cultural country with no absolute majority population.

A–Z Encyclopedia

ACCORDION (SQUEEZE BOX)

The accordion, also known as the squeeze box, comes from the organ family of instruments. When the instrument is squeezed, air is pumped from the bellows through the steel reeds, producing the musical tones. German musician Friedrich Buschmann invented the accordion in 1822, one year after inventing the harmonica. The original accordion utilized a finger button keyboard. The piano keyboard was added thirty years later. Italian musician Mariano Dallape invented the button accordion in 1910. The button accordion and the melodic hooks that it produces are indispensable to Tejano and norteño music. Many scholars believe the button accordion was introduced to Texas and Mexico in the 1860s by German and Czech immigrants. The accordion is also a key instrument in other folk genres such as zydeco and Cajun. It enjoyed a resurgence in popularity in the 1980s.

ADALBERTO

Born Adalberto Gallegos, May 2, 1956, Nogales, Sonora, México

With his power and range as a vocalist, Adalberto has been one of the most respected singers in the Tex-Mex music genre. He could inject a flood of emotion into Tejano polka standards as easily as he could reinvent torchy Mexican rancheras with fresh pain and mature resignation. Adalberto Gallegos was raised in Tucson, Arizona, where his early musical influences included Mexican ranchera greats **José Alfredo Jiménez** and **Javier Solis** as well as seminal Tejano groups such as **Latin Breed.** He began his professional career in 1975 with short stints with the USA Band and **Los Fabulosos Cuatro.** In 1976 he got a chance to join Latin Breed when lead singer **Jimmy Edward** left. He fronted the band on

Adalberto
Courtesy of Voltage Entertainment & Management

the *Power Drive* and *One Way* albums, demonstrating an impressive vocal power and range. The mid-1970s, a time when Tejano was enjoying its first golden age, were perhaps also the Breed's most creative and innovative era. The Breed, like the other top groups, combined Tejano soul with inventive brass arrangements that touched on jazz and big-band flavorings.

In 1990 Adalberto signed on with Sony Discos (then CBS) and released an impressive CD, which was produced by the noted studio wiz Bob Gallarza Jr. In a field of copycat bands glumly playing by-the-numbers polkas and cumbias, Adalberto's music was like fresh air. Tunes like "El Aguacero" and "Emoción Pasajera" fused traditional Mexican rancheras with complex, multi-layered jazz-influenced horn arrangements. Though critically acclaimed, Adalberto's music was not appreciated at retail, as CD sales were sluggish. That, combined with management problems, led to Sony's decision in 1994 not to renew his contract. In 1996 he released *Esta Vez,* an album on the Spring, Texas indie label MusaDisc. The new album featured songs by Adalberto, Javier Galván of **Fama,** as well as covers of **Juan Gabriel**'s "No Me Conoces" and Ramiro Cavazos's "Yo No Puedo Dejar de Quererte."

Escúchame (Sony Discos)
Esta Vez (MusaDisc)
Me Nace (Sony Discos)

AGUILAR, ANTONIO

Born May 17, 1919, Villanueva, Zacatecas, México

In the ranchera genre perhaps **Vicente Fernández** has had the biggest international impact. But, in terms of longevity and tradition, Antonio Aguilar has been to the Mexican folkloric form what Roy Rogers was to the American cowboy genre: the quintessential singer and wholesome cowboy.

As a child growing up at the Tayahua hacienda, Aguilar helped his parents work the fields, getting a firsthand look at what it took to survive in Mexico's rural settings. While still a young boy Aguilar traveled to Mexico City and tried to get on as a ranchera singer at famed radio station XEW in the late 1940s, but the reigning *charros* of that era were **Jorge Negrete** and **Pedro Infante.** In 1950 Aguilar married the singer Flor Silvestre and the following year reinvented himself as a bolero singer accompanied by the José Sabre Marroquín Orquesta. Shortly afterward he met Eduardo Baptista, president of Musart/Balboa records, who helped him develop into a top singer. During a stop in Puerto Rico on one of his initial tours, according to folklore, Aguilar's laid-back, crooner-style bolero singing was booed and, at the suggestion of the famous composer Rafael "El Jibarito" Hernández, Aguilar switched from boleros to rancheras and so began Aguilar's career as a traditional ranchera singer.

Now feeling properly situated, Aguilar began in earnest what would lead to a prolific career, producing more than 130 recordings and appearing in more than 164 films. Aguilar pioneered the concept of the Mexican *charro* show, which was a combination *charreada* (Mexican rodeo) and ranchera concert. He often said he was inspired to produce a show on the values of folkloric traditions after working menial jobs in the U.S. He felt there was a need to give fellow immigrants pride in their culture.

By the early 1960s, Aguilar had developed and polished the show so much that it became increasingly popular, drawing sold-out houses. Aguilar began to tour internationally, including the U.S. and Central and South America. Aguilar's elaborate *charro* productions included folkloric dance performers and mariachi groups and were primarily a family affair that featured his wife, Flor Silvestre, a singer in her own right, and sons **Pepe Aguilar** and **Antonio Aguilar Jr.** who accompanied him on boleros, rancheras, and corridos in between the equestrian shows.

Flor Silvestre (born Guillermina Jiménez, August 16, 1930) came from a humble ranching family in Salamanca, Guanajuato. Her parents liked to sing at family gatherings. She sang at the local theater when she was twelve years old, and later debuted at radio station XEFO singing "La Soldadera." It became her signature song and first nickname until she discovered there was already another "Soldadera," and so she took the stage name Flor Silvestre. She appeared in her first movie, *Primero Soy Mexicana,* alongside Joaquín Pardave and Luis Aguilar.

Antonio Aguilar was also in Mexican and American movies, including the 1969 *Undefeated,* where he costarred with John Wayne and Rock Hudson. In 1994 Balboa released the first four volumes of the Rancherismo series, which contained Antonio Aguilar's greatest hits, and a new mariachi album by Aguilar, titled *Un Hombre Derecho,* which was produced by Aguilar's son Pepe. Through the years, the Aguilar family scored with such hits as "Tristes Recuerdos," "Cielo Rojo," "La Carta," and "Morenita." The family show continued to draw packed houses into the late 1990s. *Amusement Business* reported that the 1997 *Aguilar & Family Charro,* which featured a guest appearance by **Juan Gabriel,** drew a sellout crowd of 16,000 plus at Madison Square Garden.

El Charro de México (Musart)
... Con Mariachi (Musart)
En Vivo (Musart)
Mi Gusto Es.../Con Tambora (Musart)
Norteño (Musart)

AGUILAR, ANTONIO, JR.

Born October 9, 1960, San Antonio, Texas

Born into a musical family that included his parents, ranchera singers **Antonio Aguilar** and **Flor Silvestre,** and brother **Pepe Aguilar,** Antonio Jr. got his start at an early age. He made his singing debut with his parents at the age of four in the family's touring *charro* shows during a stop in New York City.

He began his solo career as a singer in the '90s, producing several albums for the EMI Latin label. His debut CD, *Toda Mi Vida,* in 1994 was produced by his brother Pepe and Adrián Posse and featured the backing of Mariachi Aguilas de América de Javier Carrido. The album showcased his mix of rancheras and boleros with mariachi orchestration and produced the first single "Por Ti No Voy a Llorar," composed by Manuel E. Castro, which broke into the Billboard Hot Latin Tracks chart in July 1994.

La Amargura del Amor (EMI)
Amor Entre Sombras (EMI)
Toda Mi Vida (EMI)

AGUILAR, PEPE

Born José Antonio Aguilar, August 7, 1978, Villanueva, Zacatecas, México

With his parents, the famous ranchera singers **Antonio Aguilar** and **Flor Silvestre,** and an older brother **Antonio Aguilar Jr.,** also a singing cowboy, Pepe Aguilar was destined to follow the musical legacy. Pepe Aguilar made his entertainment debut in his family's *charro* show when he was three years old during a performance in San Antonio, Texas. At the age of nine, he had saved enough money to buy drums, which became the first instrument he learned to play. His first interest, though, was rock music, which he pursued for five years without major luck. His parents did not support his choice, but then they did not stop him either.

Interestingly, in 1985 Aguilar created the rodeo team El Soyate (named after the family's ranch), which won several national awards. Eventually in the late 1980s, his rock days gave way to the original folkloric music that his parents had pioneered. He recorded several CDs that were moderately successful and he also developed a keen interest in record production work. He opened Pepe Aguilar Productions, where he recorded Mexican as well as rock groups. He produced CDs for his cousin **Guadalupe Pineda,** brother Antonio Jr., and his father.

Aguilar also has appeared in fourteen movies, including the most recent, *La Sangre de un Valiente*. He produced his 1998 CD, *Por Mujeres Como Tú,* whose title track reached No. 4 on the Billboard Hot Latin Tracks chart. The CD also included original songs by noted songwriters Manuel Eduardo Castro and Manuel Durán Durán, as well as Aguilar's covers of José José's "Almohada" and **Cornelio Reyna**'s "Baraja de Oro."

Cautiva y Triste (Musart)
Chiquilla Bonita (Musart)
Mariachi (Musart)
Por Mujeres Como Tú (Musart)
Recuérdame Bonito (Balboa)
Tambora, Vol. 3 (Musart)

AGUILARES, LOS

Formed 1952, San Antonio, Texas

Los Aguilares were one of the longest running conjunto entities in South Texas history. Brothers Genaro, Frank, and Emilio Aguilar began playing professionally in the early '50s when they were in the mid-teens. In 1955 older brother Frank joined the U.S. Air Force and was replaced by Joey López, who would later go on to start his own indie label Joey International.

In 1960 López left the band and it changed its name from Los Guadalupanos to El Conjunto de Los Aguilares and began to record its first sides for Discos Norteño and scored with the early hit "De Acá de Este Lado" on Frank Morante's defunct Sombrero label. In those days, the brothers like to recall, local conjuntos would stand in line up to five hours for a chance to perform, for free, on local radio stations during the remote broadcasts. Los Aguilares recorded regional hits such as "Flor del Río," "Qué Padre la Vida," "Chaparrita," and "Esta Vez es la Última Vez."

Through the years Los Aguilares have added and replaced sons, nephews, and even grandsons in the group. In the 1990s Los Aguilares often brought along their grandsons' band, Los Tejanitos, a foursome that featured Aguilar's grandson Michael, three years old, on drums, and grandson-in-law, Richard Medina, six years old, on accordion. The two were backed by their respective fathers: Michael Sr. on bass, and Richard Medina Sr. on *bajo sexto*.

Anhelos (Joey International)
Hey (Joey International)
Me Estoy Acostumbrando (Joey International)

ALEGRES DE TERÁN, LOS

Formed circa 1948, General Terán, Nuevo León, México

Los Alegres de Terán secured their place in music history when they brought vocal duo harmonies to the accordion-driven norteño genre. Los Alegres came together when accordionist Eugenio Abrego met *bajo sexto* player Tomás Ortiz during a performance in General Terán, Nuevo León.

The men formed the group and moved their base of operations first to Monterrey, later to Reynosa, and finally to McAllen, Texas. Their first record, *Corrido de Pepito,* was released in 1948 on the Orfeo label. Los Alegres's prolific output included forty 78s and 165 albums on a series of indie and major labels. Many of these albums were top sellers that garnered gold and platinum awards from their record label, then-CBS, and included such hits as "Carta Jugada," "El Güero Estrada," and "Alma Enamorada,"

Los Alegres were also part of the first Polka Festival, which was held in Chicago in 1965, and also appeared in numerous films, including 1951's *Pueblito.* In 1983 Los Alegres were inducted into the Tejano Conjunto Hall of Fame and were recognized for their contributions, including their pioneering use of two-part vocal harmonies. Abrego died in 1988.

Canijas Viejas (Sony)
Gracias de Los Alegres (Sony)
Méxicanisimo (Sony)
Vuelven (Sony)

AMBER ROSE

Born Amber Rose Zepeda, March 2, 1983, San Antonio, Texas

Amber Rose
Courtesy of Chris Borgman/Barb Wire

With a debut CD that sported pop, dance, and Tejano grooves, Amber Rose represented the new wave in Tejano upstarts when she came on the scene in 1997. With major record label support, her engaging self-titled CD had the potential to land several charts hits—not only in Tejano but in mainstream pop/dance stations. Signed in 1996 to the Dallas-based Barb Wire label, then distributed by Virgin Records, the St. John Bosco School ninth grader recorded her CD with Top 40 rock guitarist Michael Morales and his brother, producer Ron Morales. Three singles—"Candy Boy," "Tú Me Prometiste," and "Chicas Quieren Gozar" (a remake of Cindy Lauper's "Girls Just Want to Have Fun")—were played at Tejano and pop radio stations and dance clubs.

Amber Rose was only twelve years old when she won the San Antonio citywide Our Part of Town talent contest. Although her first interest was pop, she said she was inspired to go into Tejano after Selena, one of her heroes, passed away in 1995.

Amber Rose (Barb Wire)

ANA BARBARA

Born Altagracia Ugalde Mota, January 10, circa 1970, Río Verde, San Luis Potosí, México

Ana Barbara broke on radio in 1994 with the **Selena**-influenced pop-cumbia tune "Nada," the title track from her debut CD, which was produced by Aníbal Pastor. Her career received an initial boost when FonoVisa officials helped her obtain the opening slot for tours by **Los Tigres del Norte** and **Bronco.** The following year, Barbara was nominated for a Univision Premio Lo Nuestro Award for best new female artist in the regional Mexican category. Her exceptionally tall and slender figure helped her popularity, but it was her keyboard-and-percussion-driven cumbia confections—such as "No Lloraré" and "Me Asusta Pero Me Gusta," which were often written and produced by stars like Pastor and **Marco Antonio Solis,** an ex-**Los Bukis**—that kept her on *Billboard*'s charts during the late '80s and '90s.

At the age of eight she was singing backup for her sister Viviana in a local band. In the '80s she won the Miss San Luis Potosí pageant and began to sing ranchera music, gigging in bars and private parties.

Ay, Amor (FonoVisa)
Besos No Se Dan en la Camisa (FonoVisa)
Nada (FonoVisa)
Trampa (FonoVisa)

ANA GABRIEL

Born María Guadalupe Araujo Yong, December 10, 1958, Guamuchil, Sinaloa, México

Instantly recognizable because of her trademark raspy but powerful voice, Ana Gabriel impressed quickly with prolific songwriting that generated early hits "No Me Lastimes Más" and "Mar y Arena." That, combined with her record producing skills, made her an influential figure in the Latin music scene in the '90s.

Of part Chinese ancestry (her father was Mexican; her maternal grandparents were from China), Ana Gabriel began singing as a preteen when she entered local talent contests in her hometown. When she was fifteen years old, she moved to the border city of Tijuana to pursue her musical career. A few years later she participated in the Valores Juveniles Festival where she won second place. This led to the realization of her first dream—to land a record contract. Signed to CBS México in 1985, she produced two albums with marginally successful singles. She broke into the industry full-force with *¿Quién Como Tú?,* which produced the torchy hit "Hice Bien Quererte." A live album in 1990, *En Vivo,* captured her incendiary persona onstage, particularly the songs "Propuesta" and "Solamente un Vez," where Ana Gabriel plumbed new emotional depths. She followed with the roots album *Mi México,* which yielded the hits "Mi Talismán" and "Amigo Mío," her tribute to fellow Mexican songwriter **Juan Gabriel.**

Ana Gabriel's other signature hits included "Demasiado Tarde," from the Sony ranchera compilation CD *México: Voz y Sentimiento,* and "Cosas del Amor," a duet with **Vikki Carr** that was named the pop/ballad song of the year in the regional Mexican category at the 1992 Billboard Latin Music Awards.

In 1996's *Vivencias* Ana Gabriel flirted with pop rhythms, but she returned to her ranchera roots on *Con un Mismo Corazón,* a CD full of provocative meditations on love's many guises. She reinvented **José Alfredo Jiménez**'s classic "Me Equivoqué Contigo," adding searing emotional tones to this song about falling in love with someone and finding out he is an unfaithful lout. Worth the price of the entire CD, her duet with ranchera king **Vicente Fernández,** "Con un Mismo Corazón," was an interesting view of how real love survives the rocky travails of life.

In September of 1998, Ana Gabriel released another live CD, the thirty-track boxed set *En la Plaza de Toros México,* which complemented her exquisite work on the 1990 *En Vivo.* Her live renditions of her recent hits "Cosas del Amor" and "Me Equivoque" demonstrated a singer performing with a calm confidence and a fiery conviction. She also revealed a new insight on the **Jorge Negrete**–identified "México Lindo y Querido/Cielito Lindo."

Ana Gabriel teamed up with noted studio wiz Emilio Estefan Jr. to coproduce her *Soy Como Soy* CD in 1999. Again, Ana Gabriel injected pop/dance flavorings into her ranchera ballad material. She collaborated with top songwriter Kike Santander, who also helped out on production chores and wrote the first single, "Si Me Faltaras."

In a field flooded with imitations and wanna-bes, Ana Gabriel was one of the top female ranchera singers in Mexico. And as a talented songwriter and astute producer who was shrewd enough to work with top arrangers, Ana Gabriel was easily in the same league as Juan Gabriel and **Marco Antonio Solis.**

Con un Mismo Corazón (Sony México)
En la Plaza de Toros México (Sony Mexico)
En Vivo (Sony México)
Joyas de los Siglos (Sony México)
Luna (Sony México)
Mi México (Sony México)
Soy Como Soy (Sony Mexico)
Vivencias (Sony México)

ANGELES AZULES, LOS

Formed 1980, Ixtapalapa, Mexico City, México

With their smooth horn-powered boleros and vallenato-styled cumbias, Los Angeles Azules emerged as solid players in the early 1990s. Los Angeles were a thirteen-member outfit trading in romantic ballads and the cumbia-vallenata, the accordion-led music of Colombia's Atlantic coast, and impacting with solid grooves from their big horn section and percolating percussions.

The band was founded by the Mejía brothers—Alfredo, *requinto*/accordion; José, *tumbas;* and Elias, *bajo sexto.* Eventually several other family members joined. All the Mejía brothers were degreed professionals and included a surgeon, an architect, three attorneys, and two oncologists. They are all still practicing professionals who balance their work and music careers.

After a few independent releases, the band was signed on by the Monterrey-based indie DISA and they produced some fifteen albums, churning out vallenato hits "Ay Amor," "Entrega de Amor," "El Pegado," and "Te Necesito," most of which were written by Jorge Mejía Avante, the band's principal songwriter and arranger.

By the mid-1990s, Los Angeles Azules were gaining momentum and were nominated for best artist in the grupo genre by the Mexico City daily *El Heraldo.* The band's major-label debut in 1996, *Inolvidables,* which was distributed by EMI Latin, went triple platinum, landed on The Billboard Latin 50 chart, and spun off the megahit "Como Te Voy A Olvidar." That tune, "Mi Niña Mujer," and "Me Haces Falta Tú" from the 1998 *Confesiones de Amor* CD all cracked the Billboard Hot Latin Tracks chart. Los Angeles were also invited to perform at the Acapulco '97 Festival.

15 Éxitos de Colección (DISA/EMI Latin)
Confesiones de Amor (DISA/EMI Latin)
Entrega de Amor (DISA/EMI Latin)
Inolvidables (DISA/EMI Latin)

ANGELES NEGROS, LOS

Formed circa 1971, Santiago, Chile

A forerunner to the emergent grupo movement of the '70s, Los Angeles Negros were recording boleros with electric guitar and organ, giving the material a pop sheen. The early '70s belonged to this talented outfit with such major hits as "Y Volveré," "Murió la Flor," and "Como Quisiera Decirte." The original lineup included vocalist Germain de la Fuente, along with Miguel Angel Concha, Mario Gutiérrez, Jorge Hernan Evans, and Aurelio Luis Ortiz.

The group changed vocalists several times after its initial burst of fame and relocated to Mexico in the mid-1980s. De la Fuente left the group and formed his own Los Angeles Negros, putting his name in front to avoid confusion. He returned in 1995 as a solo artist with the CD *Qué De Raro?* Featuring Peruvian bolero composer Lucho Barrios, the album contained ballads, folk rhythms, and reworked some older material by both artists.

15 Melodiás Inolvidables con Sabor a los... (Odeon)
Homenaje a Los Angeles Negros (Multimusic)
Romántico (DISMEX Sonoame)
Solid Gold (DISMEX Sonoame)
Tesoros de la Música (DISMEX Sonoame)

ANGELICA MARÍA

Born Angelica María Hartman Ortiz, circa late 1940s, New Orleans, Louisiana

Angelica María was the only daughter of musician Arnie Hartman and Angelica Ortiz. When Angelica María was a child her family traveled often because of her father's musical career. At ten she appeared and sang for the first time in the movie *Mala Semilla,* with the Mariachi Perla de Occidente, which backed the famous ranchera singer **Pedro Infante.** At the age of seventeen, then the girlfriend of famed Mexican rocker Enrique Guzmán, Angelica María recorded her first album featuring rock ballads. In 1960 she debuted in her first soap opera, eventually appearing in more than a dozen, including *Cartas de Amor* and *El Callejón del Beso.*

She scored big in the mid-1960s with the Spanish rock 'n' roll hit "Eddie, Eddie." In the late '60s she was so popular, she was considered Mexico's teenage sweetheart. Her first non-rock hit was a ranchera ballad "Tú Sigues Siendo el Mismo" in the early 1970s, which was written by a then-unknown **Juan Gabriel.** She later got on the charts in Mexico with "Cuando Me Enamoré." She pioneered the ranchera ballad at a time when the bolero ranchero was more popular. Aside from singing and appearing in more than sixty films, she has also been in soap operas, TV shows, and in theater.

20 de Colección (Sony)
Juan Gabriel/Inspira (FonoVisa)
Pero Amaneció (RCA)
Personalidad (Sony)
Reina y Cenicienta (Sony)

ARCARAZ, LUIS

Born Luis Arcaraz Torras, December 5, 1910, Mexico City, México; died June 1, 1963, San Luis Potosí, San Luis Potosí, México

Luis Arcaraz was principally a songwriter, and a prolific one at that, but few singers could interpret his material as he could, with emotional depth and exquisite phrasing. His signature hits were mostly boleros, including "Viajera," "Sombra Verde," "Bonita," and "Muñequita de Esquire."

Arcaraz's father, who died when Arcaraz was four years old, wrote *zarzuelas* (Spanish operas) and owned the Teatro Principal in Mexico City. When he was in college in Spain, he studied mechanical engineering, but he eventually switched to music, studying harmony, composition, and orchestral direction.

In 1928 Arcaraz played with a small group in the Teatro Palma in Tampico, Tamaulipas and he later played on radio stations XEG and XEFO. He eventually organized an orchestra and began touring the United States, gaining enough popularity to be considered alongside the big-band leaders, such as Tommy Dorsey, Glenn Miller, and Duke Ellington. After a while the cost of running a large orchestra got to be prohibitive and Arcaraz began touring as a soloist.

Of the more than 200 songs he wrote, many became bolero hits, including "Mentira," "Olvida," "Prisionero de Amor," and "Quinto Patio." Among his collaborators were José A. Zorrillas and Mario Molina Montes. It was during a trip from Monterrey to Mexico City that Arcaraz was killed in an auto accident on La Central Highway just outside of San Luis Potosí.

Camden: Colección del Siglo (RCA)
Grandes Éxitos de Luis Arcaraz (RCA)

ARNULFO JR. REY Y AS

See Reyes del Camino, Los

ASTUDILLO, PETE

Born December 1, 1963, Laredo, Texas

Selena's backing vocalist Pete Astudillo played weddings and private parties near Laredo with keyboardist Joe Ojeda in the local band Bad Boys. It was at a February 1989 concert that they were asked to open for Selena y Los Dinos at the Roxy nightclub. Ojeda and Astudillo impressed the group enough to get hired and they appeared on Selena's first three CDs for EMI Latin. In early 1994 Astudillo went solo, signing with the Q Productions indie label, which was then distributed by EMI.

Astudillo's first solo CDs—*Entrégate a Mí* and *Como Nadie*—had no impact on the national charts. However, within a few months after Selena's tragic death in March of 1995, Astudillo wrote "Cómo Te Extraño" as a tribute to his late mother and Selena. It became a heavily played single on Tejano radio and reached No. 2 on the Billboard Hot Latin Tracks chart in early 1996. The momentum also helped Astudillo capture most promising band honors at the 1996 TMAs. Astudillo continued to record in the 1990s, but he never came close to matching the success of his Selena tribute.

Como Nadie (EMI)
Cómo Te Extraño (EMI)
Si Tú No Estás (EMI)

AYALA, JOSÉ LUIS

See Humildes, Los

AYALA, PEDRO

Born June 29, 1911, General Terán, Nuevo León, México

One of the earliest conjunto pioneers, Pedro Ayala was credited with popularizing the use of the *tololoche* in the recording studio.

Self-taught, Ayala began playing the drums at the age of six and by his early teens he was learning the guitar and accordion. His family moved to the United States where they settled in Donna in the Rio Grande Valley in Texas. He played with his brothers and with his father, Emilio Ayala, in their band on nights and weekends. During the day, they worked in the cotton and vegetable fields. Ayala got his break in 1947, when he began recording for a small label. Over the ensuing years Ayala recorded ten CDs and wrote about seventy compositions for different record companies.

In 1982 he was in the charter group of inductees into the Tejano Conjunto Hall of Fame. In 1984, after recovering from open-heart surgery, Ayala continued to tour, albeit on a much reduced schedule. In September of 1988 he was honored with a National Heritage Fellowship Award. Ayala's three sons—Ramón, Pedro Jr., and Emilio—followed in their father's footsteps and started their own band, Los Hermanos Ayala (not to be confused with **Los Humildes,** which for a brief period used the name Los Hermanos Ayala).

15 Éxitos (RYN)
Polkas, Redowas, y Schotis (Roy Sales)

AYALA, RAMÓN

Born Ramón Covarrubias Jr., December 8, 1945, Monterrey, Nuevo León, México

In the norteño genre, few artists have proved as durable and influential as accordionist Ramón Ayala. Like the venerable **Los Tigres del Norte,** Ayala has thrived for more than thirty years, inspiring dozens of bands from Mexico's **Los Tucanes de Tijuana** and **Los Tiranos del Norte** to neo-trad acts **Los Palominos** and **Intocable.**

Ayala was born in the Monterrey neighborhood of Colonia Argentina, where he learned to play the accordion at the age of five from his father, Ramón Covarrubias, who worked as a steel mill worker by day and played with his group Los Jilgueros de Marín by night.

(Interestingly, Ayala's last name is actually Covarrubias. Ayala's father switched from Covarrubias to Ayala because, in order to get a job in the steel mill, one needed to have family or know someone who was already working there. So a friend let Ayala's father use his last name. Therefore, Ayala the norteño singer and accordionist is actually Jr.; his son Jr. is actually Ayala III; and his grandson Ramón III is actually Ayala IV.)

Ramón Ayala y Sus Bravos del Norte; with accordionist Ramón Ayala (fourth from left)
Courtesy of Freddie

While still a preteen Ayala begged his father to sit in with the band. He did and was eventually designated as the band's mascot. During Ayala's teens, however, the family endured hard economic times, moving first to El Control, and later to Reynosa, Tamaulipas where, according to family lore, Ayala bought a shoe-shine kit to help out. It was during one of Ayala's frequent trips to La Central square in Reynosa that he would run into local musicians and trade off accordion licks and musical knowledge. In 1960 a fifteen-year-old Ayala ran into *bajo sexto* player **Cornelio Reyna** and accordionist Juan Peña of Dueto Carta Blanca at the Cadillac Bar. While Reyna and Peña practiced, Ayala begged for a chance to show his prowess on the accordion. Peña was doubtful, but Reyna relented and Ayala strapped on the accordion. As the story goes, Ayala whipped out a fanciful rendition of the polka "Rosa Ana." Reyna and Peña were suitably impressed, but it would be another year before Reyna and Ayala actually teamed up as a conjunto. The start was difficult, gigs were few and far between. But in 1963 the men were discovered by Paulino Bernal who signed them to his fledgling BEGO Records. And so **Los Relámpagos del Norte** was born.

Los Relámpagos scored right out of the box with the hits "Llora" and Bruno Villarreal's "Ingratos Ojos Míos." It was a solid eight-year run that saw several more hits—mostly by Reyna, who evolved into a prolific songwriter—that became norteño standards, such as "Me Caí de las Nubes" and "Mi Tesoro."

In 1971, however, the two split. Reyna became a solo singer in a mariachi group and eventually a film actor. Ayala formed his own group, Los Bravos del Norte, and scored quickly with "La Pura Manía." Through the years Ayala secured several top singers, including Tony Sauceda, José Martínez, and **Eliseo Robles,** who also played with Los Satelites (the band of Ayala's brother Fidel). Robles split from the group in the mid-1980s and was replaced by Juan Antonio Coronado. In the '90s, Ayala took over as lead singer.

Through almost three decades Ayala, first through Los Relámpagos and then with his Los Bravos, became one of norteño's seminal artists. What the Mexican legend **Vicente Fernández** is to rancheras, Ayala is to norteño. He is among the most widely recognized and biggest selling proponents. From the beginning, Ayala diverged little from his original norteño style—plaintive vocals and crisp accordion runs over typical foot-stomping rhythms. The basic norteño repertoire is the polka and corrido, but

Ayala sprinkled a variety of cumbias, rancheras, and other musical styles to keep things interesting. In live performances Ayala delivered fluid accordion runs and harmonic vocals on melancholy songs, typically about the hopes and dreams of Mexican immigrants. He demonstrated his prowess on other standards, such as "Cruz de Madera," producing new readings by slowing the verses down or by extracting additional colors and nuances from his rhinestone-studded Gabanelli accordion. A minor downside was Ayala's use of a disc jockey sidekick, common in norteño groups, whose seemingly constant between-song banter only detracts from the performance.

Ayala's hit bag included "Besos y Caricias," "La Rama del Mesquite," "Un Rincóncito en el Cielo," "Un Puño de Tierra," and "Tragos Amargos." In the '90s Ayala received several Grammy nominations, including one in 1998 for "En las Alas de un Ángel," a tribute to his former partner, Cornelio Reyna, who died in 1997. Ayala's brother José Luis (not to be confused with **Los Humildes**'s **José Luis Ayala**) also became a prolific producer, helming CD projects by his brother, Intocable, and **Intenso.**

In the late 1980s, Ramón Ayala Jr. (born March 6, 1969, Alice, Texas) was studying accounting at the University of Texas Pan American when he decided to join his dad. He was hired as a roadie and in 1992 sang in a duet with his father on "Cuánto Me Cuesta." With Garth Brooks–on-a-diet good looks and production help from dad, the younger Ayala landed a contract with Sony Discos in 1993. His hits included "Monterrey de Mis Amores" and "Sabor Amargo."

RAMÓN AYALA

Arráncame el Corazón (Freddie)
Corridos Auténticos (Freddie)
Lágrimas (Freddie)
Somos Norteños... Total (Freddie)

RAMÓN AYALA JR.

Lágrimas de Amor (Sony Discos)
Príncipe (Sony Discos)

AYALA, RAMÓN, JR.

See Ayala, Ramón

BAJO SEXTO

Like the accordion, the *bajo sexto,* a twelve-string bass guitar, is a primary instrument in Tejano music, particularly in genuine traditional conjunto. The *bajo sexto* has a thicker neck than a regular guitar and has a feature called a "cutaway," which improves resonance. The electric bass replaced the *bajo sexto*'s bass function in many conjuntos in the 1950s, and today the *bajo sexto* mainly serves as a rhythm instrument. Scholars are unclear about whether the instrument, which is likely a descendant of the Spanish mandolin, reached Texas in the nineteenth century by way of Spain or Mexico. Unlike accordions, which for the most part are made in Germany or Italy, *bajo sextos* are made in Texas and Mexico. Handmade *bajo sextos,* such as those made by the Macias family in San Antonio, carry prestige. The *bajo sexto* is considered to be the brother of the accordion in conjunto music, because both are indispensable to a "real" conjunto.

BANDA

In its simplest terms, banda means band in Spanish, but in music industry usage it typically refers to the big brassy bands that originated from the northern Mexican state of Sinaloa, where the tradition was born. European musical customs, especially German customs, made a major impact on Mexican culture in the late nineteenth century. European immigrants brought along many industrial skills, as well as cultural traditions—from proper beer making to stately dancing. They also brought their brass bands. Often boasting over a dozen members, Mexico's boisterous bandas record songs in all popular Mexican styles—from cumbia to corrido, bolero to *huapango*. Early in the century, bandas were not known for utilizing a lead vocalist. **Banda El Limón** claimed it was the first to use vocals but, in the absence of hard documentation, it cannot be confirmed.

A traditional banda—say **Banda El Recodo de Cruz Lizárraga** or Banda El Limón from Sinaloa—utilizes core instruments like trumpets, trombones, tubas, and percussions, although a few also include the clarinet. In the early '90s, the banda movement shot to prominence thanks to its association with an athletic, fast-rhythm dance called *la quebradita* and the incorporation of electric bass and keyboards, the latter leading to the phenomenon known as techno-banda or electro-banda. The rise of *la quebradita* was a '90s phenomenon. Its name means "little break," referring to the back-bending contortion the female dancing partner makes as the male swings her toward the floor. *La quebradita,* which combines country-western, *lambada,* and flamenco, is an exciting form to watch, much like the exaggerated tango was in its cinematic heyday. *Quebradita* also refers to a fast rhythm used by many bands.

Perhaps because *la quebradita* was a contemporary form, developed and finessed by its own culture, it shot to dance-craze status among Wrangler-clad Mexican youth. Notable hits from banda's '90s revival were *quebraditas* "Provócame" by **Banda Vallarta Show** and "Al Gato y al Ratón" by **Banda Machos.** Both groups kept respectable brass sections despite using electric bass. Banda El Méxicano, known for its *quebradita* "No Bailes de Caballito," was the most extreme exponent of techno-banda, replacing the brass section with a synthesizer and electric percussion.

BANDA ARKANGEL R-15

Formed circa 1990, Las Varas, Nayarit, México

With tropical-flavored percussions, rapid rhythm changes, and bright horn blasts, Banda Arkangel R-15 rose above the herd of copycat bandas, exploding onto the scene in the 1990s when the genre enjoyed a massive renaissance.

Banda Arkangel R-15
Courtesy of Luna

Lead singer/*bajo sexto* player José de Jesús Navarro was central to the group's sound, which also featured excellent work by trumpet players Hilario Ortega, Antonio Palomera, and José Luis López. The band reportedly picked its name because the members considered themselves like archangels and the R-15 represents a powerful gun. They recorded their first album, *Tu Desastre,* for the small independent label Kora Records in 1990. But Kora's small size led the band to sign on with Luna Records in 1991 for better record distribution. They scored right out of the box with the single/title track from their first Luna album, *Tu Desastre.* The band followed up with the hits "Fue Tan Poco Tu Carino," "La Quebradita," "Sufriendo A Solas," "Bailame Quebradito," "El Merecumbe," and "Pago al Contado."

The band received its first gold record from Luna in November 1994 for sales of its fourth CD, *De Donde Es la Quebradita.* The same CD produced the hit "El Onceavo Mandamiento," which cracked the Billboard Hot Latin Tracks chart. Navarro wrote that tune as well as "Sea por el Amor de Dios" in 1996. The following year the album *La 4x4* produced the hit "Voy a Pintar la Raya," which lasted twenty-four weeks on the Billboard Hot Latin Tracks chart in 1998. The CD marked the band's first incursion into the romantic ballad genre.

Corridos (Luna)
Reyes de la Quebrada (Jupiter)
Sólo para Adoloridos (FonoVisa)
Voy a Pintar la Raya (Luna)

BANDA EL LIMÓN

Formed 1965, El Limón de Peraz, Sinaloa, México

Originally known as Banda Limón de Salvador Lizárraga, the sixteen-member group began by playing in Mazatlán for parties and conventions. The band toured extensively at the outset, but that became a problem for some of the original band members, who were eventually replaced by musicians from Mazatlán. The original lead singer, Julio Preciado, later went on to **Banda El Recodo de Cruz Lizárraga.** Among the band's biggest hits were "Que Se Te Olvidó," "El Jardinero," "Oiga Usted Mi General," and "La Bola."

15 Éxitos (Fonorama)
Me Caíste del Cielo (Fonorama)
Puro Sinaloa Compás (Fonorama)

BANDA EL RECODO DE CRUZ LIZÁRRAGA

Formed 1938, Mazatlán, Sinaloa, México

Banda El Recodo was one of the longest-running groups in the history of banda. The fifteen-member banda utilized the classic authentic sound—lots of trumpets, trombones, tubas, and percussions, but no keyboards.

When bandleader Don Cruz "Crucillo" Lizárraga (born 1918, Mazatlán, Sinaloa; died 1995, Mazatlán, Sinaloa) formed Banda El Recodo in 1938, it was rooted in Sinaloan folklore and through the years has covered a wide range of popular Mexican rhythms. The band's early hits came in the 1940s: "La Patrulla Americana" and "Sanson y Dalila." Additional hits included "El Sinaloense," "El Sauce y la Palma," and "Nereidas." El Recodo also appeared in movies, including *Yo el Valiente* and *Qué Me Entierren con la Banda.* El Recodo has accompanied luminaries such as **Lola Beltrán, Lucha Villa,** and **José Alfredo Jiménez.** When Lizárraga passed on, his son Germán Lizárraga took over directing chores. Germán's brother Luis Alfonso was a vocalist in the banda.

In the 1990s El Recodo continued to be a solid presence on the banda scene, scoring with the **Marco Antonio Solis** composition "Qué Solo Estoy sin Ti" in 1997. Its 1997 live double album, *En Vivo desde el Río Nilo,* included classics such as "Si Es Pies Abajo" as well as **Juan Gabriel** ballads "Mi Fracaso" and "Te Sigo Amando."

Banda El Recodo de Cruz Lizárraga (FonoVisa)
De Parranda con la Banda (FonoVisa)
Desde de Cielo Para Siempre (FonoVisa)
Tributo a Juan Gabriel (FonoVisa)

BANDA MACHOS

Formed 1990, Villa Corona, Jalisco, México

The banda phenomenon exploded in Southern California in 1990, and from late 1991 to 1993 banda music was the rage, although the music did not catch on elsewhere. Banda Machos were one of the few successful bands to break out big beyond the West Coast. Banda Machos became so popular that they helped propel KLAX-FM, in the space of six months, from being an unknown station to the No. 1 general market spot in Los Angeles. And, though Banda Machos made some gains in other urban areas—such as Chicago, Texas, and Florida—the heart of their music was always in Los Angeles. Banda music runs from romantic ballads to up-tempo merengues, but instrumentally bandas have a hot, brass-heavy sound akin to marching bands. This sound originates from the northern Mexican state of Sinaloa. This format includes the synth-driven pop ballads of Mexican grupos and the traditional Mexican song forms, such as ranchera and norteño.

In a genre packed with hundreds of sound-alike, unimaginative bands, Banda Machos stood above the pack with inspired takes on classic boleros and percussive cumbias. The twelve-man ensemble was led initially by lead singer/songwriter Raúl Ortega, who displayed a talent for producing upbeat tunes with melodic hooks and nifty vocal harmonies.

The 1992 release of *Quebradita* got Banda Machos extensive airplay, but their international breakthrough came on *Machos También Lloran,* a CD swirling with carnivalesque atmospherics, torchy rancheras, and seductive boleros. The band was unafraid to tackle classics like **Javier Solis**'s "Entrega Total" and "Esclavo y Amo" and to personalize them with their own brand of horn-fueled dynamics.

Gracias Mujer, the band's fourth CD, took Banda Machos another step in their evolution toward the complete big-band approach.

Employing the familiar, out-front bass and brass lines to power perky cumbias and slow-shuffling rancheras and boleros, the band cleverly employed more vocal harmonies in order to distinguish themselves from the pack. While the banda movement subsided considerably by 1994, Banda Machos remained one of the most popular proponents, keeping up with a heavy touring and recording schedule. After five albums in seven years, Raúl Ortega left the group in 1995, claiming internal conflicts, and was replaced by band percussionist José Morfin. Ortega formed his own ten-member Banda Arre and released albums on FonoVisa, leaning toward a more keyboard-driven banda mix.

BANDA MACHOS

Gracias Mujer (FonoVisa)
Machomanía (FonoVisa)
Machos También Lloran (FonoVisa)
Quebradita (FonoVisa)

RAÚL ORTEGA

Andan Diciendo (FonoVisa)
El Maestro (FonoVisa)

BANDA MAGUEY

Formed 1991, Villa Corona, Jalisco, México

This tight-knit, highly disciplined twelve-man group rose to prominence with its highly stylized *banda rítmica* music, a potent blend of basic brass-over-bass banda that freely mixed with galloping cumbias, brooding boleros, and even mambos and merengue-flavored tunes. This free-spirited approach was best appreciated when watching the band live. Dressed in identical *charro* suits, the band members keyed off each other onstage as they injected choreographed dance steps, all while delivering precise chops in blistering, fast-paced sets. Particularly impressive was the band's powerful seven-man horn section: two trombones, two saxophones, and three trumpets.

Key to the group's success was front man Ernesto Solano, who handled lead singer/songwriter duties and also produced the band's CDs. Banda Maguey's third studio album, *Tu Eterno Enamorado,* propelled the group into larger venues on the strength of the hit singles "Porque Es Amor," and the title track. Subsequent hits "Pero Te Amo," "Los Melones," "Tu Eterno Enamorado," "Si Tú No Estás," "La Estrella de los Bailes," and "Corazón de Oro" solidified the group's standing as one of the best and youngest banda outfits in the market. In 1997 the band signed on with BMG/U.S. Latin and quickly launched its debut, *Lágrimas de Sangre,* from which the chart single "Quiero Volver," written by Solano, went up the Billboard Hot Latin Tracks chart. Also notable on the CD were the swinging "María María," with its sweaty reggae dance fever, and the thundering cumbia "1000 Vueltas."

In late 1998, FonoVisa capitalized on the band's new momentum on BMG by releasing a three-CD greatest hits collection that extensively spanned Banda Maguey's career, including the early hits such as "Cecy" and "Borracho," as well as the Solano-penned tunes "El Primer Beso," "Baila Nena Baila," and "Linda Muchachita." It also included the band's energetic take on **José Alfredo Jiménez**'s "Mano de Dios," a wistful tune about everlasting love, and Daniel Garzes's "Mujer Paseada," on resisting temptation.

As the '90s closed out, Banda Maguey was positioned to become the genre's leading representative thanks to the group's original tunes, solid musicianship, and dynamic stage presence.

30 de Colección (BMG)
Éxitos en Vivo (Live) (BMG)
La Estrella de los Bailes (FonoVisa)
Lágrimas de Sangre (BMG/U.S. Latin)
El Mundo Gira (FonoVisa)
Tumbando Caña (FonoVisa)

BANDA VALLARTA SHOW

Formed 1988, San José del Valle, Nayarit, México

Banda Vallarta Show was known for its elaborate *vaquero* outfits, energetic choreography, and electro-banda approach, substituting electric bass for the tuba and incorporating keyboards for harmony. Alongside **Banda Machos,** Banda Vallarta was part of the leading wave of bandas that helped revitalize the genre in the mid-1990s.

Aspiring to become better known, the band, directed by Pablo Mejía, relocated from Nayarit to Los Angeles. In 1991 it released its first album on FonoVisa, *Te Ves Bien Buena.* The banda covered El General tunes like "Muévelo" and hit big with the now-standard "Provócame" and "Esa Chica Me Vacila." The band soldiered on after vocalist **Ezequiel Peña** split to go solo in late 1994, but never quite regained its momentum.

Esa Chica Me Vacila (FonoVisa)
La Fiesta (FonoVisa)
Provócame (FonoVisa)
Te Ves Bien Buena (FonoVisa)
El Tirador (FonoVisa)

BARRON, PACO, Y NORTEÑOS CLAN

Formed 1987, Apatzingan, Michoacán, México

With a postmodern norteño sound that leaned toward bubblegum pop, Norteños Clan started as Los Vaqueros del Norte led by *bajo sexto* player Ezequiel Barron, Paco Barron's father. After relocating from Michoacán to Nuevo León in 1993, it recorded its first CD for DISA, *Copa Rota.* Though the group has recorded rancheras and corridos, it carved a niche with its live cumbia medley of hits by **Luis Miguel,** Enrique Iglesias, **Juan Gabriel, José Guadalupe Esparza,** and Leo Dan. A family group, the band also included Barron brothers—Plutarco "Paco," lead singer/accordion; Salvador, drums; and Artemio, percussions—and Ignacio Méndez on bass. The band broke onto the Billboard Hot Latin Tracks chart with the hits "Potpourri de Quique" and "Amor de Miel." In 1998 the band finally went beyond potpourri predictability on the CD *Mil Rosas en el Cielo,* which was produced by Tirzo Paiz and which contained no medleys.

Copa Rota (DISA/EMI Latin)
Mil Rosas en el Cielo (DISA/EMI Latin)
Norteños de Corazón (DISA/EMI Latin)
Norteños de Medianoche (DISA/EMI Latin)
Norteños de Rodeo Puro (DISA/EMI Latin)
Potpourri: Adiós Amigo Bronco (DISA/EMI Latin)

BELTRÁN, GRACIELA

Born December 29, 1973, Costa Rica, Sinaloa, México

Graciela Beltrán began singing when she was only six years old and was known by the stage name Gracielita. When her family moved to California she continued making appearances at area festivals, attracting increasing attention.

On her first few albums she experimented with a variety of styles—from banda and norteño, to ranchera and pop. Her early hits included "Róbame un Beso," "Adiós Amor," "Mi Corazón Es Tuyo," "Tesoro," and "Están Lloviendo Lágrimas." She also appeared in five movies, including one with **Los Tigres del Norte.**

Beltrán got a major sales and promotional boost when she appeared on a hit compilation with **Selena** in early 1995 titled *Las Reinas del Pueblo,* a month before the popular Tejano queen died. Selena's death then created an incredible demand for her music—anything with her name on it sold out. But, Selena's coattails can only take one so far. Beltrán's subsequent CDs have only produced a few hit singles, including "Tuya" and "Le Pediré Perdón," though both of these landed on the Billboard Hot Latin Tracks chart.

Con la Banda Culiaca (EMI)
Graciela Beltrán (EMI)
Mi Corazón Es Tuyo (EMI)
Tesoro (EMI)
Tuya (EMI)

BELTRÁN, LOLA

Born María Lucila Beltrán Alcayaga, March 7, 1932, Rosario, Sinaloa, México; died March 24, 1996, Mexico City, México

Lola Beltrán became world famous for the exquisite power and control of her voice and for singing Mexico's rancheras, heartland folk music akin to American country music. Her signature songs, "Cucurrucucu Paloma" and "Paloma Negra," were prototypical rancheras—late laments for love gone but not forgotten.

Over the years Beltrán became known as "Lola la Grande" (Lola the Great) for her ability to inject so much emotion and theatrics into her mariachi songs. She captivated her audiences. On stage she projected a majestic presence, dressed in elaborate folkloric costuming and jewelry and dramatically gripping her ubiquitous *rebozo,* or shawl.

And whether she was singing to poor Mexican immigrants in between cockfights at the earthy *palenques* (county fairs) or performing before European kings or American presidents, Beltrán was a charming diva. She was fond of stopping the orchestra midmeasure with a hand gesture to emphasize a lyric or dramatic moment.

One of seven children born to María de Los Angeles Ruíz del Beltrán and Pedro Beltrán Felix, Beltrán grew up in the rural nondescript town of Rosario in the Pacific state of Sinaloa. At the age of eight she began singing at mass and in the church choir, where a church teacher exposed her to **Pedro Infante**'s and **Agustin Lara**'s romantic ballads "Solamente una Vez," "Granada," and "Valencia."

After graduating from high school she pursued a degree as a commercial secretary. In 1953, fresh with her secretarial certificate and chaperoned by her mother, Beltrán traveled to Mexico City to look for work. By then she was already intrigued by the stars of the day and was excited when she visited the studios of famed radio station XEW.

In interviews Beltrán liked to tell the story that it was on one of those visits that she begged station officials to let her sing on the airwaves. Each day there were dozens of similar wanna-bes at XEW so Beltrán was thrilled when, through the timely intervention of noted songwriter Tomás Méndez, she got her chance. By coincidence Méndez, then with Los Diamantes, had witnessed Beltrán's rude dismissal by the station and through his connections got her an audition. She impressed station music director Amado C. Guzmán enough to land a job—as his secretary. A year later, Beltrán entered a contest to sing opposite **Miguel Aceves Mejía** on the weekly radio program *Así Es Mi Tierra.* Beltrán won, was christened Lola Beltrán, and launched her career with Discos Peerless. Her first 45 contained two **José Alfredo Jiménez** originals: "Cuando el Destino" and "Por un Beso."

Beltrán's forty-plus year career included seventy-eight albums, and eventually appearances in more than fifty films. But it was through her association with famed composers Tomás Méndez, Agustin Lara, José Alfredo Jiménez, Rubén Fuentes, and others that Beltrán recorded the songs that defined her as the preeminent female interpreter of Mexico's vernacular music. She had an impeccable sense for choosing material that was best suited to her voice and style and in which she could capture life's melancholy essence. She sang with a knowing calmness about loneliness, suffering, and abandonment. Her biggest hits were "Cucurrucucu Paloma," "Cielito Lindo," "Paloma Negra," "Si Nos Dejan," and "No Volveré"—touching songs that ignited the hopes and soothed the hardships of the millions of peasants, workers, and migrants who adored her.

Beltrán was the first ranchera singer to perform at El Palacio de Bellas Artes in Mexico City, which had previously only hosted classical concerts. She was also the only Mexican artist to perform at the Olympia Theater in Paris. She enjoyed a lengthy run as the premiere ranchera singer, impressing with such passion and feeling. She influenced dozens of folkloric and pop artists, including **Juan Gabriel, Angeles Ochoa,** and even pop/rock singer **Linda Ronstadt,** who called Beltrán "a world-class singer, up there rubbing shoulders with Billie Holliday and Edith Piaf."

In 1988 her song "Soy Infeliz" was the opening theme for Pedro Almodóvar's hit motion picture *Women on the Verge of a Nervous Breakdown.* For Beltrán, there was no difference performing on stage or in films. "Any good singer is already an actress," Beltrán said. "If you're doing things properly, you are projecting. And as you project, people are feeling the drama and the emotion that pours out of you."

Beltrán married bullfighter Alfredo Leal. They divorced after their daughter, María Elena, was born.

Beltrán had been working on the Juan Gabriel–produced *Las Tres Señoras* album when she died of a stroke at Mexico City's Hospital Los Angeles. The subsequently released CD also featured Amalia "La Tariácuri" Mendoza of **Trío Tariácuri, Lucha Villa, Vicente Fernández,** and Las Jilguerillas.

20 Éxitos de Colección (Sony)
Canta a José A. Jiménez (RCA)
En Vivo/Desde el Teatro Olympia (Sony)
Las Inmortales de... (Sony)

BERNARDO Y SUS COMPADRES

Formed 1972, Laredo, Texas

In the world of genuine foot-stomping conjunto outfits, Bernardo y Sus Compadres have always been considered solid contenders. Although they never scored hits like other better known acts such as **Mingo Saldivar** or **Rubén Naranjo,** Los Compadres consistently scored regular airplay with the winning polkas "Esa Mujer," "Ella," and "Padre Ingrato."

Bandleader/singer Bernardo Martínez Jr. organized the group while he was a high school senior in his hometown of Laredo, Texas. Two years later the band recorded their first 45 single in Corpus Christi, Texas on conjunto pioneer/Tejano Conjunto Hall of Famer **Tony De La Rosa**'s indie label. And with good reason, De La Rosa was one of their earliest influences and it showed in the band's playing. With Gregorio González on accordion and Bernardo Martínez III on drums, the fivesome blended De La Rosa's *tacuachito* (possum) style with their own percolating grooves. Bernardo and his father wrote most of the material for the band, which later on signed with San Antonio's Joey International. The other compadres are Armando Garza on *bajo sexto* and Rudolfo Reyes on bass.

Me Gusta Estar Contigo (JB)
Tres Generaciones (JB)
Tres Generaciones, Vol. 2 (JB)

BOLANOS, TATIANA

Born Tatiana Beatriz Bolanos, December 16, 1988, Los Angeles, California

Like **Gerardito Fernández,** Tatiana Bolanos was a child singing star who impressed with her ability to interpret rancheras—passionate songs that are traditionally more suitable for mature singers. Although she had been singing for several years, Bolanos was "discovered" by Don Francisco, host of the

TV show *Sábado Gigante,* on which she won the Miss Chiquita contest. By 1998 she had appeared on nearly all the major talk shows on English- and Spanish-speaking networks.

Her 1998 debut album, *La Chiquita Divina,* released by Sony, was coproduced by noted helmsmen Rigoberto Alfaro and Antonio Zamora. The CD featured the single "Debajo de los Puentes" and contained new songs by well-known composers such as Eva Torres, Teodoro Bello, and Zamora. Six tracks were recorded in Los Angeles, the other six in Mexico City.

La Chiquita Divina (Sony)

BOLERO

The word bolero can mean many things, depending on which Latin American country one might be in. But the bolero referred to in regional Mexican music is not the fast-paced dance form from Spain.

The Mexican bolero is a slow, romantic ballad that originated in Santiago, Cuba in the late 1800s. Usually sentimental and reflective, the bolero is considered by some to be the equivalent to the jazz ballad. While many norteño and mariachi groups include boleros in their repertoire, the trios of the 1940s and 1950s, mostly notably **Trío Los Panchos,** are considered the best interpreters of the genre. **Agustin Lara** was perhaps the first widely known Mexican bolero composer. Prolific, he wrote numerous classics from the mid-1920s through the 1960s. He is best known for the hits "Imposible" and "Solamente una Vez." Other notable boleros included Consuelo Velásquez's "Bésame Mucho," Roberto Cantoral's "Reloj," and **Armando Manzanero**'s "Somos Novios," covered by Perry Como as "It's Impossible."

In the late 1950s the bolero ranchero, a more melodic bolero, was popularized by **Pedro Infante** and **Javier Solis.**

Bolero enjoyed a major renaissance in the '90s thanks to Mexican pop singer **Luis Miguel**'s huge-selling bolero albums *Romance, Segundo Romance,* and *Romances,* each of which was certified as having sold more than one million copies in the U.S. by the Recording Industry Association of America (RIAA).

BRAVO, JOE

Born José Jasso Bravo, July 2, 1945, San Antonio, Texas

Joe Bravo was one of the early 1970s Tejano heroes when he scored with a series of hits, including "Patita de Conejo," "Qué Casualidad," and "It's Okay."

As a teen at Harlandale High School, Bravo was influenced by Fats Domino and Jimmy Clanton and His Rockets, whose hit "Just a Dream" Bravo had memorized and sung when he helped form Little Joe and the Harlems. In 1962, at the age of seventeen, Bravo stepped up into the Chicano/Tejano market when he took over the lead vocal spot for **Sunny Ozuna** in the Sunglows band and was featured on the albums *The Fabulosos Sunglows* and *Corazón Salvaje*. In 1968 Bravo left to form his own group Joe Bravo y Su Orquesta and was signed with Johnny Gonzáles and El Zarape records. Bravo produced a series of albums, including the seminal *Playboy '70* and *Simplemente* and later with Freddie Records the CD *Joe Bravo Is Back,* which contained the megahit "Qué Casualidad," written by Carlos Cárdenas.

Bravo faded from the scene in the early '80s after he was arrested for possession of a controlled substance in Austin and sentenced to eight years at the federal penitentiary in Bastrop, Texas. Bravo was released after two-and-a-half years. But because of various parole violations he was sent back and released two more times.

Joe Bravo
Courtesy of Freddie Records

In the early 1990s Bravo produced a couple of albums on the indie Manny Music, but he could not match his earlier success. In addition to the Tejano hits, he was known for other regional hits, including "Irma Linda," "Te Regaña Tu Senora," "La Parranda," "María Kantú," and "Qué Bien Te Ves."

Amorcito de Mi Amor (Freddie)
Joe Bravo Is Back (Freddie)
Playboy '70 (Freddie)

BRONCO

Formed 1978, Apodaca, Nuevo León, México; disbanded 1997

Patterned after the highly popular norteño outfit **Los Tigres del Norte,** Bronco exploded on the scene in 1990 with a series of early hits such as "Adoro," "Que No Quede Huella," and "Sergio el Bailador." Like Los Tigres, Bronco dressed in matching cowboy hats and brightly colored, fringed cowboy suits, used elaborate western-themed stage props, and specialized in the norteño staples: corridos and rancheras.

Bronco's live concerts were more like huge barn hall dances than concerts. Fans would crowd the front of the stage, but there were also hundreds of couples dancing farther away.

However, unlike Los Tigres, Bronco also wrote songs for children—such as "El Sheriffe de Chocolate," "El Carretón de Bronco," and "Amigo Bronco"—with matching cartoon videos that were shown on huge screens during their performances. Bronco's children's songs were typically cumbias, but they were characterized by funny story lines or anecdotes.

The four members of Bronco—**José Guadalupe Esparza,** singer/bass/songwriter; Javier Villarreal, guitar; **Ramiro Delgado,** accordion/keyboards; and José Luis Villarreal, drums—met in the late '70s in their hometown of Apodaca in Monterrey, Nuevo León. For a few years the band was a struggling local outfit and did not begin its recording career until 1985.

Although Esparza was the principal songwriter (he wrote most of the hits), the group also used outside songwriters, including **Armando Manzanero,** Martin Urieta, Gil Rivera, and others. The band's other adolescent influences included Renacimiento '74, **Los Bukis,** and **Los Angeles Negros,** who helped the band create a new grupo norteño fusion.

While the band was proficient in writing melancholy corridos and solid rancheras, it made sure each album contained perky cumbias ("La Hechicera," "El Ruego") and romantic ballads ("¿Para Qué Vuelvas?" "Déjame Amarte Otra Vez").

Accolades came fast and furious in the early '90s. The band was named best new group at the Billboard/Premio Lo Nuestro Awards in 1990 and in consecutive years was given the Cerro de la Silla Award in Monterrey for consistently being the highest ticket-selling group in the genre. High peaks included attracting 60,000 people at the Río Nilo grounds in Guadalajara and, in 1993, selling out (for the first time) the Plaza de México in Mexico City.

The band appeared in the late '80s Mexican film *Los Penitentes de PUP* and its members played themselves in the 1991 *Bronco* film.

By 1993 Broncomania was at a feverous pitch as the band scored a number of unique accomplishments, including becoming the only Mexican group to get a comic book based on its adventures, appearing as themselves in the highly popular Mexican soap opera *Dos Mujeres, un Camino,* and even having a street named after the band in the entertainment capital of Las Vegas (Bronco Street).

In December of 1996 the members of the group shocked the music world when they announced their retirement.

"Two years ago, we discussed how we would end this some day, and we always felt we wanted to go out on top," said Esparza in an interview. "It is better to go now, before we run out of the energy that has kept Bronco galloping so intensely for so long."

They did.

Their final farewell was planned to the last detail. Their last album was titled *Adiós! La Última Huella* (Goodbye: The Last Footprint), with the title track, written by Esparza, as the first single. Their worldwide *Gira de Adiós* (Goodbye Tour), which launched on February 11 in Monterrey, covered some eleven countries, including the U.S., Ecuador, Bolivia, Argentina, and Paraguay.

The 150-city concert tour came to an end on December 21, 1997 at the 115,000-capacity Estadio Azteca in Mexico City. In early 1998, Esparza and Delgado launched solo careers, on the FonoVisa and BMG/U.S. Latin record labels respectively.

Adiós! La Última Huella (FonoVisa)
Animal (FonoVisa)
Bronco Super Bronco (FonoVisa)
Cien Por Cien Norteño (FonoVisa)
Pura Sangre (FonoVisa)
Rompiendo Barreras (FonoVisa)

BRYNDIS

Formed 1989, Santa Paula, California

Sharp-looking, youthful, and oozing with professionalism, Bryndis made big noise in the mid-1990s with romantic pop-cumbias sung by José Guadalupe Guevara's angst-ridden tenor, though sometimes it sounded like a poor man's **Los Temerarios.** Bryndis's first CD to reach a mass audience was 1992's *A Su Salud* on DISA. Most of the band members were natives of San Luis Potosí and Oaxaca and they wrote most of their own material. Among the band's biggest hits were the cumbias "Te Esperaré," "Olvidemos Nuestro Orgullo," and the ballad "Te Vas Con El." The group experimented with interspersing spoken prose into its biggest hits on *Poemas* (Vols. 1 & 2). Additional hits included "Amor Prohibido," "Te Esperaré," and "Te Juro Que Te Amo."

Así Es el Amor (EMI)
Mi Verdadero Amor (EMI)
Poemas (EMI)
Tu Amor Secreto (EMI)

BUKIS, LOS

Formed 1970, Ario de Rosales, Michoacán, México

Led by enigmatic singer/songwriter/producer **Marco Antonio Solis,** Los Bukis enjoyed a solid twenty-year run as Mexico's most prolific hit makers in the romantic pop/grupo genre, scoring with such melodic monster hits as "Quiéreme," "Chiquilla Bonita," and "Como Fui A Enamorarme de Ti."

Los Bukis; with singer/songwriter/producer Marco Antonio Solis (seated, right)
Courtesy of FonoVisa

Through the years the band's synthesizer-drenched cumbia/ballad approach inspired dozens of bands from **Bronco** and **Bryndis** to **Ladrón** and **Liberación.** Even Los Bukis' casual-but-cool coat and tie look was imitated by many. But while copycats and duplicators abounded, no one could approach the killer grooves in original songs woven by "El Buki" Solis. His superb knack for compelling lyrics was surpassed only by a sharp instinct for melodic synth-pop hooks. In terms of longevity, impact, and influence, Los Bukis are comparable to the Rolling Stones in the rock world. Los Bukis were the quintessential grupo years before the Latino music press coined the term to describe Mexico's keyboard-driven romantic pop bands.

Los Bukis came together in the early '70s when Solis, then only twelve years old, and his brother Joel formed Los Hermanos Solis in the small town of Ario de Rosales in the southern state of Michoacán. In 1975 the band became Los Bukis, which means "the kids in their hometown," and debuted professionally with the LP *Falso Amor.* The title track was a big hit and set the band on a solid course to the top of the charts. *Falso Amor* had the sound that would become Los Bukis' signature: richly melodic and easily danceable romantic pop music with Solis's plaintive vocals. Almost formulaic, the Bukis sound generated so many sleek, sulky, and syrupy hits it is no surprise that they have inspired so many followers—among the most successful are **Los Yonics** and **Los Temerarios.** At the outset, the band, which was led by the Solis brothers on guitar and vocals, included Eusebio "El Chivo" Cortéz, bass; Pedro Sánchez, drums; Roberto Guadarrama, keyboards; and his brother José Guadarrama, percussions and keyboards.

The '80s belonged to Los Bukis who, under Solis's direction (he wrote ninety percent of the material and produced the albums), completely dominated the pop *grupero* music scene in Mexico. Other hits followed in quick succession—"Te Tuve y Te Perdí," "Me Siento Solo," "Una Noche Como Ésta," "Quiéreme," and "El Celoso." The band fine-tuned its music, with thumping percussions and just the right amount of synthesizer fills to give its sound a modern high-tech sheen.

In 1989 Los Bukis delivered one of their biggest hits, *Tu Carcel,* which, according to their label, became the first record in Mexican history to sell one million copies. Later that year they followed up with another chart-topper "Como Fui Enamorarme de Ti" from their *Y Para Siempre* CD. "Como Fui" was so successful that it spawned a movie with the same title that featured the group.

Constantly touring, Los Bukis also intrigued on elaborate stages with complicated light shows and huge videos to amplify their songs. Out front leading the band, Solis resembled a messianic agent with his ever-present full beard, shoulder-length black wavy hair, and thin, usually cape-clad build, especially when he raised his hand to the crowd as if in benediction. Musically, Solis cited Chicago, the Animals, the Eagles, and Santana as influences. Snippets of each of these groups and more came through in their music, which featured not only standard romantic tunes but also electrified cumbias, snappy *huapangos,* and chugging boleros.

Beyond his success with Los Bukis, Solis also wrote songs for and produced the work of other artists, including **Rocío Durcal, Lucero,** and Marisela.

In late 1995, citing the need for new challenges, Solis departed from the band for a solo career. He immediately signed on with the same label—FonoVisa. The remaining Los Bukis huddled briefly, re-emerged as **Los Mismos** or The Same Ones, and signed on with EMI Latin. Few will question that during their twenty-year reign, Los Bukis were the undisputed kings of Mexico's romantic pop/grupo genre.

16 Éxitos de Siempre (1997) (FonoVisa)
A Través de Tus Ojos (FonoVisa)
Inalcanzable (FonoVisa)
Por Amor a Mi Pueblo (FonoVisa)
Quiéreme (FonoVisa)
Y Para Siempre (FonoVisa)

CABALLERO, LORENZO

Born 1919, San Antonio, Texas

At the age of eleven, while serving as an altar boy, Lorenzo Caballero learned to play the church organ. By 1937 he joined **Don Santiago Jiménez** y Sus Veladores and recorded on RCA. Caballero also performed with **Lydia Mendoza,** Pedro González, Beatrice "La Chata" Nolesca, as well as sang with **Javier Solis** and La Prieta Linda.

After a stint with the U.S. Army in the early '40s, Caballero reunited with Don Santiago Jiménez in 1946 and shortly afterward formed his own three-piece group El Conjunto Estrella. In 1950 the group signed a five-year contract with RCA and changed its name to Lorenzo Caballero y Su Grupo de Estrellas.

Caballero was nicknamed "Guitar Wizard" because his stage act included pulling a cat, a mouse, and other living objects from his guitar. He was also known for setting his guitar on fire. Caballero continued playing and touring through the early '70s. In 1990 Caballero was inducted into the Tejano Conjunto Hall of Fame.

Appears on:

Lydia Mendoza, First Queen of Tejano Music (Arhoolie)
Mexican American Border Music, Vol. 1, 1928–1958 (Arhoolie)
Narciso Martínez, Father of Tex-Mex Conjunto (Arhoolie)

CADETES DE LINARES, LOS

Formed April 1974, Linares, Nuevo León, México

Los Cadetes de Linares were a second-tier norteño pioneer group whose rural, nasally-sung norteño corridos and rancheras found their largest audience in the '70s alongside **Los Alegres de Terán.** Dozens of groups, including **Los Tigres del Norte,** cited Los Cadetes, Los Alegres, and **Los Tremendos Gavilanes** as fundamental and influential groups in the genre.

Founded by Homero Guerrero Sr., who occasionally wrote songs, and Lupe Tijerina, Los Cadetes delivered smooth but muscular boleros, jouncy corridos, and rhythmic cumbias in their music. Many of their hit tunes were written by noted songwriter Raúl Ramírez García, including "Despedida con Mariachi," "Una Flor para Mi Madre," "Descansa General" (a tribute to Pancho Villa), and "Adiós María."

Guerrero Sr. died in the early '80s and shortly thereafter Tijerina and Guerrero's son Homero Guerrero Jr. went their separate ways, each using the Cadetes de Linares name. Both groups continued recording and touring in the '90s with moderate success.

14 Éxitos de Ayer, Hoy, y Siempre (Sony)
15 Hits (Hacienda)
Los Dos Amigos (PolyGram)
Éxitos/El Chubasco (PolyGram)

CAMINANTES, LOS

Formed 1983, San Francisco del Rincón, Guanajuato, México

This slick-suited fivesome combined big horns and keyboard-driven cumbias/ballads to produce early hits "Cuando Dos Almas," "He Sabido," and "Porque Tengo Tu Amor." Originally the group was founded by four brothers—Agustin, Horacio, Brigido, and Martin Ramírez. The band was signed in 1983 by Abel de Luna to record on his Luna label. Their first CD, *Supe Perder,* produced the hit title-track single. In 1986 an auto accident forced the retirement of keyboardist Brigido Ramírez, who was replaced with Mario Sotelo. Shortly thereafter the band began its first U.S. tour behind the single "Amor sin Palabras" from the *De Guanajuato... para América* CD.

The band's momentum of consistent hits and major tours was blunted the following year when another auto accident resulted in the death of Martin Ramírez. But the band pressed on, recording the tribute LP *Gracias Martin,* which produced the top single "Todo Me Gusta de Ti."

In 1991 the band was featured in the autobiographical film *Caminantes... Si Hay Caminos.* Later that year, Los Caminantes released a greatest hits collection, *14 Románticas,* which also included their cover of the Luis Silva–penned, **David Marez**–identified "Entre Más Lejos Me Vaya," a bitter ballad about love's addiction. In 1996 Los Caminantes took a left turn, recording an album backed by mariachis. The effort produced a hit single "Pobre Millonario," which peaked at No. 31 on April 13, 1996 on the Billboard Hot Latin Tracks chart.

14 Románticas (Luna)
Con Tinta del Corazón (Luna)
Corridos Bravos (Luna)
Cumbiando con los Chulos (Luna)
De Guanajuato... para América (Luna)
Gracias Martin (Luna)

CAMPANAS DE AMÉRICA

Formed 1978, San Antonio, Texas

Mariachi Campanas de América have been one of the most versatile and prolific recording mariachi troupes in the United States. Founded by director Juan Ortiz and longtime school instructor Belle Ortiz San Miguel, Campanas de América were among the first mariachis to add a full drum set in their instrumentation.

In the mid-1990s the troupe became a featured attraction at the Fiesta Texas theme park in San Antonio, playing a mix of traditional mariachi and contemporary rock, pop, and country music. That sense of musical adventuresomeness has always been a Campanas trademark, and it comes through on their albums. Their debut CD on the Dallas-based indie Barb Wire featured a merengue-flavored cumbia, ("Mujeres Coquetas"), a *son huapango* ("La Mariquita"), a big-band polka ("Déjame Llorar Solo"), and a torchy ranchera ("Cómo La Quiero"). Their signature hits included "Reynalda," "Chango Wango," and "Lone Star Medley."

Campanas, christened by **Mariachi Vargas de Tecalitlán,** have also been featured on a host of albums by such artists as **Little Joe, Rubén Ramos, Flaco Jiménez,** Willie Nelson, and **Vikki Carr.**

Campanas de América (Capitol/EMI Latin)
Lo Que Quiero Es Bailar (Tejano Discos)

CAMPEROS DE NATI CANO, LOS

Formed circa 1963, Tijuana, Baja California Norte, México

One of the few commercially recorded mariachi troupes in the United States, Los Camperos de Nati Cano helped spread mariachi music throughout the U.S. for almost four decades. Los Camperos were one of four mariachi troupes that backed up **Linda Ronstadt** on her historic *Canciones de Mi Padre* CD, which won a Grammy for best Mexican American performance in 1988.

Nati Cano (born 1933, Ahuisculco, Jalisco) studied violin at the Academia de Música in Guadalajara. At the age of eight, he played in his father and grandfather's mariachi band. In his teens, while playing in a Mazatlán orchestra he heard of the rapidly growing Mexican population in Los Angeles and decided to move there.

After years of playing in local bars, Cano was hired at the famed downtown Million Dollar Theatre, which backed touring Mexican stars. The theater gig required occasional touring and it was during one of those tours in a stop at Lubbock, Texas that Cano was refused service at a restaurant. He vowed to start a restaurant where all nationalities were welcome. Seven years later, Cano opened La Fonda restaurant in the MacArthur Park area of L.A.

In 1996 the state government of Jalisco in Mexico honored him with the Silvestre Vargas Award, named after the founder of the legendary **Mariachi Vargas de Tecalitlán.** Cano lectured on ethnomusicology at University of California at Los Angeles (UCLA) and, in 1990, he received a National Heritage Fellowship Award from the National Endowment for the Arts.

Canciones Para Siempre (Polydor)

CANALES, LAURA

Born August 19, 1954, Kingsville, Texas

In the mid-1970s as the Tejano genre enjoyed its first golden age, Laura Canales broke through the traditionally male-dominated market with her smooth, clear voice. By the mid-1980s, Canales had won a series of TMAs, earning her the nickname of "La Reina de la Onda Tejana" (Queen of the Onda Tejana).

Canales, who cited her high school choral director Milicent Wiley as her biggest influence, made her debut with Los Unicos in 1973. After a short stint with **El Conjunto Bernal,** she joined the Ramiro de la Cruz–led Snowball & Co. and produced the hit single "Midnight Blue," a remake of the classic song. Snowball eventually became Felicidad, but the band split in two in June of 1981 with one half becoming Romance, the other Laura Canales and Encanto.

That year Canales married drummer Balde Muñoz; they divorced in 1982.

Canales/Encanto's 1981 album debut, *Si Viví Contigo,* produced the title-track hit single that established Canales as a top female singer. Starting in 1983 Canales won the TMA female vocalist and entertainer honors for four consecutive years, a record broken only by **Selena** in the 1990s.

On December 22, 1985, at Billy Bob's in Fort Worth, Canales performed for the last time with Encanto, citing managerial reasons. Drummer Muñoz and the remnants of Encanto went on to form **Fandango USA.** Canales temporarily faded, but in 1989 she signed on with EMI Latin and later with FonoVisa but subsequent CDs produced only regional hits such as "Cuatro Caminos," "Dime Si Tú Me Quieres," "Dame la Mano," "Me Dan Ganas de Ti," "Frente a Frente," and "Dile a Tu Esposa."

Dile a Tu Esposa (EMI Latin)
Midnight Blue (Freddie)
La Reina (Freddie)
Si Viví Contigo (Freddie)

CANTA A LA VIDA

Recorded September 1996, San Antonio, Texas

Patterned after the hugely successful We-Are-the-World-type project from the mid-1980s, Tejano industry officials produced the *Canta a la Vida* all-star project as a fund-raiser and awareness vehicle for the AIDS epidemic. Proceeds from the CD went to the central Texas region administered by the San Antonio AIDS Foundation. The brainchild of nightclub owner/concert promoter Arjon Tabatabai as a message "about hope and healing," the CD featured spoken messages from comedian Paul Rodríguez and actor Edward James Olmos. The all-star cast included **Mazz**'s Joe López, **Emilio, Nydia Rojas, Rubén Ramos,** Elida Reyna (of **Elida y Reyna**), **Roberto Pulido,** George Rivas, **Ramiro Herrera, Campanas de América, Los Desperadoz**, **Bobby Pulido,** Joe Jama, Ricardo Castillon, and others. The first single, "Tenemos Que Abrir los Ojos," was written by Humberto Ramón, while Rick Orozco penned the English-language counterpart "Let's Not Look Away."

Canta a la Vida (Southwest Wholesale)

CARDENALES DE NUEVO LEÓN, LOS

Formed 1982, Monterrey, Nuevo León, México

The traditional norteño fivesome Los Cardenales de Nuevo León began by playing small clubs in Monterrey. Lead singer/*bajo sexto* player Cesareo Sánchez Chávez named his band after the defunct '60s group Los Cardenales de Linares.

In 1987 Los Cardenales was signed by the DISA record label and their first record *Si Yo Fuera El* produced the hit single "Vestido Blanco." With a genuine sound that included the accordion and *bajo sexto,* Los Cardenales scored with their signature hits, including "La Perra Madura," "¿Y, Cómo Es Él?" "Amor de Unas Horas," and "Y, ¿Qué Más Da?" Their 1994 album *Fuego contra Fuego* included the song "Soy lo Peor," which was written by **Armando Manzanero,** and "Para Olvidarme de Ti," which was written by Sergio Villarreal, singer of **Ladrón.** Percussionist Eduardo López Gallegos's father was Arnulfo Sánchez López, lead singer/founder of **Los Traileros del Norte.**

Boleros de Recuerdo (FonoVisa)
Compraron una Cantina (EMI)
Fuego contra Fuego (FonoVisa)
Sucedió en un Pantalón (DISA)

CÁRDENAS, GUTY

Born Augusto Alejandro Cárdenas Pinelo, December 12, 1905, Mérida, Yucatán, México; died April 5, 1931, Mexico City, México

As a young boy Guty Cárdenas learned to play the mandolin, upright bass, saxophone, piano, and guitar, the latter becoming his favorite instrument. He later studied in Mexico City and earned a degree in accounting. It was after meeting noted composer Tata Nacho, back in Mérida in 1926, that Cárdenas was persuaded to return to Mexico City and begin his artistic career.

He recorded for Columbia Records in New York City in 1928 and by 1931 he was featured on the Mexican radio station XEW, on the *Calendario Artístico* program accompanied by the Orquesta del Maestro Guillermo Posadas. He quickly became a top artist. In April of 1931 Cárdenas was on an XEW radio program where he recorded "Para Olividarte." After the show he went to the Bach bar in Mexico City, where an altercation with a Spaniard turned into a gunfight. Cárdenas was killed. During his funeral procession, fans pelted his casket with flowers and sang his songs. His biggest hits included "Por la Maña," "Pasión," "Blanca Rosa," "Hoy Que Vuelves," and "Peregrino de Amor." Cárdenas's last studio recording was **Agustin Lara**'s bolero "Otra Vez."

Inmortales de la Trova Yucateca (Sony)
El Ruiseñor Yucateco (Arhoolie)

CARR, VIKKI

Born Florencia Bisenta de Casillas Martínez Cordona, July 19, 1942, El Paso, Texas

Vikki Carr was the oldest of seven children. She was born in El Paso but was raised in East Los Angeles, where her father made a living working construction and picking strawberries. Carr's father had aspired to be a singer and he was instrumental in encouraging her career path.

Carr's first pop hits were "Country Rebel," "It Must Be Him," and "With Pen in Hand." Through the years she performed for presidents and royalty, including a 1967 performance for Queen Elizabeth II in London. It was not until 1972, though, that her Spanish-language career began in earnest with her album *Vikki Carr en Español.* In 1985 she won her first Grammy for *Simplemente Mujer* and in 1992 she won her second for *Cosas del Amor.*

A devoted follower of **Javier Solis,** Carr paid tribute to the legendary singer by recording *Recuerdo a Javier Solis,* on which she sang his classics "Sombras," "En Mi Viejo San Juan" (a duet with Danny Rivera), "Llorarás, Llorarás," "Payaso," and "Amanecí en Tus Brazos," which through the marvel of modern studio technology was recorded as a "duet" with Solis. The CD won Carr her third Grammy in 1995.

Brillantes (Sony)
Brindo a la Vida, al Bolero (Sony)
Cosas del Amor (Sony)
Recuerdo a Javier Solis (Sony)
Simplemente Mujer (Sony)

CHAVELA Y SU GRUPO EXPRESS

Formed 1980, Fresno, California

During the '80s, Chavela (born Isabela Salaiza Ortiz, circa 1952, Fresno, California; died October 7, 1992, San Jose, California) was one of the first and few successful female accordionists in the conjunto genre. In 1987 she was nominated for a Grammy for her 1987 *El Rey del Barrio* and had gained enough fame as a recording artist that she was invited to play the 1988 Tejano Conjunto Festival in San Antonio.

Chavela grew up in East San Jose, California and acquired her love of music from her family. At the age of nine, she began to play accordion with Las Incomparables Hermanas

Ortiz ,which included her mother on *bajo sexto,* her grandfather on electric bass, and her sister Stella on drums. The group disbanded in 1968 but Chavela continued to play with area bands. In 1976 she joined the group Brown Express, playing accordion and singing. In 1980 she went on her own and formed Chavela y Su Grupo Express. Later she married Jorge Hernández, lead singer for norteño heroes **Los Tigres del Norte.**

Chavela went into a coma when she fell from a horse and hit her head on a rock during a publicity shoot in Milpitas, California and died on October 7, 1992.

El Rey del Barrio (FonoVisa)

CHELO

See Laure, Mike, y Sus Cometas

CONJUNTO

In its purest essence, conjunto is happy dance music fueled primarily by the earthy accordion. Traditional conjunto music has a lot in common with two other original American genres—blues and zydeco. All three genres are folk-based musical forms that originated in rural, country settings from people or cultures in a distinct region of the U.S.

Conjunto, which means "group" or "ensemble" in English, is the folksy predecessor of the modern Tejano genre, whose biggest proponents in the '90s included **Selena, Emilio,** and **Bobby Pulido.** Conjunto is also the American equivalent of the Mexican norteño genre. The two styles are nearly identical except that norteño singers generally have more distinct nasal qualities and Mexican accents. The basic instrumentation includes a *bajo sexto* (twelve-string Spanish guitar), drums, and, at the heart of the music, the indispensable button accordion, which defines conjunto much in the same way the fiddle might define Western swing music. In conjunto's infancy, musicians used the *tambora de rancho,* a homemade drum.

Conjunto's origins date back to the turn of the century when German and Czech immigrants first settled in Texas and northern Mexico and lived side by side with native Mexicans. All along the Texas-Mexican border musicians mixed Mexican string-based rancheras with the German/Czech polkas and waltzes.

Before World War II, first-tier conjunto pioneers such as **Narciso Martínez** and **Don Santiago Jiménez** began recording for small independent labels. Before 1950 conjunto music was mostly instrumental and accordionists were occasionally hired to provide backup music for top singers. However, followers of the big-band Orquesta Tejana style, whose '50s stars were **Beto Villa** and **Isidro López,** derided the genre as cantina music because of its folk roots. By the '60s conjunto music fell out of favor as a new generation of Tejano groups looked to popular culture for inspiration. But while the form faltered, it never died.

By the mid-1980s, a renewed interest in roots and world music helped the music's resurgence. Also critical to the music's resurrection was the establishment of the annual Tejano Conjunto Festival and its Hall of Fame, which showcases pioneers and young turks alike. The seven-day event typically draws more than 35,000 people to San Antonio's Rosedale Park every year. The international resurgence of the music can also be credited to the guest appearances of conjunto accordionist **Flaco Jiménez** on albums by the Rolling Stones, Ry Cooder, and the Mavericks. Annual European and Asian tours by such artists as **Texas Tornados, Steve Jordan, Valerio Longoria,** and **Santiago Jiménez Jr.** have also spread the style's popularity.

CONJUNTO BERNAL, EL

Formed 1952, Raymondville, Texas

With its twin chromatic accordion attack, beautiful but haunting vocal harmonies, and matching suit-and-tie outfits, El Conjunto Bernal emerged as the premiere ensemble in the '60s. Alongside peers **Tony De La Rosa** and **Los Relámpagos del Norte,** the group helped commercialize the folksy conjunto music into a vibrant and exciting genre.

Paulino Bernal (born June 22, 1939, Raymondville, Texas) was raised in poverty, quitting middle school to help with family finances. He grew up listening to accordion greats **Narciso Martínez** and **Valerio Longoria.** When a friend of his received an accordion as a gift, it was Bernal who practiced on it and became an accomplished player. His mother, a divorcée, moved Bernal, and his brothers, Eloy and Luis, and his three sisters to Kingsville where they picked cotton and crops. After Eloy (born March 11, 1937) received a *bajo sexto* from his father, he and Paulino started their musical career in 1952 as Los Hermanitos Bernal. Paulino impressed with his ability to use the accordion's full range and he also used four- and five-row chromatic models. Soon they were discovered by Armando Marroquín with Discos Ideal and became El Conjunto Bernal. Periodically, Paulino Bernal also played in other groups, including bandleader **Chris Sandoval.** Initially they backed up such artists as Carmen y Laura, but by 1955 they headlined for the first time and released a 78 record with the songs "Mujer Paseada" and "Desprecio."

They recorded for Ideal between 1955 and 1960, producing tunes such as "Mi Único Camino" and "Sentimiento." The former became the band's signature hit because of its dark message of abandonment and beautiful two- and three-part vocal harmonies. This was an important development because it was the first time harmonies were used in conjunto music. Later hits included "Buena Suerte," "Me Regalo Contigo," "Punto Final," and "Por Amor de Dinero." Marroquín started Nopal Records in 1960 and took Conjunto Bernal with him. Shortly afterward, El Conjunto relocated to McAllen and, after working with Victor González, founded Bego Records.

In the late '60s, González bought out Paulino Bernal's share of Bego Records and Bernal founded his own company, Bernal Records. He quit performing and took over administrative duties. A series of singers then took lead vocals, including Joe Ramos, Rúben Perez, Manuel Solis, Cha Cha Jiménez, accordionist Oscar Hernández, and later a young singer named **Laura Canales.** Pressures of the road, though, had already taken their toll on Bernal, who had difficulties with alcohol and drugs. In 1972, influenced by a cook who was hired to work in a restaurant he owned, Bernal became a born-again Christian. Bernal gave up alcohol and drugs and resumed his career as an accordionist, forming a new record company—Bernal Christian Records. Bernal constantly experimented with the accordion and was able to play the entire scale on it, something that the three-row button accordion is not supposed to do. In his book *The Texas-Mexican Conjunto,* music scholar Manuel Peña notes that El Conjunto Bernal had a major impact on conjunto music through "their innovative genius, polished sound, and vocal harmonies." On April 22, 1998, at the age of sixty-one, Eloy was killed when his tour bus flipped just south of Corpus Christi, Texas.

Hijo de Dios (Hacienda)
Mi Único Camino (Arhoolie)
Para Siempre (Freddie)

CORRIDO

Another song form steeped in folk tradition, the corrido is a narrative ballad or story-song that in its early days could be considered the social conscience of Tex-Mex music. Corridos first became popular in Mexican culture during the Mexican Revolution, which created events that were tailor-made for these folk ballads. The corridos initially dealt with heroes and historical events. Eventually, the anti-hero corridos became more popular, and more controversial, as they glamorized the lives of bandits, outlaws, and coyotes (smugglers of illegal immigrants).

Usually sung to a waltz or polka beat, most corridos have similar melodies and incorporate minimal conjunto instrumentation. American song equivalents would include Marty Robbins's "El Paso" and even the Charlie Daniels Band's "The Devil Went Down to Georgia."

During the '40s and '50s, the corrido was a popular style on both sides of the border and was recorded by norteño acts such as **Los Alegres de Terán** and conjunto artists like **Tony De La Rosa.** Corridos of that age frequently glorified Mexicans who battled or resisted Anglo domination. However, corridos largely faded from American conjunto sets after the civil rights movement of the '60s.

Los Tigres del Norte recorded the first narco-corridos, corridos that deal with drug smuggling, in 1971 with the now classics "Contrabando y Traición" and "Camelia la Tejana." By the '80s though, Los Tigres switched gears and retained their incredible fan loyalty when they began recording corridos about Mexican pride, particularly the plight of poor immigrants facing discrimination in America with songs like "La Jaula de Oro" (The Golden Cage). In the '90s norteño acts like **Los Tucanes de Tijuana** ("La Piñata") and the late **Chalino Sánchez** began churning out corridos about braggadocio-filled tales of the drug trade. The lyrics, though rarely vulgar, drew comparisons to gangsta rap and some corridos were banned from radio playlists.

CUEVAS, AIDA

Born circa late 1950s, Mexico City, México

In high school her teachers said she would not make it as a singer because she "was too thick and strong." But it was not long before she proved them wrong, singing popular rancheras on the radio program *Taller de XEW* in Mexico City. In the 1980s Aida Cuevas recorded three songs from the Mexican Revolution for the twenty-LP set *La Historia de México A Través de la Música.*

Cuevas reached a widespread audience with the **Armando Manzanero**–penned hit "Te Juro Que Andas Mal," the theme song for the film *Te Solté la Rienda.* In 1996 she recorded a half-bolero, half-ranchera album with her brother, bolero singer Carlos Cuevas.

Aida Cuevas Canta a Juan Gabriel (RCA)
Canciones de Mi Pueblo (DISMEX Sonoame)
Dueto del Siglo (IMD)

CULTURAS

Formed 1992, San Antonio, Texas

Culturas came together when drummer Joe Martínez, who played with **Patsy Torres** and Joe Posada, pulled together singer/songwriters Dee Burleson (born March 3, 1958, San Antonio, Texas), who played with La Franz and Blue Harmony, and Delia Gonzáles (born circa early 1960s, Crystal City, Texas), who played with Kompania, to form a band that would become known for its multi-culturalinfluences and dynamic stage shows.

Dee y Grupo Valiente; with singer/songwriter Dee Burleson (center)
Carlito Miranda/Courtesy of Tejas Records

The group was signed by Manny Music in late 1992 and its self-titled debut album produced the original hits "Ay Mamá" and "Bésame." But it was the band's energetic shows, which featured an eclectic mix of full-throttle pop covers and traditional polkas, that gained the group a loyal following. Burleson was an engaging singer/showman whose manic stage antics included jumping, juking, and dancing with his long dreadlocks flying everywhere. Meanwhile, Gonzáles was the straight woman, balancing the show with slower ballads.

The band's lineup at various times included guitarist/songwriter Luis Ortis (who played with **Jimmy Edward**); bassist Xavier Michael Macías (who played with Henry Rivas); keyboard/composer Carlos Silvas (who played with **Sunny Ozuna, Rene y Rene,** and **Joe Bravo**); saxophonist Kevin Russell; and accordionist Candor Tovar (who played with Rancheras Alegres).

In 1993 Culturas were named most promising band at the TMAs and later that year their sophomore CD, *Culture Shock,* produced the original hit singles "Loco Loco," "Candyman's Jam," and "Golpe Traidor." The following year Culturas released their third and final album, *Baba Dice,* which featured a cover of **Pedro Infante**'s "Amorcito Corazón." In 1995 they were named TMA showband of the year and broke up temporarily at the end of that year.

Burleson went on to form Dee y Grupo Valiente and was signed to BMG/U.S. Latin. Gonzáles kept the name and regrouped as Delia y Culturas, producing a CD on EMI, and later signing with Freddie Records, but eventually fading from the scene. Burleson grew up in San Antonio's West Side listening to the norteño and Tejano rhythms of the barrio as well as the R&B/funk music on the radio. His 1980–1991 tenure with the local pop/R&B outfit La Franz helped Burleson fine-tune his stage presence, as he learned to put on a fast-moving, dynamic performance. His 1996 BMG/U.S. Latin debut, *Valiente,* produced the regional hit "Un Poquito Más." In 1998 Burleson signed with Tejas Records.

Burleson was only one of three African Americans to have performed frontline duty in a Tejano band. First there was Bobby Butler (aka "El Charro Negro," The Black Cowboy) who sang for **Little Joe y La Familia** from 1964 to1975. The other singer was **Ruth,** whose 1996 BMG/U.S. Latin debut featured the hit cumbia "El Toquecito."

CULTURAS

Baba Dice (WEA Latina)
Culturas (Manny Music)
Culture Shock (WEA Latina)
Simplemente Delia (WEA Latina)

DEE Y GRUPO VALIENTE

Dee y Grupo Valiente (BMG/U.S. Latin)

DELIA Y CULTURAS

Una Nueva Aventura (EMI)

CUMBIA

With its trotting pace and hip-swaying moves, the cumbia, like the polka, is one of the most popular dance rhythms in Tex-Mex music. Deceptively simple, the rhythm, which is one of many developed on Colombia's Atlantic coast by African slaves in the eighteenth century, has been compared to a horse trot. But the simplicity gives percussionists liberty to fill in the gaps with syncopated riffs. Occasionally cumbias feature repeating keyboard patterns, a practice borrowed from salsa. The seminal Colombian group **Sonora Dinamita** helped internationalize the cumbia in the 1960s, especially in Mexico.

Tex-Mex cumbias are often simpler than their Colombian counterparts and usually substitute brass instrumentation with accordion. Cumbia also refers to the dance form, which features couples dancing counterclockwise, separately, but in synch. It has sprouted countless varieties, though the shuffling steps common to it may have come, as folklore tells us, from slaves who were dancing while wearing leg irons and chains.

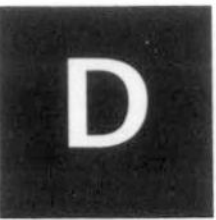

DANDYS, TRÍO LOS

Formed 1957, Mexico City, México

Trío Los Dandys came on the scene late in the golden age of trios, but, musically, they were on par with the greats like **Trío Los Panchos.** Los Dandys, ironically a quartet, achieved fame for boleros such as "Gema," "Tres Regalos," "Negrura," and "Alma de Cristal," most of which were written by José Luis "Guicho" Cisneros, who was considered to be the "fifth" Dandy during the group's early years. Original members included José Luis Segura, director/ singer/guitar; Armando Navarro, *requinto;* Francisco Escamilla, backing vocals; and Joaquín Ruíz Martínez, vocals.

During its heyday, the group played at the prestigious Follies Bergere and Teatro Lírico theaters in Mexico City and the Million Dollar Theater in Los Angeles. Segura died in 1963 and was replaced by his son, who was also named José Luis Segura. By then, Cisneros was a member of the group and Escamilla had left. In the mid-1960s, Cisneros left to form Trio Gema with Escamilla and Florentino Cruz. Martínez died in 1995 at the age of sixty-one, but Cisneros continued to lead a new version of the group called Guicho y Sus Dandys.

Las Estrellas del Fonógrafo (RCA)
Gema (Musart)
Grandes Boleros (Hemisphono)
Homenaje a José Alfredo (Orfeon)
Más Románticos Que Nunca (FonoVisa)

DE LA ROSA, TONY

Born Antonio De La Rosa, October 31, 1931, Sarita, Texas

With his two-row button accordion producing dynamic and beautifully harmonic accordion runs, Tony De La Rosa helped popularize the tradition-bound conjunto music—that foot-stomping, polka-based border dance music that enjoyed a major renaissance in the late '80s along the American Southwest. De La Rosa also composed some of the unforgettable instrumental polkas that have become part of the conjunto canon: "Atotonilco," "Sarita," and "Rosa Ana."

Tony De La Rosa
Frank Estrada/Courtesy of the National Endowment for the Arts

Born in a worker's hacienda on the King Ranch in South Texas, De La Rosa was one of twelve children in a family of field laborers.

At the age of sixteen, De La Rosa took up the accordion, a two-row model he ordered from a Montgomery Ward catalog for seven dollars.

As a teen he was influenced by **Narciso Martínez,** who by the late '30s was already a major force in border conjunto music (interestingly, De La Rosa and Martínez were born exactly twenty years and two days apart). Martínez's early recordings for the Bluebird label, including the standard "La Chicharronera," were recorded at San Antonio's Bluebonnet Hotel. In the '30s it was common practice for representatives from the "race music" divisions of major labels to travel to cities across the country to record local artists during marathon sessions in hotels. De La Rosa was also inspired by the western swing/country music that he heard while working in the fields. He liked the music enough that he joined a country band playing local honky-tonks in Kingsville.

In 1949 De La Rosa formed his own band, which included the celebrated Amadeo Flores on *bajo sexto,* and recorded his first hit polkas, "Sarita" and "Tres Ríos," and other minor hit singles on a series of indie labels, including Arco and Discos Ideal. In his book *The Texas-Mexican Conjunto,* noted scholar Manuel Peña credited De La Rosa with introducing a slower style of polka that resulted in the *tacuachito* (possum) dance, which featured couples dancing counterclockwise in slow, gliding movements. De La Rosa was also credited with other innovations, including being the first bandleader to replace the *tololoche* (upright bass) with an electric bass and adding drums and amplification as regular elements in his sound.

In 1951 De La Rosa recorded with Armando Marroquín's Discos Ideal again. In 1953 he recorded the bolero "Adiós Amor" with the duo Carmen y Laura and eventually produced another series of hit singles, including "El Circo," "Paloma Negra," "Los Frijoles Bailan," "La Periodista," "El Sube y Baja" (a remake of the **Los Donnenos** classic), and the ubiquitous "Atotonilco," which was an instrumental interpretation of an old Mexican polka by Juan José Espinoza that De La Rosa had learned as a boy while listening to his mother play it on a harmonica. Learning "Atotonilco" was almost considered a rite of passage for accordion students. Interestingly, "El Circo" was actually a remake of Red Foley's "Alabama Jubilee," which became a Top 10 hit on *Billboard*'s country charts in 1951.

Throughout the years De La Rosa ran through a series of notable lead singers, including Joe Ramos, Cha Cha Jiménez, his brother Adán De La Rosa, and others, many of whom went on to form their own conjuntos. In 1989 another former lead singer, Greg Paredes, formed Grupo Badd, which later became Los Hombres, with Raymond García (who played with **Augustin Ramírez, Freddie Martínez,** and Angel Flores), Manuel Vargas (who played with **Roberto Pulido**), and Rene López, son of Tejano Conjunto Hall of Famer **Juan López.**

In 1982 De La Rosa was inducted in the Tejano Conjunto Hall of Fame. During his career he has produced more than seventy-five albums. In 1998 the National Endowment for the Arts presented De La Rosa with a National Heritage Fellowship Award, the highest honor bestowed on a cultural artist.

15 Éxitos para Siempre (Freddie)
Así Se Baila en Tejas (Rounder)
Atotonilco (Arhoolie)
Éste Fue Mi Adiós (Hacienda)

DEE Y GRUPO VALIENTE

See Culturas

DEL RÍO, YOLANDA

Born May 27, circa late 1950s, in Pachuca, Hidalgo, México

In 1972 ranchera singer Yolanda Del Río launched her career with the hit single "La Hija de Nadie," which sold more than eighteen million copies by the late '80s and made her one of RCA's best-selling ranchera artists. Ironically, she also starred in eleven movies, but the first, which launched her career as an actress, was a spin-off of her album *La Hija de Nadie.* While filming the 1980 *El Canto de los Humildes,* Del Río was courted on and off screen by **Los Humildes** drummer Juan Manuel Ayala and days after they finished filming they were married. In 1984 she was nominated for a Grammy in the Mexican American performance category for the album *Un Amor Especial.* By the late '90s, Del Río had produced thirty-five albums.

25 Años (Balboa)
Con Mariachi (Balboa)
Mejor de Juan Gabriel (Balboa)
Mi Destino Fue Quererte (FonoVisa)
Te Voy a Esperar (FonoVisa)
Yolanda Del Río (BMG/U.S. Latin)

DELGADO, RAMIRO, Y LOS CAZADORES

Formed circa early 1980s, Monterrey, Nuevo León, México

At a young age, Ramiro Delgado learned to play instruments at home because his father, Roosvelt Delgado, a member of the famed Rancheritos del Topo Chico, would let him play with the band's instruments after the group rehearsed. Delgado and singer Cacho Cantú led Los Cazadores del Norte in the Nuevo León area before Delgado went on to join **Bronco** on accordion/keyboards in the late '80s.

Like the Beatles in pop music, Bronco's spectacular ten-year run at the top was phenomenal and seemingly ended too short. But Delgado shared the spotlight equally with band mates singer/bass/songwriter **José Guadalupe Esparza**, guitarist Javier Villarreal, and drummer José Luis Villareal.

When Bronco disbanded in 1997, Delgado and Cantú reformed Cazadores, dropped "del Norte" from the band's name, added Ramiro's name, and quickly signed on with BMG/U.S. Latin, releasing a self-titled debut CD in 1998. It featured a norteño grupo concept utilizing a mix of cumbias, ballads, charangas, and boleros. The group's first single, "Lágrimas," was a norteño cumbia. Other heat-generators on the CD included the ranchera standard "De Que Sirve" and the gritty but euphonious polkas "Vas a Casarte con Otro" and "Ya No Puedo Más." Delgado said he picked the name Los Cazadores (The Hunters) because it pays tribute to the mythical Diana the Huntress.

Ramiro Delgado (BMG/U.S. Latin)

DELIA Y CULTURAS

See Culturas

DESPERADOZ, LOS

Formed 1990, in San Antonio, Texas

Los Desperadoz are a family unit of three Villarreal brothers—Mike, accordion/vocals; Lee, *bajo sexto*/guitar; and P.J., drums/vocals. Their roots and the band's name go back to their paternal grandfather, Librado Villarreal, a locally prominent musician in the '50s outfit Los Hermanos Villarreal. In the late '80s, because of their affinity for pumping iron, the boys changed the band's name from Los Hermanos Villarreal to Los Test Tube Babies and took to performing on stage bare chested. By 1990, though, the group decided to take a more serious approach, changing their name to Los Desperadoz and focusing on the neo-traditional style.

In the ensuing years, the band developed a loyal following in the Central and South Texas area, particularly on the strength of their stylized takes on classics like "Canción Mixteca" and **Cornelia Renyo**'s "Sufriendo Penas." The band's *Breaking the Barrier* CD sparkled with the brothers' inspired rendition of **José Alfredo Jiménez**'s "Alma de Acero" and the reflective ballad "Llorando en Silencio." In early 1999, the band left EMI and was quickly signed by the upstart label Tejas Records, run by producer/A&R scout Chris Lieck.

Signed to Bob Grever's Cara Records, Los Desperadoz produced a self-titled debut album in '90 that featured the hit single "Borracho Perdido" and later scored with the tunes "Enamorado Estoy de Ti," "Retrato," and a country song, "Another Party Night."

13 Greatest Hits (EMI)
Breaking the Barrier (EMI)
Los Desperadoz (EMI)
Rawhide (EMI)
Rough Rider (EMI)

DIFERENZIA, LA

Formed circa 1989, La Pryor, Texas

When La Diferenzia debuted on the upstart label Arista/Texas, the group impressed with its versatility, easily segueing from fast-tempo cumbias to foot-stomping polkas. Singer Ricardo Castillon (born March 22, 1971, Lubbock, Texas) also shone with his vocal power and range, especially on "Hay Unos Ojos," his duet with mariachi singer **Nydia Rojas.**

The first version of La Diferenzia came together in the mid-1980s in La Pryor, Texas when brothers Ricardo and Ramiro Castillon produced a series of albums on the indie Manny Music. In 1991 Ramiro was killed in an auto accident and the group disbanded for two years. During this period Castillon worked odd jobs cleaning offices and flipping hamburgers while supporting his family in San Antonio.

La Diferenzia; with lead singer/founder Ricardo Castillon (third from left)
Courtesy of BMG/ U.S. Latin

In 1994, infused with new energy and inspiration, Castillon returned, assembled a new band, and signed with Arista. His first albums produced several radio hits, including "Si Lo Quieres," "Linda Chaparrita," "Soy Feliz," "Tú No Tienes Corazón," "Antonieta," and "Mundo sin Guitarras," which was written by Humberto Ramón and which won song of the year at the 1998 TMAs.

In 1995 La Diferenzia's self-titled debut CD was nominated for a Grammy for best Mexican American performance. Later that year La Diferenzia was named TMA's most promising band and was nominated for a Univision Premio Lo Nuestro Award for best new artist of the year in the regional Mexican category. The band's 1997 CD *Canta Conmigo,* which debuted at No. 9 on The Billboard Latin 50 chart, featured an adventurous mix of spine-tingling, spirit-lifting cumbias and polkas.

Canta Conmigo (Arista)
Diferenzia (Arista)
Fue Mucho Más Que Amor (Arista)

DINASTÍA NORTEÑA

Formed circa 1995, Acapulco, Guerrero, México

A serious devotee of norteño heroes **Ramón Ayala** and **Cornelio Reyna,** Dinastía Norteña produced two tribute CDs, *Relampagueando* (1995) and *Relampagueando II* (1995), and followed up with *Homenaje a un Grande* (1997), a homage to Reyna, who died in early 1997. *Relampagueando* referred to **Los Relámpagos del Norte,** the legendary conjunto formed by Ayala and Reyna. Made up of brothers Justino, Fidencio, and Alvaro Gómez, and songwriter Salvador Soto, the foursome supplemented the traditional conjunto lineup with Alvaro's electric bass. Based in Los Angeles, Dinastía Norteña made the Billboard Hot Latin Tracks chart in 1998 with "Acabo de Enterarme" from its *Cien Por Cien Norteño* album on Platino Records. The group was nominated in 1998 for a Univision Premio Lo Nuestro Award for best new artist in the regional Mexican category.

Especialmente para Ti (FonoVisa)
Homenaje a un Grande (FonoVisa)
Nostalgia Norteña (FonoVisa)
Relampagueando (FonoVisa)
Relampagueando II (FonoVisa)

DINNOS, LOS

See Dinnos-Aurios, Los

DINNOS-AURIOS, LOS

Formed 1987, San Francisco, California

Pop-balladeers Los Dinnos-Aurios spiced their MOR melodic tunes with percussions and utilized two-part vocal harmonies to stand out from the grupo pack. Four of the group's five members, including vocalist César Valdosiera, are from Aguililla, Michoacán, but they did not meet until they immigrated to San Francisco.

The band stepped up to the plate nicely in 1995 with the cool "El Taxista," about a philosophical cabbie detailing his view of inner city life written by **Joan Sebastián,** which peaked at No. 3 on the Billboard Hot Latin Tracks chart. And while the group has also flirted with techno-banda and other styles, its prime specialty was rhythmic ballads with melancholy lyrics about the lives of the lonely and heartbroken.

The band started out as Los Dinnos, but had to alter its name temporarily in the early '90s to avoid confusion with **Selena**'s band Los Dinos. The group's other chart hit, "No Lloraré por Ti," made No. 16 on the Billboard Hot Latin Tracks chart in 1996. Additional hit singles include "Maldita Suerte," "Dame Tu Amor," "Camionero," and "Te Conozco," a cover of Ricardo Arjona's original ballad, from the 1998 *Tiempo de Amar* CD on Platino Records.

A Bailar (FonoVisa)
Amor (FonoVisa)
Chica de Mis Sueños (Luna)
Enamorado del Amor (Sony)
Hoy Te Amo (FonoVisa)
Soledad (Luna)
Tiempo de Amar (FonoVisa/Platino)

DONNENOS DE MARIO Y RAMIRO, LOS

Formed 1948, Donna, Texas

Nuevo León natives, accordionist Mario Montes, and vocalist/*bajo sexto* player Ramiro Cavazos (born 1927, Garza Ayala Los Ramones, Neuvo León) of Los Donnenos de Mario y Ramiro began recording with Discos Falcon in 1948. One of the earliest norteño duos/conjuntos, they were named Donnenos because they were from Donna, Texas. They later signed with Torero Records of Corpus Christi.

After establishing commercial success with material written mostly by Cavazos, they returned to Mexico in 1957 to sign with CBS Columbia, a label that had stopped recording Spanish artists in the U.S. In 1962 they competed with more than eighty groups in Ciudad Victoria, winning the title Campeones Nacionales de la Música Norteña. In 1973 they signed with DLB in Monterrey. After returning to the U.S. in the mid-1970s, they began recording with Discos RYN of McAllen, Texas. Among their biggest hits was the Mexican traditional folk song "Canción Mixteca."

50 Años (Sony)
Donnenos (Sony)
Mario y Ramiro (RYN)

DOS GILBERTOS, LOS

Formed 1965, Edinburg, Texas

Los Dos Gs, as fans know them, are known for their solid rhythm section, genuine foot-stomping grooves and vocal harmonies. Accordionist Gilberto García Sr. was a master player and his exhilarating instrumental piece "Redoblando" was one of the most covered tunes in the genre.

García (born 1948) originally formed his own group when he was fifteen years old, but two years later he teamed up with Gilbert López, then a well-known Rio Grande Valley–based accordionist, to form Los Dos Gilbertos. The four-man group played the local circuit for several years until 1975 when they landed their first recording contract with Discos Falcon. Their first single was a hit, a remake of **Valerio Longoria**'s "El Rosalito."

Los Dos Gilbertos; with founder/ accordionist Gilbert García Sr. (left) and accordionist Gilbert López (right)
Courtesy of Hacienda Records

By the mid-1970s López's deteriorating health forced him to leave the group. García took over on accordion and his son Gilberto Jr. became the band drummer—and so they kept the moniker. Through the '80s Los Dos Gilbertos recorded on numerous indie labels and scored more than a dozen regional hits, including "Por Mala Mujer," "Lucerito," "Paloma Negra," "La Gata Blanca," "Te Recomiendo Esa Ingrata," "El Viejito Parrandero," and "Palabra de Hombre."

In 1981 Los Dos Gs were awarded a TMA for best conjunto album for *Una Mala Mujer* and repeated the next year for *Querida Reynosa*. One of their best CDs was 1995's *Los Dos Gilbertos Live,* recorded in Houston and featuring the band's original singer, Rubén Garza.

La Conocí en la Pulga (RCA)
Los Dos Gilbertos Live (EMI)
Niña Mujer (EMI)
El Viejito Parrandero (Freddie)
Viejos Amigos (Hacienda)

DURCAL, ROCÍO

Born María de los Angeles de las Heras Ortiz, October 4, 1944, Madrid, Spain

The oldest of six sisters, Rocío Durcal carved a niche as a top pop-ranchera singer in the '80s after a short, but prolific, film career. Though she gained fame as a pop singer, Durcal became a Mexican idol through a series of Mexican folkloric albums. Unlike singers who simply go through the motions in interpreting rancheras, Durcal impressed with the amount of emotion she could pour into her songs, especially on the **Juan Gabriel** standard heartbreaker "Amor Eterno."

When Durcal was ten years old, her grandfather took her to a local radio program *Conozca a Sus Vecinos,* where she impressed the audience with her singing. At the age of fifteen, she appeared on the TV show *Primer Aplauso,* where she won first place and officially changed her name to Rocío Durcal. She appeared in her first movie, *Canción de Juventud,* in 1962 and followed up with another sixteen films through 1976.

By the early '80s she had quit films and had dedicated herself full time to music. It was at an Ariola/BMG/U.S. Latin record company dinner in Mexico in the early '80s that Durcal met noted singer/songwriter Juan Gabriel. The meeting led to her first ranchera album, *Canta a Juan Gabriel,* which included ten Gabriel originals. After producing four more ranchera albums, Durcal helped revitalize the ranchera genre internationally and the Mexican music industry bestowed on her the honorary title of Ambassador of Mexican Music.

Durcal then began a series of pop ballad albums, working with Rafael Pérez Botija and later with noted singer/songwriter **Marco Antonio Solis** (of **Los Bukis**). The collaboration produced the benchmark albums *Como Tu Mujer* and *Si Te Pudiera Mentir.*

In 1995 Durcal was nominated for a Grammy in the Latin pop category for *Hay Amores y Amores,* produced by Roberto Livi. In 1997 she reunited with Juan Gabriel to record the double LP *Juntos Otra Vez,* which included nine duets with him. Among her career hits were "Te Amo," "El Gato Bajo la Lluvia," "Falso," "La Guirnalda," "Me Duele Que Así Te Vayas," and Juan Gabriel's classic "Amor Eterno."

16 Grandes Éxitos (RCA)
20 Éxitos, Vol. 2 (RCA)
Como Tu Mujer (RCA)
Desaires (RCA)
Lo Mejor (RCA)

ELIDA Y AVANTE

Formed July 1992, Mercedes, Texas

Elida Reyna met arranger Noel Hernández at Pan American University in Edinburg, Texas to form Elida y Avante in 1992. Two years later, they signed with Houston's Voltage Discos and released their debut CD, *Atrévete,* which included the hit "Luna Llena." This album impressed with imaginative arrangements and Reyna's smooth, but affecting, vocals.

Elida y Avante; with lead singer Elida Reyna (center)
Raven Photography/Courtesy of Tejas Records

Conflicts with Voltage Discos led to a lengthy delay and eventually to her signing with San Antonio's Tejas Records for her long awaited sophomore effort, *Algo Entero,* whose single "Lágrimas de Amor" was a melodic ballad that again showcased Elida's distinctive vocals. In 1996 the band was named best new artists at the Billboard Latin Music Awards.

Algo Entero (Tejas)
Atrévete (Sony/Voltage)
Tú Llegaste Remixes (Tejas)

EMILIO

Born Emilio Navaira III, August 23, 1962, San Antonio, Texas

His smooth good looks and plaintive vocal stylings helped make Emilio one of the most popular artists in Tejano's '90s rise. But it was the combined efforts of his crack team that propelled him to the top—including skillful songwriting by his brother Raúl Navaira, aggressive backing by the EMI label, and savvy marketing by Stuart Dill/Refugee Management (who also worked with the **Texas Tornados** and Holly Dunn).

It was the same talented cadre that helped Emilio make a successful foray into the world of country music in 1995. His country debut *Life Is Good* CD sold nearly 400,000 copies within a year of its release and charted three singles on *Billboard*'s country charts, more than sufficient proof that Emilio was a bona fide country artist.

Emilio grew up at home listening to the Tejano music of his parents: **Little Joe, Latin Breed,** and **Roberto Pulido.** But at school and with his friends Emilio preferred rock/pop heroes like Extreme, Kiss, the Cars, as well as country stars George Strait and Randy Travis. He played sports, but his first love was music, and he was good enough to earn a music scholarship at Southwest Texas State University in San Marcos. Initially he wanted to teach music, but when **Ramiro Herrera** vacated the lead vocalist spot for **David Lee Garza y Los Musicales,** Emilio was offered the post. Emilio still had one more year to get his degree, but he decided to follow in George Strait's shoes, and halted his studies to jump into a music career. The union produced numerous hits and awards for Garza. But with Emilio getting most of the attention while singing stagefront, a parting of the ways was inevitable.

Emilio quickly formed Grupo Río, which included Raúl, and signed on with EMI. Their debut CD, *Sensaciones,* produced three hit singles, including the title track. It was

Emilio
Chris Borgman/Courtesy of EMI Latin

the beginning of a successful run that included "Quédate," "Naciste Para Mí," "Juntos," "Mi Destino," "Y Se Pasan los Años," and "Cómo Le Haré." Emilio and Raúl found a way to produce a new style of pop polkas that moved feet and hips but included melodic vocal hooks that made it easy for fans to sing along. By their third CD, Emilio and Raúl had come into their own with original and irresistible polkas ("Cómo Le Haré"), rock-edged Tejano ("Te Deseo Bien"), acoustic ballads ("Juntos"), and their first country tracks ("South of the Border" and "We Had It Made in Mexico").

By 1994 Emilio was dominating the annual TMAs, winning almost half a dozen awards each year and he played the Astrodome for the Houston Rodeo's Go Tejano Days, setting attendance records each time. Already at the top of his game in Tejano, Emilio looked to country for new frontiers.

Emilio's debut country CD in 1995, *Life Is Good,* which was produced by Barry Beckett and which included a mix of emotive ballads and catchy shuffles, came as no surprise as Tejano and country music have many similarities—both musical genres rely on honest emotion, heartbreak ballads, and fast-paced shuffles. The CD's first single, "It's Not the End of the World," was a slow-starting ballad with an insidious but subtle hook that built into an anthemic chorus. It was a powerful tale about a man coming to the stark realization that he was facing life alone. Emilio flooded the tune with blues-tinged emotional tones. His instincts were finely-tuned; he honed in on the soul of a song and found a way to make it come alive.

Emilio's follow-up country CD, *On the House,* produced again by Beckett, offered more of the same—mature reflective ballads and feel-good shuffles. On the simple "Somebody Stop Me," Emilio described the pain of being addicted to someone who no longer cares, injecting a bluesy and resigned been-down-that-black-hole-before tone. Emilio sang the melodic and up-tempo "The Bottom of It" and "Take It from Someone Who Knows" from the I-feel-your-pain/best friend stance. Overall, Emilio's country CDs featured the same characteristics that sold his best Tejano material: excellent songwriting, sharp musicianship, and soulful singing.

By 1997 a minor backlash against Emilio's country move by some Tejano fans led to his slowdown in the Tex-Mex market. His previously undisputed position as Tejano No. 1 was taken over by two new younger stalwarts—**Bobby Pulido** and **Michael Salgado.** In early 1998, Emilio and his manager Stuart Dill parted ways and it seemed his country career had stalled out.

Emilio Live (EMI)
Life Is Good (Capitol Nashville)
Quédate (EMI)
Sensaciones (EMI)
Shoot It (EMI)
Soundlife (EMI)
Unsung Highways (EMI)

ESMERALDA

Born Esmeralda Jaime, December 28, 1970, Salt Lake City, Utah

When she entered the Tejano market in 1991, Esmeralda claimed a solid stake with her powerful and melodic vocals, especially on the fiery rancheras "No Soporto Más" and "Tu Muñeca."

Esmeralda launched her career at the age of five when she won a talent contest in San Antonio that led to her first album with RCA Victor International. In 1979 she signed with CBS Columbia, where label officials changed her name to Lolita. She recorded two albums with Juan González as "Juancho y Lolita." In 1990, at the age of twenty, Esmeralda sang lead vocals on the song "Sabor de Engaño," with the Liberty Band, which led to a recording contract with Manny Music. Her debut album, *Tu Muñeca,* produced the hit title track. Her sophomore effort resulted in the title-track hit, "No Soporto Más," a bolero ranchero sparkling with Esmeralda full-bore emotional singing. Esmeralda temporarily "retired" in 1993 to devote more time to her growing family.

Lo Mejor de Esmeralda (EMI)

ESMERALDA

Born Alma Graciela Herrejon, circa 1927, Morelia, Michoacán, México; died August 25, 1992, Mexico City, México

Esmeralda became known as one of the best interpreters of noted bolero/ballad songwriter **Agustin Lara.** After studying in Mexico City, Esmeralda launched her career first under the name of Alma Graciela and later, when contracted to sing at XEW with host Robert G. Treviño, she changed her name to Esmeralda. At her peak in the '40s and '50s she toured extensively, including Central America, Cuba, and the U.S. She also starred in television and in films, including *Dos Pesos Dejada.*

Mejores Chotis (Balboa)

ESPARZA, JOSÉ GUADALUPE

Born October 12, circa late 1940s, Francisco I. Madero, Durango, México

Talented singer and prolific songwriter/ producer José Guadalupe Esparza was the major engine that drove the success of **Bronco** in the early '90s. Although the other members sang, too, it was Esparza's smooth light tenor that was heard on most of the band's superhits, including "Adoro," "Que No Quede Huella," "Sergio el Bailador," and "Quien Pierde Más."

José Guadalupe Esparza
Courtesy of BMG/México

Beyond tight musicianship and melodic hooks, the central appeal for Bronco was its lyrics, which dealt with everyday workingman concerns—from the usual found-the-girl, lost-the-girl, recovered-the-girl material to songs about class conflicts and social ambitions. During Bronco's rise, Esparza worked closely with noted producer Homero Hernández to create the clear melodic norteño sound that became Bronco's signature. Hernández was killed in a bus accident in 1994 but Esparza continued to mold the Bronco sound, a sound that was evident on his solo self-titled CD. Esparza quickly signed on with FonoVisa after Bronco finished its farewell tour in 1997. The first single, "Deja Que Te Quiera," was one of six tracks written by Esparza in the 12-track CD *Mi Historia.* "Deja" peaked at No. 20 on the Billboard Hot Latin Tracks chart. Backed by the Mariachi Aguilas de América, Esparza delivered a mix of fiery rancheras and perky cumbias with his smooth tenor. As a teen, Esparza's big idol was ranchera singer **Antonio Aguilar** and he realized his longtime dream of someday becoming a ranchera singer.

Mi Historia (FonoVisa)

FABULOSOS CUATRO, LOS

Formed 1964, McAllen, Texas

Los Fabulosos Cuatro's career spans four decades during which time they became known for their vocal harmonies and were credited for helping introduce keyboards and the organ into *la Onda Chicana* in the early '70s. The band was formed by the heart of the group, drummer Juan Hinojosa (born April 17, 1950, Monterrey, Nuevo León) and his nephew, keyboardist/arranger Armando Hinojosa (born March 29, 1950, McAllen, Texas). Los Fabulosos have been fronted by a series of singers, all of whom went on to prominence in other bands, including Carlos Guzmán, who recorded "Vestida de Blanco," and Joe López, who recorded "Prieta Linda" and who would go on to lead **Mazz** in the '80s. Other notables included Cha Cha Jiménez, **Laura Canales,** and Adalberto and Marcos Orozco. The band's other hits were "El Pájaro Negro," "El Embrujado," "Le Ando Siguiendo los Pasos," and "De Corazón a Corazón."

On Our Own (EMI)
Simplemente Fabulosos (EMI)

FAMA

Formed 1989, Houston, Texas

The spark that led to the birth of Fama was ignited by Miguel Treviño, who taught his nephews—brothers Javier, Oscar, and Edgar Galván—how to play music.

Born in Mexico and raised in Houston, the Galván brothers and neighborhood friend Eddie Gonzáles, began as a garage band. After a year, the group gained recognition when they wrote, produced, and released their first two singles, "Guardado en Mi Corazón" and "Por Favor," which came to the attention of Sony Discos. Sony quickly signed Fama to a multi-record contract and released the band's debut album *Amor, Amor, Amor,* which included the above mentioned hits.

Fama; with lead singer/songwriter Javier Galván (front row, center)
Courtesy of Sony Discos

Lead singer Javier Galván wrote most of the band's hits and won a songwriter award from BMI in 1994. In early 1992, Fama signed on with the Houston-based Voltage Entertainment, a booking/management agency. Later that year, the group released its second album, *Como Nunca,* which, according to the label, sold more than 100,000 copies and produced the hit "Ojitos Color Café," which was an instant hit and gave Fama its signature sound. The song featured a bouncy keyboard riff, catchy sing-along chorus, and Javier's raspy but melodic vocals.

Fama's third album, *En Grande,* debuted at No. 10 on The Billboard Latin 50 chart and included hits "Llorando" and "Boulevard de

Sueños." In 1994 Fama was named best new artist in the regional Mexican category at the Univision Premio Lo Nuestro Awards in Miami. In 1998 Oscar Galván left the band in an organizational shift that saw the band move to San Antonio.

Al Punto (Sony)
Amor, Amor, Amor (Sony)
Como Nunca (Sony)
En Grande (Sony)

FANDANGO USA

Formed 1986, Pharr, Texas

Fandango was founded by brothers Balde and Oscar Muñoz from remnants of what originally started as **Laura Canales** and Encanto. When Canales decided to break away and return to academics, the group hired singer/arranger Hugo Guerrero (who played with **Johnny Hernández**). They added USA after discovering a similarly named female group recording in Mexico.

Fandango USA
Courtesy of Freddie

A twenty-five-year career pro, Balde Muñoz played in the '70s with Los Únicos. In 1981 Muñoz married Canales; they divorced in 1982. The band scored with the song "Yo No Te Pido la Luna" from its debut self-titled album, which also helped Fandango nab the 1987 TMA for most promising band. Guerrero left briefly to record three solo albums, but rejoined by 1992. The 1993 CD, *Class Act,* included the megahit "La Charanga," a remake of the 1940 cumbia classic by Calixto Ochoa. According to the band, "La Charanga" was a last minute addition to the album. Additional regional hits included "Me Gustas y Te Deseo," "Baila Compadre Juan," and "Te Amare un Millón de Veces." In 1997 the band's *10th Anniversary* CD was nominated for a Grammy.

10th Anniversary (Freddie)
Charanga Kings (Freddie)
Class Act (Freddie)
Felicidades (Freddie)
Matanga la Changa (Freddie)
Pura Alegría (Freddie)
Solid (Freddie)

FARÍAS, JODY, Y INCREÍBLE

Formed circa 1996, Kenedy, Texas

Young bloods Jody Farías y Increíble emerged as a promising Tejano outfit with a heavy norteño slant just as the market for Tejano was deflating and the thumpy norteño was gaining favor everywhere. Their sophomore CD, *Ni una Lágrima,* was produced by John Martínez and regional hits included the title track and "Nadie Te Ama Como Yo."

Jody Farías y Increíble; with lead singer Jody Farías (third from left)
Courtesy of Freddie

Jody Farías y Increíble (Freddie)
Ni una Lágrima (Freddie)
Quiero Estar Contigo (Freddie)

FENDER, FREDDY

Born Baldemar Huerta, June 4, 1937, San Benito, Texas

Freddy Fender became one of the first, and one of the few, successful Mexican American crossover artists in 1975 when he scored a No. 1 hit on the Billboard Top Country Singles Sales chart with "Wasted Days and Wasted Nights" on June 21, 1975.

Before Fender, **Johnny Rodríguez** had enjoyed similar success. In the '90s Rick Treviño—and, to a lesser extent, **Emilio**—were able to cross over in the country market, landing albums and singles on *Billboard*'s country charts.

In 1947 a ten-year-old Fender had his first radio appearance at KGBS-AM in Harlingen, Texas singing "Paloma Querida," which, folklore has it, won him a tub of food worth about ten dollars. His parents were migrant workers and a young Fender traveled with them on the circuit to Arkansas, Ohio, Michigan, Indiana, and other points north, wherever there were crops to pick. The family worked alongside fellow black workers, some of whom sang pretty well, Fender later recalled. It was in those fields that Fender was first influenced by the blues. After a stint in the U.S. Marines in 1953, Fender returned home and began recording as the "Bebop Kid," singing Elvis Presley and Gene Vincent covers in Spanish, including "Don't Be Cruel" and later Harry Belafonte's "Jamaica Farewell." These and Fender's other early bilingual rock 'n' roll songs from that period are included in the compilation *Canciones de Mi Barrio,* which was released by Arhoolie Records in the early '90s.

By 1960, at the behest of record label marketing honchos, Fender (who was still using his given name, Baldemar Huerta) took on his stage name. The choice of "Fender" was inspired by the headstock of his Fender electric guitar; he added the first name Freddy because it was alliterative—making his new name easy to remember and to pronounce. During this period Fender's singles "Mean Woman" and "Holy One" had moderate success. Later he made his first recording of "Wasted Days and Wasted Nights," but the single had minimal impact. That year Fender was arrested in Baton Rouge, Louisiana for possession of marijuana and was sent to Angola State Prison for two and a half years.

When Fender got out he worked for Paco Betancourt at Discos Ideal (a job was condition of his parole) and he went from sweeping the sidewalks to sorting out records. Fender later recalled that in 1964, while working as a engineer in the label's studio, he recorded a session with the famed norteña singer **Lydia Mendoza.** Fender was impressed with a technique that Mendoza used—while rehearsing she whispered her parts, but when it came time to record she belted out the songs.

"I couldn't believe the strength of that woman! She knew that her energy was very precious and she was saving it for the right time," Fender observed.

Fender struggled for several years before hitting the big time in 1975 with "Before the Next Teardrop Falls," which reached No. 1 on both *Billboard*'s country and pop single charts. He followed that with a second recording of "Wasted Days" in June, a remake of Doris Day's "Secret Love" in October, and a remake of Barbara K. Lynn's "You'll Love a Good Thing" the following February. All three songs went to No. 1 on the Billboard Top Country Singles Sales chart and Fender was named best male artist in *Billboard*'s year-end issue. Fender also appeared in a few films, including *Short Eyes, She Came to the Valley,* and Robert Redford's 1987 *Milagro Beanfield War.*

In 1989 he joined the **Texas Tornados,** which included **Flaco Jiménez,** Doug Sahm, and Augie Meyers, and they produced several hits, including "Soy de San Luis," "Who Were You Thinking Of?" and "Little Bit Is Better Than Nada," which was featured on the soundtrack for the 1996 movie *Tin Cup,* starring Kevin Costner and Rene Russo.

Aquí Estoy Yo (Hacienda)
Canciones de Mi Barrio (Arhoolie)
El Hijo de Su (Hacienda)
In Concert (Hacienda)
Mean Woman (Hacienda)

FERNÁNDEZ, ALEJANDRO

Born April 24, 1971, Mexico City, México

Being the son of a world famous ranchera singer (**Vicente Fernández**) may have been intimidating to Alejandro Fernández when he first began his career, but within a few quick albums, the younger Fernández rose to genuine superstar status as perhaps the best bolero ranchero singer in North America. With a light, but emotion-drenched, tenor that recalled the late great **Javier Solis,** Fernández proved he had not packed the force of his father's vocal chops but, instead, through his own maturity, he understood the power of subtlety and understatement.

The younger Fernández was only four years old when his father first brought him on stage during a San Antonio performance. Fernández studied architecture for a while but the allure of the music world proved irresistible. He developed his craft performing at small *palenques* (Mexican rodeo fairs that include the famed cockfights), where his working-class fans were only a few feet away.

Fernández debuted in 1990 in a duet with his father on "Amor de los Dos" on the *Voz y Sentimiento* Sony compilation CD. On the series' second volume Fernández debuted as a soloist on "El Andariego." Fernández sharpened his delivery and versatility on his first three albums, which included a range of mellow romantic ballads and fiery rancheras. With each album his velvety vocal tones, especially on the soft tunes, explored new depths and colors.

Alejandro Fernández and Nydia Rojas
Joe Rico/Courtesy of Olivia Rojas

In 1997 Fernández reached a creative peak with his *Muy Dentro de Mi Corazón* CD, on which he fully realized his smooth baritone style. Later that year he teamed up with Emilio Estefan Jr. to produce the roots-ranchera CD *Me Estoy Enamorando,* blending a superb mix of pop ballads and slow-burning bolero rancheros that demonstrated that Fernández would not be content to merely fill his father's shoes. Both albums produced simultaneous hit singles on the Billboard Hot Latin Tracks chart, including "Si Tú Supieras," "No Sé Olvidar," "Yo Nací para Amarte," and "En el Jardín," a duet with Gloria Estefan.

Fernández married América Guinart in 1991. The couple had three children but were briefly separated in 1997.

Alejandro Fernández (Sony Discos)
Grandes Éxitos (Sony Discos)
Me Estoy Enamorando (Sony Discos)
Muy Dentro de Mi Corazón (Sony Discos)
Piel de Niña (Sony Discos)
Que Seas Muy Feliz (Sony Discos)

FERNÁNDEZ, GERARDITO

Born Gerardito Cuevas Cobos, August 24, 1985, Guadalajara, Jalisco, México

Directed by his father, José Luis Cuevas, Gerardito Fernández began recording at the age of six. This was not unusual, given that his older brother, ranchera crooner **Pedro Fernández,** also started young. Gerardito was a name to watch out for in mariachi music, a genre that enjoyed a renaissance in the '90s. Fernández's first two albums gained minor notice, notably the 1995 album *La Niña Popis* with the singles "Papá" and "La Mariquita Linda." His major label debut on EMI Latin in 1998, *El Consentido,* was produced by Cuevas and Juan Mares. The CD incorporated cumbias into its mariachi arrangements and the young Fernández was able to project mariachi's traditional sentiment with uncanny maturity beyond his age. By 1998 Fernández had appeared on numerous TV shows and performed at Fiesta Broadway in Los Angeles.

El Consentido (EMI Latin)
La Niña Popis (Alacran)
Sangre de Charro (Alacran)

FERNÁNDEZ, PEDRO

Born José Martin Cuevas Cobos, September 28, 1969, Guadalajara, Jalisco, México

Pedro Fernández was only seven years old when he began his acting career in the movie *La de la Mochila Azul.* Like **Luis Miguel,** Fernández was prolific early in his career, becoming a popular actor in Mexican films and novelas. Although he was mostly a pop singer, Fernández became a serious devotee of Mexican folkloric music. His idols were **Pedro Infante** and **Vicente Fernández** and he changed his stage name as a tribute to them. In 1996 he recorded *Querida,* an entire album of **Juan Gabriel** songs.

Pedro Fernández
Courtesy of Arjon's

Fernández recorded more than two dozen albums and among his biggest hits were "Quien" and "La Mujer Que Amas," a Spanish-language version of Bryan Adams's "Have You Ever Really Loved a Woman?" Fernández's 1997 CD, *Un Mundo Raro,* was a tribute to legendary Mexican composer **José Alfredo Jiménez.**

1992 La de la Mochila Azul (Sony)
1993 Lo Mucho Que Te Quiero (Philips)
1997 Un Mundo Raro (PolyGram)
1996 Querida (Sony)

FERNÁNDEZ, VICENTE

Born February 17, 1940,
Huentitán el Alto, Jalisco, México

For more than thirty years Vicente Fernández has been the most important and influential ranchera singer in the world. His reign as the king of the ranchera rivals Frank Sinatra's stature in the American pop standard genre. Fernández has not been at it as long as Sinatra, but he has had a greater impact with sold-out shows and chart-topping albums well into the late '90s.

As young as six years old, Fernández dreamed of becoming a singer. When he received a guitar at the age of eight he quickly learned how to play and began studying folkloric music. His ambition drove him to enter an amateur contest in Guadalajara, and he won first place. Emboldened, he began playing in local restaurants and at weddings, receiving rave reviews from family and friends.

In late 1965 Fernández traveled to Mexico City, making the rounds at the various record labels. He received rejection after rejection, but he continued to hang around the then-CBS studios, hoping for an audition. In one of those storied traditions, a mariachi troupe that had backed up another singer was waiting around between sessions when Fernández approached them. He begged them to back him up on a few songs while the record label executives were in the area.

As it happened, the executives relented. Perhaps they felt sorry, or maybe it was their attempt to finally get rid of him, in any case the record executives listened—for all of two songs.

"Then one of the guys came up to me, shaking his head, and told me, 'Son, you'd be better off selling peanuts in the streets or something,' " Fernández later recalled in a *San Antonio Express-News* interview, with the glee that comes with post-success hindsight.

Undaunted, Fernández soldiered on. A few months later, Fernández's fate would change forever. At 5:30 A.M on April 19, 1966, **Javier Solis,** the most popular bolero ranchero singer in Mexico, died of complications from a gallbladder operation.

For the third time in thirteen years, Mexico had lost a national hero.

First there was **Jorge Negrete.** Tall and handsome, an operatic singer and popular actor, Negrete was widely considered to be the quintessential Mexican *charro.* He died of a liver infection at the Cedars of Lebanon Hospital in Los Angeles in December 1953. With Negrete's death, **Pedro Infante,** who had been Negrete's chief rival, became a cultural icon. But on the morning of April 15, 1957, Infante was killed when the cargo plane that he was copiloting crashed on the outskirts of Mérida, Yucatán.

Javier Solis had already been recording for five years when Infante died, but afterward Solis's star began to rise quickly. From the 1950s through the mid-1960s, Solis was Mexico's biggest ranchero singer.

The world of music has always driven image and perception, luck and opportunity. And so it was for Fernández when Solis died in 1966. Many of the same record labels that had rejected Fernández just months previously began calling. It was in the summer of 1966 that Fernández signed on with CBS México, recording his first hits: "Perdóname," "Tu Camino y el Mío," and "Cantina del Barrio."

However, it would be ten years before Fernández would become the new undisputed ranchera king. Songwriter Fernando Z. Maldonado had penned a ranchera tune with a new twist about a macho who accepted blame and acquiesced in a relationship. The angle may have been new but the song impacted. "Volver, Volver" went on to become an anthem in the mariachi ranchera canon. In late 1976, the song blasted out of car radios, home stereos, and jukeboxes as hundreds of groups in the U.S., Mexico, and Central and South America covered the song.

The song pole-vaulted Fernández to international star status and began his string of unforgettable hits. In the ensuing years Fernández recorded a half dozen other standards, including "La Ley del Monte," "El Rey," and "El Peñal."

Vicente Fernández
Courtesy of Sony

By the early '80s the Mexican music press coined a new title for Fernández—"El Idolo de México"—and it stuck. Through the years Fernández's success generated hundreds of imitators, but no one could match his operatic power and range as a singer. His benchmark works include *Recordando a los Panchos,* his take on bolero classics, and *Las Clásicas de José Alfredo Jiménez.* The latter was pure fire, not a filler track in the bunch. Fernández fascinates when he reinvents Jiménez's chestnuts such as "Yo," "Ella," "Tu Recuerdo y Yo," and "Alma de Acero."

Fernández also appeared in some twenty movies, many of which carry the title tracks of his top albums, including *La Ley del Monte* and *El Rey.* He took pride in being loyal to his record company, Sony Mexico, and has recorded more than fifty albums with the label. In 1998 *Billboard* inducted Fernández into its Latin Music Hall of Fame.

Aunque Me Duela el Alma (Sony Discos)
El Charro Méxicano (Sony Discos)
Javier Solis (Sony Discos)

Lástima Que Seas Ajena (Sony Discos)
Motivos de Alma (Sony Discos)
Ni en Defensa Propia (Sony Discos)
Recordando a los Panchos (Sony Discos)

FIEBRE, LA

Formed 1986, Pasadena, Texas

When Tejano exploded in the early '90s a few key bands were responsible for attracting youth to the music. La Fiebre, with its rock-tinged music and dynamic stage shows, represented the new wave with such magnetic hits as the intoxicating ballads "Borracho de Besos" and "Por Tu Culpa."

In 1985 the five founding members (Rudy Rocha, Rick Garza, Joe Reynosa, Pete Espinoza, and Johnny Tristán) started as Pride of Pasadena. In 1986 Ricky Patiño and Rudy Ramírez joined the band and they changed the name to La Fiebre. At this time the band mostly played rock 'n' roll, performing at small local clubs and private parties. Ramírez and Patiño soon left, with Patiño joining **La Mafia.**

In 1987 the band self-produced the LP *Contagious,* which included the hits "Vestida de Color de Rosa" and "Por Tu Culpa," and distributed it on their own label, L.F. Records. With the success of *Contagious,* the band members decided to go into venture full time and quit their jobs. Later that year, they were signed by Cara Records, then the biggest Tejano indie label, and distributed by Sony Discos. According to the label, the band's second LP, 1993's *On the Rise,* sold more than 100,000 copies on strength of hits "Sólo un Sueño" and "Borracho de Besos." The CD landed on The Billboard Latin 50 chart. The band's 1990 LP *Out of Control* produced the hit "Si Mañana Viene o No." That year the band signed directly with Capitol/EMI Latin and won TMA's most promising band in 1991.

La Fiebre
Chris Borgman/Courtesy of Freddie

La Fiebre's signature rock-guitar-edged sound was directly influenced by Van Halen, Bon Jovi, and Ozzy Osbourne. Band members sported long hair, pierced earrings, leather boots, and studded jackets. They combined polka-based Tejano with strains of melodic rock, including drum-crashing effects and guitar-fueled metallic wailing. The band lost serious momentum in 1992 during a legal dispute between Freddie Records and Capitol/EMI Latin. The former was accused of illegally tampering with La Fiebre, which was then signed to EMI. The lawsuit dragged in the courts for three years, during which time La Fiebre's visibility faded.

After the lawsuit was settled, La Fiebre released two more CDs and they were finally released from EMI in 1996. The following year they were picked up by Freddie Records and produced the CD *Fenomenal,* which included regional hits "De Cantina en Cantina" and "Qué Tal Si Te Compro," which was written by the late **Cornelio Reyna.** By this time key members, including sax player Erik Jiménez and drummer Rick Garza, had left the group.

Hasta el Final (EMI)
No Cure (EMI)
Nuestras Mejores Canciones (EMI)
Young Generation (Hacienda)

FIGUEROA, JOSÉ MANUEL

See Sebastián, Joan

FILIS, LOS

See Mier, Los

FLASH, GRUPO

Formed 1986, Nueva Rosita, Coahuila, México

Led by the throaty baritone of lead singer/musical director José Luis Garza, the cumbia outfit Grupo Flash was one of the top merchants of brash, heavily-syncopated cumbias. Flash regularly drew packed houses and jammed dance floors in the 1980s and 1990s. The group's early hits included "Cuco el Perruco" and "El Profesor Rui Rua." In the 1990s the band scored again with two cumbia hits penned by **Ladrón**'s Sergio Villarreal: "Las Cartas de la Baraja" and "Tu Pelo Tu Piel." In the mid-1990s, the group added young tenor Fernando Arturo Mendiola to its lineup. After Grupo Glash left the indie DISA, it independently rereleased its late 1990s albums, including the 1998 CD *Tu Saborcito,* whose title track, a tropical cumbia, achieved respectable airplay.

15 Éxitos (JE)
Nuevo Camino (FonoVisa)
Tu Saborcito (JE)

FREDDY'S, LOS

Formed 1962, Guadalajara, Jalisco, México

Los Freddy's emerged in the early '60s as a rhythmic pop-ballad group. By the '70s Los Freddy's, which were then competing against early grupos Los Babys and Los Solitarios, were getting regular airplay with hits "Sin Tu Amor," "Déjenme Llorar." Later they got airplay with "Recuerda Prieta." The group received a Grammy nomination in 1988 for the album *Vida Nueva.*

By 1991 Los Freddy's had recorded twenty-nine albums. At that time, according to director and occasional composer Pedro Iñiguez, the group started to worry that its songs were beginning to sound alike and so they used new composers for the release of *Los Freddy's '91*. The single from that CD, "Pero Acuérdate de Mí," reached No. 23 on the Billboard Hot Latin Tracks chart.

On the band's 1998 album, *Locuras de Amor,* Iñiguez teamed up with noted producer Sergio García to forge a crisper sound, particularly on the ballads "Para Olivar Qué Me Olvidas" and "Acaricia Mis Lágrimas."

In 1999, Los Freddy's were teamed up with the venerable grupos Los Solitarios, Los Apson, and Los Terricolas on a live compilation album—*El Baile del Recuerdo en Vivo*. Los Freddy's contributed "Sin Tu Amor," "Si Acaso Vuelves," and "Aquel Amor."

16 Éxitos (Peerless)
Con Banda (Peerless)
Emociones (Musart)
La Leyenda Continúa (FonoVisa)
Locuras de Amor (Universal)

Appear on:

El Baile del Recuerdo en Vivo (BMG/ U.S. Latin)

FUGITIVOS, LOS

Formed 1991, Santa Maria, California

Los Fugitivos shot to the upper echelons of the *onda grupera* scene in the mid-1990s with the rock-guitar-edged, pop-leaning hits "La Loca" and "Diablo."

Brothers Jaime and Edi Espinoza, both natives of Tepic, Nayarit, formed the nucleus of the band in 1985 as Grupo Kariño. But in 1991, with the addition of the New York City–born, Mexico City–raised singer/keyboardist Roberto Nieto, the band became Los Fugitivos. The five-man outfit, led by singer/bassist/songwriter Jaime, specialized in a lusty blend of traditional rancheras, cumbias, and rock-guitar-fueled ballads.

The title track of the group's debut album, *Esperando Por Ti,* was a cover of American rocker Richard Marx's "Right Here Waiting." In 1993 Los Fugitivos retooled José Luis Perales's ballad "La Loca," which landed on the Billboard Hot Latin Tracks chart and elevated the band to headliner status. The band followed up with the cumbia/rock tune "Diablo," the melodic ballad "Vanidosa," and the catchy cumbia "Lobo," about a nightclub hound. Their 1998 album *Secretos* featured a rockish, percussive cover of Roberto Carlos's "Pájaro Herido."

In early 1999, keyboardist Nieto departed and was replaced by Hekar Rivero, just as the band left PolyGram and signed on with Sony Discos.

Their debut Sony CD *Mi Última Tentación,* was coproduced by the group and studio helmsman Pepe Mota and contained few surprises. Evident everywhere was the band's trademark sound: keyboard-driven cumbias and airy pop ballads.

In promotional tour interviews, singer Jaime Espinoza noted that the band prided itself on that distinct ballad sound, and counted among its musical influences the bands Kansas, Journey, Chicago, and Air Supply. "In fact, when we were starting out, we were called the Mexican Air Supply," Espinoza said.

Dios (PolyGram)
Ilusiones (PolyGram)
Mi Última Tentación (Sony Discos)
Secretos (PolyGram)
Vanidosa (PolyGram)

GARCÍA, ELSA

Born Elsa Laura García Gutiérrez, January 19, circa 1956, Monterrey, Nuevo León, México

Elsa García began singing at the age of four and she cites her mother, Hermelinda Escamilla (who used the stage name Linda La Norteña), as her major influence. García produced six albums without much luck in the late '80s before she got on the Tejano map in 1993 with the catchy polka "Ya Te Vi." García also got radio play with "Tus Desprecios," from the Bob Gallarza–produced *En Familia* CD. García self-produced her most recent CDs, including *Escápate Conmigo,* for which she also picked the material.

Diez (EMI)
Escápate Conmigo (EMI)
Ni Más, Ni Menos (EMI)

GARZA, DAVID LEE, Y LOS MUSICALES

Formed 1980, Poteet, Texas

David Lee Garza y Los Musicales emerged in the late '80s with a big band Orquesta Tejana approach—featuring the accordion, *bajo sexto,* keyboards, and saxophone—to produce foot-stomping polkas, rhythmic cumbias, and solid rancheras.

Garza (born February 15, 1957, Jourdanton, Texas) began playing the accordion at the age of eight and his biggest influence was his dad, Tony Garza, but the group also drew inspiration from **Roberto Pulido.** By the age of eleven, Garza was playing with his father in the band Margarito Hernández y Su Conjunto. In 1968 the band, then called David Lee Garza y Su Conjunto, recorded its first 45: "Al Baile Me Fui," a father and son duet. By then the band included Garza's brothers Richard on bass and Adam on drums.

Garza married in 1975 and continued playing weekends. To help make ends meet, Garza installed storm windows from 1976 to 1978. The band was signed to Bob Grever's emerging Cara Records in 1984. By this time, Garza was on his second lead singer, Emilio Navaira. Navaira had been preceded by **Ramiro Herrera** (1980–1983) and was succeeded by Oscar G. (1988–1990), **Jay Pérez** (1990–1994), and Marcos Orozco (1995 to present). Herrera, Navaira, and Pérez all went on to successful solo careers. (Navaira became known by his first name, **Emilio.**) By the mid-1980s Garza began winning numerous TMAs, including most promising band (1982), best conjunto album for *Award-Winning Musicales* (1985), and best album for *Cuántas Veces* (1987). The group also won the 1993 TMA Tejano Country Award for "She's Not Alone," and best showband. Some of the band's biggest hits included "Tonta," "Amor de Madrugada," "Cuántas Veces," and "Qué Tristeza."

When Jay Pérez was Los Musicales's lead singer in the early '90s, the band produced the landmark albums: *Con el Tiempo* and *1392.* The albums featured a tight rhythm section, floor-rattling drums, and lively accordion runs. Pérez's torchy vocals soared over the potent mix in songs about love's discovery and betrayal. In 1993 Garza teamed up with **Selena** at the Astrodome for the Houston Rodeo. Los Musicales continued producing popular albums and winning TMAs, including best conjunto album *Ya Me Cansé* (1995) and instrumental for song "David Lee's Favorites" (1996).

1392 (EMI)
Algo Diferente (EMI)
Con el Tiempo (EMI)
Especialmente para Ti (Hacienda)
Todavía No Me Muero (Hacienda)
Ya Me Cansé (EMI)

GATOS, LOS

Formed 1992, Osaka, Japan and Kyoto, Japan

Los Gatos are a four-man conjunto band that originally formed in Osaka and Kyoto in western Japan. The group was originally known as the Gamblers but then changed its name to Los Gatos in 1992.

Los Gatos were formed by lead vocalist and accordion player Kenji "El Gato" Katsube, who started out as a rock guitarist. But in 1975 Katsube discovered the accordion while listening to Ry Cooder's *Showtime* CD, which featured accordionist **Flaco Jiménez,** and he decided to start his own conjunto band. For years he looked for an accordion player in Japan without luck until finally, in 1989, he decided to learn to play the accordion himself. He imported a Hohner Corona II accordion from Germany and taught himself how to play by listening to conjunto recordings again and again.

By the early '90s Jiménez, **Steve Jordan, Mingo Saldivar,** and other conjunto greats had toured Japan, further spreading the music.

In 1994 Los Gatos traveled halfway across the world to attend that year's Tejano Conjunto Festival. After listening to a demo tape of the group, festival organizer Juan Tejeda said, "They really weren't that good, but I was really impressed with their enthusiasm." That led to their first appearance at the next year's festival, during which they featured inspired performances of conjunto classics such as "Atotonilco" and "El Sube y Baja." They generated such a feverish reaction from the crowd that they have been back to the TCF each year since.

It was on one of those trips to Texas that Los Gatos signed on with the Corpus Christi–label Hacienda Records and susequently produced three albums. Famed conjunto legend **Tony De La Rosa** produced Los Gatos's second album, which featured their cover of Daniel Garzes's "El Mosquito Americano" sung in Spanish and Japanese and the **Vicente Fernández**–identified ranchera "Volver, Volver." Los Gatos's third album, *Son Mentiritas,* was also produced by De La Rosa.

Gatos de Japón (Hacienda)
Lo Mejor de los Gatos (Hacienda)
Son Mentiritas (Hacienda)

GONZÁLEZ, EDDIE

Born Eddie Gonzáles, October 9, 1975, San Antonio, Texas

With an exhilarating stage show that included lots of female-rousing dance moves and youthful, emotion-laden vocals, Eddie González generated interest and enthusiasm when he burst on the scene in 1992. González clicked on all cylinders with his revamped versions of **Cornelio Reyna**'s "Botoncito de Cariño," and "El Disgusto," which featured fluid saxophone notes and rippling accordion runs all while the band went through its hip-shaking, pelvic-thrusting dance moves that made **Emilio**'s shuffle look stiff and dated.

González first fancied that he could sing when he was eight years old and recorded his own version of "We Are the World" on his parents' portable radio. At the age of eleven, when he met guitarist Frank Tarin, who used to play an old **La Mafia** song "Tú, Sólo Tú," González realized that he liked Tejano music and could sing it. Afterward, he would ask to join in with the bands at area weddings and family gatherings.

In October of 1992, González teamed up with Tim Villanueva to form **Grupo Vida** and they premiered at Burbank High School. Eventually, the band was brought to the attention of then–Sony Discos A&R rep Luis Silva who signed the band to a recording contract. González y Grupo Vida's debut CD, *100% Tejano,* produced the hits "Sólo Tuyo Nada Más" and the rock-tinged Tejano polka "Cómo Te Deseo." González's real name ended with an "s," but because of a typo on his debut album from Sony Discos he began using the "z" version of the spelling of his name.

In live performances, González y Grupo Vida turned heads with spirited renditions of norteño and conjunto classics, such as

Eddie González
Courtesy of Sony

"Un Rinconcito en el Cielo," "Viva Seguin," and "Atotonilco." The band created magic when it combined lively accordion runs, flowing saxophone solos, and a solid bottom section. The group also thrilled its mostly female crowds with elaborate stage choreography that featured almost constant twisting, turning, and jumping movements.

In 1996 González y Grupo Vida were named best new artist at the Billboard Latin Music Awards and in 1998 won the TMA Showband Award. The latter was ironic because González y Grupo Vida had gone their separate ways just months before, citing irreconcilable personal differences. In early 1998 González quickly assembled a new band under his own name and released *Mi Charchina.*

100% Tejano (Sony Discos)
10 Years of Tejano Music (Sony Discos)
Ay Cariñito (Sony Discos)
El Disgusto (Sony Discos)
Mi Charchina (Sony Discos)

GORME, EYDIE

Born Eydie Gormezano, August 16, 1931, New York, New York

Early in her career, Eydie Gorme sang with the Tex Beneke band while attending night school at New York's City College and working as an interpreter for the United Nations. She got her first break in 1953 when she auditioned and was chosen for *The Steve Allen Show,* replacing a singer who knew only five songs. She married Steve Lawrence in 1957, and they stepped onstage in 1960 as Steve and Eydie. Both became regular cast members of *The Steve Allen Show.* The duo won a Grammy in 1960 for their *We Got Us* album on ABC.

In 1964 Gorme recorded *Amor,* a landmark Spanish album with **Trío Los Panchos** that included several hit boleros, including "Nosotros" and "Sabor a Mí." Gorme won a Grammy in 1966 for her solo single "If He Walked into My Life." Gorme has also appeared on stage and on television and has won several Emmy Awards. Gorme and Lawrence were honored with a Lifetime Achievement Award from the Songwriters Hall of Fame and the duo performed with Frank Sinatra during his Diamond Jubilee world tour.

50 Años (Sony)
Canta en Español (Sony)
Eydie Gorme & Trío Los Panchos (Sony)
Personalidad Discos (Sony)

GRUPO

Grupo is a loosely defined term for a genre that enjoyed prominence in Mexico in the early '90s. Generally, grupo refers to the "band concept," mostly within the keyboard-driven romantic ballad subgenre, and occasionally within tropical cumbia. The term "band concept" refers to a group that does not give any member top billing, as does **Emilio** or **Ramón Ayala.**

Known collectively as *la onda grupera,* the genre's prototypical grupos include **Los Bukis, Los Temerarios, Liberación,** and **Los Fugitivos.** However, grupos usually have one or two better-known members, often the vocalist and musical director plus a few interchangeable players. By some accounts, the term grupo has its origins in the '60s Mexican pop ballad/rock groups (Los Babys, **Los Angeles Negros,** Enrique Guzmán, Los Locos del Ritmo, **Los Freddy's**) that imitated American and English rock groups like the Beatles, the Rolling Stones, and the Beach Boys.

The grupo phenomenon peaked in the early '90s when it became part of another rising trend in Mexico—huge, Woodstock-style dance concerts in major cities like Monterrey and Guadalajara that drew up to 100,000 fans. These marathon concerts would typically feature up to five stages (to minimize delays between bands) and typically ran from 7 P.M. to 7 A.M. Norteño and Tejano groups like **Mazz,** Ramón Ayala, **La Mafia,** and **Selena,** made inroads on *la onda grupera*'s popularity in the mid-1990s.

GRUPO VIDA

Formed 1997, San Antonio, Texas

With the Tazmanian antics of Sonny Sauceda and a solid rhythm section, Grupo Vida was one of the few Tejano bands that survived the loss of a charismatic lead singer.

In late 1997, lead singer **Eddie González** y Grupo Vida went their separate ways in an acrimonious split. Personal conflicts between them had become increasingly heated in the months leading up to the final blow-out backstage at **Emilio**'s Tejanos for Children benefit festival at Sunken Garden Theater in San Antonio.

Grupo Vida; with accordionist Sonny Sauceda (third from left)
Chris Lieck/Courtesy of Tejas Records

Grupo Vida had backed González from the very beginning—his 1994 debut, *100% Tejano*—and along the way earned a reputation as one of the most dynamic stage bands in the biz. Eddie González y Grupo Vida shows were excitement-filled concerts that featured González's passionate vocals and elaborate choreography and the wild theatrics of Sauceda, who would spin, jump, and juke while playing his accordion. During the March 1998 SXSW music festival showcase in Austin, Texas, Sauceda wowed the Austin Music Hall crowd when he swung the twenty-pound accordion around by his teeth. The show was ultimately more important, though, because it featured the capable vocals of new singer Art Tigerina and the cohesiveness of Vida's dynamic live shows—high energy levels and elaborate shoulder-swaying, hip-shaking choreography—were still intact.

Grupo Vida's debut CD, *Vida,* on Tejas Records showcased the band's tight musicianship and creative spark on songs such as "Sin Buenas Condiciones" and "La Charchina."

Vida (Tejas)

GUADALUPANOS, LOS

See Aguilares, Los

GUARDIANES DEL AMOR, LOS

Formed 1992, Los Angeles, California

The youthful pop-influenced Los Guardianes del Amor were formed when Mexican lead singer/accordionist Arturo Rodríguez and renowned Argentinian songwriter Aníbal Pastor decided to start a romantic/pop grupo. Rodríguez quickly recruited drummer Oscar Saúl Cervantes, keyboardist Daniel Poplawsky, guitarist Pablo Calderón, and bassist Ernesto García—all ex-members of other local bands in Monterrey and Mexico City.

Their debut 1994 CD, *Cuatro Palabras,* which, according to their label, sold more than 200,000 copies in Mexico, generated the hit "Los Ángeles Lloran" and the title track, both written by Pastor. Los Guardianes also claim to be the first Mexican grupo to have played in Spain. The band's 1995 sophomore work, *Camino al Cielo,* revealed a more romantic approach with mellower keyboard-driven ballads. The CD also featured a duet with the noted balladeer Marco Antonio Muñiz on "Un Amor entre Dos." The album *Por Siempre y Para Siempre* yielded two noteworthy hits, "El Perro, el Gato y Yo," and a duet with **Bronco**'s **José Guadalupe Esparza,** "No Somos Nada." Pastor wrote the majority of the group's songs.

Camino al Cielo (BMG/U.S. Latin)
Cuatro Palabras (BMG/U.S. Latin)
Por Siempre y Para Siempre (BMG/U.S. Latin)
Te Amo Todavía (BMG/U.S. Latin)

GUERRERO, LALO

Born December 24, 1916, Tucson, Arizona

Singer/songwriter Eduardo "Lalo" Guerrero became a major entertainment figure in the '40s when his song "Canción Méxicana" was recorded by the late ranchera great **Lucha Reyes,** then in her prime. He was also in film and television, singing and playing guitar beside Jane Russell, Robert Mitchum, and Gilbert Roland. Four of his 1940s songs about Chicano "Zoot Suiters" were used in the 1979 musical *Zoot Suit.* Politically attuned, Guerrero wrote *No Chicanos on TV,* which addressed the lack of Mexican American actors in prime roles. Offstage he was an activist, urging farmworkers to register and vote, encouraging children to improve their minds for a brighter future.

In 1949 **Agustin Lara** recorded Guerrero's song "Pecadora," which established him as a major Latino artist. Guerrero also scored hit singles in the '50s and '60s, including his 1955 crossover hit "Pancho López," which established him as a bicultural musician. His best-selling recordings include fifty children's Spanish albums recorded under the name Las Ardillitas (The Squirrels). He has received several Lifetime Achievement Awards from organizations such as Nosotros and the United Farm Workers. Among his biggest hits were "Barrio Viejo," "Chicas Patas Boogie," "Muy Sabroso Blues," and "El Chicano." In 1991 Guerrero was inducted into the Tejano Music Award's Hall of Fame and his former grade school in Tucson, Arizona was renamed after him.

Las Ardillitas de Lalo (EMI)
Cenzontles con Su Permiso, Señores (Arhoolie)
Los Lobos Papá's Dream (Music for Little People)

GUERRERO, MANUEL

Born June 17, 1937, San Antonio, Texas; died January 22, 1991, San Antonio, Texas

Manuel Guerrero was a self-taught guitarist/accordionist whose dual twenty-plus career as a singer/accordionist and a sergeant in the U.S. Army earned him the nickname "El Sargento Que Canta" (The Singing Sergeant).

Born into a musical family that included his uncle Jesús García, who played upright bass or *tololoche,* and his mother, Dolores, who used to sing rancheras, Guerrero was already playing the accordion and winning local contests by the time he was ten years old. In 1951, at the age of fourteen, he was recruited as accordionist for noted singer/songwriter Daniel Garzes and **Los Tres Reyes.** In 1957 Guerrero joined the U.S. Army where after a few years he was placed in the Special Services Division and was part of several USO tours, playing conjunto music in the far-flung locations of Germany, Korea, and Vietnam. During his leaves, Guerrero returned home to record albums with Toby Torres for a series of indie labels, including Corona, Río, Ideal, and Discos Falcon. Guerreo retired from the army in 1977 and immediately formed Manuel Guerrero y Su Conjunto.

He recorded with several more labels, including Capitol México, Pan American, and Del Bravo; and among his biggest regional hits were "El Viejo Chivo," "Abre el Corazón," "Soy Albañil," and his 1984 hit "Dos Corazones," a duet with his daughter María Elena Guerrero. In 1991, Guerrero was inducted into the Tejano Conjunto Hall of Fame.

Mis Polkas Favoritas (JB)
Yo Tenía Dos Corazones (BLD)

GUIZAR, TITO

Born April 8, 1908, Guadalajara, Jalisco, México

Although he grew up in a rural setting, Guizar studied medicine for two years in Milan, Italy. Back in Mexico City he appeared in the operettas *Naughty Marietta* and *The Student Prince.*

Like **Jorge Negrete,** Guizar was intrigued by the chance to break into stardom in New York City, then a hotbed for actors and singers in the exciting early days of TV and radio. Under the pretext of enrolling in the Columbia School of Medicine, he got his parents' permission to move to the Big Apple in 1929. In New York he sang in Prohibition-era nightclubs and later, after an audition got him a spot on the Columbia Broadcasting System (CBS), he dropped out of school.

He moved to Los Angeles, where he lived for twenty-eight years. There he signed with CBS, where he was billed as "The Mexican Troubador." In a career that paralleled that of the quintessential American cowboy Roy Rogers, Guizar sang at Carnegie Hall and appeared in dozens of Mexican and American films, working with such stars as Dorothy Lamour and Roy Rogers. Along with Jorge Negrete, **Pedro Infante,** Pedro Armendariz, and María Felix, Guizar was part of Mexico's golden age of cinema. His output included mostly Mexican folkloric songs as well as Cuban, Puerto Rican, and South American ballads. Guizar was also a regular interpreter of **José Alfredo Jiménez**'s songs. The 1938 *Allá en el Rancho Grande* was his best-known Mexican film and signature hit. His brother was the composer José "Pepe" Guizar, who was famous for the songs "Guadalajara," "Cuando México Canta," and many others.

Rancheras Originales (Boingo Latino)

GUZMAN, JOEL

See Little Joe y La Familia

HERMANAS MENDOZA, LAS

Formed circa early 1940s, San Antonio, Texas; disbanded 1951

Younger sisters of **Lydia Mendoza,** Juanita and María became known for their vocal harmonies on Mexican corridos and rancheras from the early 1940s through the early '50s. Prominent on the *carpa* circuit, tent shows that brought entertainment to migrant worker communities, the sisters also played San Antonio bars when World War II's gas rations limited touring. In 1946 Las Hermanas Mendoza, along with sister Lydia, signed with Azteca Records and, though they rarely performed together live, Lydia frequently backed the group up on record with her twelve-string guitar. When María married in 1951, the group dissolved, but Lydia and Juanita occasionally recorded together afterward as Las Hermanas Mendoza. The sisters' signature hits were "Por Última Vez" and Luis Moreno's "Mis Pensamientos."

Mendoza Sisters (Arhoolie)

HERMANOS AYALA, LOS

See Humildes, Los

HERMANOS BARRON, LOS

Formed 1970, Nueva Rosita, Coahuila, México

Formed by two of the Barron brothers—singer Joaquín and saxophonist Oscar—Los Hermanos Barron were a venerable norteño-tropical crew whose live shows impressed with solid chops and a combination of nimble accordion runs and wicked sax licks to produce feverish metallica-cumbia grooves, attracting followers and inducing dance fever. There is no pop sheen on this mature bunch, just straight-ahead rhythmic polkas and quick-trotting cumbias with a rubbery, *charanga* feel. A perennial fixture at dance halls along the Tex-Mex border, Los Hermanos Barron spiced up classics like "El Mariachi Loco" and **Ramón Ayala**'s "Qué Suerte la Mía." Los Barron also scored with "Borrachera," "Tengo Mi Segundo Frente," and their signature hit, "El Mojarras."

The journeyman band recorded more than twenty albums for various indies. Notable recent hits include "Cha Cha Cha del Tren," which manages to incorporate nearly every state in Mexico in the lyrics, and "El Rococo," from 1996's CD *Va de Nuez* on AFG Sigma records. The five-man group, which also features third brother Francisco Barron on *bajo sexto* and nephew Oscar Barron Jr. on drums, released *Un Amanecer Tropical* in 1997.

Ahora Si Baila el Muñeco (Freddie)
Bájate del Macho (Freddie)
Burrito Moro (DISA)
La del Moño Colorado (Freddie)
El Mojarras (Freddie)
Rueditas de Amor (DISA)
Sinaloense (DISA)
Un Amanecer Tropical (Simitar)
Viborón (Freddie)

HERNÁNDEZ, JOHNNY

Born Johnny DeLeon Hernández, November 24, 1944, Temple, Texas

After years of playing second fiddle to his brother, Tejano legend Joe Hernández of **Little Joe y La Familia,** during the band's heyday, the younger Hernández decided to strike out on his own in 1984. He produced a few solo albums as Johnny Hernández and Third Coast, but his only hits were remakes of the **Tito Guizar** classic "El Rancho Grande," the **Isidro López**–identified "Díganle," and "Canta Canta."

Hernández got his start at the age of sixteen when his older brother Little Joe asked him to sing lead on the song "Por un Amor" during a recording session (despite the name, the younger Hernández was not in the band). The song became a major hit in 1961 and launched the group, which was then performing as the Latinaires, to a national audience. Johnny also sang with Little Joe on the band's bigger hits, including "Las Nubes," "Cartas Marcadas," and "Viajera." Eventually the band was renamed as Little Joe, Johnny y La Familia.

Although Johnny Hernández had left by 1984, from time to time the brothers would perform together in informal reunions. In late 1995 Johnny Hernández moved to New Mexico and released his *Hostile Takeover* CD, for which he wrote nine songs, including his cover of **Cornelio Reyna's** "Me Caí de las Nubes."

Canta Canta (Hacienda)
Poquita Fe (Hacienda)

HERNÁNDEZ, RAÚL

Born circa late 1950s, Mocorito, Sinaloa, México

One of the founding members of the top norteño group **Los Tigres del Norte,** Hernández departed from the group in early 1996 to pursue a solo career. Like his brothers, Hernández was inspired as a teen by older brother Jorge Hernández to join the band. Raúl was on some thirty Tigres albums, his last being *El Ejemplo.* His last show with the band was in Oakland, California on January 1, 1996. Signed to FonoVisa, Hernández's debut solo album, *Rancheras y con Banda,* did well, reportedly selling more than 200,000 copies, and generated the hit singles "Amor Prisionero," "Con Letras Rojas," and "La Abuela de Mis Hijos."

Norteño de Corazón (FonoVisa)
Rancheras y con Banda (FonoVisa)

HERRERA, RAMIRO

Born January 9, 1960, San Antonio, Texas

His smooth vocals and knack for finding the essence in romantic ballads quickly established Ramiro "Ram" Herrera as a bright star in the mid-1980s Tejano scene. In 1985 his signature song "Rosa para una Rosa" elevated him swiftly from regular player status to rising star.

Ramiro Herrera
Courtesy of Sony Discos

Herrera was born on the South Side of San Antonio to Manuel Herrera and María Portales. He began singing in the seventh grade when he tried out for a solo in the Terrell Wells Middle School choir. Later on Herrera would credit his choir teacher, William Sánchez, for encouraging him and giving him singing tips. In 1973 Herrera recorded his first single—a rendition of "Ben," which was featured in the middle school fund-raising album.

While Herrera got his initial voice lessons in middle school and later on at McCollum High School (other notable McCollum graduates included **Emilio,** Yolanda Saldivar, and the Farías brothers, who later became **La Tropa F**), he honed his chops in the late '70s in area Top 40 bands, including Chicano Brass and Monte Cielo. In 1978 he married his high school sweetheart, Isabel "Bella" Hinojosa, who would later become Herrera's manager.

In 1980 Tony Garza, father of David Lee Garza, offered Herrera the lead singing position in his son's band **David Lee Garza y Los Musicales.** In later interviews, Herrera said that he only accepted because Los Musicales were then touring with seminal Tejano conjunto figure **Roberto Pulido.** Herrera ran with the Musicales posse until 1983, during which time he recorded three albums with the band and helped it win the TMA's most promising band category in 1983. After increasing personal conflicts with Garza (Herrera felt that as lead singer he was not getting enough credit), Herrera left in 1983 to join the local fledgling band Montana, which was under the direction of veteran manager Joe Ríos. Ríos was looking for a new singer because his then-singer **David Marez** (ex-**Royal Jesters**) was about to leave. In 1985 Herrera recorded his biggest hit—the romantic polka "Rosas para una Rosa" (Roses for a Rose), which was written by Homer Hernández. The song generated heavy airplay all over the Southwest and it made Ram Herrera a household name. In the ensuing tour, Herrera established his tradition of opening his shows with "Rosas" and handing out more than a dozen fresh roses at every performance.

Herrera's hot streak continued with Roger Contreras's "Entre Cantina y Cantina," a saloon song about being unable to forget that special love. In 1988 he reached the peak of his career, winning five of twelve honors at that year's TMAs, including best male vocalist, entertainer, album (for *Ram Herrera*), and song/single (for "Amor Querido") of the year. The following year Herrera left Montana and started his Outlaw band, which included several Montana members.

But by the early '90s, through a combination of personal and industry developments, Herrera's momentum had completely dissipated. In the fast-living, high pressure world of entertainment, the temptations of booze, drugs, and other vices are evident every day and everywhere. In a *Houston Chronicle* interview in late 1992, which came out as he was releasing his *Pensamientos* CD, Herrera admitted to having a drug problem and added, "It's a big problem in the industry. It's widespread.

"I've learned through trial and error, making mistakes and learning not to do them again. I am finally going straight."

Compounding things was the industry shake-up in early 1990 when EMI Latin purchased the Tejano powerhouse indie Cara Records, which had entered a distribution deal with Sony Discos. Herrera signed with Sony, but he still owed two albums to Cara/EMI. Herrera, like David Marez and **La Mafia,** suffered from the two-year wait between fulfilling Cara obligations and beginning anew on a different label.

In 1994 Herrera teamed up with noted producer Bob Gallarza to produce a new version of Delaney and Bonnies' "Neverending Love," which gained massive airplay. That same year, Herrera reached another milestone when he teamed up with **Selena** to play before 60,000-plus fans at the Astrodome for the Houston Rodeo.

10 Years of Tejano Music (Sony Discos)
Cuenta Conmigo (Sony Discos)
Insuperable (Sony Discos)
Neverending Love (Sony Discos)

HINOJOSA, TISH

Born Leticia Hinojosa, December 6, 1955, San Antonio, Texas

Tish Hinojosa grew up listening to the pop melodies of the Beatles and the Byrds and the folk rhythms of traditional Mexican singers like **Lola Beltrán.** These cross-cultural influences helped shape and define Hinojosa's musical outlook as she wove a bilingual, bicultural tapestry of folk songs in her music.

Hinojosa began singing after school at coffee houses and folk masses while attending Providence High School. After graduating she attended San Antonio College and sang radio jingles. Later she signed a singles deal with the local Cara Records, but they had only regional impact. Hinojosa was already writing her own songs when, in 1979, she moved to Taos, New Mexico and later that year won the New Folk Songwriters Competition at the Kerrville Folk Festival. In 1986 she released the single "I'll Pull You Through" on Curb Records and it was chosen as the theme song for the Red Cross that year.

In the late '80s Hinojosa recorded music that incorporated a bilingual mix of conjunto rhythms, western swing, and border folk tunes on such albums as *Aquella Noche* and *Culture Swing.* Her seventh album, *Fronteras,* on Rounder featured guest musicians **Flaco Jiménez,** Brave Combo, Peter Rowan, Robert Skiles, **Santiago Jiménez Jr., Mingo Saldivar,** and **Eva Ybarra.** In 1996 she released *Cada Niño* (Every Child), a bilingual album for children, on the Rounder label.

Aquella Noche (Watermelon)
The Best of the Sandía: Watermelon 1991–1992 (Watermelon)
Cada Niño (Rounder)
Culture Swing (Rounder)
Fronteras (Rounder)
Memorabilia Navideña (Watermelon)
Soñar del Laberinto (Warner Bros.)

HOBBS, GARY

Born Gary Lee Hobbs Jr., January 5, 1960, Amarillo, Texas

Raised in Eagle Pass, Texas, Hobbs learned piano at the age of seven. Later he sang in his high school choir and played trumpet in the band. In 1971 he became a soloist in his church choir. After short stints with local bands Chicano Breed and Starlite, he teamed up with future **Mazz** keyboardist Brando Mireles in 1980 and started the Hot Sauce Band. Early hits included "Mentiras" and "Sálvame." Hobbs was signed by EMI Latin in 1991 and his most successful CDs have been *Te Vas a Acordar,* which spun off the singles "Maldito Amor," "Tres Rosas," "Chiquitita, Chiquitita," and the title track. Later minor hits came in "Por Favor Corazón" and "Quiero Que Vuelvas."

Miradas (EMI Latin)
Soy el Mismo (EMI Latin)
Te Vas a Acordar (EMI Latin)

HOMETOWN BOYS, THE

Formed 1970, Lubbock, Texas

The Hometown Boys were among the best of the traditional Tejano/conjunto ensembles at a time when most groups were exploring new directions. However, the Homies, as their fans called them, drew a large and loyal following through their music, which featured infectious polkas and irresistible foot-stomping rhythms.

The band was started as El Conjunto Internacional by brothers Ricky and Joe Martínez (born 1964) in their native Lubbock, Texas. Older brother Roman Martínez Jr. motivated his younger brothers to learn new music by giving them five dollars every time they learned a new song. The band members grew up with music in the house as their father, Roman Martínez Sr., and mother, María Dolores, were members of the original conjunto group Los Madrugadores del Valle. In 1990 El

Conjunto became the Hometown Boys and in 1991 they were signed by Capitol/EMI Latin.

The Hometown Boys; with the late accordionist Joe Martínez (left)
Courtesy of FonoVisa/Discos MM

The Homies gained a reputation as a traditional conjunto that played with a raw and primitive intensity. They produced such irresistible grooves that the dance floors were always packed. Among the band's signature hits were "Somos Dos Gatos," "Hombre Inocente," and "Mire Amigo." Accordionist Joe Martínez, who wrote some of the songs, had a tendency to rip up accordions, which thrilled the crowds.

Their debut album, *El Poder de una Mujer,* produced a single by the same name. The band produced four more albums before moving on to sign up with FonoVisa in 1995. Their second FonoVisa CD, *Mire Amigo,* went gold (sold 50,000 copies) in its first four days of release, and generated the single "Mi Deseo" and the title track. Later that year they received a TMA for *Tres Ramitas,* for best album (conjunto-traditonal). In 1996 the Hometown Boys were the first Mexican Americans inducted into the West Texas Walk of Fame. The Homies were honored in ceremonies that also included Buddy Holly and the Crickets, Angela Strehli, Butch Hancock, the Maines Brothers, Joe Ely, and Terry Allen.

At the 1997 TMAs, the song "Joe's Special No. 10" was named best instrumental of the year. In October of that year, percussionist Roman Jr. died of cerebral palsy. Shortly afterward Joe Martínez left the band because of a contractual disagreement with the record label, but the band continued producing music.

Martínez went on to form a band called Joe Martínez y Dream and produced his first album, *A New Beginning* on the Houston-based Toka Records label. During a January 22, 1998 Hometown Boys performance at Hulabaloos nightclub in Houston, Martínez (though officially no longer part of the band) went onstage to join his brothers for a jam. After twenty minutes he collapsed and was rushed to an area hospital where he was pronounced dead from cardiac arrest.

THE HOMETOWN BOYS

Hombre Inocente (EMI)
Live (EMI)
Mire Amigo (FonoVisa)
Somos Dos Gatos (EMI)
Tres Ramitas (EMI)

JOE MARTÍNEZ Y DREAM

A New Beginning (Toka Discos)

HUMILDES, LOS

Formed 1972, Modesto, California

Los Humildes were originally founded as a grupo/norteño foursome by the three Ayala brothers: José Luis, Alfonso, and Juan Manuel, all natives of Zamora, Michoacán, Mexico. The fourth founding member was Rodolfo Flores, from Coahuila, Sinaloa, who left in 1987. The band debuted with the album *Ambición,* beginning a lengthy career that saw some fifteen-plus albums in the solid bass-thumping norteño tradition.

The band peaked in 1975, being named among the most popular bands in a year-end survey by *Billboard*. From 1976 until the mid-1980s the band was in seven movies. In 1985 Los Humildes, who were also known as Los Hermanos Ayala and Los Humildes de Los Hermanos Ayala, were nominated for the twenty-eighth annual Grammy Awards for *13 Aniversario/13 Éxitos*. Drummer Juan Manuel, who had married **Yolanda Del Río,** left the band in 1990. Led by singer/guitarist José Luis Ayala, Los Humildes scored with the single "Lagrimitas" in 1991 and "Un Beso Para Llevar," which reached No. 26 on the Billboard Hot Latin Tracks chart in April 1997.

LOS HUMILDES

Con la Banda San Miguel (FonoVisa)
Donde Estará (Freddie)
Cuando Vaya P'al Pueblo (Freddie)
Igual Que Ayer (Discos Caminan)
Ni Me Viene ni Me Va (FonoVisa)
Por dentro y por Fuera (FonoVisa)
Siempre (FonoVisa)

JOSÉ LUIS AYALA

Como Te Extraño (FonoVisa)
En el Cielo del Olvido (FonoVisa)
Entre Pecho y Espada (FonoVisa)

HUMILDES DE LOS HERMANOS AYALA, LOS

See Humildes, Los

HURACANES DEL NORTE, LOS

Formed 1969, San Jose, California

A veteran norteño outfit that played in the traditional style, complete with matching western outfits, the band was originally called Los Cuatro del Norte when it was formed in 1969 by the García brothers: Heraclio, Jesús, Francisco, and Asunción Rubalcava, all natives of Tanganzicuario, Michoacán.

They had emigrated as teens to San Jose, California and worked in the fields picking seasonal crops, a job they still performed during the band's lean early years. In 1972, they added the youngest García brother, Guadalupe, and renamed themselves Los Huracanes del Norte. A year later they recorded their debut album, which had regional success with the song "El Corrido de Daniel Treviño."

By their second album, *La Gavilla del Burro Prieto,* the hit single, "Son Tus Perfumenes Mujer," helped spread their popularity through the American Southwest and northern Mexico. By the late '70s, Los Huracanes were producing a steady stream of hit songs, including "La Musiquera," "El Corrido de Juan Martha," "Amanda, Ciérrale," and "El Ranchero Chido," most of which were written by Martin Rubalcava. Los Huracanes, now based in Portales, New Mexico, soon started appearing in films—by 1997 they had been in seven movies.

In 1995 they signed with FonoVisa and their 1997 album *Top Norteño* sold more than 200,000 copies and featured the hit "El Clavo." Additional radio hits followed: "911," "El Sexenio de la Muerte," and "El Gato de Chihuahua."

Aires de Mi Norte (FonoVisa)
Corridos (FonoVisa)
Jugada Norteña (FonoVisa)
Una Explosión Musical (Sony)
Verdades Norteñas (FonoVisa)

IGLESIAS, JULIO

Born Julio José Iglesias de la Cueva, September 23, 1943, Madrid, Spain

When Julio Iglesias began his career in the early '70s he was a smooth romantic pop balladeer whose moans and yells in concert elicited screams from female audiences. By the '80s Iglesias transformed into a suave crooner and then made his move to become a household name in America. In the interim, he sang rancheras, boleros, and even tangos.

During the mid-1960s, Julio Iglesias played professional soccer for the Real Madrid team, but his career was cut short by a near-fatal car accident. During his recovery, Iglesias learned to compose music, play the guitar, and sing, winning the 1968 Spanish Song Contest with "La Vida Sigue Igual." His rise in Latin America was swift, and it was accelerated by his ability to sing in a wide variety of languages, which also made him a star throughout Europe and eventually in Asia. In the late '70s Iglesias recorded a series of romantic albums that impacted in Mexico, including *El Amor,* and *A México,* which included his takes on classic boleros and rancheras "Cucurrucucu Paloma," "No Me Amenaces," "Ella," "Cuando Vivas Conmigo," "Solamente una Vez," and others. He followed with the gigantic hit "Hey!" which cemented his triumph in Mexico and, in 1984, he made his American conquest with his crossover CD *1100 Bel Air Place,* a collection of duets that included the Top 10 hit duet with Willie Nelson "To All the Girls I've Loved Before."

1100 Bel Air Place (Columbia)
A Flor de Piel (Sony)
América (Sony)
A México (Sony)
A Mis 33 Años (Sony)
El Amor (Sony)
Begin the Beguine (CBS Discos)
Crazy (Columbia)
De Niña a Mujer (Sony)
Hey! (Sony)
In Concert (Columbia)
Tango (Columbia)

INCOMPARABLES DE TIJUANA, LOS

Formed circa 1980, Guamuchil, Sinaloa, México

Traditionalists in style, Los Incomparables have recorded songs that are alternatively amusing ("Andamos Borrachos Todos") and message-oriented ("No a las Drogas").

In 1982 the group moved to Tijuana and recorded its first album on the independent label Linda. Founding members Tello Higuera, Guadalupe Quintero, and Mariano Quintero are fathers/uncles of the members of **Los Tucanes de Tijuana,** which pole-vaulted to the top of the charts in the mid-1990s.

Included among their biggest hits are "Sentencia," "Pista Secreta," "Clave 5-8-5," "Destino Ingrato," "Las Morenitas," "La Gavilla de Beltrán," and "Traficantes Michoacános." In the mid-1990s the group signed with major label EMI Latin, bringing them wider distribution and exposure.

Corridos Prohibidos Clave Nueve (EMI Latin)
Dedos de Oro (EMI Latin)
De Nueva Cuenta (EMI Latin)
Incomparables de Tijuana (Linda)

INDUSTRIA DEL AMOR

Formed 1982, Oxnard, California

Industria del Amor was a youthful, keyboard-driven band that mined the same romantic pop field dominated by **Los Bukis.**

The band impacted on the charts with "¿Dónde Estarás?" "Mi Dulce Compañera," and "Te Tengo Que Olvidar."

Industria del Amor
Courtesy of FonoVisa

The six-member band was formed by the sons (all from the state of Michoacán) of migrant workers who picked strawberries in southern California. In fact, three of the members picked fruit as well as worked in construction. The group got its name from radio station DJ Pepe Reges. Band members initially objected to the name, but eventually warmed up to the idea. The band signed on with Ramex Records and produced a series of albums in the mid-1980s that generated its first hits such as "Mi Dulce Compañera" and "Vuelve." In 1991 the group signed with FonoVisa and immediately released the album *Para Ti.* Later hits included "Rey de Oros" and "Me Quedé Llorando."

Founding members—Roberto Verduzco, vocalist/director; Salvador Vasquez, guitarist/composer; and Francisco Javier Solis, drummer/composer—took the grupo concept one step further when they added elaborate costuming and choreography to their synth-driven romantic pop music. Although the band used outside songwriters, Vasquez and Solis often contributed tunes, including "Lloraré Por Ti" and "Ingrata Mujer." In 1995 *Reencuentro* earned Industria del Amor a double platinum record (selling over 200,000 copies), according to the label FonoVisa.

In 1996 Roberto Verduzco released a solo CD, *Unidos,* with mariachi, and in 1997 produced *Remembranzas Musicales,* but continued performing with the band.

INDUSTRIA DEL AMOR

Feliz Navidad (FonoVisa)
Para Ti (FonoVisa)
Sueños de Amor (FonoVisa)
Verano de Amor (FonoVisa)

ROBERTO VERDUZCO

Remembranzas Musicales (FonoVisa)
Unidos (FonoVisa)

INFANTE, PEDRO

Born Pedro Infante Cruz, November 18, 1917, Guamuchil, Sinaloa, México; died April 15, 1957, Mérida, Yucatán, México

In the history of Mexican pop culture, there has never been an artist who has captured the hearts and minds of Mexicans like the ranchera singer/film actor Pedro Infante. His film roles almost always cast him as the hopeless romantic, the adventurous hero, the sexy singer, or the tough macho with a heart. He recorded hundreds of rancheras and boleros, many of which became classics, including his signature hits "Cien Años" and "Amorcito Corazón."

Infante always had a smile, he was handsome (he resembled American actor Eli Wallach), and his image was everywhere (he starred in fifty-nine movies).

Yet, despite the wild and unending adulation of his fans around the world, Infante was also admired for his easily approachable, common-man demeanor. Working class Mexicans identified with him because, like many of them, Infante came from rural roots that were marked by grinding poverty and class struggles. In spite of his massive success at the box office and in record stores, Infante never distanced himself from his fans.

Because of his humble family background, Infante worked a variety of jobs—as a carpenter, waiter, boxer, and barber. He sang for the first time in 1937 in a local fiesta in Sinaloa. His first wife, María Luisa León, encouraged him, urging him to go to Mexico City to seek his fortune. There, after his first break on radio station XEB, Infante began playing local clubs, including a lengthy stint at Hotel del Prado. He made his first recording, "El Soldado Raso," in 1943 with Peerless, the only record label for which Infante would ever record. His early hits included "El Durazno," "Dulce Patria," "Rosalia," "Corazón, Corazón," and "La Que Se Fue." He recorded tunes from the top songwriters of the day, including **Cuco Sánchez,** Rubén Fuentes, Alberto Cervantes, and **José Alfredo Jiménez.**

Many music historians credit Infante with introducing the bolero ranchero into Mexican pop music in the '40s. It was a stylized subgenre that **Javier Solis** would mine with much success in the '60s.

In 1955 Infante debuted on the radio program *Así Es Mi Tierra* on XEW. As his popularity increased, Infante toured widely, including all of Mexico, the U.S., and Central America.

His film debut came in 1942 with *La Feria de las Flores,* which was not met with much fanfare. Still, Infante would go on to work in some fifty-plus films, including *Jesusita en Chihuahua, Sobre las Olas, ¿Qué Te Ha Dado esa Mujer?* and *Reportaje.* But it was Infante's film trilogy about bittersweet poverty—*Nosotros los Pobres, Ustedes los Ricos,* and *Pepe el Toro*—that most endured him to Mexican fans. He was awarded an Ariel, the equivalent of Hollywood's Oscar, by the Academia de Ciencias de Artes Cinematográficas de México for his role in the 1956 film *La Vida No Vale Nada.* He starred with María Felix in his last film, *Tizoc,* for which he was also awarded a Golden Bear Award at the Berlin Festival in Germany.

Infante's penchant for daring adventures and his willingness to live life to the fullest attracted fans. An avid motorcycle fan, Infante rode a Harley Davidson. The Mexico City Police Department made him an honorary member of its Motorcycle Patrolmen's Squadron when he filmed *A Toda Máquina.* In 1951 Infante developed a passion for flying, obtaining his license and eventually buying several airplanes. Ironically, Infante (then called "Capitán Cruz" by friends) was involved in two airplane crashes before the third, fatal accident in Mérida, Yucatán.

Pedro Infante was known for being a playboy and his indiscretions were covered by the celebrity-hungry media in Mexico. According to lore, Infante was not yet divorced from first wife, María León, when he married the young Irma Dorantes. His divorce appeal to the Mexican Supreme Court failed and the incident caused a media storm. It was precisely during his attempt to meet with León and negotiate a divorce that Infante decided to fly from Mérida to Mexico City in the early morning hours of April 15, 1957. With a copilot, Infante took off in a converted World War II bomber, owned by the TAMSA airlines of which he was part-owner. Shortly after takeoff, at about 8 A.M. local time, the plane started to nosedive and crashed on the outskirts of Mérida.

Infante died six months shy of his fortieth birthday.

Like **Jorge Negrete**'s death before him, Infante's sudden death at the peak of his career stunned the entertainment world and caused a national day of mourning in Mexico. TV and radio stations ran his movies and music continuously for days. His funeral in Mexico City jammed the streets with thousands of mourners as well as dozens of TV, radio, and recording stars. In a final serenade, more than a dozen mariachis sang his signature song, "Amorcito Corazón."

For Mexicans everywhere, the quintessential Infante images include the movie roles when he played the common man struggling against the odds or the romantic fool trying to get the girl. Romantics were enthused by his affecting bolero rancheros when he sang of the intoxicating power of love's discovery, or of the good love gone but never forgotten. For all of his movies and all of his music, Infante will be remembered as the preeminent Mexican hero.

39 Aniversario: 60 Rancheras Inmortales (Peerless)
Adiós Mis Chorreadas (Peerless)
Amorcito Corazón (Peerless)
Boleros, Vol. 1 (Orfeon)
Canta a José Alfredo Jiménez (FonoVisa)
Mejores Rancheras, Vol. 1 (Peerless)
Mi Cariñito (Peerless)
Música de Sus Películas (Sony)
¿Qué Pasa, Compadre? (Peerless)
Rancheros (Peerless)
Las Románticas (Sony)
Tu Recuerdo y Yo (Peerless)
Voz y Sentimiento (Peerless)
Viejos Amigos (Sony)

INTENSO, GRUPO

Formed 1997, Rio Grande City, Texas

This five-man group, which writes and records most of its own music, was cut from the same mold as **Los Tigres del Norte**—with its *bajo sexto*/accordion–fueled polkas and corridos, and matching western-themed suits. Lead singer Rogelio Campos delivered the requisite plaintive tones on the group's songs, especially its first single, "Duele."

Grupo Intenso
Courtesy of Sony Discos

Although the members—Campos, singer/*bajo sexto;* Rubén Núñez, percussion; Domingo Garza, accordion/arranger/producer; Leonel García, drums; and Gabriel Salinas, bass—are all natives from the farming community of Cerralvo, Nuevo León, the band was formed in Rio Grande City, Texas.

Mixing norteño cumbias with Tejano polkas, Intenso produced its debut album at Pro Sound Studios in McAllen, Texas. After securing a management/booking contract with Promociones Serca, one of the most influential agencies in northern Mexico, the group was signed by Sony Discos in 1997. The band's CD *Regalo del Cielo* included songs written by Josué Contreras ("Duele") and Eduardo Alaniz ("Sabor a Miel").

Regalo del Cielo (CBS/Sony Discos)

INTOCABLE

Formed 1993, Zapata, Texas

When Tejano was peaking in popularity in the early 1990s Intocable took a left of center approach by playing a new norteño/Tejano hybrid. Alongside **Michael Salgado,** Intocable injected a freshness into the increasingly predictable Tejano sound with norteño corridos and polkas that employed a new crunch and tension on songs like "¿Dónde Estás?" and "La Mentira." The band's music featured bluesy boleros, harmonic accordion runs, and engaging vocal harmonies.

Intocable was formed when Ricardo "Ricky" Muñoz and friends that he had known since junior high school came together in the tiny border town of Zapata, Texas. Muñoz, singer/accordionist; Rene Martínez, drummer; and percussionist, Sergio Serna forged the sound that used the raw norteño rhythms and upbeat Tejano polkas as the foundation and topped it with a rock 'n' roll sensibility and Beatlelike vocal harmonies.

The band floundered on Freddie Records before signing with EMI in 1993 and producing the EMI debut, *Fuego Eterno,* in 1994. The band followed up with *Otro Mundo,* which was produced by **Ramón Ayala**'s brother José Luis Ayala and which hatched the chart toppers "Besos Sin Condición" and "La Mentira," a bluesy bolero. By 1996 Intocable was rapidly becoming a major player, attracting full houses and ecstatic crowds with the band's almost constant touring. In 1997 the group released *Llévame Contigo.* It produced two Billboard Hot Latin Tracks chart toppers—the single "No Te Vayas," which peaked at No. 5 in August 1996, and title track, which peaked at No. 20 in October 1996. Other chart hits included "Parece Que No" and "Y Todo, ¿Para Qué?" According to EMI officials, by late 1998 the band had sold a combined total of one million albums in the U.S. and Mexico.

In late 1997 internal conflicts led to the departure of *bajo sexto* player/songwriter Johnny Lee Rosas and accordionist Albert Ramírez Jr. (who were replaced by Danny Sánchez and Silvestre Rodríguez Jr. respectively). Rosas and Ramírez went on to form **Masizzo.** Muñoz and Intocable lost no momentum, releasing the already completed *Intocable IV* album, which generated the hits "Eres Mi Droga" and "Vivir sin Ellas." In March of 1998 Intocable reached another milestone when it teamed up with **La Mafia** at the Astrodome for the Houston Rodeo, drawing 50,000 plus fans.

On January 31, 1999 onstage MC José Ángel Farías (at the age of twenty-three) and bass player Silvestre Rodríguez Jr. (at the age of twenty-six) were killed in a car crash outside Monterrey, Nuevo León.

Intocable IV (EMI)
Intocable (EMI)
Llévame Contigo (EMI)
Otro Mundo (EMI)

INVASORES DE NUEVO LEÓN, LOS

Formed 1980, Monterrey, Nuevo León, México

This five-man norteño outfit began its career in 1978 when accordionist/music director Javier Ríos assembled the group in Monterrey, Nuevo León. TKR radio station DJ Rogelio García named the group Los Invasores during a name-the-band contest. The group was discovered while playing a wedding by veteran band manager/booking agent Servando Cano, who helped Los Invasores get signed to a record label. The band became known for its traditional sound, which went beyond the *bajo sexto* and accordion, and featured vocal harmonies.

At the outset Lalo Mora was the lead singer, but he was replaced by Rolando Marroquín. During the band's initial phase Cano got it opening slots on **Ramón Ayala**'s tours, which helped the group get wider exposure and recognition. Los Invasores's first hit came in 1982 with "Mi Casa Nueva." The CD by the same name was their first gold record, selling more than 50,000 copies. That success opened the doors for their first U.S. tours. The band followed up with a series of hits that included "Aguanta Corazón," "Laurita Garza," and "Qué Valor de Mujer." In 1995 Los Invasores generated heavy airplay with the single "El Barón del Golfo" from their *Corridos* album. The band also appeared in eleven movies.

In 1997 the band released *Ventanas al Viento,* which included songs by **Cornelio Reyna,** Paulina Vargas, Ramiro Leija, and Jorge Mascorro. Reyna died in early 1997 and his "Ventanas al Viento," the title track of the CD, was reportedly the last song he wrote.

1997 Grandes Éxitos, Vol. 3 (EMI)
Corridos (FonoVisa)
¿Para Qué Volver? (FonoVisa)
Ventanas al Viento (EMI)

JAIME Y LOS CHAMACOS

Formed 1979, Alice, Texas

Jaime y Los Chamacos became top players in Tejano circles in the late '80s with a combination of swirling accordion runs, sweet vocal harmonies, and lively foot-stomping polkas. The four-man unit, piloted by lead singer/accordionist Jaime De Anda, enjoyed a streak of hit singles, but it was their live dynamic stage show that drew the loyal crowds.

De Anda (born January 3, 1965, Houston, Texas) began playing the drums at the age of five and at the age of thirteen he learned to play the accordion from musicians Chema Sánchez and Vidal Jamie, his father's compadres. While a young teen De Anda played in his father's band—Las Estrellas de Houston. In 1979 the family moved to Alice, Texas and the band became Los Chamacos de Raúl de Anda and was an all-family affair.

By the late '80s Los Chamacos began a streak of hit singles, including "Como Pude Enamorarme de Ti," "Qué Le Vas a Dar," "Pretty Baby," "Mi Música Favorita," "Un Complejo," "El Monito," and "X-Novia." All these hits were rhythmic polkas that featured the dulcet vocal harmonies of the foursome, which at the time included bassist Eduardo Ordonez; *bajo sexto* player **Juan P. Moreno;** and drummer Manuel Alvarado Jr. In 1991 Hector Tello Jr. replaced Alvarado and Johnny Lee Rosas replaced Moreno (who went on to join **David Lee Garza** for a couple of years before venturing on a solo career). In 1995 Rosas left and became one of the original founders of **Intocable.**

Jaime y Los Chamacos; with lead singer/founder/accordionist Jaime De Anda (second from left)
Jay Salazar/Courtesy of Freddie

As one of the young turks in the early '90s Tejano explosion, Los Chamacos created excitement in their lively shows, which featured De Anda dancing, prancing, spinning, and jumping—all while belting out songs and playing the accordion. Its momentum increasing, the band relocated in 1990 to San Antonio, which is the recording capital of Tejano and conjunto music, and became regular performers at the annual Tejano Conjunto Festival.

Los Chamacos won their first TMAs (for best album of the year) in 1994 for *Unrivaled* and in 1995 for *Tren,* which was named best instrumental of the year. The band was twice nominated for a Grammy Award in the Mexican American category for best performance: in 1996 for *No Se Cansan* and in 1997 for *En Vivo Puro Party Live.*

En Vivo Puro Party Live (Freddie)
Mi Muñequita (Freddie)
No Se Cansan (Freddie)
Unrivaled (Freddie)

JARA, CARMEN

Born Carmen Luz Jara Barra, March 12, circa 1975, Cuidad Obregón, Sonora, México

Banda singer Carmen Jara started her career as a teen when she left her hometown to perform in bars in Cancún, singing boleros and bossa novas. In 1991 she moved to Los Angeles and worked in Latin clubs just as the resurgence of banda was beginning. After Jara recorded her first album on an indie label, FonoVisa signed her in 1992 for the follow-up, *La Mujer... El Nuevo Folklore de México,* which spun off the hits "Reina y Cenicienta" and "Sin Fortuna." The latter was a duet with Jorge Hernández, who was the lead singer of **Los Tigres del Norte.**

Insisting on performing with the genuine Sinaloan sound, Jara was backed up by the nineteen-member Banda San Miguel. Jara liked to claim she was the only female musician doing authentic Sinaloan music—which, unlike techno-bandas, eschews keyboards for a full, six-piece horn section. Later Jara scored with hits "Como Tu Mujer" and "La Denuncia." Jara's *Con Sentimiento Jara* was a mariachi-styled CD that was produced by former **Bronco** singer **José Guadalupe Esparza.**

1996 12 Kilates Musicales (FonoVisa)
1997 Con Sentimiento Jara (FonoVisa)
1994 La Mujer... El Nuevo Folklore de México (FonoVisa)
1996 Mujer Enamorada (FonoVisa)
1994 Y Tú Te Quedas (FonoVisa)

JENNIFER Y LOS JETZ

Formed 1995, Corpus Christi, Texas

After videotaping herself singing **Selena**'s hits and sending it to Selena's family, Jennifer Peña (born 1983, San Antonio, Texas) was picked to perform at the May 1995 Selena Tribute at the Houston Astrodome. Jennifer, then twelve years old, signed up with Abraham Quintanilla's Q Productions, which had a promotion and distribution agreement with EMI Latin.

In early 1996, she released her debut album, *Dulzura,* which produced the hits "Pura Dulzura" and "Ven a Mí." According to EMI Latin, that debut CD eventually sold more than 200,000 copies. Her second album, *Jennifer y Los Jetz,* featured several covers, including the Doris Troy hit "Just One Look" (Yo Te Vi), which is often identified with **Linda Ronstadt;** the Shirelles's "Will You Still Love Me Tomorrow?" (Cuando Me Despierte Mañana); and Rick James's "Superfreak" (Corazoncito Ven a Mí).

In 1997, Jennifer won a TMA for best female entertainer of the year. Jennifer's voice was overdubbed in the singing scenes of the young Selena in the movie *Selena.*

Dulzura (EMI)
Jennifer y Los Jetz (EMI)

JIMÉNEZ, DON SANTIAGO

Born April 25, 1913, San Antonio, Texas; died December 2, 1984, San Antonio, Texas

Don Santiago Jiménez, who was nicknamed "El Flaco" (The Skinny One), was considered to be one of the first-tier pioneers of Tejano/conjunto music. His mix of Mexican rancheras and accordion-fueled German polkas helped make him a popular draw from the 1940s through the mid-1950s. His signature hits included "Margarita," "Viva Seguin," and "La Piedrera."

Jiménez's father, Patricio Jiménez, was a local accordionist who mixed the Mexican rancheras with the German polkas, mazurkas, and waltzes for his audiences, which varied from Mexican Americans to German and Polish Americans. Jiménez was only ten years old when his father taught him the basics of the accordion and later he accompanied his father to many dances, learning by watching.

In 1935 Jiménez bought his first two-row accordion and produced his first album in the mid-1930s on Decca Records called *El Aguacero Polka.* In 1936 he married his wife, Luisa, and the couple had eight children, including two sons who would go on to become famed accordionists in their own right—**Flaco Jiménez** (who appropriated his father's nickname) and **Santiago Jiménez Jr.**

(from left to right) Don Santiago Jiménez (with accordion), Juan Viesca (with bass), and Flaco Jiménez (with* bajo sexto*)
Courtesy of Chris Strachwitz/Arhoolie Records

Though he was on local radio constantly in the late '30s, he supported his family by working as a janitor at San Antonio's Fort Sam Houston. From 1940 to 1952 he played every Saturday night at Perales Nite Club. During World War II, the majors slowed record production substantially and the smaller indie labels picked up the slack. During this period, Jiménez scored his biggest hits—"Viva Seguin" and "La Piedrera." The latter was a song that he had composed about his San Antonio neighborhood, which was nicknamed "La Piedrera" because it was next to a rock quarry. Jiménez is recognized by scholars for introducing the *tololoche,* the upright or double bass, to Tejano/conjunto music.

In 1950 he recorded the song "Margarita," which became popular and was covered by dozens of bands. In 1952 he quit playing gigs and later moved to Dallas, where he worked at a seminary for eleven years before he retired in 1978. In 1977 he was part of the important documentary *Chulas Fronteras,* which was produced by Les Blank and Chris Strachwitz and which featured **Los Alegres de Terán, Lydia Mendoza,** Los Pinguinos del Norte, and others. Jiménez also wrote "Ay Te Dejo San Antonio," which was rerecorded by Flaco Jiménez and won a 1986 Grammy for best Mexican American performance. Another Jiménez original, "Soy de San Luis," was rerecorded by the **Texas Tornados.** It won a Grammy in 1990 for best Mexican American performance.

In 1979 he returned to San Antonio and played steadily at Jimmy's Mexican Restaurant, where he also worked until his death in 1984. In 1982 Jiménez was in the charter group of pioneers that were inducted in the first year of the Tejano Conjunto Hall of Fame.

His First and Last Recordings: 1937–1979 (Arhoolie)

JIMÉNEZ, FLACO

Born Leonardo Jiménez, March 11, 1939, San Antonio, Texas

What B. B. King is to the blues or, say, George Jones is to traditional country, Grammy-winning accordionist Flaco Jiménez is to the world of Tex-Mex conjunto. Jiménez was universally recognized as the leading exponent of authentic South Texas conjunto. While there are many masters of the accordion along the Texas-Mexican border, none have toured Europe, Japan, and other points overseas or recorded with as many pop, rock, and country artists as Jiménez has. By all accounts, Jiménez was an international icon for the accordion-fueled conjunto genre.

Born Leonardo Jiménez, the son of famed conjunto pioneer **Don Santiago "El Flaco" Jiménez Sr.,** the younger Jiménez grew up in the Tejano conjunto capital of San Antonio. The family lived in the La Piedrera (rock quarry) neighborhood, and one of senior Jiménez's original polkas was named after the quarry, "La Piedrera."

Jiménez's earliest influences included classic norteño outfits like **Los Alegres de Terán** as well as his father's peers, artists like **Narciso Martínez** and **Juan López.** But he also had a keen interest for things new and different like jazz, country, and rock music. Jiménez learned to play the accordion at the age of seven by watching his father, and by the age of fourteen he was performing professionally.

By 1954 he had already appropriated his father's nickname "Flaco" when he teamed up with **Henry Zimmerle Jr.** in Los Caporales for a short stint before moving on to the local conjunto Los Caminantes (not to be confused with the Mexican group of the same name) with Mike Garza and Richard Herrera. But in 1962 Jiménez was drafted into the army and he was replaced in Los Caminantes by another accordion great—**Mingo Saldivar.** When Flaco returned in 1964 from Korea, he rejoined Los Caminantes for a year, then left to record with various musicians, including Alfredo Ojeda, Manuel Pacheco, Toby Torres, and Joey "Canelo" López.

In 1974 Jiménez turned in an impressive performance in the highly acclaimed international documentary *Chulas Fronteras,* produced by Les Blank and Arhoolie/Folklyric producer Chris Strachwitz. Two years later Jiménez teamed up with folk guitarists/musicologist Ry Cooder on his album *Chicken Skin Music,* which led to an appearance on *Saturday Night Live.* Jiménez then hooked up with singer/songwriter Peter Rowan on a Flying Fish release that included the comedy song "Free Mexican Airforce."

Flaco Jiménez
Courtesy of Chris Strachwitz/Arhoolie Records

Although he had learned to play traditional conjunto by watching his father, Jiménez quickly took to incorporating other influences into his music. That naturally led to performing and touring with Rowan, Cooder, and other rock and country artists. In 1988 Jiménez worked with Dwight Yoakam and Buck Owens to record the hit single "Streets of Bakersfield." By then Jiménez had already won his first Grammy (best Mexican American performance) for his version of his father's song "Ay Te Dejo en San Antonio."

In 1990 Doug Sahm (of the Sir Douglas Quintet) organized the **Texas Tornados,** which also featured Augie Meyers, **Freddy Fender,** and Jiménez. Their self-titled debut CD won a Grammy (best Mexican American performance) that year for the track "Soy de San Luis," which was also written by the senior Jiménez.

Dividing his time between the Tornados and his prolific solo career, Jiménez's next project was the all-star CD *Partners,* which featured a dozen guests, including **Linda Ronstadt, Los Lobos,** Dwight Yoakam, Emmy Lou Harris, Stephen Stills, and others.

In the ensuing years, Jiménez collaborated with numerous pop and rock musicians, including the Rolling Stones in 1994 on the Mick Jagger–written track "Sweethearts Forever" from their *Voodoo Lounge* CD. That year Jiménez was inducted into the Tejano Conjunto Hall of Fame and recognized for his outstanding contributions and steadfast dedication to spreading the conjunto gospel around the world.

In 1995 Jiménez signed on with the new Austin-based label Arista/Texas and his self-titled debut won him his third Grammy (best Mexican American performance) for his self-titled CD. His follow-up CD, *Buena Suerte, Señorita,* offered a return to the raw, foot-stomping conjunto sound that Jiménez grew up with. Solid tracks included the irresistible, life-affirming "Borracho No. 1" and "Contigo No Más," the whipping polka stomp "El Gallo Copetón," the supremely sad "Mis Brazos Te Esperan," and the electrifying accordion runs on the boleroish "Mala Movida." The music was stripped down and free from pretension, but Jiménez delivered engaging songs full of melodic hooks and compelling lyrics.

Throughout his career, Jiménez has always remained dedicated to creating music that moves people. On his style of accordion expressiveness, Jiménez has a simple philosophy: "Even [for] just one note you have to punch it with heart." On playing genuine conjunto music he is known for saying:

"Si no hay bajo sexto, you don't have conjunto." In 1999 Jiménez won a Grammy for his Barb Wire debut album, *Said and Done,* in the new Tejano performance category. That same year Jiménez also won a Grammy as part of **Los Super Seven** in the Mexican American performance category for the band's self-titled CD on RCA.

Ay Te Dejo en San Antonio (Arhoolie)
Buena Suerte, Señorita (Arhoolie)
Flacos Amigos (Arhoolie)
Flaco Jiménez (Arhoolie)
Un Mojado sin Licensia (Arhoolie)
Said and Done (Barb Wire)
Seguro Que Hell Yes (Arhoolie)

JIMÉNEZ, JOSÉ ALFREDO

Born José Alfredo Jiménez Sandoval, January 19, 1926, Dolores Hidalgo, Guanajuato, México; died November 23, 1973, Mexico City, México

Over the course of twenty years and some 400 songs, José Alfredo Jiménez earned his undisputed standing as the most important and prolific songwriter of contemporary Mexican folkloric music. Many of his songs became standards in the ranchera canon: "Ella," "Yo," "Un Mundo Raro," "La Mano de Dios," "Cuatro Caminos," and many others.

Jiménez's chief skill was his ability to describe the fears and frailties, hopes and dreams in romantic affairs of everyday Mexicans. His lyrics dealt with simple yearnings: a faithful love, a better life. He had an uncanny sense for insight and directness in his lyrics. "Ella," an anthem for ranchera singers, was a frank tale of accepting one's destiny. Jiménez also spun tales of looking back ("Tu Recuerdo y Yo") and the forks in the road of life ("Cuatro Caminos"). Jiménez specialized in the proud macho posture in such songs as "Yo," "La Media Vuelta," "El Rey," and "La Ley del Monte."

Jiménez was born to a middle-class family in the working-class city of Dolores Hidalgo. He was one of four children of Carmelita Sandoval and Agustin Jiménez Albo, a bacterial chemist who owned the only pharmacy in the city. From an early age, Jiménez demonstrated an affinity for songwriting. His first compositions, though primitive, were about his favorite animals. While in elementary school Jiménez and his best friend, Jorge Gabilondo Soler, the son of the entertainer Cri Cri, dreamed of being bullfighters. Jiménez, who also developed a passion for soccer, was only ten years old when his father passed away and the family moved to Mexico City.

While still a teen, Jiménez got a job as a waiter at the luncheonette La Sirena in the San Cosme area in Mexico City, but he still pursued his dream of writing and singing his own songs. He convinced the son of La Sirena's owner to help him start the trio Los Rebeldes, which featured Jiménez, the son, Jorge Ponce, and brothers Enrique and Valentine Ferrusca. The trio played in local restaurants and bars, making little noise beyond the neighborhood. Like most songwriters, Jiménez wrote from a combination of personal experience and everyday observations. At the age of eighteen, he had his first serious heartbreak with a young girl whose parents forbade her to go out with him because he was a lowly waiter. This young woman, and this class conflict, became the subject of "Ella."

By that time Jiménez was making daily excursions to radio station XEW, pitching his songs to the stars of the day, including **Pedro Infante, Jorge Negrete, Miguel Aceves Mejía,** and others. In 1948 Jiménez got his chance to sing on famed radio station XEX and, months later, on XEW with Los Rebeldes. The first group to record his material was the Hermanos Samperio, but his first hit came in 1950 when Andrés Huesca y Sus Costenos recorded "Yo," a powerful tune of desperation and control.

In June of 1952 Jiménez married his longtime girlfriend Paloma Gálvez. The singer Miguel Aceves Mejía was their witness.

Maturing as a songwriter, Jiménez also wrote about tragedy. "Camino de Guanajuato" was based on a real-life episode—his brother's death in that city. As luck would have it, the subject of his song "Ella" came back into his life in 1955. But this time he brushed her off and wrote about it in the "Tú y Las Nubes." The story told in this song was later turned into a movie by the same name.

Jiménez became increasingly prolific, producing the hits "No Me Amenaces," "Paloma Querida," "Cuando Vivas Conmigo," "Pa Todo el Año," "Un Mundo Raro," and others. As Jiménez's hits increased, so did the list of artists who sought him out. Pedro Infante, Jorge Negrete, **Pedro Vargas, Javier Solis, Vicente Fernández,** and others recorded his music. Jiménez composed "Corrido de Martin Corona," for Pedro Infante. The story told in this song later became a movie by the same name.

Yet, having top stars interpret his material was not enough. Jiménez insisted on singing his songs, too. His vocal qualities were average, but what Jiménez lacked in finesse, he compensated for with intensity and approach. Because Jiménez wrote the lyrics, he understood each song's essential message. And he used this to his advantage, injecting a fiery mix of emotion and intonation to sing his stories with conviction and dramatic impression. He eventually got a recording contract with RCA. Jiménez performed on radio, TV, films, in country fairs, and onstage. He toured all of Mexico, the U.S., and Central America.

Jiménez also had his controversies. He drank heavily throughout most of his life. He wrote about alcoholism on "Llegó Borracho el Borracho," which, though banned from the radio, only helped to make him more popular. When he became a celebrity, Jiménez was also challenged by the temptations of fame. There were reports of infidelities and indiscretions. But through it all he never divorced his first wife. Reportedly he did this to guarantee that his children would receive his inheritance. In 1968 Jiménez was diagnosed with cirrhosis of the liver. For the next few years he was on medication that helped him feel better and sing better, but he eventually began drinking heavily again. Ironically, Jiménez may have foreshadowed his own death, composing his gratitude song "Gracias" in 1972. On November 23, 1973, Jiménez died in Mexico City.

The Mexican folkloric song form had first peaked in the 1930s with composers such as Pepe Guizar, **Guty Cárdenas,** and Manuel Esperón. By the late '40s, the genre was already fading. Younger Mexicans considered folk music quaint and better suited for museums. Jiménez is remembered for helping to revive the native musical forms. With his rich trove of incredibly frank songs of loving and losing, of solitude and reflection, Jiménez provided fresh inspiration for a new generation.

Brillantes (Sony)
Homenaje: 16 Éxitos Originales (CBS)
Javier Solis (Sony)
Personalidad (Sony)
Viejos Amigos (RCA)

JIMÉNEZ, SANTIAGO, JR.

Born April 8, 1944, San Antonio, Texas

Like his brother **Flaco Jiménez,** Santiago Jiménez Jr. was also fundamentally inspired by his father, **Don Santiago Jiménez,** and his paternal grandfather, Patricio Jiménez. However, while Flaco blazed a path by playing a flashy hybrid of trad-conjunto fused with rock, jazz, country, and pop elements, Santiago stuck to the simple but graceful old style.

Jiménez was fourteen years old when he learned to play the accordion after watching his father practice in the living room. Jiménez dropped out of Rhodes Junior High School in the ninth grade and at the age of sixteen he began working at weddings and parties. A year later he recorded his first single, "El Príncipe del Acordeón," on one of his father's sides for Discos Grande. For the next few years, Jiménez played for area venues and recorded several records for local indie labels. In 1977 Jiménez, his father, and his brother were part of the documentary *Chulas Fronteras,* which also featured **Lydia Mendoza** and **Los Alegres de Terán.**

Santiago Jiménez Jr.
Courtesy of Chris Strachwitz/Arhoolie Records

In 1980 Jiménez opened El Chief Studios in his home and began to teach accordion lessons. One of his career highlights was composing the song "El Corrido de Henry Cisneros" for Henry Cisneros's 1981 mayoral campaign in San Antonio. After Don Santiago died in 1984, Jiménez began rerecording as a tribute as many of his father's songs as he could remember or locate on vinyl. Like his father, Jiménez favored the old-style tradition with sincere, simple conjunto melodies and he faithfully rerecorded the original versions. In 1985 he formed the Santiago Jiménez Jr. Conjunto and, later that same year, he was nominated for a Grammy for best Mexican American performance for *Santiago Strikes Again.* In 1990 he was again nominated for a Grammy for best Mexican American performance for *Familia y Tradición.* Through the years, Jiménez's hits have been "Los Barrandales del Puente," "Viva Seguin," and "La Piedrera." The latter two were rerecordings of his father's classics. In the late '80s and early '90s Jiménez was also one of a half dozen South Texas accordionists who regularly toured England, Germany, and other European countries.

In the '90s Jiménez worked with the Bad Livers' Mark Rubins, who played upright bass on Jiménez' albums. Jiménez has been a fixture at the annual Tejano Conjunto Festival and periodically teaches accordion classes at the Guadalupe Cultural Arts Center in San Antonio.

Canciones de Mi Padre (Watermelon)
Corazón de Piedra (Watermelon)
Corridos de la Frontera (Watermelon)
Familia y Tradición (Rounder)
El Gato Negro (Rounder)
El Mero, Mero (Arhoolie)
Música de Tiempos Pasados, del Presente (Watermelon)
Navidad en San Antonio (Watermelon)
Santiago Strikes Again (Arhoolie)
Purely Instrumental (Arhoolie)

JIMMY EDWARD

Born Santiago Eduardo Treviño, March 16, 1951, San Antonio, Texas

After playing in numerous bands in high school, Jimmy Edward helped form the original **Latin Breed** in 1969. Disorganization led to the group's disbanding, though, and it was not until 1973—when several key members, including saxophonist Gilbert Escobedo, left the **Sunny Ozuna** band because of salary disputes—that it finally reunited. The union produced several albums—the popular *Return of Latin Breed* and *Más Latin Breed*—as well as perhaps the first Tejano anthem, the song "El Tejano Enamorado."

Jimmy Edward went solo in 1975 and his debut album, *Memories,* which contained mostly English cuts but which also featured the megahit/title track, a remake of the old Mexican classic "Diez y Seis Años." The single reached No. 4 on *Billboard*'s regional charts. In 1982 he scored again with the hit "Tú, Prieto," but subsequent albums failed to chart. In the '90s he began singing Spanish-language Christian music for local gospel labels.

Amor Viajero (EMI)
Ayer y Hoy (Sony)
Cristianos (EMI)
Memories (EMI)
Todo de Ti (Sony)

JORDAN, STEVE

Born Esteban Jordan, February 23, 1939, Elsa, Texas

Esteban "Steve" Jordan played his music the way he lived his life—free-spiritedly and adventurously, injecting the various elements of rock, jazz, and blues into his basic conjunto, polka, and ranchera repertoire. Jordan mesmerized audiences. He played his accordion with such energy and intensity that he was often called "The Jimmy Hendrix of the Accordion."

Jordan was one of fifteen children in a family of migrant farmworkers in the Rio Grand Valley. At birth Jordan was blinded in his right eye when a midwife mistakenly put contaminated eye solution in his eyes. His black eye patch lead to the nickname "El Parche" (The Eye Patch). The impairment often left him at home while his family worked in the fields.

At the age of seven he learned to play the guitar and a year later picked up the accordion after he saw conjunto legend **Valerio Longoria** perform. Longoria frequently played for appreciative crop pickers in the labor camps of the migrant circuit. Jordan eventually learned to play thirty-five instruments. His first recording, "Squeeze-box Man," was a big crossover regional hit in the 1960s. Through the '60s and early '70s he played rock 'n' roll and jazz guitar with high profile musicians in California and New York. By the late '70s he returned to his accordion roots and was considered one of the best squeeze box players.

He was inducted into the Tejano Conjunto Hall of Fame in 1982, making him one of the first inductees and, at forty-three years old, one of the youngest. In 1987 he was nominated for a Grammy for his album *Turn Me Loose* on Hacienda Records. He appeared on Cheech Marín's *Born in East L.A.* and on *True Stories*. In 1988 Jordan was invited to play at the Berlin Jazz Festival. Later that year, he was contracted by the Hohner Accordion Company to design the "Tex-Mex Rockordion." His biggest hits were "My Toot Toot" and "Turn Me Loose."

Ahorita (Hacienda)
Lo Mejor, Vol. 1 (Hacienda)
Many Sounds of Steve (Arhoolie)
Soy de Tejas (Hacienda)

JUAN GABRIEL

Born Alberto Aguilera Valadez, January 7, 1950, Paracuaro, Michoacán, México

In the late '80s Juan Gabriel became one of the most commercially successful and prolific singer/songwriters Mexico has ever known. His biggest hit ballads were pop staples that were recorded by dozens of top stars—from Roberto

Carlos and **Rocío Durcal** to **Guadalupe Pineda** and Yuri. His Mexican folkloric songs—like "Querida," "Amor Eterno," and "Hasta Que Te Conocí"—became part of the ranchera canon and were considered standards by mariachis everywhere.

In the '90s Juan Gabriel began a prodigious sideline as a studio producer, directing albums by Angela Carrasco, Guadalupe Pineda, and Rocío Durcal.

He was born Alberto Aguilera Valadez to a family of very modest means in Paracuaro, Michoacán. His parents, Gabriel Aguilera Rodríguez and Victoria Valadez Rojas, were poor peasants who struggled to support Alberto and his nine older siblings. According to family folklore, friends suggested to his parents that they name him Alberto after Alberto Limonta of the soap opera *El Derecho de Nacer* on radio station XEW in Mexico City.

When he was still a young teenager, Alberto's mother moved the family to the border city of Tijuana, across from El Paso, Texas. There the family moved in with a family friend in a house that would eventually become the Semajase Music School, a private orphanage established by Juan Gabriel in 1978.

The economic situation was hard and Juan Gabriel helped out wherever he could. For a while he worked with his sister selling tortillas in downtown Juárez and he sang in local church choirs.

His larger ambitions lay in music, though, and he aspired to someday sing onstage like his idols Enrique Guzmán, **Lola Beltrán,** and **Agustin Lara.** Eventually his persistence paid off and he landed an appearance on the local TV show *Noches Rancheras,* where he took his first stage name—Adán Luna. At just sixteen years old, he made his public debut at the famed nightclub El Noa Noa, a place he would immortalize years later with a hit song by the same name.

His hopes perked and over the next few years he traveled to Mexico City, trying to secure a recording contract with a major label, but success escaped him. Times were tough and for a while he slept at night in Avenida Central, the railroad station, and in the Basílica de Guadalupe. At one point he was falsely accused of robbery and was briefly imprisoned. These events were detailed in his autobiographical movie, *Es Mi Vida,* which was released in 1978.

After his jail episode, he was introduced to Queta Jiménez, "La Prieta Linda," who introduced him to officials at RCA. She became the first artist to record his music with the song "Noche a Noche."

In late 1971 he made his first pop ballad recording for RCA, scoring big with the hit "No Tengo Dinero," and emerged professionally as Juan Gabriel, the stage name that would last the rest of his life. He began writing songs for Spanish pop/ranchera singer Rocío Durcal, a collaboration that would last for years. In quick succession, he appeared in two movies, *Del Otro Lado del Puente* and *Noa Noa.*

By the early '80s Juan Gabriel gained major momentum, expanding his music to include mariachi and disco songs for Ariola Discos, and scoring bigger hits, including "Costumbres" and "Querida," which reached No. 1 in Mexico in 1984. He became one of the very few Mexican artists to play the Universal Amphitheater in Los Angeles, selling out five consecutive shows in 1983. In 1986 Los Angeles Mayor Tom Bradley proclaimed a day in early spring to be Juan Gabriel Day, as Juan Gabriel toured the U.S. behind his latest CD, *Pensamientos.*

But it was not all good news. Juan Gabriel was seriously shaken when his mother died in 1988. He wrote the ode "Amor Eterno" as a tribute to her. The song became a monster hit and was covered by more than a dozen top artists, including Rocío Durcal, **Ana Gabriel,** and **Vicente Fernández.**

As the '80s came to a close, Juan Gabriel had a solid reputation as one of the top live performers. He typically presented two-and-a-half-hour shows that featured several costume changes and almost nonstop dancing and singing. But not all was rosy for the then almost forty-year-old singer. He changed management, but not before the IRS filed a petition in U.S. Tax Court alleging that Juan Gabriel owed $1.5 million in back taxes. A dispute with his record company delayed the creation of any studio album for years. In the interim he released perhaps his career high-water mark—his 1990 double CD *Juan Gabriel en El Palacio de Bellas Artes.*

Hailed critically, the concerts featured backing by the seventy-piece Mexican Symphonic Orchestra, a top-notch mariachi, and Juan Gabriel was in impeccable shape. His inspired interpretation of "Querida" elevated the song into a form of worship and Juan Gabriel plumbed new emotional depth in "Amor Eterno," a song about a dear one gone but not forgotten.

In 1991, at only forty-two years old, he was honored with a Lifetime Achievement Award at that year's Billboard/Univision Latin Music Awards. In 1992 he played a then-record of ten consecutive sold-out dates at the Auditorio Nacional in Mexico City.

In the ensuing years it becames readily apparent that Juan Gabriel had hit a creative lull. He gained weight and the wild dancing of the past was relegated to slow movements and shuffling onstage. But, if as an artist things were slow, he was still in demand as a songwriter and producer. More artists—like Isabel Pantoja and José José—were recording his songs than ever before. Others—like Pandora, **Pedro Fernández,** and Lorenzo Antonio—were recording complete albums of his music.

In 1994 he was inducted into the Billboard Latin Music Hall of Fame. That same year, after an eight-year waiting period, Juan Gabriel released his first studio album, the synth-driven *Gracias por Esperar,* for which he wrote all eleven tracks. Reviews were mixed, but the public was hungry and sales propelled the CD up *Billboard*'s charts.

When the Mexican ranchera great Lola Beltrán died in Mexico City on March 24, 1996, Juan Gabriel was already working on the album *Las Tres Señoras,* which featured Beltrán, **Yolanda Del Río,** and Amalia "La Tariácuri" Mendoza of **Trío Tariácuri.** The CD would be released to great fanfare later that year.

After an absence of a few years, Juan Gabriel produced a new album in 1996 with Rocío Durcal, appropriately titled *Juntos Otra Vez.* The title track, a duet, gets solid airplay on the radio, but the CD has faded from the charts.

Through the years Juan Gabriel's impact has been felt beyond the stage. The Mexican chapter of ASCAP (the American Society of Composers, Authors, and Publishers) lists him as the No. 1 royalties revenue generator. He also has the most songs registered with the chapter and was the No. 1 covered artist in the country.

Debo Hacerlo (RCA)
Juntos Otra Vez (RCA)
Juan Gabriel en El Palacio de Bellas Artes (RCA)
Lo Mejor de Juan Gabriel con Mariachi (RCA)
El México Que Se Nos Fue (BMG/U.S. Latin)
Recuerdos (RCA)
Siempre Estoy Pensando en Ti (RCA)

LADRÓN

Formed 1991, Monterrey, Nuevo León, México

This fresh faced, youthful foursome plowed the *onda grupera* genre in the early '90s with moderate success, thanks to a fresh keyboard-driven ballad approach on their debut CD, *Corazón Desvalido,* which was produced by the noted composer **Armando Manzanero.** The group's sophomore effort, *No Tengo Lágrimas,* generated several radio singles, including "Tú Me Quieres Lastimar" and the title track. Lead singer/guitarist Sergio Villarreal wrote most of the band's material. Later hits included "Pienso en Ti," "Vengo a Pedir Tu Mano," "Celos Por Ti," and "Te Casaste."

Corazón Desvalido (EMI)
No Tengo Lágrimas (EMI)
Piden Tu Mano (EMI)

LALO Y LOS DESCALZOS

Formed 1990, Los Angeles, California

A native of Jerez, Zacatecas, Eduardo "Lalo" Enríquez (born 1959) moved to Los Angeles in 1984 and joined the local group El Tiempo, learning the basics of the *grupera* scene. In 1990 Enríquez tried his hand forming his own group and secured a record label deal with WEA Latina. His debut album, *Para Matar el Aburrimiento,* yielded the hit "La Traición." The group continued in the cumbia/ballad vein throughout the '90s.

Camino al Cielo (EMI)
Dejando Huellas (WEA Latina)
El Orgulloso (WEA Latina)

LARA, AGUSTIN

Born Agustin Lara Aguirre del Pino, October 30, 1897, Mexico City, México; died November 6, 1970, Mexico City, México

During Mexico's golden age of popular music in the '30s and '40s and during the later bolero renaissance, Agustin Lara emerged as one of the most prominent singer/songwriters of the age, alongside **José Alfredo Jiménez** and **Armando Manzanero.** His signature hits—including "Granada," "María Bonita," and "Flor de Lys"—have been among the most covered in the world.

Although Lara was born in Mexico City in 1897, he liked to claim he was born in Tlacotalpan, Veracruz in 1900, a strange quirk that is perhaps attributed to his wish to have been born in his mother's hometown.

His family wanted him to be a doctor like his father, Joaquín Lara, but Lara's musical talents were soon obvious. He was a piano prodigy at the age of sixteen, the same age that he left home to join the *villistas* in the Mexican Revolution. With his slight build—5'10", 110 pounds—he did not last long as a soldier. He tried his hand at bullfighting, but eventually was hired as the piano player at the cabaret Santa María la Redonda, where he spent most of his time getting inspirations for his songs. He would eventually write more than 500 songs, including some of the all-time classic boleros, such as "Farolito," "Imposible," "Entrega," "Sola," "Contraste," "Mujer," "Sevilla," and "Mi Novia."

In 1930 he was hired at XEW to host his own show, *La Hora Intima de Agustin Lara,* where he debuted many of his songs. In 1933 he teamed up with singers **Pedro Vargas** and Ana María Fernández and began touring Latin America. During a tour of Brazil, he ran into a good friend, José Mojica, who was suffering during a separation from a girlfriend, and whose experience inspired Lara to write the song "Solamente una Vez."

Lara also appeared in two dozen films, including *La Mujer Que Yo Amé, Novillero, Perdida,* and *Coqueta.*

With his rakishly handsome looks (some consider him to look like a cross between Humphrey Bogart and Valentino), Lara became a sex symbol in Mexico. He wrote "Mujer" for his first wife, Angelina Bruschetta. His second marriage in Caracas, Venezuela to actress Carmen Zozaya produced the song "Cuando Vuelvas." He divorced Zozaya in 1946 to marry the actress María Felix, who subsequently divorced him and later married **Jorge Negrete.** Heartbroken, Lara wrote the classic "María Bonita."

Lara married three additional times. More by some accounts.

Éxitos (Sony)
Nostalgia (Sony)
Serie Retrato (RCA)
Su Voz, Su Piano, Sus Canciones (Sony)

LARES, SHELLY

Born Michelle Yvette Lares, November 13, 1971, San Antonio, Texas

Shelly Lares was only nine years old when Jimmy Jiménez asked her to front his local Hot Tamales Band. In 1985 she and her cousin Tony Lares formed the New Generation Band, which eventually became the Shelly Lares Band by the time Lares graduated from Providence High School in 1989.

Only seven months younger than **Selena,** Lares ran on a parallel course with the late singer. Both were managed by their fathers and recorded in the mid-1980s for small indie labels with minimum success. In 1989 Lares had a young guitarist who was also helping her write songs—Chris Pérez, who would later join Selena's band and eventually marry her.

Shelly Lares
Courtesy of Sony Discos

But while Selena's career took a marked upward curve in the early '90s after she signed with EMI Latin, Lares seemed relegated to the minor leagues, despite constant recording and touring. For years Lares was nominated for best female entertainer and vocalist at the TMAs, and each year Selena grabbed top honors. Even after Selena's death on March 31, 1995, Lares would still have to wait until 1998 for her first female vocalist award. In 1996 and 1997 respectively Selena (posthumously) and newcomer Jennifer Peña won the female categories.

Lares began to attract a following in the early '90s with "Enamorada" and "Tú Solo," which were both from albums that featured her keyboardist, J. J. Reyes, as songwriting partner. In early 1996 Lares got on board with Sony Discos. Her debut, titled simply *Shelly,* produced the regional hits "Siempre Lo Esperaré" and "Mr. Right" and also featured a duet with **Jay Pérez** on "All I'll Ever Need."

Aquí Me Encuentro (Sony Discos)
Shelly (Sony Discos)

LATIN BREED

Formed 1969, San Antonio, Texas

In the summer of 1969, tenor sax player Rudy Guerra, trumpet player Charlie McBurney, and bass player Pete Garza founded Latin Breed, a band that would go on to become one of the finest horn-fueled ensembles in the history of Tejano. The band ranks first among those that stretched the envelope, due to their unique fusion of jazz, blues, soul, and funk elements with Tejano.

Because of disorganization the first aggregation of the band lasted only eight months. The Breed was reformed in 1973, this time with Guerra, Garza, and sax player Gilbert Escobedo, plus several other musicians who had split from the **Sunny Ozuna** and the Sunliners group. They, along with singer **Jimmy Edward,** produced music on benchmark albums that are no longer in print, such as *Return of Latin Breed, Más Latin Breed, Latin Breed Minus One,* and *Latin Breed USA*. The *Return of Latin Breed* album reached No. 1 on *Billboard*'s regional charts in the winter of 1973. Their hits from the '70s included "Qué Chulos Ojos," "Todos Dicen," "Si Yo Pudiera," "Yo Vendo Unos Ojos Negros," and perhaps the first Tejano anthem—"El Tejano Enamorado."

In 1974 Guerra left the band to pursue gospel music. Jimmy Edward followed in 1975 to go solo, subsequently recording another monster hit, "Memories," a bilingual remake of the Mexican oldie "Diez y Seis Años"; he was replaced in the Breed by **Adalberto Gallegos** (ex-**Fabulosos Cuatro**). In a year-end survey of the best-selling tracks of 1976 by *Billboard,* the albums *Latin Breed USA, Memories,* and *Power Drive* were in the top three positions.

In the early '80s the Breed faded into obscurity and changed its name to Fantasia, playing the local nightclub circuit and occasionally resurfacing as the Latin Breed for special events. In 1989 Escobedo, Garza, and others reunited to record the benchmark album *Breaking the Rules,* which was produced by Gilbert Velasquez and which was easily one of the best Tejano albums of the decade. The album featured a young **Jay Pérez** on vocals and went on to win album of the year at the 1990 TMAs. The single "Ay Mujer" won song of the year. Other hits off the album were "Qué Chulos Ojos," "No Naciste Para Mi," and another Tejano anthem—"Don Luis El Tejano."

Breaking the Rules (EMI)
Qué Chulos Ojos (SOI)
Todos Dicen (SOI)

LAURE, MIKE, Y SUS COMETAS

Formed circa 1960, El Salto, Jalisco, México

With his mix of tropical percussions and horns and rock 'n' roll energy, Mike Laure, called "El Rey del Trópico" (The King of the Tropics), was widely considered to be the father of the tropical/cumbia genre. His successors include a line of distinguished acts—from **Rigo Tovar y Costa Azul** and Renacimiento '74 in the '70s to **Fito Olivares** and **Aniceto Molina** in the '80s.

Mike Laure (born Miguel Laure Rubio, September 29, 1939, El Salto, Jalisco) was into the American rock 'n' roll scene as a teen in the mid-1950s. His chief idol was Bill Haley. Laure named his band los Cometas after Haley's band, Bill Haley and the Comets. But by the early '60s Laure had also been influenced by the raging percussive and whip-sharp horns of Colombia's **Sonora Dinamita** and Cuba's Orquesta Aragón, both of which made major splashes in Mexico in the early '60s.

The result was the emergence of a new musical fusion called *chunchaca,* which was marked by bright trumpets, rippling percussions, and Laure on the *güiro,* firing off the classic salsa *soneo* (call-and-response exchange). Laure scored quickly in the mid-1960s with a series of hits that included "Banda Borracha," "El Mochilón," "Rajita de Canela," "Zero 39," and "Tiburón, Tiburón."

Mike Laure
Courtesy of Balboa/Discos Musart

An integral part of his band was Chelo (Consuelo Rubio), his cousin, who had sang lead and backing vocals in Los Cometas before she left in the early '70s to front her own group. She eventually switched to rancheras and recorded for the Musart label. Later hits for Laure included "Cosecha de Mujeres," "Mazatlán," "Amor de Chapala," and "Veracruz."

By the late '70s Laure had lost momentum, although he kept playing through the '80s. In 1990 he suffered a major stroke, which left him partially paralyzed. He quit playing for a few years but, after some recovery, he resumed playing, albeit on a semi-retired basis. Fito Olivares and Aniceto Molina easily give him credit for pioneering the tropical/cumbia movement. In the '90s younger groups also gave tribute to Laure, in particular **Yahari,** which recorded several medleys of Laure's hits.

MIKE LAURE

15 Exitazos (Musart)
Al Ritmo de Mike Laure (Musart)
Banda Borracha (Musart)
Boleros con... (Musart)
Boleros de Ayer y Hoy (Musart)
Cumbias Picosas (Musart)
Secretaria (Musart)

CHELO

Chelo con Mariachi (Musart)
Chelo y Cornelio Reyna (Musart)
Mucho Corazón (Musart)
Norteño (Musart)
Voz Tropical (Musart)

LIBERACIÓN

Formed November 9, 1976, Monterrey, Nuevo León, México

Liberación emerged as a top player in the mid-1970s in the same field that was dominated by **Los Bukis**—the pop-cumbia, keyboard-swept genre known as *grupo rómantico.*

Led by founder/keyboardist Virgilio Canales, Liberación eked out a niche early on with the energetic tune "Corazón Prisonero." Canales was a member of Los Brillos and later joined Monterrey's **Banda Machos** before he formed Liberación. He named the group Liberación to reflect the movements of the time—the feminist liberation movement and the Palestinian liberation movement.

The band's signature hits included the ballads "Cómo Duele" and "Enamorado de un Fantasma." Additional hits included "Llegaste Tú," "Para Estar Contigo," "Doble Engaño," and "Nunca Supe Más de Ti."

The group has created more than twenty albums and has appeared in several films, including *Los Peseros* and *Matadero,* whose soundtrack included the band's hit "El Muñeco." In 1997 Liberación's album *Un Loco*

Romántico was an interesting mix of rancheras and cumbias and included the top single "La Viuda Magdalena," the group's first attempt at vallenato.

15 Super Éxitos (EMI)
Mi Gusto Es el Mariachi (FonoVisa)
Super Éxitos (FonoVisa)
Un Loco Romántico (EMI)

LÍMITE, GRUPO

Formed 1995, Monterrey, Nuevo León, México

The sound and the look of Grupo Límite sparked a wave of imitators in the Tejano and norteño camps when these young turks blew out of the chute in 1995. The childlike voice of lead singer/songwriter Alicia "La Güera" (The Fair-haired Girl) Villarreal (born Martha Alicia Villarreal Esparza, August 31, 1974, Monterrey, Nuevo León) was a key ingredient for this young dynamic group. Grupo Límite's unique sound featured energized cumbias, pop-leaning norteña rancheras, and the novelty of a female-led norteño act. Villarreal's standard outfit included blue jeans, boots, and cowboy hats. With her long, braided light brown hair, toothy smile, and expressive eyes, Villarreal projected an innocence that belied her deep, versatile vocals.

Villarreal began singing in hotel lobby bars while still in high school in Monterrey. From 1989 until 1994, Villarreal recorded and performed with a series of bands, including Banda Musical, Alaska, Candela, and Conspiración 11. Villarreal's experience with Conspiración 11 involved recording a CD at the hands of producer/composer Juan H. Barron, but Barron died before it was completed.

Eventually Villarreal teamed up with accordionist Gerardo Padilla and *bajo sexto* player Jesús Cantú to form the nucleus of what would become Grupo Límite. After recording a demo, the band approached all the labels in Monterrey, but it was during a trip to Mexico City that Grupo Límite attracted the serious attention of PolyGram. The band was signed up in 1995 and, shortly afterward, Límite produced its debut album, *Por Puro Amor.* According to PolyGram, the CD sold over one million copies in the U.S. and Mexico, spinning off the hits "Te Aprovechas," "Con la Misma Piedra," and "El Príncipe," which were all Top 10 singles.

Grupo Límite's lead singer/songwriter Alicia Villarreal
Courtesy of Rafael Montiel

The group's sophomore album, *Partiéndome el Alma,* continued its success, producing the *Billboard* chart singles "Solo Contigo" and "Juguete." The album climbed to No. 3 on The Billboard Latin 50 chart and stayed on the chart for more than thirty weeks. The band reached another milestone in February of 1997 when it joined **Emilio** at the Astrodome for the Houston Rodeo performance, setting an attendance record of 62,939, almost 1,000 more than the previous record set by Emilio and **Selena** in what turned out to be her last performance there in February 1995 (Selena was killed March 31, 1995).

Límite's third album, *Sentimientos,* produced by Jesús "Chuy" Carillo, also sold well and charted on the Billboard Hot Latin Tracks chart with the song "Hasta Mañana." The group captured a Univision's Premio Lo Nuestro Award in 1997 for best regional Mexican group and in 1998 the band won a TMA for best Tejano norteño group.

Partiéndome el Alma (PolyGram)
Por Puro Amor (PolyGram)
Sentimientos (PolyGram)

LITTLE JOE Y LA FAMILIA

Formed 1959, Temple, Texas

With his big-band approach and marvelous knack for recording hard-hitting rancheras, Little Joe rose to the top of Tejano music in the mid-1970s, a wild boomtown period considered to be the genre's first golden age. At his peak Little Joe evoked a dangerous edge in his music, combining the power of the blues and the freewheeling spirit of rock to propel his robust fusion of the blistering Mexican ranchera and the life-affirming Tejano polka.

When at the top of their game, Little Joe y La Familia concerts were a time to celebrate *en los bailes grandes* with soul-drenched party music fueled by a crack horn section. But sometimes when Little Joe sang bittersweet songs like "Cuando Salgo a los Campos" or "Las Nubes," which recount the daily struggles of Mexican Americans, one could sense the political frustrations simmering underneath the surface.

Little Joe (born José María DeLeón Hernández, October 17, 1940, Temple, Texas) was the son of sharecropper parents whose roots went back to the Mexican Revolution. His paternal grandfather, Colonel José María DeLeón, served in Pancho Villa's army. His father, Salvador "La Cotorra" (The Parrot) Hernández, worked on the railroads for thirty-five years and did weekend music gigs. When his father was arrested in 1955 for possession of marijuana and sentenced to twenty-eight months in prison, Little Joe, at the age of fifteen, became head of the family, many of whose members worked picking crops in the fields around Temple.

That same year Little Joe bought his first guitar for fourteen dollars. At the age of sixteen he joined the Waco Musician's Union and began playing with David Coronado and the Latinaires. He often mentioned that his last day of picking cotton (during which he harvested a record 600 pounds) was on his seventeenth birthday. From there, he worked in a factory with younger brother Jesse, who played bass for the band.

In 1959 Coronado left for Walla Walla, Washington and the group became Little Joe and the Latinaires (Little Joe sang and played guitar). In 1961 Jesse quit the factory to become a full-time musician and he challenged Little Joe to decide his future. It was a pivotal moment, Little Joe later recalled, that led him into music as a serious enterprise. On March 15, 1964, Jesse was killed in an auto accident and, according to Little Joe, he later made a graveside vow that he would make it to the top.

The Latinaires started out as a Top 40 act, dressing in glitzy tuxedos and performing with choreography and vocal harmonies that recalled the rock 'n' roll acts of the period. Little Joe recorded his first hit single, "El Corrido del West," in San Antonio. By the early '70s the band moved to California and Little Joe was inspired by the hotbed of rock, pop, jazz, and other music strains flowing everywhere. It was the era of Vietnam, Watergate, civil rights, and the Chicano Movement. Against this fertile backdrop Little Joe rediscovered his roots, renaming the band José María DeLeón Hernández y La Familia. He produced one of his most important albums, the seminal *Para la Gente.* The album included a song, "Las Nubes," that secured Little Joe's stature not only as a beloved performer but as an eloquent spokesman for Mexican Americans. Like Bruce Springsteen's "Born in the U.S.A.," "Las Nubes" had catchy, anthemic choruses soaring over stark lyrics of solitude, despair, and disillusionment. This song became, arguably (along with **Latin Breed**'s "El Tejano Enamorado"), a national anthem for the Tejano culture.

In the late '70s, Little Joe returned to Temple and formed his own record label, Buena Suerte, and built Brown Sound studios. In the early '80s, Little Joe was a frequent winner at the TMAs, picking up multiple honors for male vocalist and entertainer and album for his 1980 *Live for Schlitz*. The latter drew minor controversy because it appeared as though Joe had sold out to the commercial establishment after years of supporting the militant Chicano Movement.

In 1986 he became the first Tejano artist to be signed by a major—CBS/Sony Discos. Later that year he became the first Tejano musician to perform at Willie Nelson's Farm Aid. He went on to release such landmark albums as *25th Silver Anniversary,* a live recording, and the 1988 *Timeless,* which was on the *Billboard* charts for fifty-seven consecutive weeks. Both albums were produced by noted guitarist Bob Gallarza, whose previous stints included working with Marilyn McCoo and Billy Davis Jr. and the Fifth Dimension. Little Joe's period hits included "Los Laureles" and "Las Isabelas."

In 1990 Willie Nelson sang on "You Belong to My Heart" and "Marie" from Little Joe's *Tu Amigo* CD. That same year Little Joe brought Nelson with him for his Astrodome for the Houston Rodeo performance. In 1992 Little Joe became the first Tejano act to win a Grammy for best Mexican American performance for his *16 de Septiembre* CD. Shortly after he left Sony Discos and started another label, Tejano Discos, which signed a few local acts but none enjoyed any chart success. Little Joe's office complex in Temple included a studio and his own museum and memorabilia collection.

Through the years Little Joe's band spawned a number of notable musicians, including highly respected keyboardist/accordionist/producer Joel Guzmán and trumpet player/bandleader Tony "Ham" Guerrero, who formed Tortilla Factory, a big-band outfit that played jazz and salsa-tinged Tejano during the '70s.

16 de Septiembre (Sony)
25th Silver Anniversary (Tejano Discos)
Borrachera (Freddie)
Live for Schlitz (Freddie)
Las Nubes (Roy Sales)
¿Qué Pasó? (Tejano Discos)
Reunión '95 (Tejano Discos)

LOBOS, LOS

Formed 1973, Los Angeles, California

Los Lobos were born when East Los Angeles High School buddies (César Rosas, David Hidalgo, Louie Pérez, and Conrad Lozano) came together as a Mexican folk quartet playing at weddings and social gatherings. These self-taught musicians got their first break in 1981 while opening up for the rock band the Blasters, which included saxophonist/keyboardist Steve Berlin, who later joined Los Lobos. In 1983, Slash Records released *And a Time to Dance,* which was a half-rock, half Mexican American album that included Grammy-winning single "Anselma."

In June of 1987 Los Lobos played on the title track of the *La Bamba* movie soundtrack. The single, which featured a scorching guitar solo by Hidalgo, put them over the top when it reached No. 1 on the Billboard Hot 100 Singles Sales chart. The song received three Grammy nominations (including song of the year) and won the MTV Video Music Award for best video from a film. A second single, "Come on Let's Go" reached No. 21 on the Billboard Hot 100 Singles Sales chart. The soundtrack for *La Bamba* went to No. 1 on The Billboard 200 chart.

In 1988 Los Lobos followed up with the mostly acoustic *La Pistola y el Corazón,* an album of folk songs from Guerrero, Veracruz, Michoacán, and other Mexican states that was cowritten by Hidalgo and Pérez. The album led to the band's second Grammy for best Mexican American performance. Additional soundtrack credits included scores on *Desperado,* a Robert Rodríguez border-town action film, *Mi Vida Loca,* which was about female Chicano gang members in Los Angeles, and the Keanu Reeves romantic comedy *Feeling Minnesota.*

Throughout their eclectic career, Los Lobos have always been known for mixing music styles and freewheeling experimental fusions. Though fueled by their love for roots rock and rhythm and blues, Los Lobos injected a spicy mix of Mexican norteño, Tex-Mex funk, and folksy music for a distinctive sound.

In late 1998 Hidalgo and Rosas were part of **Los Super Seven,** a Mexican American all-star band that included **Flaco Jiménez, Freddy Fender,** Joe Ely, Rick Treviño, and **Rubén Ramos.** The collaboration led to an album by the same name, which was released on RCA. A tribute to the musicians' roots and influences, the album included interpretations of Woody Guthrie's "Deportee" and **Agustin Lara**'s "Piensa en Mí."

By the Light of the Moon (Warner Bros.)
Colossal Head (Warner Bros.)
How Will the Wolf Survive? (Warner Bros.)
The Neighborhood (Warner Bros.)
La Pistola y el Corazón (Warner Bros.)

LONGORIA, VALERIO

Born March 13, 1924, Clarksdale, Mississippi

A top-notch accordionist and influential stylist, Valerio Longoria was one of the bedrock figures in the evolution of Tejano conjunto music.

Longoria began playing the accordion at the age of seven by watching conjunto pioneer **Narciso Martínez.** As a teen he played local weddings and parties in Harlingen, Texas. He was drafted into the U.S. Army in 1942 and at the end of World War II he was stationed in Germany, where he managed to get an accordion and play in local nightclubs. In 1945 he moved to San Antonio and he began recording for Corona records. His first recordings were "El Polkerito" and "Chiquitita." Later hits included "Jesús Cadena" and "El Barrilito."

Valerio Longoria
Courtesy of Chris Strachwitz/Arhoolie Records

Throughout his career Longoria has been a major part of the development of conjunto. Among the many recognitions Longoria received in noted scholar Manuel Peña's book *The Texas-Mexican Conjunto,* he has been credited with being the first musician to play standing up, to use modern drums in conjunto (this was considered a radical innovation), and to introduce boleros into his repertoire. He also was the first to experiment with octave tuning.

In 1982 he was among the first inductees into the Tejano Conjunto Hall of Fame and in

1986 he was awarded the National Heritage Fellowship Award, the nation's highest honor given to folk artists.

Longoria's sons Valerio Jr. and Flavio and grandson Valerio IV played with him in his band. Over his sixty-year-long career, he has more than 200 recordings on several labels. Like most of the first-tier conjunto pioneers, Longoria was not a flashy stage performer, choosing instead to pour all his energies into his accordion, producing expressive and colorful melodies that move. His standard repertoire included the basics—polkas, rancheras, cumbias, corridos, boleros, *redowas,* or even occasional country and jazzy blues tunes. Longoria taught weekly accordion classes at the Guadalupe Cultural Arts Center and, in addition to being a master accordion player, he was also skilled at repairing, tuning, and customizing them.

Caballo Viejo (Arhoolie)
Tejano Roots (Arhoolie)
Texas Conjunto Pioneer (Arhoolie)
La Piragua (Hacienda)
Prieta Consentida (Hacienda)

LÓPEZ, ISIDRO

Born Isidro Manuel López, May 17, 1929, Bishop, Texas

When Isidro "El Indio" (The Indian) López combined the Orquesta Tejana, or big band, sound with accordion-laced conjunto music in 1955, he created what we now know as modern Tejano music. From the beginning the essence of Tejano has always been a mixture of danceable Mexican polkas, rancheras, and cumbias that is highlighted with modern elements of pop, rock, and country. In its modern form Tejano has splintered into many subgenres that mostly feature keyboards, but classic Tejano employed a big horn section.

López was half Apache—his father, Pedro G. López, was a full-blooded Apache Mescalero from Riodoso, New Mexico—and his family members belonged to an Apache tribe. López's family picked cotton during the harvest season. Early in the mornings, as the family got ready to go out into the fields, López listened to the folk music of Los Madrugadores, which came from a Monterrey, Neuvo León radio station. In the fields he also heard country music artists, such as Eddie Arnold, on portable radios. When he was eleven years old, López's uncle Francisco Rodríguez taught him how to play the guitar. And later while attending Ray Miller High School in Corpus Christi, López learned to play the tenor saxophone and joined the high school band. After graduating high school, López enrolled at Texas A & I Kingsville, where he studied business administration.

In the late '40s, López began recording and playing with such pioneers as **Narciso Martínez** and **Tony De La Rosa.** Later he joined the Eugenio Gutiérrez Orchestra, which was then playing at venues up and down the Rio Grande Valley. It was not until a 1954 recording session with the Juan Colorado (real name Juan García) Orchestra at Armando Marroquín's Discos Ideal studio in Alice, Texas that López stepped up to the microphone. In those days recording sessions utilized only one channel and the bands or groups played "live"—usually producing 78s on vinyl in one or two takes. Since the regular singer, Lupe López, did not show up, Marroquín suggested that Isidro López, who had written the tune, "Díganle," sing it. He did and he was good enough to become the regular singer.

In 1956 López formed his own Isidro López Orchestra and began recording and touring. López often used some of the best musicians of the time on his recordings, including accordionists Amadeo Flores, who would go on to join Tony De La Rosa; Henry Cuesta, who later played reeds in the Lawrence Welk Band; trombonist Joe Gallardo; saxophonist Max Bernal; and trumpeter Lee Martínez Jr., who was the brother of future Tejano legend **Freddie Martínez.** Later Isidro López Orchestra graduates included Fred Salas, Pepe Compean, Luis Gasca, Manny Guerra, Roy Montelongo, and López's brother Rubén. López's early hits included "Corazón del Pueblo," "Todo o Nada," "Por Tu Cariño," and "Mí Rosita."

Isidro López
Courtesy of Arhoolie

By 1958 López had established the essential template for what became known as modern Tejano music. Narciso Martínez, who had popularized the accordion-led conjunto, became the acknowledged father of that genre. Meanwhile, **Beto Villa**—who, along with his orchestra, had popularized big-band-styled, mostly instrumental dance music—became the father of the Orquesta Tejana. But it was López who combined both styles when he added two accordions to his orchestra and, unlike Villa, also sang. These innovations were the fork in the road that led to modern Tejano music.

Later hits for López included "Nuevo Contrato," "Emoción Pasajera," "Comprende Cariño," "Desilusión," and "Sufriendo y Penando." For the next three decades López continued touring and recording until the late '70s when he went into semiretirement. In 1983 López was inducted into the Tejano Music Award's Hall of Fame. López's niece **Lisa López** gained international fame in 1981 with her hit ballad "Si Quieres Verme Llorar," which was written by Johnny Herrera.

15 Hits (Hacienda)
El Indio (Arhoolie)
La Lumbre (Hacienda)

LÓPEZ, JUAN

Born March 8, 1922, Jackson County, Texas

Juan López became known as "El Rey de la Redowa" (The King of the Redowa) because his specialty was the Polish *redowa,* a Bohemian dance that is slower than the polka. His parents, Alberto and Alberta López, moved to South Texas in 1910. López began playing the accordion when he was twelve years old, learning from his four older brothers. He turned professional at the age of eighteen and was part of the legendary music scene in Robstown, Texas in the '40s. Playing in the traditional style, López jammed with regional artists such as violinist Don Esteban Canales.

In 1948 López made his first recording on the Cuatro Estrellas records label in San Antonio, and later recorded for several independent labels, including Imperial, Ideal, Peerless, and RYN Records of McAllen. In 1950 he joined with his brothers to form Los Hermanos López. He wrote most of his material, including the polkas "La Polvadera," "La Palancana," "Los Camaleones," and "El Chanclazo," but was best remembered for his *redowas,* including "La Comadre Julia" and "El Porrón."

In 1989 López was inducted into the Tejano Conjunto Hall of Fame. Since then he has been a regular at the annual five-day outdoor concert series, the Tejano Conjunto

Festival, which is held every May in San Antonio's Rosedale Park.

Polkas, Redowas, Huapangos (RYN)
El Rey de la Redowa (Arhoolie)
El Rey de la Redowa (RYN)

LÓPEZ, LISA

Born October 4, 1963, Corpus Christi, Texas

Lisa López's first foray into the music world was her English-language pop recording of "Looking Back," which made local radio charts in 1979. She shifted to Spanish in 1981 and recorded her biggest hit, the single "Si Quieres Verme Llorar," which reached No. 1 on the Billboard Latin Tracks chart. Written by Johnny Herrera, the song was a touching ballad about acquiescence. That song earned her the female entertainer, song, and single of the year honors at the 1982 TMAs. She became the first Tejano artist to debut on The Billboard Latin 50 chart when the charts were initiated in October 1986. López was signed to the Sony Discos label in the early '90s and produced a few albums without major chart success.

A graduate of South San High School in 1981, López came from a musically inclined family. Her father, Rubén López, was a prominent musician in South Texas and her uncle **Isidro López** was the bandleader who was credited with helping establish Tejano music.

20 Super Hits (Hacienda)
Canciones de Amor (Hacienda)
Si Quieres Verme Llorar (Hacienda)

LUCERO

Born Lucero Hogaza León, August 29, 1969, Mexico City, México

Lucero began her career as Lucerito, a child star. In 1983 she landed roles alongside **Pedro Fernández** in the movies *Coqueta* and *Delincuente* and with **Luis Miguel** in *Fiebre de Amor.* The same year she also recorded her debut album, *Te Prometo.* She appeared with future husband, singer Manuel Mijares, in the 1987 film *La Pícara Adolescente.*

Although she made a name for herself as a pop singer, Lucero also delved into the Mexican folkloric ranchera genre. The guitar-playing youngster was noticed in 1982 by TV host Raúl Velasco, who let her sing on the show *América, Ésta Es Tu Canción.* At the age of twenty-one she changed her stage name to Lucero and recorded her first ranchera album in 1990, *Con Mi Sentimiento.* **Mariachi Vargas de Tecalitlán** arranger Rubén Fuentes produced this CD, which contained covers of hits written by **Marco Antonio Solis** of **Los Bukis.** During the '90s her ranchera hits included "Me Estás Quemando," "Siempre Contigo" (from the CD of same name), and "El Milagro." Her 1998 mariachi-roots CD, *Cerca de Ti,* which contained "El Milagro," was produced and arranged by Fuentes and Pepe Martínez, Mariachi Vargas de Tacalitlán's musical director.

Cariño de Mis Cariños (FonoVisa)
Historia de un Romance (Universal)
Lucero (FonoVisa)
Lucero de México (FonoVisa)
Piel de Ángel (Universal)
Cerca de Ti (FonoVisa)
Siempre Contigo (FonoVisa)
Sólo Pienso en Ti (Universal)

LUIS MIGUEL

Born Luis Miguel Gallego Bastery, April 19, 1970, San Juan, Puerto Rico

Perhaps no other artist deserves greater recognition for helping revive the bolero song form than pop singer Luis "Luismi" Miguel. With his enormous success on the radio, retail, and touring circuits, Luis Miguel was instrumental in introducing the bolero to a whole new generation during the '90s. His three albums of classic boleros—*Romance* (1991), *Segundo Romance* (1994, Grammy winner in the Latin pop category), and *Romances* (1997)—each sold over one million copies in the U.S., as certified by the Recording Industry Association of America (RIAA).

Mining the catalog of classic bolero songwriters like **Armando Manzanero, Agustin Lara,** and Roberto Cantoral, Luis Miguel breathed new life into the style, which had been popularized by trios four decades before. His biggest bolero hit remakes included "No Sé, Tú," "Media Vuelta," and "Sabor a Mí." The singles and albums enjoyed lengthy stays on the Billboard Latin Tracks chart and The Billboard Latin 50 chart and even made the The Billboard 200 chart.

Born to a Spanish father, singer Luisito Rey, and an Italian mother, Marcela Bastery, Luis Miguel's family was based in Mexico. A former child star, Luis Miguel began his career recording bubblegum pop, releasing his first album, *Luis Miguel: Un Sol,* in 1982. He almost immediately scored two big hits, "1+1=2 Enamorados" and "Tú y Yo." He also appeared in movies, costarring with fellow child-star-turned-adult-singer **Lucero** in *Fiebre de Amor* (1984). His '90s output has alternated between boleros and jazz- and R&B-inflected pop songs. His influences included Frank Sinatra and **Julio Iglesias.** Like most high-profile celebrity bachelors, Luis Miguel has been tied to a number of women. Despite persistent rumors of a marriage to Daisy Fuentes, they never married.

Romance (WEA Latina)
Romances (WEA Latina)
Segundo Romance (WEA Latina)
Todos Romances (WEA Latina)

MAFIA, LA

Formed 1978, Houston, Texas

Brothers Oscar (born 1963, Houston, Texas) and Leonard (born 1960, Houston, Texas) Gonzáles developed their musical talents at an early age. Their father, Henry Gonzáles Sr., owned a nightclub and discovered his sons' potential when he noticed that they often played with the instruments that the bands had left from events from the night before. Gonzáles Sr. helped his sons form Los Mirasoles in 1975.

In 1978 older brother Henry Gonzáles Jr. took over as band manager and changed the group's name to La Mafia. A series of albums on the indie labels Diana and Hacienda led nowhere until 1980 when Luis Silva and Bob Grever of the Tejano indie giant Cara Records heard the group's demo tape. The band signed with Cara and greatly benefited when, in 1986, Cara entered into a five-year promotion and distribution deal with then–CBS Discos. By the mid-1980s, La Mafia, heavily inspired by the visceral power of MTV, had earned a reputation as a top showband with spotlights, fog, towering speaker banks, and flashy outfits.

By the mid-1980s there was a bitter rivalry between the group and labelmates **Mazz.** Their mutual dislike was such that it led to a celebrated fistfight in December 1986 between members of the two groups in Laredo, Texas during the final stop in the *Shootout* concerts series. According to police reports, the fight started at Roli's Dance Hall, but continued inside the Laredo police station.

La Mafia; with guitarist Leonard Gonzáles (standing, left) and lead singer Oscar de la Rosa (seated, center)
Courtesy of Sony Discos

When EMI Latin bought Cara Records in 1990 and signed Mazz, La Mafia opted to jump ship and signed on with rival CBS/Sony Discos. However, La Mafia still owed two CDs to Cara/EMI Latin. La Mafia duly delivered the material, but not without some controversy. Their final master tapes were accepted by EMI, but ultimately instrumental tracks on some of the songs were changed (against La Mafia's wishes) before the CD was released.

La Mafia's first three albums on Sony, *Estás Tocando Fuego, Ahora y Siempre,* and *Vida* were very successful and all generated gold album status (50,000+). These albums established La Mafia's new sound and its shift from a Tejano group to a keyboard-driven ballad/cumbia outfit. The new hits included "Me Estoy Enamorando," "Vida," "Cómo Me Duele, Amor," and "Me Duele Estar Solo."

In February of 1992 La Mafia and the **Texas Tornados** set an attendance record of 55,970 at the Astrodome for the Houston

Rodeo. Later that year the group was awarded best group and song (for "Cómo Me Duele, Amor") at the Billboard/Univision Premio Lo Nuestro Awards. In *Billboard*'s year-end survey, La Mafia's "Me Estoy Enamorando" was named hot Latin track of the year.

In 1995 Henry Gonzáles resigned as the band's manager and started his own Voltage Discos record label/booking agency. The label was distributed by Sony Discos and the initial roster included **Juan P. Moreno** and **Elida y Avante.** Later that year Oscar took his mother's maiden name, de la Rosa, as his stage name. Also in 1995 La Mafia's song "Vida" reached No. 1 on the Billboard Hot Latin Tracks chart, just two weeks after its release. In 1997/1998, the group received Grammys for *Un Millón de Rosas* and *En Tus Manos,* the best-selling albums that produced the hits: "Enamorada," "Amiga Cruel," "Solo," "Me Duele Estar Solo," "Yo Quiero Ser," and "Mejores Que Ella," a duet with Marc Anthony.

On December 2, 1998 La Mafia announced its retirement.

Ahora y Siempre (Sony Discos)
Estás Tocando Fuego (Sony Discos)
En Tus Manos (Sony Discos)
Éxitos en Vivo (Sony Discos)
Un Millón de Rosas (Sony Discos)
Vida (Sony Discos)

MANDINGO

Formed circa 1992, Monterrey, Nuevo León, México

The six-man grupo made headlines in Mexico in 1995 when **Bronco**'s lead singer **José Guadalupe Esparza** admitted that Mandingo's singer Mario Alberto Esparza was his younger brother. The older Esparza wrote and produced much of Mandingo's early output. Dressed in casual outfits, Mandingo was set in the grupo mold, using keyboards and percussions to drive their cumbias with a bouncy, rapid backbeat. The band's hits included cumbias "Seguiré Tu Huella," "Suavecito," and "Para Ti," which was written by José Guadalupe Esparza.

In 1995 the album *Rompiendo Corazones* was released on the FonoVisa label. The CD included a duet with Mario and José Guadalupe Esparza on the single "Vamos a Amarla los Dos." In 1997 Mandingo released another album *Como Nunca Para Ti,* which included the song "Para Ti," which was written by José Guadalupe Esparza. From this album the single "Juntos" was also released as a video.

Como Nunca Para Ti (FonoVisa)
De Corazón Viajero (FonoVisa)
Rompiendo Corazones (FonoVisa)

MANZANERO, ARMANDO

Born Armando Manzanero Canche, December 7, 1935, Mérida, Yucatán, México

One of Mexico's most prolific songwriters of the twentieth century, Armando Manzanero's stature was akin to **Agustin Lara** and **José Alfredo Jiménez.** Manzanero's classics—such as "Contigo Aprendí," "Adoro," "Voy a Apagar la Luz," and "Somos Novios"—have become part of the bolero canon. These songs were recorded in the '50s by **Trío Los Panchos** and in the '90s by Mexican pop singer **Luis Miguel,** and covered by hundreds of artists in between.

Manzanero studied piano at the age of ten, although his parents were initially against his desire to pursue a music career. Nonetheless, he enrolled in La Escuela de Bellas Artes de Mérida and later began playing with local groups. In 1957 he moved to Mexico City where he studied harmony and musical composition with Rafael de Paz and José Sabre Marroquín. At this time he began writing his first songs and produced "Nunca en el Mundo" and "Llorando Estoy." In 1958 Lucho Gatica recorded his "Voy a

Apagar la Luz," which became an instant hit. An accomplished pianist, he then began his first tours in 1960 with **Angelica María,** Daniel Riolobos, and Gatica.

Manzanero continued pouring out more boleros, including "Esta Tarde Vi Llover," "No," and others, which began to get recorded increasingly by artists such as Olga Guillot, Marco Antonio Muñiz, and Roberto Ledesma. Eventually American pop artists recorded his material, including Perry Como, Frank Sinatra, Elvis Presley, and Shirley Bassey. Through the years Manzanero has tried his hand at producing albums, working with such artists as Sonia López, Dyango, **Luis Miguel,** and **La Sonora Santanera.**

Las Canciones Que Quise Escribir (RCA)
Canto Sólo Para Enamorados (RCA)
Carinosamente Manzanero (Sony)
Mientras Existas Tú (RCA)
Serie Platino (RCA)

MAREZ, DAVID

Born August 18, 1949, Mathis, Texas

With his range and control David Marez emerged as one of the most soulful singers in the Tejano genre. He went solo after building a resumé that included tenure with the **Royal Jesters.**

Marez's earliest musical experiences came in church, where he sang gospel in the choir. As a teen, soul, jazz, and funk also impressed him. In the early '60s Marez enjoyed stints with the local Top 40 groups the Eptones and Gilbert and the Blue Notes. In 1967 he joined the Royal Jesters, who were then just becoming a force in Central Texas with a series of English hits, including "We Go Together," "Lady Sunshine," and "That Girl." His singing career was interrupted in 1968 when he joined the U.S. Navy, returning four years later to rejoin the group. In the late '70s he formed his own group, People, which included future notables saxophonist Joe Posada, drummer Richard Solis, and guitarist Gilbert Velasquez.

David Marez
Courtesy of Sound Mex

In 1983 talent scout/publisher/label owner Bob Grever signed Marez to his Cara Records, a label that was then emerging as a dominant force in Texas. In the '80s Marez's biggest success came with the singles "Tus Perfumes," "Inseparables," and "Entre Más Lejos Me Vaya," which dominated radio in 1986 and won TMA's song of the year in 1987. In 1989 Marez again won TMA's song of the year with "Fíjate" from his *Sold Out* CD, which was also named album of the year. In 1990 Marez was named the TMA male vocalist and later that year he signed on with Sony Discos, although he still owed two albums to Cara/EMI Latin. In 1994 he recorded his last album for Sony Discos, *Todo por Amor,* and in 1997 he released *Back to Basics* for the San Antonio indie Sound Mex, also run by Grever, but the album failed to generate any significant chart activity.

Back to Basics (Sound Mex)
Qué Sentimientos (EMI)
Revival (BGS)
Soy Tuyo (Sony Discos)

MARGARITA

Born Margarita Huerta, July 23, 1976, Harlingen, Texas

With her clear, emotive vocals, Margarita turned a few heads with her debut CD in early 1998. Coproduced by **Mazz**'s guitarist/producer Jimmy González and studio veteran Gilbert Velasquez, her self-titled album bristled with rhythmic cumbias and perky polkas. The first single, "Te Juro," was written by Juan Vivero and additional songs were written by Humberto Ramón and Richard Allen. In high school Margarita sang and played violin in mariachi groups. In 1996 Margarita got an opportunity to open for Mazz, which led to a record contract with EMI.

Margarita (EMI)

MARÍA VICTORIA

Born María Victoria Gutiérrez, circa 1925, Guadalajara, Jalisco, México

Born in an artistic family, María Victoria was in entertainment all her life. In 1940 she began singing professionally on a Monterrey radio station and later moved to Mexico City where she sang at XEX and appeared in a musical revue. Signed to RCA in 1950, she recorded her debut single, "Soy Feliz," which was written by Juan Bruno Tarraza, and her signature hits were "Amor Perdido" and "Todavía No Me Muero." With **Luis Arcaraz,** she toured Mexico, Central America, and the U.S. She appeared in five films, including *Mi Querida Mujercita.* She also played the character "La Criada Mal Criada" on Mexican soap opera for many years. María Victoria sang for many seasons at Teatro Blanquita in Mexico City.

Boleros Inmortales (Sony)
Estrellas del Fonógrafo (RCA)
María Victoria (Sony)
Voz con Sentimiento (Sony)

MARIACHI

The heartland music of Mexico, mariachi originated before the turn of the twentieth century as a traditional folk form and evolved into a symphonic ensemble that included harp, violin, guitar, *guitarrón,* and *vihuela.*

In its ultimate expression, modern mariachi music is like a mini-orchestra, complete with strings, horn sections, and sophisticated arrangements. But its roots are folk-based and today, *charros* and mariachis are as easily identified with Mexico as cowboys and country music are with America.

The term mariachi refers to an individual or an actual ensemble, but not necessarily a musical style. Mariachis usually perform musical genres that can be played in a variety of cadences: *son, huapango,* ranchera, and *vals* or waltz. The main repertoire includes the boleros, polkas, and corridos, although the favored form is the bolero ranchero—a chugging, bluesy ballad. A basic mariachi generally consists of bass *guitarróns,* violin, *vihuela,* trumpet, and flute.

Scholars' theories about the origin of the word mariachi vary, but a common explanation places it during Mexico's Napoleonic period of 1864 to 1867, which was when French aristocracy hired the ensembles to play at weddings and parties. The groups became associated with weddings (which are called *mariages* in French) and the word got a Mexican twist, becoming "mariachi." Early mariachis, which were known as *conjuntos de arpa,* used harps and violins. Due to the harp's lack of portability, traveling mariachis substituted it with the *guitarrón,* a bass guitar that has four to six gut strings. They also incorporated the *vihuela,* a small guitar with a v-shaped back that produces a high sound.

Mexico's most important mariachi, **Mariachi Vargas de Tecalitlán,** was formed in 1898 in Tecalitlán, Jalisco, by Gaspar Vargas. The trumpet, which is so integral to today's mariachi, did not appear in the ensemble until the 1930s, when Emilio Azcarraga Vidaurreta, founder of Mexico City radio station XEW, insisted on it because strings sounded too thin on the radios of that time. At about the same time, mariachi outfits changed from peasant clothing to the *charro* outfits that have become a mariachi trademark. In the '40s and '50s mariachis accompanied the great singing *charros* of Mexico's golden age of cinema, like **Pedro Infante** and **Jorge Negrete.**

During the 1950s, Rubén Fuentes, director of Mariachi Vargas de Tecalitlán, upgraded the level of musicianship in the genre by requiring that all members of Mariachi Vargas read music. In the American Southwest mariachi enjoyed a major renaissance in the late '80s with a series of mariachi festivals and the introduction of mariachi instruction at the high school and college level. **Linda Ronstadt**'s 1987 Grammy-winning release *Canciones de Mi Padre* and her 1991 follow-up *Más Canciones,* roots-ranchera albums with participation from Mariachi Vargas, helped give widespread exposure to the music.

Important mariachis in the 1990s included Los Angeles–based **Mariachi Sol de México,** which recorded with the Beach Boys in 1998, and San Antonio–based **Campanas de América.** Mostly, mariachis were backing units for solo singers like **Vicente Fernández** and **Antonio Aguilar.** With perhaps the notable exceptions of **Lucha Reyes** and **Lola Beltrán,** few women have made as strong an impact on the mariachi scene as their male counterparts.

MARIACHI COBRE

Formed 1971, Tuscon, Arizona

One of the most professional Mexican American mariachis in the U.S., Mariachi Cobre has accompanied **Lola Beltrán, Lucha Villa, Linda Ronstadt, Ana Gabriel,** and **Guadalupe Pineda.** Formed by brothers Randy and Steve Carrillo, Mack Ruíz, and musical arranger Frank Grijalva, Mariachi Cobre organized the first International Mariachi Conference in 1981 and since 1982 has performed regularly at Disney World in Orlando, Florida. The group's self-titled debut CD was released in 1991. The group recorded sporadically on independent labels during the '90s, focusing on classic mariachi covers.

Éste Es Mi Mariachi (Kuckuck)
Mariachi Cobre (Kuckuck)
XXV Aniversario (Black Sun)

MARIACHI CUARTETO COCULENSE

Formed circa late 1890s, Cocula, Jalisco, México

Mariachi Cuarteto Coculense was the first mariachi to have been recorded—in 1908, one year before the outbreak of the Mexican Revolution. The quartet was led by musical director, Justo Villa, on vocals/*vihuela* with Cristóbal Figueroa on vocals/*guitarrón* and brothers Hilario and Cresencio "El Tirilingue" Chanverino on violins. In 1905 Coculense became the first mariachi to play in Mexico City, fascinating the urban dwellers with its traditional peasant clothing.

The early recordings consisted of twenty-one *sones abajeños,* all of which were recorded for the only major U.S. phonograph companies of the time—Columbia, Edison, and Victor. These recordings remain in print on the folk label Arhoolie, taped off the original cylinders, which predated vinyl. Despite the poor sound quality, the lyrics—with their double entendres, sentimentality, and stories of daily life—still resonate. There was a spiritual quality in this folk, almost tribal, music that dates from the days when mariachi was an obscure regional style. Classic songs from the sessions included "La Malagueña," "El Arriero," and "Arenita de Oro."

Mexico's Pioneer Mariachis, Vol. 4 (Arhoolie)

MARIACHI REYNA DE LOS ANGELES

Formed 1993, Los Angeles, California

Mariachi Reyna de Los Angeles gained fame quickly as the most popular and successful all-female mariachi group in the U.S. The troupe was founded by **Mariachi Sol de México** founder/director José A. Hernández with help from bandleader Laura Sobrino. The thirteen females were accomplished mariachis who deftly played violins, *vihuelas,* trumpets, guitars, *guitarróns,* and the harp.

Mariachi Reyna de Los Angeles
Courtesy of PolyGram

Mariachi Reyna delivered an impressive debut on PolyGram titled *Sólo Tuya,* which featured a few originals and some inspired readings of old classics, such as "Serenata Huasteca" and "Mucho Corazón." The troupe reached its zenith on the touching tribute to **Selena,** "Bidi Bidi Bom Bom/No Me Queda Más," an amazing interpretation that arguably outshined the original. The group also tackled the **Rocío Durcal**–identified, **Juan Gabriel**–penned original "Amor Eterno," perhaps the best tribute to a love gone but not forgotten.

Sólo Tuya (PolyGram)

MARIACHI SOL DE MÉXICO

Formed 1981, Los Angeles, California

One of the most prolific recording mariachis in the country, Mariachi Sol de México also evolved into a versatile, top performing troupe. Mariachi Sol has recorded and/or performed with **Linda Ronstadt, Selena,** the Beach Boys, and **Vikki Carr** as well as played with the Los Angeles Philharmonic Orchestra and other *orquestas* in Sacramento and San Jose, California, as well as in Albuquerque, New Mexico.

José A. Hernández (born 1958) was a native of Mexicali, Baja California Norte and was raised in Los Angeles. He initially founded Mariachi Sol in 1981 as a recording group that could back up Mexican pop stars such as **Juan Gabriel.** Hernández was a fifth-generation mariachi who dates his family mariachi tradition to his great paternal grandfather, Monico Ledesman, who played in a mariachi at the turn of the century in Jalisco. Hernández's grandfather was part of Mariachi Chapala, which was established in 1938.

In 1995 Hernández arranged and produced two songs that Selena sang for the film *Don Juan de Marco,* including the original Felipe Valdéz Leal song "Tú Solo Tú." The latter was included on Selena's *Dreaming of You* crossover CD, which reached No. 1 on the Billboard Hot Latin Tracks chart. He also contributed music to the film *Old Gringo* with Jane Fonda and Gregory Peck.

In 1998 Hernández collaborated with the Beach Boys to record a revamped bilingual version of "California Girls" as the title track for his album *Acapulco Girls.* The CD also included a remake of "Kokomo."

Acapulco Girls (EMI)
Corazón, Buenas Noches (EMI)
La Nueva Era (EMI)

MARIACHI VARGAS DE TECALITLÁN

Formed 1897, Tecalitlán, Jalisco, México

Founded by Gaspar Vargas in 1897, Mariachi Vargas consisted of original members Manuel Mendoza, harp; Refugio Hernández and Lino Quintero, violins; and Vargas, *guitarra de golpe* (five-string guitar). This was the same instrumentation used by the *conjuntos de arpa* of the period, such as Los Campesinos de Michoacán. *Conjuntos de arpa* typically included the violin, harp, and *guitarra de golpe.*

In 1921 Gaspar's son Silvestre joined the mariachi with the violin and in the early '30s he took over the mariachi. He changed the direction of the music by adding trumpets and, in 1941, hired the first permanent trumpet player—Miguel Martínez. In 1931 Mariachi Vargas, while still under Gaspar's leadership, was contracted to play in Tijuana. This was an important step because it was the farthest away from home they had ever played. And it was the first time that they appeared in costumes, which consisted of loose-fitting white cotton pants, red sash belts, muslin shirts tied at the waist, straw sombreros, and red bandanas. This was the traditional period clothing for natives and peasants of Jalisco. Mariachis would later evolve into the modern *traje de charro* or *traje de gala,* which feature tight-fitting pants with ornamental buttons, matching jackets, broaches, and wide-brimmed hats, all embroidered with equestrian designs.

Early Mariachi Vargas signature hits included "El Tren" and "La Mariquita" and by 1933 the troupe, which by now had grown to eight members, moved to Mexico City. Later that year they won an important mariachi contest in Guadalajara. In 1934 they played at the inauguration of President Lazaro Cárdenas. Cárdenas subsequently employed Mariachi Vargas as the official musical group with the Mexico City Police Department, a post that they held for twenty years.

In 1937 Mariachi Vargas appeared in the first of some 200 movies, *Así Es Mi Tierra.* Also that year, the group recorded its first sides for Peerless Records and in 1938 the group signed with RCA Victor Méxicana, officially becoming Mariachi Vargas de Tecalitlán.

By 1944 Rubén Fuentes Gasson (born in Cuidad Guzmán, Jalisco), a trained musician, was hired to play the violin and he soon became the musical director for Mariachi Vargas. Fuentes, with Vargas's help, standardized the arrangements of many traditional songs for many of the singers and songwriters that the mariachi collaborated with, including **Pedro Infante,** Miguel Aceves Mejía, **Lola Beltrán,** and **José Alfredo Jiménez.** Fuentes would also compose some of the most popular boleros of the '50s, including the evergreens "Cien Años," "Tu Amor y Mi Amor," and "Tu Vida es Mi Vida," all with lyrics by Alberto Cervantes, as well as "Divino Tormento," "Donde Encontrarás," and "Luz y Sombra," which became a major hit for Marco Antonio Muñiz. Fuentes also wrote "Escándalo," which became a **Javier Solis** classic.

By the mid-1950s Fuentes's insistence that all musicians should read music changed the way mariachi music moved from one group to another. In time Fuentes became one of Mexico's most prolific composer/arranger/producer/conductors. He was important in the development of Mexican folkloric music, especially rancheras and boleros. Mariachi Vargas continued to evolve by adding two trumpets, a classical guitar, and more violins, which made it a complete adaptable orchestra.

In 1987 Fuentes helped produce *Canciones de Mi Padre,* the landmark roots-ranchera album by **Linda Ronstadt** that also featured Mariachi Vargas. The following year Mariachi Vargas accompanied Ronstadt on her *Canciones de Mi Padre* tour. Through the years, signature Mariachi Vargas hits included "Son de la

Negra," "Canción Mixteca," "El Mariachi Loco," and "Jalisco Está de Fiesta."

In 1997 Mariachi Vargas had a year-long celebration of its 100th anniversary.

Aniversario 100/Las Canciones (PolyGram)
La Fiesta del Mariachi (PolyGram)
Mi Historia (PolyGram)
Serie 20 Éxitos (RCA)
Their First Recordings: 1937–1947 (Arhoolie)

MARTÍNEZ, FREDDIE

Born Alfredo Ricardo Martínez, April 15, 1942, Corpus Christi, Texas

Freddie Martínez became a superstar in the early '70s with his Tejano classics "Te Traigo Estas Flores" and "Botoncito de Cariño," but it was his gamble to start an independent record label that elevated him into pioneer status.

Freddie Martínez
Courtesy of Freddie Records

Martínez's grandfather, bandleader Ralph Galván, opened Corpus Christi's first ballroom, where Martínez grew up listening to a lot of touring bands. At the age of eleven, his father, Lee Martínez, sent him to a music professor for voice lessons and Martínez later learned the trumpet from Bernave Alvarado. In 1954 he began as a fill-in trumpet player for his grandfather's orchestra. While still at Roy Miller High School, Martínez formed the Freddie Martínez Orquesta and recorded his first single on Armando Marroquín's Discos Ideal label. In 1964, after having gone through four lead singers, he decided to sing lead.

A series of records on indie labels led nowhere and, in his frustration, he formed Freddie Records in 1969 and later opened Marfre Publishing to register his own songs. That year he also released his first single, "Necesito Tu Amor," which he wrote and followed with "Botoncito de Cariño," which was written by Johnny Herrera. Both became solid hits. Other Herrera songs that Martínez released as hit singles were "Muñequita de Canelo" and "Un Par de Ojitos." But in 1971 his signature hit arrived—"Te Traigo Estas Flores," which was written by his bass player Joe Mejía. A simple tune about bringing flowers to a girlfriend, the song impacted with its jumpy hook and feel-good atmospherics.

In 1973 Martínez became one of the first Tejano artists to play in the Hollywood Palladium and in New York City's Madison Square Garden and later appeared in the movie *La Muerte de Pancho Villa.* Martínez retired in 1978 as a touring musician to devote all of his time to his growing record label, which included a recording studio. However, in 1988 Martínez appeared on the CD *Los Dos Reyes* with norteño singer **Ramón Ayala.** In March of 1997 Martínez was inducted into the TMA's Hall of Fame and the following year he produced the oldies project *Leyendas y Raices,* with his '70s contemporaries Carlos Guzmán, **Sunny Ozuna,** and **Augustin Ramírez.** The first single/title track was an extended medley of their greatest hits: "Vestida de Blanco," "Reina de Mi Amor," "Tres Ramitas," and "Te Traigo

Estas Flores." The success of the medley led to a limited Southwest tour.

Época de Oro (Freddie)
El Inoldivable (Freddie)
Te Traigo Estas Flores (Freddie)
Ven a Mí (Freddie)

MARTÍNEZ, JOE, Y DREAM

See Hometown Boys, The

MARTÍNEZ, NARCISO

Born October 29, 1911, Reynosa, Tamaulipas, México; died June 5, 1992, San Benito, Texas

Known as "El Huracán del Valle" (The Hurricane of the Valley), Narciso Martínez was credited for combining *bajo sexto* with the diatonic or push-button accordion, taking the embryonic conjunto beyond its simple and original Germanic style. As a result, Martínez is often called the father of conjunto music. Martínez also set the basic template for modern conjunto and norteño music when he played accompaniment behind the vocal duos of the day, including Carmen y Laura.

It is in keeping with the bicultural nature of the Texas/Mexican conjunto/norteño duality of this music that while Martínez was born in Mexico and never became an American citizen, he spent almost his entire life in the U.S.

Martínez learned to play the accordion when he was seventeen years old after his older brother had played it. By 1936 Martínez began his career playing locally and, as his popularity grew, he caught the attention of furniture store owner Enrique Valentine, who helped Martínez advance in his career. By now Martínez was playing regularly with Santiago Almeida (born July 25, 1911, Skidmore, Texas) on *bajo sexto,* an evolutionary development in conjunto, which heretofore had only used accordions. Valentine took Martínez to San Antonio to make his first recordings on Bluebird Records. Family folklore has several reasons for Martínez's nickname of "El Huracán del Valle." According to one, Martínez played in a fast style, faster than his contemporary **Don Santiago Jiménez.** Another myth has it that there was a major hurricane in 1934 in the Rio Grande Valley.

Narciso Martínez
Courtesy of Ramón Hernández

According to Arhoolie Records owner, Chris Strachwitz, Martínez recorded twenty titles in San Antonio's Bluebonnet Hotel on October 21, 1936, for which Martínez was paid $150. Interestingly, five weeks later, on November 27, 1936, future blues legend Robert Johnson (born May 8, 1911, Hazelhurst, Mississippi) arrived in San Antonio by train from Mississippi to record seven blues sides (he only recorded twenty-nine songs in his lifetime) also for Bluebird Records. Among Johnson's biggest songs was "Crossroads."

Martínez's first recordings were sold under his own name in Chicano areas, under "Louisiana Pete" in Cajun areas and as "Polski Kwartet" in Polish areas. He was one of the first conjunto musicians to tour outside of Texas. Martínez peaked in popularity when he backed the duo Carmen y Laura. He continued recording for Bluebird until the late '40s, when major companies lost interest in the genre. Martínez's later hits included the instrumental "La Chulada" and "Vidita Mia." By the mid-1950s, he was playing music on weekends and working during the week as an agricultural worker and a truck and tractor driver. His popularity grew once again when he became the house accordionist for Discos Ideal and played with **Beto Villa, Isidro López,** and **Lydia Mendoza.** Villa and Martínez teamed up to record the polkas "Madre Mía" and "Monterrey" as well as two waltzes, "Rosita" and "Morir Soñando." After another slow period in the mid-1960s, Martínez moved temporarily to Florida to pick tomatoes and other produce.

Returning to Texas in 1973, Martínez took a job at the Gladys Porter Zoo in Brownsville, feeding the animals. Around that time, filmmaker Les Blank and producer Chris Strachwitz included Martínez in an acclaimed documentary about Texas Mexican border music called *Chulas Fronteras*. In 1977 Martínez left the zoo and settled for a small pension, playing dances nearly every weekend.

In 1982 Martínez was among the first inductees in the Tejano Conjunto Hall of Fame. In 1983 he received the National Heritage Fellowship Award from the National Endowment for the Arts, the highest honor for folk musicians, and in 1989 he received a Grammy nomination for *Narciso Martínez: El Huracán del Valle,* the rerecording of his earlier hits on Arhoolie Records. In 1993 the Tejano Conjunto Hall of Fame officially named the award statue given to its inductees the Narciso Martínez Award in commemoration of the artist's lifetime contribution to conjunto music. His signature hits included "La Chicarronera," "El Barrilito," "El Callito," "Lupita," "La Parrita," "La Polvadera," "Florecita," "La Chulada," "Vidita Mía," and "El Arbolito." On June 5, 1992, Martínez died of leukemia in his hometown of San Benito, Texas.

Father of Tex-Mex Conjunto (Arhoolie)
El Huracán del Valle (RYN)
El Huracán del Valle (Roy Sales)

MASIZZO

Formed 1997, Dilley, Texas and Zapata, Texas

The new Masizzo was born when *bajo sexto*/singer/songwriter Johnny Lee Rosas and accordionist Albert Ramírez Jr. left **Intocable** and joined brothers bass player Bryan Ramírez and drummer Roger Ramírez.

Masizzo
Courtesy of Sound Mex

Rosas had spent two years with **Jaime y Los Chamacos** before joining Intocable in 1992. Bryan and Roger were original members of Masizzo along with Albert Ramírez Sr., Bryan's father. Rosas and Ramírez Jr. coproduced and coarranged the band's debut album, *La Otra Mitad* on Sound Mex label, which spawned the hit "Te Quiero Tanto." The song was No. 1 on *Radio y Música*'s Tejano chart for twelve weeks, and another song off the album, "Por Tu Capricho," also scored on charts. Daniel Martínez replaced Roger Ramírez, who left to join Trueno in early 1998.

La Otra Mitad (Sound Mex)

MAZZ

Formed 1977, Brownsville, Texas

The story of Mazz begins in Brownsville in 1950. Singer Joe Manuel López and guitarist Jimmy González were born thirty minutes apart in the same hospital on August 28, 1950. Their families lived across the street from each other and both López and González graduated from Hanna High School in 1969. At 450 pounds, González was a hefty guy. In various interviews he attributed his weight to a glandular disorder.

In 1966 López and González formed Little Joe's Group. They changed the band's name several times in the next few years (Los Glares, Phases, Belaire Band). López was drafted by the U.S. Army in 1970 and served two years. In 1974 he joined the group **Los Fabulosos Cuatro** and recorded his first album. In 1975 López took two years off to study criminal justice at Texas South Most College. In 1977 López/González formed a group called Brown Express and it was during a house gig at a local Holiday Inn that Luis Silva and Bob Grever of the powerful Tejano indie Cara Records "discovered" the group. After changing its name to Mazz, the band was signed on.

The band's first two albums received little recognition, but the third album, which was released late in 1981, included the hit single "Laura Ya No Vive Aquí," which reached No. 1 on *Billboard*'s regional charts. In 1985 Mazz released the benchmark LP *No. 16,* which reached No. 4 on The Billboard Latin 50 chart. The LP produced the hits "Decídelo," "¿Por Qué? ¡Dios Mío!" "Perdóname," and "Porque Te Quiero," which was the theme song for the Univision network soap opera *Cristal*.

In 1990, when Cara was purchased by EMI Latin in a move that shook up the industry, Mazz elevated its music further. The band produced a series of albums that impacted and influenced the industry. Mazz's album *Para Nuestra Gente* included the hits "Soy Como Soy" and "Canciones de Amor." The 1991 Grammy-nominated *No Te Olvidaré* album contained the mariachi potpourri "Canciones del Corazón," and the 1993 *Mazz Románticos Que Nunca* included the "Bolero Medley." Both albums foreshadowed the industry trend of bands to increasingly focus on folkloric music.

Another Mazz landmark album, *Lo Haré por Ti,* in 1992 delivered the hits "Vuelvo," "Lo Voy a Hacer por Ti," "Qué Sera," "No Soporto Más," and "Ayer y Hoy." This album showed a band at the peak of its creative power. Subsequent albums produced an occasional hit or two, but none has matched this moment.

The secret to Mazz has always been the sharp musical punch (rhythmic cumbias and melodic polkas) that are engineered by guitarist/producer Jimmy González and the appealing vocals and looks of front man Joe López, who has a passing resemblance to the actor Tom Selleck. Although not first to do so, Mazz was credited with utilizing the synthesizer and blending rock 'n' roll influences into traditional Tejano music in the '80s.

The band has won more than two dozen TMAs. At its peak, the group won a record six of thirteen awards both in 1991 and 1992. Additional signature hits included "Que Me Lleven Canciones," "No Te Olvidaré," "Traicionera," and "Estúpido Romántico."

Joe López of Mazz
Chris Borgman/Courtesy of EMI Latin

Part of Mazz's appeal has been its controversial nature, which led to its nickname "The Bad Boys of Brownsville." The band generated negative publicity when Joe López was arrested for misdemeanor drug charges (marijuana) in 1995 in Kleberg County. (López got off when the band offered to play a benefit dance for community organizations.) Mazz gained a reputation as a "no show" when it canceled or did not bother to show up for performances and López earned a well-known and publicized reputation for paternity suits.

In the summer of 1998 Mazz split into two groups—lead singer Joe López plays under the name Joe López y Nuevo Imagen Mazz while guitarist Jimmy González tours under the name Original Grupo Mazz.

Al Frente De Todos (EMI)
Lo Haré por Ti (EMI)
No Te Olvidaré (EMI)
Para Nuestra Gente (EMI)
¿Qué Esperabas? (EMI)

MEJÍA, MIGUEL ACEVES

Born November 13, 1917, Chihuahua, Chihuahua, México

Miguel Aceves Mejía rose to the top of Mexican pop culture in the late '50s as a prolific film actor and ranchera singer known as "The Golden Falsetto."

While working as a youngster at an auto factory, Mejía got his first break when his boss got him a singing gig on a show that he sponsored at radio station XEFI. Later Mejía signed on with Monterrey station XET, earning nine pesos per month. There he formed a trio with Emilio Allende and Carlos Sorolla. Mejía later moved to Los Angeles, where, as a soloist, he developed the falsetto singing style that became his trademark. He returned to Mexico City in 1940, joining the roster of the prestigious radio station XEW.

Mejía's first LPs for RCA were tropical, but a 1946 strike of studio musicians forced him to record with mariachi. With the tunes "Ya Se Va La Embarcación" and "Carabina 30-30" he found his musical niche. He began film work in the 1947 *De Pecado en Pecado,* where his voice was dubbed over actor José Pulido's singing parts. Mejía was a frequent collaborator with the prolific songwriter **José Alfredo Jiménez** and he recorded Jiménez's tunes "Perla," "Cuatro Caminos," and "Alma de Acero." Additional rancheras that became identified with Mejía included "Hay Unos Ojos," "Paloma Negra," "El Pastor," "La Malagueña," "Cucurrucucu Paloma," "El Jinete," and "Canción Mixteca."

Mejía got his first major role in 1954's *Los Cuatros Vientos,* the film that made him a movie star. With his good looks and trademark white shock of hair, he was instantly recognizable. During Mexico's golden age of cinema in the '50s, he costarred with legendary performers, including María Felix, Pedro Armendariz, **Lola Beltrán,** and Amalia "La Tariácuri" Mendoza of **Trío Tariácuri.** He eventually appeared in more than forty movies.

12 Éxitos Rancheros (RCA)
15 Huapangos de Oro (RCA)
Corridos y Caballos (RCA)
Mejía Miguel Aceves (RCA)
Las Rejas No Matan (RCA)

MENDOZA, AMALIA "LA TARIÁCURI"

See Trío Tariácuri

MENDOZA, JUAN

See Trío Tariácuri

MENDOZA, LYDIA

Born May 13, 1916, Houston, Texas

Lydia Mendoza
Courtesy of Arhoolie Records

Lydia Mendoza's biggest influence was her mother, Leonar Samarripa Reyna, who taught her to sing and play guitar. Mendoza learned to play violin, mandolin, and two-string guitar. In the mid-1920s, she began her career singing with her family in El Cuarteto Carta Blanca at barbershops and restaurants in the Rio Grande Valley. In 1928 the family responded to a newspaper ad and landed a recording session at the now defunct Bluebonnet Hotel in San Antonio with the OKEH label, which generated ten sides, or five singles.

In 1934 Mendoza won a Pearl beer radio talent contest and landed her family a contract with Bluebird Records. She was then asked to record several solo cuts, which generated her biggest hit, "Mal Hombre." The hit resulted in a tour and earned Mendoza the nicknames "La Cancionera de los Pobres" and "La Alondra de la Frontera." Other hits for Mendoza were "Amor de Madre," "Celosa," and "Puño de Tierra."

Mendoza recorded more than fifty albums and 200 songs, including boleros, rancheras, and tangos on the labels RCA, Columbia, Azteca, Peerless, El Zarape, Discos Falcon, and Norteño. She also recorded and performed with the likes of **Beto Villa, Narciso Martínez,** and **Valerio Longoria.** She sang for former president Jimmy Carter at the John F. Kennedy Center in Washington, D.C.

Mendoza was credited with uniting intimate folk songs with more polished, commercial performances that typify dance hall and theatrical music in the '30s and '40s. In 1971 she performed at the American Folklife Festival in Montreal, Canada, an invitation that was extended from the Smithsonian Institution. In 1982 she received a National Heritage Fellowship Award from the National Endowment for the Arts. She was inducted into the TMA's Hall of Fame in 1985 and into the Tejano Conjunto Hall of Fame in 1991. In 1988 Mendoza suffered a stroke that left her partially paralyzed. In 1993 her autobiography, *Lydia*

Mendoza: A Family Autobiography, was published by University of Houston's Arte Publico Press.

20 Éxitos de Ayer (Arhoolie)
First Queen of Tejano Music (Arhoolie)
La Gloria de Tejas (Arhoolie)
Vida Mia (Arhoolie)

MEZA, BECKY LEE

Born October 2, 1985, Harlingen, Texas

Like many little girls throughout the Southwest, Becky Lee Meza was also inspired by **Selena.** As a preteen Meza would ad-lib to songs from the radio, using her grandfather's cane as an imaginary microphone. In the spring of 1996, several thousand little girls in San Antonio, Miami, Chicago, and Los Angeles tried out for the role of young Selena for the film about the pop star's life. Director Gregory Nava picked Meza, who played the wide-eyed, playful, and aspiring little Selena.

Becky Lee Meza
Al Rendon/Courtesy of Barb Wire

A&R scout Jerre Hall signed up Meza in early 1997 to record a debut album, *Vive Tu Sueño,* on his Dallas-based indie label Barb Wire, which was then distributed by Virgin Records. The album was released to coincide with the release of the Selena movie, *Dreaming of You,* with the first single being "Sueño." Produced by Wyatt Arp, the CD featured eleven tracks, mostly teen pop bilingual tunes.

Vive Tu Sueño (Barb Wire/Virgin)

MIER, LOS

Formed circa early 1980s, Santiago, Nuevo León, México

The Mier brothers—Hector, Eduardo, Alejandro, and Rocardo—were scions of Nicandro Mier, director/founder of venerable norteño group Los Montaneses del Alamo. Originally formed as Grupo Armonia and then later as Los Hermanos Mier, the tropical cumbia keyboards/percussion group, led by singer/ director /songwriter Hector Mier, got on the map in the mid-1980s with early hits "Cachito de Luna," "Silencio, Corazón," and "A Que Sí, Te Acuerdas."

Los Mier returned to the Billboard Hot Latin Tracks chart in the mid-1990s with a trio of radio-friendly, keyboard-driven cumbias, including "Te Amo," "Bordada a Mano," and "Tímida." In the mid-1990s, the third generation of Los Mier jumped into the music scene in the form of the new group Los Filis on the EMI label.

Cuando Creí en el Amor (FonoVisa)
Dedicado a Ti (FonoVisa)
Rosas y Mujeres (FonoVisa)
Te Amaré (TH-Rodven)

MISMOS, LOS

Formed late 1995, Ario de Rosales, Michoacán, México

Los Mismos were born from the ashes of **Los Bukis,** Mexico's top romantic pop band in the '80s that disbanded in late 1995 when their intriguing and inspiring bandleader **Marco Antonio Solis** took off for new pastures. In short order, though, the remaining band members regrouped and decided to soldier on.

It was a considerable challenge, however, considering that Solis was the main songwriter, producer, and lead singer. But the band—Joel Solis, guitar; Roberto Guadarrama, keyboards; José "Pepe" Guadarrama, percussions; Pedro Sánchez, drums; and Eusebio "El Chivo" Cortéz, bass—was lucky to find someone quickly to replace Solis. They were lucky in the sense that new singer Pedro Velázquez, from San Felipe, Baja California Norte, sounded a lot like Solis on record and in live shows. He was also tall, slim, and handsome.

The band quickly signed on with EMI Latin (Solis had signed with their old label, FonoVisa) and in a smart marketing move, christened themselves Los Mismos (The Same Ones) and ironically named their debut CD *Juntos Para Siempre* (Together Forever). This CD produced the hit single "Dependo de Mi Trabajo." With their slick coat-and-tie outfits and their keyboard-driven romantic pop songs, Los Mismos looked and sounded the same as Los Bukis, so it was no surprise that they drew the same crowds on their initial U.S. and Mexico tours. Guadarrama still cranked out synth-drenched rhythms to propel their cumbia/ballads and "El Chivo" Cortéz still danced manically onstage while playing his bass. In 1997 their second CD, *Te Llevas Mi Vida,* produced the title track and "Adiós y Buena Suerte" as chart hits and included a duet with **Graciela Beltrán** on "Gracias por Todo."

Juntos Para Siempre (EMI/Latin)
Te Llevas Mi Vida (EMI/Latin)

MR. CHIVO

Formed 1974, Miguel Alemán, Tamaulipas, México

The amusing tropical cumbia outfit Mr. Chivo was formed in a small border town across the Rio Grande Valley from Roma, Texas. The group's specialty has been funny cumbias with catchy phrases and lots of sticky dance hooks.

Mr. Chivo scored its signature hits during the mid-1980s, including "Ron Con Coca-Cola," "Chevere," and the bolero "Si No Me Quieres Igual." The key to the group was the stage antics of singer Juan Carlos Pérez, who punctuated songs with English asides and hoarse laughter. In live shows Pérez frequently changed costumes to match the central character of the group's novelty cumbias, which include "Soy Drácula" and "Mi Abuelito." Because of its stage animation and costuming, the band appeals to children.

Buenas Noticias (Sony)
Facetas (AFG Sigma)
Mister Chivo Otra Onda (Sony)
Por dentro y por Fuera (Sony)
Signos Vitales (EMI)

MODELO, GRUPO

Formed 1978, Oxnard, California

Led by singer/guitarist/producer/arranger Hector Fregoso, whose vocals bear an uncanny resemblance to former **Los Bukis** front man **Marco Antonio Solis,** Grupo Modelo came together when the members were in their teens. All of the band members were natives of San Martin de Bolaños, Jalisco.

To casual fans, Modelo could have been mistaken for Los Bukis. The keyboard-driven pop ballads, the mod suits, and hip hairstyles—they were all there. The band cut its first album in 1984, but it would be a few years before the group signed with a major label (FonoVisa) in

1990. Aided perhaps in their similarity to the Bukis sound, the hits came in quick succession: "Guardaré Tu Recuerdo" and "Aquí Esperándote," which was a cumbia-styled cover of Richard Marx's "Right Here, Waiting" in 1994. Another notable song, "Te Sigo Extrañando," was a duet with **Graciela Beltrán** that was featured in the band's 1995 effort *Quiéreme Más*. Besides romantic ballads and cumbias, Modelo also plays rhythmic *huapangos* and, on "Te Esperaré," fused cumbia, salsa, and flamenco.

12 Novedades de Modelo (FonoVisa)
Adiós por Teléfono (FonoVisa)
Aquí Esperándote (FonoVisa)
Quiéreme Más (EMI)
Te Acordarás de Mí (EMI)

MOJADO, GRUPO

Formed circa 1990, Matamoros, Tamaulipas, México

Guitarist and composer Felipe Barrientos helped launch Grupo Mojado in the early '90s with singer José Luis Davila. The band carved a solid niche through its originality and creativity.

The band trademark sound was best exemplified on the rapid-fire vocal delivery on Mojado's first hit, the cumbia "Tonta," which helped put the group on the map. The single also helped the band win the 1992 Billboard/Univision Premio Lo Nuestro Award for best new artist in the regional Mexican category. Led by the multi-talented Barrientos, the group experimented with banda on *Mojado con Banda* in the mid-1990s. For the band's 1994 album *Sin Fronteras* noted Bukis bandleader **Marco Antonio Solis** handled producer chores and contributed three original songs, including "Ya No Quiero."

The band evolved further on its 1996 CD *Sueño y Realidad,* incorporating reggae, rock, and vallenato into its cumbias, and generating four hit singles, including "Motivos" and "Caldo de Pollo." In 1998 the band's album *Como Pez en el Agua* featured songs by Barrientos and drummer Francisco Javier Gutiérrez.

Como Pez en el Agua (FonoVisa)
La Gorda (FonoVisa)
Mojado con Banda (FonoVisa)
Romántico Mojado (FonoVisa)
Sin Fronteras (FonoVisa)

MOLINA, ANICETO

Born April 7, 1939, El Campano, Colombia

Aniceto Molina was a premier accordionist in the vallenato genre, the accordion-led music from Colombia's Atlantic coast. Molina's specialty was mixing Afro-Cuban salsa rhythms, percussion-driven cumbias, and soulful boleros into one smooth blend. In live performances Molina's band, Los Sabaneros, utilized vocal harmonies as well as two saxophones, timbales, and congas (instead of the traditional drum set) to produce nonstop dance music.

Born in the coastal town of El Campano, Colombia, Molina was exposed to the accordion by his brother, Anastasio. By the time he was twelve years old, Molina learned to play the instrument with fluidity and grace. The brothers formed a band to play in local wedding and parties.

In 1961 Molina began his recording career with four 78s in Barranquilla, Colombia and toured continuously. In 1969 he signed with Musart/Mexico, a development that led to his moving to Mexico City a few years later where he hooked up with the band Los Corraleros del Majagual. He followed with a short tenure in 1995 with the indie label DLB, which produced his *Aniceto Molina en México* album, which included the hit singles "Josefina" and "La Burra Tuerta." Shortly afterward Molina joined forces with La Luz Roja de San Marcos, an area band that, years earlier, had lost the majority of its members in an accident. They immediately recorded an LP, which generated the hit singles

"La Brujita," "Perro con Rabia," and "Carmencita." In 1979 the band became Aniceto Molina y Los Sabaneros and produced several more hits, including "El Campanero," "La Paisana," and "Caballito de Palo."

In the early '90s Molina moved to San Antonio, Texas and signed up with DISA/EMI Latin, producing several best selling albums, including *El Tigre Sabanero.* Molina was booked to play one of the biggest venues in his career at the Los Angeles Sports Arena on April 1, 1995.

He never played it. **Selena** was the scheduled headliner, but she had been killed the day before in a Corpus Christi, Texas motel and the show was canceled.

15 Años de Éxitos (Hemisphono)
Mis 14 Éxitos de Oro (PolyGram)
Las Mujeres de Aniceto Molina (EMI)
Puro Vallenato (Joey International)
El Tigre Sabanero (EMI)
Vallenato (EMI)

MONTECLARO, LORENZO DE

Born Lorenzo Hernández, September 5, 1939, Cuencame, Durango, México

Norteño singer Lorenzo de Monteclaro was known for his light tenor and vibrato and his signature hit was "El Ausente." He got his first break on the Torreón, Coahuila radio station program *Aficionados de los Ejidos.* He scored with his first single, "El Caminante," and began a prolific film career, appearing in forty-plus movies, including *Me Caí de las Nubes* with **Cornelio Reyna.** He experimented with a *pop-grupera* sound on 1995's *Digan Lo Que Digan.* He returned to his typical style on 1998's *Raices de la Música Norteña,* which included a dozen norteño/conjunto evergreens, including "Mi Único Camino" and "El Sube y Baja."

El Ausente (Sony)
Mexicanísimo (Sony)
Para Corridos con Banda (Sony)
Raices de la Música Norteña (PolyGram)

MORENO, JUAN P.

Born Juan Pablo Moreno, September 30, 1965, Twin Falls, Idaho

Juan P. Moreno
Courtesy of Voltage Discos

Juan P. Moreno began playing *bajo sexto* professionally at the age of fourteen when he joined his uncle Fernando Rodríguez's band La Familia Méxicana in Twin Falls. After his family moved to Alice, Texas, where he completed high school, Moreno landed his first local gig playing *bajo sexto* and singing background vocals for the late songwriter Juan Sifuentes. Moreno later joined the young conjunto outfit **Jaime y Los Chamacos,** which was then based in Houston. After seven-and-a-half years with the band, during which they released the top-selling albums *Qué Le Vas a Dar* and *Playing with Fire,* Moreno was fired in 1991 over a salary dispute. The next day, according to Moreno, he hooked up with **David Lee Garza y Los Musicales,** where he played *bajo sexto* and sang backing vocals for lead singer **Jay Pérez.** In 1993 Pérez left the band and shortly thereafter Moreno went solo.

Signed to Houston's Voltage Discos label in 1994, Moreno released his debut solo album, *Front and Center,* which generated the single "Cuando Yo Te Conocí," a song he wrote to his wife, Janie. On his sophomore CD, *Dichoso Soy,* the title track featured a duet with Jay Pérez. From 1995 to 1998 Moreno received several TMA industry honors, including best *bajo sexto* player (for four consecutive years) and best male rising star.

Dichoso Soy (Sony)
Front and Center (Sony)
Quien (Toka Discos)

NARANJO, RUBÉN, Y LOS GAMBLERS

Born February 22, 1945, Alice, Texas; died October 12, 1998, Alice, Texas

Rubén Naranjo began playing the *bajo sexto* when he was fifteen years old but switched to the accordion in 1962 when accordionist Chano Cadena invited him to play accordion in his group. Cadena's second accordionist had just left the group and Cadena wanted to keep the tradition of having two accordionists in his band.

In 1972 Naranjo formed his own group—Los Gamblers—and began touring with Eligio Escobar. He recorded several records with the Dallas-based indie El Zarape records, one of which produced the hit single "La Estrella." By the mid-1970s Naranjo signed on with Freddie Records and produced a series of records that resulted in his signature hits: "Besos Callejeros," "Preso Sin Delito," "Ángel de Mis Anhelos," and "Dos Caracoles."

Through the years Naranjo has been called "The Clark Gable de la Onda" because of his uncanny resemblance to the late American actor.

Acaba con Mi Dolor (Freddie)
Ese Es Tu Orgullo (Freddie)
Mi Jovencita (Freddie)
Que Te Vaya Bonito (Hacienda)
Señora de la Noche (Freddie)

NEGRETE, JORGE

Born Jorge Alberto Negrete Moreno, November 30, 1911, Guanajuato, Guanajuato, México; died December 5, 1953, Los Angeles, California

There have been only a few truly great mariachi/ranchera singers in the history of Mexico—**Pedro Infante, Javier Solis,** and **Vicente Fernández.** And the debate has raged for years about just who was the greatest. What cannot be argued is that Jorge Negrete was Mexico's first national ranchera hero known as "El Charro Cantor" (The Singing Cowboy).

Negrete was tall, handsome (he resembled English actor David Niven) and he fit the elegant posture of the noble, gallant *charro* (Mexican cowboy) perfectly. He recorded some 200 songs and starred in thirty-eight movies, becoming Mexico's first major movie star during the '40s and '50s—Mexico's golden age of cinema.

His signature song was "México, Lindo y Querido," a patriotic song whose verse about dying away from the homeland became prophetic for Negrete.

Befitting the status of a true legend, Negrete lived large. He began his recording career in Mexico City in the '30s and later, when he traveled to New York City, he worked for the National Broadcasting Company. After his highly successful singing career was established, he launched a prolific film career. He married three times, first the stage dancer Elisa Christy, then the film actresses Gloria Marín, and finally María Felix, who was considered the Elizabeth Taylor of Mexico. Negrete fathered his only child, Diana Negrete Christy, from his first marriage. At a time when the terms "media star" and "paparazzi" were not yet in existence, Negrete became one of Mexico's biggest celebrities and music ambassadors, with his life splashed across the major newspapers and magazines of the day.

But unlike other superstars of his time, Negrete sincerely cared for his fellow actors. In the early '40s, he helped found the Asociación Nacional de Actores (ANDA), which was comparable to the American Screen Actors Guild. From 1949 to 1950 he was the association's secretary. Beyond the seemingly unimportant title, though, Negrete was a major force in ANDA's development. He channeled the power of his own political connections and even contributed his own funds to help establish ANDA. ANDA officials would later repay him when, after completing their new gleaming offices at Altamirano 127 in Mexico City, they named the theater at the new location Teatro Jorge Negrete.

On the morning of December 5, 1953, Negrete died in the Cedars of Lebanon Hospital in Los Angeles from cirrhosis of the liver, an illness he had suffered for years. He had just arrived in L.A. to perform a five-day run at the famed Million Dollar Theater on one of his many U.S. tours. On the day of his death five minutes of silence were observed in his honor at all Mexican theaters. For the next seventy-two hours the Mexican film industry ceased production. Tens of thousands of Los Angelinos paid their last respects during Negrete's wake at the Cunningham O'Conner Funeral Home. The Mexican government sent a C-47 commercial transport plane to bring his remains home. His wife María Felix reportedly rejected the gesture, sniffing that the plane was beneath Negrete's stature. The tiff lasted only eight hours. The plane, with Negrete's body, left Los Angeles the evening of December 8.

In Mexico City mobs greeted the plane's arrival at the airport. More than 100,000 people filled downtown streets in one of the biggest funerals in the history of Mexico. Fellow cinematic and ranchera hero Pedro Infante, dressed in a policeman's uniform, led the motorcycle police escort for the funeral procession. The funeral service at Panteón Jardín featured a galaxy of Mexican stars, many of whom sang Negrete hits.

Born to an upper-class military family, Negrete grew up in Guanajuato, Guanajuato and later in San Luis Potosí. His father, David Negrete Fernández, was a lieutenant colonel in the Mexican Army during the Mexican Revolution. Through his connections he got a teaching post at Mexico City's German College, where the young Negrete enrolled and learned five languages, including German, English, and French. After graduating with a bachelor's degree, Negrete entered the Heroico Colegio Militar, which was considered to be Mexico's equivalent of West Point. There he reached the rank of lieutenant and joined the Mexican Army.

He took voice lessons under José Pierson and developed a taste for opera. In 1930 Negrete got his first opportunity in show business, landing a singing post at radio station XEW. Things did not go well initially. Negrete was an operatic singer, which did not lend itself well to singing rancheras. Still, ingrained perhaps with the self-discipline he had learned in military school, Negrete persevered. In 1934 he sang at the inauguration of El Palacio de Bellas Artes in Mexico City and the following year he resigned from the army to dedicate himself fully to the arts. In 1936 an opportunity presented itself when fellow singer Emilio Tuero Armengod could not make an engagement in New York City. Negrete replaced him and quickly landed a singing job at NBC. Negrete made fast friends with Chucho Navarro Moreno and Alfredo Gil, of the future **Trío Los Panchos,** who helped him by letting him stay at their Hotel Belvedere apartment. Negrete began getting regular bookings at Latino clubs, and he later collaborated on a song with Xavier Cugat.

It was in New York City that Negrete met his first wife, Elisa Christy, who was working as a cabaret dancer at the Club Madrid-Havana. When Christy was pregnant with their daughter, Diana, she had a bad experience at a New York hospital and it was reportedly this transcendent event that moved Negrete to work on behalf of struggling actors. Negrete felt compelled to establish an organization like ANDA in order to provide legal, financial, and medical help for actors. In New York, Negrete also ran into cinematographer Ramón Peon, who helped him land his first film in Mexico in 1937, *La Madrina del Diablo.* His career underway, Negrete would go on to create thirty-eight movies, including his 1942 signature *Ay Jalisco No Te Rajes,* a highly popular movie that projected Negrete's "El Charro Cantor" image worldwide. Later that year Negrete appeared in *El Peñón de las Ánimas,* during the filming of which he first met and worked with actress María Felix. Ten years later, on October 18, 1952, Negrete married María Felix in a very public ceremony that received worldwide attention, thanks to the emerging print, TV, and radio media of the age. It was called by many "the wedding of the century." In 1952 Negrete appeared with another Mexican film and music giant, Pedro Infante, in *Dos Tipos con Cuidado.*

Negrete recorded some 200 songs, including his biggest hits "Paloma Querida," "El Hijo del Pueblo," "San Luis Potosí," "Ella," and "Amor con Amor Se Paga." At his peak Negrete enjoyed the same international stature as tango master Carlos Gardel or film actor Valentino.

12 Éxitos Rancheros (RCA)
Fiesta Mexicana (RCA)
México, Lindo y Querido (IMD)
Serie Retrato (RCA)

NOEMY

Born Noemy Torres Esparza, May 26, 1971, Las Cruces, New Mexico

Tall, with model looks, and hard working, Noemy made an impact when she began her career in 1996. Her debut CD, *Eternamente,* produced the hit singles "Mentiras" and "Dímelo," and gave her initial momentum. But perhaps more important was her smart choice of management in veteran Sonny Flores. Quickly signed to a five-year contract with FonoVisa, Noemy was given the choice opening slots for **Los Tigres del Norte** and **Bronco,** which gave her exposure and recognition.

Although initially she gained popularity in Tejano circles, Noemy smartly played the bigger regional Mexican gamut of rancheras, boleros, and polkas. "Mentiras" reached No. 17 on the Billboard Hot Latin Tracks chart in early 1997. Her 1998 CD, *Encadenada,* featured her melodic cover of **Juan Gabriel**'s "Así Fui" and the title track, which was one of three songs that she wrote for that album.

Encadenada (FonoVisa)
Eternamente (FonoVisa)
Presa de Su Amor (FonoVisa)

NORTEÑITOS DE OJINAGA, LOS

Formed 1986, Ojinaga, Chihuahua, México

This six-man band played traditional norteño but added sax, electric bass, and two drummers to stand apart from the norteño herd. Led by accordionist/director Luis Armando Sánchez Valles, Los Norteñitos de Ojinaga got a boost in the late '80s when they opened for ranchera singer **Lorenzo de Monteclaro.** Los Norteñitos's hits included "Carta Mortal" and "El Corrido de Pablo Acosta," which featured lead singer Hector Abelardo Sánchez Valles's nasal delivery.

Al Rojo Vivo (Ramex)
Ay Amor (Ramex)
Bonita (Ramex)
Encadenada a Mí (Ramex)
Ese Arbolito (Ramex)
La Resbalosa (Ramex)
Se Me Derrumba el Alma (Ramex)

NORTEÑO

In its rudimentary form, norteño (which is Spanish for "northern") is the Mexican counterpart to Texas-based conjunto music. As with conjunto, norteño has folk-based rural origins, and a genuine, traditional norteño group must have two essential elements—the accordion and the *bajo sexto* (twelve-string bass guitar). Like conjunto, norteño was influenced by the introduction of the accordion and European dance forms like the waltz and *Schottische* by German and Czech railroad engineers. The most popular norteño outfits, like **Los Tigres del Norte,** added other instrumentation, such as the electric bass and sax. On the pop end of the spectrum were **Bronco** and **Grupo Límite,** which also used keyboards. However, they all retained the accordion and *bajo sexto.*

A few characteristics distinguished norteño groups from their Tejano peers. Most norteño outfits, except some on the pop side, recorded story-songs known as corridos ("Camelia la Tejana," "Gabino Barrera"), which have fallen out of favor with modern conjuntos. However, polkas, rancheras, and cumbias were ubiquitous to both.

To casual fans, there is no discernable difference between the genres. But astute followers can distinguish nuances. Norteño singers typically exhibit a more pronounced Mexican accent and a pinched, nasal quality. In addition, the polka backbeat tended to be less pronounced than in Tejano music and norteño accordionists generally lent more subtlety to their riffs. **Los Relámpagos del Norte**'s success was largely due to their mastery of both styles—**Ramón Ayala**'s signature nasal vocals coupled with brilliant accordion riffs. Their sound is still copied by such neo-traditional outfits as **Intocable** and **Michael Salgado.**

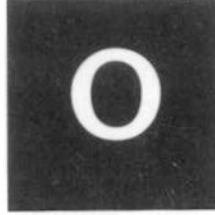

OCHOA, ANGELES

Born Angeles Nayibeth Ochoa Leduc, October 2, 1972 in Tijuana, Baja California Norte, México

Her clear, powerful vocals and impressive knack for being able to get inside a song made Angeles Ochoa one of the most promising young ranchera singers in Mexico in the early '90s. Typically performing in a *charro* outfit and singing the traditional bolero rancheros (her specialty), Ochoa was often compared to her idol, famed singer **Lola Beltrán.**

Angeles Ochoa
Courtesy of PolyGram

Ochoa became intrigued with folkloric music when, at the age of six, she listened to her grandmother talk about mariachi and ranchera music. She made her first public performance at a local church fund-raiser. At the age of eight, she saw Lola Beltrán on television and told her parents that one day she would sing with a mariachi. Years later, her childhood dream came true as she sang with the famed group **Mariachi Vargas de Tecalitlán.** In 1982 Ochoa performed in the fourth Festival de la Canción Ranchera and in Festival OTI, both of which were in Mexico City.

Ochoa was just twelve years old when she signed with CBS México in 1982, but internal label problems resulted in her being able to make only two albums through 1989. In the interim, Ochoa hosted a radio show, *México en Marcha,* on XEW in Mexico City.

In 1990 she turned heads with her impressive album *Vine Solo a Cantar,* with the radio hits "Déjame en Paz" and "Aunque Tenga Que Llorar." In 1994 she recorded *Sentimiento Norteño,* which was produced by norteño hero **Ramón Ayala.** In 1995 Ochoa left Sony to sign on with PolyGram and quickly recorded the album *Ayúdame a Pasar la Noche,* which was produced by her longtime collaborator, producer Homero Patron.

Ayúdame a Pasar la Noche (PolyGram)
Cancionero (Sony)
Sentimiento Norteño (Sony)
Sólo Vine a Cantar (Sony)

OLIVARES, FITO

Born Rodolfo Olivares, April 19, 1947, Ciudad Miguel Alemán, Tamaulipas, México

Fito Olivares learned to play the saxophone at the age of seven from his father, Mucio Olivares, who played in a local band in Ciudad Camargo. Olivares admired the way his father played the instrument and considered him a pivotal influence.

While still a teen Olivares played in various local groups, including Dueto Estrella, for which he wrote his first ranchera, "Ya No Eres

Mía." In 1979 Olivares and his brothers—Javier, singer/percussionist; and Jaime, keyboardist—and brother-in-law Jacinto Treviño, guitarist, joined Argelio Cantú in Sabinas Hidalgo to form the Mexican cumbia outfit **Los Tam y Tex,** for which Olivares wrote his first hits, including "La Musiquera," which later was the inspiration for a movie by the same name.

Fito Olivares y La Pura Sabrosura; with saxophonist Fito Olivares (front row, center)
Courtesy of EMI Latin

A year later Olivares and his brothers moved to Houston, where they formed Fito Olivares y La Pura Sabrosura. Olivares continued writing songs that became regional hits and kept the fledgling band going. In 1986 Olivares wrote the monster hit "Juana la Cubana," a rhythmic cumbia that topped charts everywhere and spawned more than a hundred cover versions by bands from Mexico and the United States to Central and South America.

Olivares's early influences were '70s greats and seminal Cuban-influenced tropical/cumbieros Pedro Estrada, **Mike Laure,** Pérez Prado, Orquesta Aragón, and then-young balladeers Roberto Carlos and Camilo Sesto. His predominant inspirations though were the Afro-Cuban mambos and Afro-Caribbean *charangas* that have always shown up in his music, resulting in a fusion of the cumbia's rapid percussions and the saxophone's brassy swirls. Among Olivares's biggest hits have been "La Güera Salomé," "Mi Profesión," "Rosa la de Reynosa," "Mi Caballito," and "La Gallina."

After recording fifteen albums with the small Houston indie label Gil Records, Olivares, who had by then emerged as an influential tropical/cumbiero, signed on with the major Mexican label FonoVisa in 1993. Subsequent singles that cracked the Billboard Hot Latin Tracks chart included "La Ranitas, "El Colesterol," "El Paso del Canguro," and "Cupido Bandido."

By the early '90s Olivares had perfected his blend of norteño cumbias with *charangas* and mambos, which he liked to describe as *guapachosa,* contagious or catchy. Oddly, Olivares had a penchant for titling his songs after animals or women, which, he stated in media interviews, provided his main inspiration as a songwriter.

In 1997 Olivares was signed by EMI Latin and produced his EMI debut, *Con Amor y con Sabor,* which produced the hits "La Pulguera" and "Winnona."

Con Amor y con Sabor (EMI Latin)
Con Mucha Sabrosura (FonoVisa)
La Güera Salomé (FonoVisa)
La Negra Catalina (FonoVisa)
La Pura Sabrosura (FonoVisa)
Tambores y Sabor (FonoVisa)

ORQUESTA TEJANA (BIG BAND)

Before modern Tejano music there were earthy, accordion-fueled conjuntos and genteel Orquestas Tejanas, which combined American, Mexican, and Latin cultural elements, reflecting the biculturalism of the Mexican American middle class during the 1940s and 1950s.

Orquestas Tejanas were heavily influenced by the American big bands led by Glenn Miller and Tommy Dorsey, as well as by the conjunto accordion and Mexican ranchera lyrics. Purist conjunto fans derided *orquesta* music as *jaiton,* high-toned, considering it snobby. But the *orquestas* were versatile, playing Latin styles such as the bolero, mambo, and *danzón,* and American styles like the fox-trot and swing.

Beto Villa was arguably the father of the Orquesta Tejana genre. In 1932, while still in high school, the Falfurrias, Texas, native formed his first group, the Sonny Boys, which took musical cues from the popular big bands on radio. After a World War II stint in the navy, Villa launched his career in earnest. Recording for Discos Ideal in 1946, he recorded polkas with ranchera lyrics put to a big-band backdrop. His combination proved commercially successful. He recorded "Rosita" with conjunto accordionist **Narciso Martínez** and racked up hits such as "Monterrey," "Las Gaviotas," "La Picona," and "Tamaulipas" during the late 1940s. Calm and confident as his *orquestas* became increasingly popular, Villa opted to explore a wider variety of rhythms, and required all band members to be able to read music. His repertoire expanded into popular Latin and American big-band dance styles of the day, though he continued to record polka rancheras.

During the 1950s the young saxophone and clarinet player **Isidro López** emerged on the scene. López added accordions to his band, and adapted mariachi instrumentation to his music, in a style he dubbed *Texachi.* His biggest hits included "Desilusión," "Díganle," and "Sufriendo y Penando," most of which he cowrote. With this stylistic fusion, López created what would become known as Tejano music.

Though never achieving an audience size comparable to conjunto, Orquesta Tejana's most popular bandleaders, like López, knew how to mix conjunto into their sets. Other prominent bandleaders of the era were **Chris Sandoval,** Balde González, Mike Ornelas, Darío Pérez, Eugenio Gutiérrez, and Pedro Bugarin. The formal *orquesta* setup faded along with American big bands after the late 1950s when rock began to dominate. However, the tradition of the big-band horn section carried on with seminal Tejano artists like **Little Joe** and **Sunny Ozuna.**

ORTEGA, RAÚL

See Banda Machos

OZUNA, SUNNY

Born Ildefonso Fraga Ozuna, September 8, 1943, San Antonio, Texas

In the late '60s and early '70s, Sunny Ozuna became one of the dominant singers in Chicano/Tejano music with big-band hits "Reina de Mi Amor" and "Cariñito." But it was Ozuna's English-language pop hits "Talk to Me" and "Smile Now, Cry Later," in the early '60s that first put him on the national map.

Raised in the South Side of San Antonio, Ozuna was in Burbank High School in 1957 when he formed his band the Galaxies. During the summer of 1958, Ozuna and Rudy Guerra formed Sunny and the Sunglows, which included one African American, two Anglo-Saxons, and two Mexican Americans. They sang strictly in English because they were influenced by the emerging rock 'n' roll scene. While still at Burbank, the Sunglows began playing five-cent dances in the barrio and at church gatherings and sock hops. That same year, they made their first record, *Just a Moment.*

Early in the summer of 1963, Sunny and the Sunglows recorded Little Willie John's "Talk to Me," which enjoyed regional success. Then an internal dispute led to Ozuna's separation from the Sunglows. **Joe Bravo** replaced Ozuna, who had gone to Houston and picked up the members of Jesse Villanueva's Rockin' Vees to form Sunny and the Sunliners. By late 1963 "Talk to Me" had begun to climb the national charts, peaking at No. 11 on the Billboard Hot 100 chart. Both the original Sunglows and the Sunliner's versions were credited in the rock books. By then the success of the single earned Ozuna an appearance on the TV show *Dick Clark's American Bandstand,* making Ozuna the first Mexican American on the popular dance show. Ozuna later scored additional songs on the Billboard Hot 100 chart. "Rags to Riches," "Out of Sight, Out of Mind," and "Peanuts" reached No. 47, No. 71, and No. 64 respectively.

Sunny Ozuna
Courtesy of Freddie Records

Ozuna's gold rush in the English pop market stalled by the late '60s, eventually leading Ozuna to mine the then-expanding Chicano market. In the early '70s, Ozuna got lucky again, producing the hit singles "Reina de Mi Amor," "Cariñito," "Árbol Seco," and "Mi Chulita." Through the '70s and '80s, Ozuna formed and re-formed a series of bands and created more than two dozen records on a variety of independent labels, but he never matched his earlier successes. In the late '80s Ozuna had repeated surgeries for throat problems, which affected the quality of his singing. In 1991 Sunny was signed by Manny Music and produced *Mr. Magic,* which generated the single "Que Se Vayan al Diablo." In 1998 Ozuna was part of the *Leyendas y Raices* reunion project, which also featured his contemporaries **Freddie Martínez,** Carlos Guzmán, and **Augustin Ramírez.**

Éxitos/Tejano Hits (SOI)
Mr. Magic (WEA Latina)
No Tengo Dinero (WEA Latina)

PALOMINOS, LOS

Formed 1985, Uvalde, Texas

Los Palominos
Courtesy of Sony Discos

Los Palominos had been plugging away for years in their hometown, Uvalde, Texas—first as Los Tremendos Pequeños and later as Los Tremendos de Johnny Arrela—before they were "discovered" in 1990 by **La Mafia**'s Armando Lichtenberger and Oscar de la Rosa. The allure of this neo-trad conjunto came from its old-time, minimalist style, as well as its solid rhythm section and sweet vocal harmonies on polkas, rancheras, and boleros.

Los Palominos were formed by the Arreola brothers—James, *bajo sexto*/vocals; Johnny, vocals/accordion/keyboards; Jesse, drums; and George, bass. Lichtenberger and de la Rosa helped Los Palominos produce a demo and eventually land a deal at Sony Discos. Each album consistently produced hits and the early ones included "La Llama," "Donde Está la Puerta," and "Eres Lo Que Más Quiero," a duet with Oscar de la Rosa from their 1995 album, *El Ganador*. Later hits included "Duele el Amor" and "La Carta Que Nunca Envié."

Corazón de Cristal (Sony Discos)
Duele el Amor (Sony Discos)
El Ganador (Sony Discos)
Te Seguiré (Sony Discos)

PALOMO, EL, Y EL GORRIÓN

Formed circa 1970, Aramberri, Nuevo León, México

The brothers Miguel "El Gorrión" (The Pigeon) Luna and Cirilo "El Palomo" (The Sparrow) Luna were inspired to go into music by their mother, who played the guitar and sang. While they were still preteens, their father, Jesús Luna Rojas, took them to plazas and other public places to sing to audiences where they were known as Los Generalitos.

El Palomo y El Gorrión have over sixty recordings on Discos Paygo, which was their label for twenty years. The group was invited to perform at the White House and it performed for three different Mexican presidents. The Universidad de Nuevo León in Monterrey published a book about them, titled *Ingratos Ojos Míos*. Their signature hits include "Es Toda la Chapa," "Ingratos Ojos Míos," and "La Elisa."

15 Éxitos (EMI)

PANCHOS, TRÍO LOS

Formed 1944, New York, New York

In the Latin world, *música de trío,* or trio music, has always been considered the most romantic genre. The basic song form is the bolero, a slow, sentimental dance song that originated in Cuba but that is now considered international. Some consider the bolero to be similar or equivalent to the jazz ballad.

In the '50s the bolero enjoyed a massive resurgence in Latin America and *música de trío* enjoyed a golden age. Trio music is essentially three guitarists singing soft ballads in two- or three-part Beatle-esque vocal harmonies. During the '50s and '60s the preeminent trio was Trío Los Panchos, which toured widely, bringing the music to a worldwide audience.

Los Panchos were born when Mexicans Jesús "Chucho" Navarro Moreno and Alfredo "El Güero" (The Fair-skinned One) Bojagil (which he shortened to "Gil") ran into Puerto Rican Hernando Aviles on Broadway. Navarro and Gil, who had already played in a group called Felipe Gil y Sus Caporales, were looking for a third partner to form a trio. They named themselves Los Panchos in tribute to famed Mexican revolutionary Pancho Villa.

Los Panchos debuted on May 14, 1944 in New York City's Teatro Hispano. From the beginning the group drew rave notices. Their appeal centered around their beautiful boleros, dulcet vocal harmonies, and, in particular, the ringing qualities of the *requinto,* a small high-pitched stringed guitar that Alfredo Gil developed in 1947. The *requinto* was smaller than a regular guitar and it could play higher notes. On Los Panchos's classics, like "Sin Ti" and "Rayito de Luna," Gil plucked the guitar strings to introduce the melody that immediately identified the songs. It was Los Panchos's signature sound, and one that would be emulated by later trios, especially by masters such as Gilberto Puente of **Los Tres Reyes** and Guillermo Rodríguez of Los Embajadores.

Los Panchos's initial success in New York's Latin community was duplicated in Mexico when they first toured there in 1948 and played at the famed radio station XEB, and later at the nightclub El Patio in Mexico City. Subsequent tours to Colombia, Brazil, Argentina, Chile, Puerto Rico, Spain, and even Japan cemented their reputation as the finest trio in the world. They played the most prestigious venues, including Radio City Music Hall, the Waldorf Astoria, and the Paramount in New York City. They impacted with a series of hit boleros, many of which they wrote, including "Perdida," "Rayito de Luna," "Una Copa Más," "Mí Último Fracaso," "Reloj," "Sin Ti," "La Mentira," and others.

By 1951, though, Aviles was tired of the road life, and he left the group abruptly during a tour of South America. Gil and Navarro found Raúl Shaw Moreno in Brazil to fill Aviles's shoes, but he lasted less than a year. From that point a succession of singers came and went through the late '80s, including Julio Rodríguez, Johnny Albino (at eleven years, he lasted the longest), Enrique Caceres, Ovidio Hernández, and Rafael Bazurto Lara. Aviles went on to form his own group, Cuarteto Aviles, without much success, and in the late '50s he formed Los Tres Reyes with the brothers Gilberto and Raúl Puente.

Aviles died in 1986. Navarro passed away in 1993.

In the history of the bolero, there has never been a more popular or successful trio than Los Panchos. During their extensive career, they recorded some 2,500 songs on 250-plus albums, including six in Japanese and two in Greek, and they appeared in fifty films. They sold millions of albums and their music is still played on classic format radio stations in Mexico.

In 1998 Los Panchos were honored with the Excellence Award at the Univision Premio Lo Nuestro Awards in Miami.

Since the '80s the bolero and trio music has enjoyed another resurgence thanks to other artists who record the classic, seemingly timeless boleros such as "Sin Ti" and "Reloj." Mexican pop singer **Luis Miguel** recorded three entire albums dedicated to the boleros, while emerging ranchera giant **Alejandro Fernández** specializes in the bolero ranchero.

50 Años (Sony)
Época de Oro (Sony)
Leyendas, Vol. 1 (Sony)
Tesoros Musicales Discos (Sony)

PAVOS REALES, LOS

Formed 1957, San Antonio, Texas

Los Pavos Reales were influential conjunto pioneers known for their vocal harmonies and signature polkas "Todos Dicen" and "Acábame de Matar."

As young boys, the Torres-García brothers were influenced by their father, Arturo Ramírez García, who was an accordionist from the Hacienda de Guadalupe in Rosita, Coahuila.

In 1945 accordionist Salvador Torres-García (born June 15, 1933, Seguin, Texas) formed the Conjunto Hermanos Torres-García with his brothers Pedro on guitar; Jesús "Jesse" on *bajo sexto;* and Nieves on string bass. The brothers played small gigs in the area until 1957, when younger brother Eduardo "Lalo" (born September 24, 1939, Clear Spring, Texas) joined on *bajo sexto* and the group became Los Pavos Reales.

The group gained a reputation as a solid unit, with precision playing on the accordion and *bajo sexto,* two instruments that were fundamental to the development of modern conjunto. Through the years the band survived on regional hits on indie labels, including Ideal, Corona, Lira, Sombrero, Cometa, and even under their own Pavo label. Both Salvador and Eduardo became prolific songwriters. Among their biggest hits were "Qué Chulada de Mujer," "El Corrido de Seguin," and "La Huella de Mis Besos."

In 1974 the seminal Tejano band **Latin Breed** recorded Eduardo's "Todos Dicen," a macho tune about taking on a bad relationship, and made it a major chart hit. Los Pavos kept recording through the mid-1970s on additional indies Bravo, DLB, and Joey International. In 1975 Los Angeles's Mayor Tom Bradley issued an official welcome proclamation to Los Pavos Reales for their excellent music. The following year Los Pavos Reales disintegrated when brothers Salvador and Eduardo went their separate ways.

At the 1989 Tejano Conjunto Festival older brother Salvador, known as "El Pavo Grande" (The Senior Pavo), was inducted into the Tejano Conjunto Hall of Fame. Throughout his career he recorded more than 150 original songs and has a catalog of fifty-plus albums. He performed on the same stage with international superstars such as **Pedro Infante, José Alfredo Jiménez, Lola Beltrán, Jorge Negrete, Trío Los Panchos,** and **Javier Solis.** He also appeared in the movie *La Mafia de la Frontera.* Accordionist/ songwriter **Nick Villarreal** credits Salvador with teaching him the intricacies of songwriting. Salvador was among the first to be invited to tour thirty-five states with the Smithsonian-sponsored Folklife American Tour.

Early Hits (Arhoolie)

PEGASSO DE POLLO ESTEVAN

See Pegasso, Grupo

PEGASSO, GRUPO

Formed 1980, Cerralvo, Nuevo León, México

Singer/musical director Emilio Reyna Villarreal formed the original version of Pegasso, a name taken from the Greek god Pegasus. Pegasso traded in organ-propelled cumbias and romantic ballads to angle its way into the top tier of the modern *onda grupera* age, influencing northern Mexican bands Toppaz and Zaaz. Pegasso's early hits included "Se Tambalea," "Para Olvidarme de Ti," and "Tu Imagen," written by keyboardist Oscar Mata Zavala.

But by the mid-1980s the group split up into Pegasso de Emilio Reyna and Pegasso de Federico "Pollo" Estevan, the original group's ex-guitarist. The groups took to fighting each other in the press and on album covers, in a mild precursor to the public feud by rappers Eazy-E and Dr. Dre. Eventually, Estevan's group won the exclusive right to the name Pegasso in 1996. They signed on with DISA/EMI Latin in 1997 and released *Rompiendo el Silencio.* In 1998 the band released *Soy el Mismo.*

Pegasso de Emilio Reyna changed its name to Pega Pega in 1996 and scored a comeback hit on Reyna's indie label JE Records with "Cosas del Amor." Reyna liked to claim his group was the first *onda grupera* outfit to join the anti-drug campaign, recording the just-say-no song *Pesadilla,* which was written by Mata, and making the video of the same name in conjunction with the Nuevo León Prosecutor General's office in 1991.

GRUPO PEGASSO

Sentir y Fantasía (PEG)
Solamente Baladas (FTA)

PEGASSO DE POLLO ESTEVAN

Rompiendo el Silencio (DISA/EMI Latin)
Soy el Mismo (DISA/EMI Latin)

PEÑA, EZEQUIEL

Born Ezequiel Peña Avalos, circa 1967, San José del Valle, Nayarit, México

As the lead singer for the **Banda Vallarta Show,** the upbeat and energetic Ezequiel Peña helped engineer the rise of the group as one of the most popular bandas in the early '90s.

Banda Vallarta—along with Banda Móvil and **Banda Machos**—was among the hottest groups when the banda genre exploded in Southern California in the early '90s. Peña left the band in late 1994 to pursue his solo career and recorded his first CD, *El Tirador,* with noted producer **Marco Antonio Solis.** His second CD included Peña's first hit, the title track, "Yo Vendo Unos Ojos Verdes."

Ezequiel Peña
Courtesy of FonoVisa

The youngest of twelve children, Peña was born on a ranch called San José del Valle in Nayarit. He started singing in school at the age of seven and his teacher saw that he was good, inviting him to sing for a local school celebration. His mother encouraged his singing, but his father opposed it. His mother had sung when she was young, but stopped when she met his father. At the age of fourteen Peña went to Puerto Vallarta to study accounting. He moved to California at the age of eighteen because he wanted to work in the U.S. He washed cars to buy a mariachi outfit, and later worked in a variety of jobs, including gardener, assistant bricklayer, carpenter, dishwasher, and caretaker of horses. While Peña was working as a truck driver his coworkers heard him sing and encouraged him. Peña had always counted ranchera singer **Antonio Aguilar** among his biggest idols and, using him as inspiration, he went on to win several talent shows at amateur night events.

His tenure with Banda Vallarta lasted from the group's start in 1988 to 1994. Peña's second solo CD, *Sentimiento Ranchero,* produced the song "Cuando el Destino Se Cobra," which peaked at No. 32 on the Billboard Hot Latin Tracks chart on March 8, 1996. He scored with additional hits, including "Ven y Ven," "Qué Chulada de Mujer," and "Me Fallo en el Amor."

El Tirador (FonoVisa)
No Más Contigo (FonoVisa)
Orgullo Ranchero (FonoVisa)
Yo Vendo Unos Ojos Verdes (FonoVisa)

PÉREZ, JAY

Born Jesse Pérez Jr., September 21, 1963, San Antonio, Texas

Jay Pérez
Courtesy of Sony Discos

Jay Pérez was eleven years old and had already sung in an elementary school choir when he was recruited by Mike DeLeon to join the R&B/pop group Young and Free. He later learned to play drums, but singing was his first love, something he pursued in the John Jay High School choir in San Antonio. In 1984 he got his first break when he was asked to play drums and sing for the local Top 40 cover band Mysterio. He left Mysterio in 1987 when he auditioned for and landed the lead singer position with **Latin Breed,** which had been the top Tejano group during the '70s with hits such as "Tejano Enamorado" and "Todos Dicen."

Pérez sang on the 1989 Latin Breed reunion album *Breaking the Rules,* which went on to win the 1990 TMA for album of the year. The excellent single "Ay Mujer," which featured Pérez's soaring vocals, was named TMA's song of the year.

In 1990 Pérez left Latin Breed when he got a better offer to join **David Lee Garza y Los Musicales.** Pérez was a major factor in producing Los Musicales's two landmark albums, *Con el Tiempo* and *1392,* which generated the radio hit singles "Qué Tristeza" and "Hasta Cuando" respectively. In late 1992 he left the band for a solo career with Sony Discos. Pérez organized a crack band to launch his career, including top musicians Gilbert Escobedo on sax, Gilbert Velasquez on guitar, Johnny Salazar on accordion, and Vicente "Chente" Barrera on drums. By 1998 all four would be gone, but Pérez's first three albums—all of which were produced by Gilbert Velasco— did well, generating the singles "Si Te Portas Mal," "Ven a Mí," and "Lo Que Tú Tienes." Pérez, like **David Marez** and a few other Tejano singers, has always had a healthy respect for '60s R&B artists. He recorded credible takes of Marvin Gaye's "Let's Get It On" and Al Green's "Let's Stay Together." Both songs are staples in his live shows. In 1994 Pérez was named best new artist in the regional Mexican category of the Billboard Latin Music Awards.

10 Years of Tejano (Sony Discos)
No Limits (Sony Discos)
Steel Rain (Sony Discos)
Te Llevo en Mí (Sony Discos)
The Voice (Sony Discos)

PINEDA, GUADALUPE

Born Guadalupe Lupita Pineda, circa 1962, Guadalajara, Jalisco, México

Guadalupe Pineda emerged as one of Mexico's most promising folkloric singers at the start of the '90s and she especially shined on bolero rancheros. She formed her first group, the folk band Sanampay, in 1977 and went solo in 1982. Her major influences were Mercedes Sosa, Nana Mouskuri, Aretha Franklin, and Ella Fitzgerald. Pineda showcased her torchy interpretive talents on her 1991 *Costumbres* CD, whose title track was her cover of the **Juan Gabriel** classic. Pineda also shone on the evergreen bolero "Cien Años." The album, which was produced by Tino Geiser, featured guest artists from Trío Los Sobaneros and Mariachi 2000.

Así como Tú (RCA)
Costumbres (RCA)
De Nuevo Sola (RCA)

PINKYS, LOS

Formed 1993, Austin, Texas

Polish American accordionist/*bajo sexto* player Bradley Jaye Williams's interest in conjunto music dates back to his teens when he was growing up in Saginaw, Michigan. His mother played polka music at home, his father was a jukebox distributor. In the early 1990s, Williams moved to San Francisco and joined the band Movie Stars, playing mandolin/button accordion.

In 1993 Williams moved to Austin and ran across accordionist/*bajo sexto* player Isidro Samilpa, whose credits include **Los Pavos Reales,** playing the local club circuit. The two shared their mutual appreciation of the accordion and conjunto polkas and teamed up as Los Pinkys. They produced two albums for Rounder, *Seguro Que Sí,* which produced the regional hit "Rosa Anna," and *Esta Pasión.* The latter was self-produced at Corpus Christi's Hacienda Studios. In 1998 Los Pinkys released an independently produced cassette, *Los Senderos,* and were looking for a record deal. The band won *Austin Chronicle*'s Music Award for best Tejano/conjunto band of the year in 1994 and 1995.

Esta Pasión (Rounder)
Seguro Que Sí (Rounder)
Los Senderos (Los Pinkys)

POLKA

Despite its European roots, the basic polka was appropriated by Mexican musicians at the turn of the century and reinvented as a native dance form. Polkas and rancheras, the primary song forms of Tejano and conjunto music, exhibit a staccato, *oompah-oompah* feel. Polka skips along at 110 to 120 beats per minute. In conjunto, it is sometimes accompanied by a shuffling dance called the *tacuachito* (little possum). The polka originated around 1840 in Bohemia, which is now the western Czech Republic. The dance, characterized by a jump step, quickly spread throughout Europe and caught on in Mexico City during the reign of Emperor Maximilian (1864–1867). As the music spread to provincial regions, it became a common rhythm in folk dances. Since then, it has remained the trademark rhythm for conjunto and norteño ensembles. Tejano and norteño groups often refer to polkas with romantic lyrics as rancheras, and to story-song polkas as corridos. Other acts have stricter definitions of the polka, often using the word to mean only accordion-led instrumentals. Tex-Mex groups also use brass and keyboards as lead instruments in their polkas.

PRISCILA Y SUS BALAS DE PLATA

Formed 1995, San Nicolás de Los Garza, Nuevo León, México

The sound and spirit of the late '90s norteño genre was invigorated by new faces like Priscila y Sus Balas de Plata, **Los Tiranos del Norte, Dinastía Norteña, Grupo Límite, Intocable,** and other young and daring groups.

The staid *norte* genre, which for years was dominated by heavy-set, middle-aged men, underwent a sound and image makeover in the mid-1990s. Now there are not only young hulks prowling the scene, but young female out in fronts singing, like Grupo Límite's Alicia Villarreal, **Carmen Jara,** and **Noemy.** Priscila, though, went one step further, she sang *and* played the accordion.

Priscila's 1995 debut CD, *Corazonadas,* generated a hit single, the melodic ranchera "Ay Corazón." Gaining versatility and confidence, the band quickly followed with its sophomore CD, *La Cantante,* which featured a Priscila original "Falsas Promesas," which also became a hit. That year the group's momentum was bolstered by a series of concerts during which it opened for norteño legends **Los Tigres del Norte** and **Bronco.**

Like the other mid-1990s sensation, Grupo Límite, Priscila specialized in the new romantic pop-norteño sound and, aiming at a new younger audience, wisely steered away from the controversial narco-corridos then in vogue among veteran norteño bands.

The band came together in San Nicolás de Los Garza, Nuevo León when Priscila, under the guidance of her father, the famed composer and producer Tirzo Paiz, teamed up with her brother Tirzo Jr. and sister Ursula. Using his connections and influence, Paiz helped his daughter to sing on national television at the age of five and later to appear in two Mexican movies. Priscila quickly learned guitar and piano. Eventually she learned accordion.

In 1994 Paiz assembled a band and, after shopping around its demo, got the group signed to FonoVisa. The group specialized in pop-norteño, a teen-friendly variation of the genre that includes country shuffles and blues-based licks along with the usual rancheras and cumbias.

Busco Novio (FonoVisa)
La Cantante (FonoVisa)

PUENTE, GILBERTO

See Tres Reyes, Los

PULIDO, ALMA

See Pulido, Roberto

PULIDO, BOBBY

Born Roberto Pulido Jr. April 25, 1973, Edinburg, Texas

Bobby Pulido successfully blended smooth vocals, smart song selection, and a solid band to rise to the top in the mid-1990s.

Despite initial criticism that he was riding on the hard-earned reputation of his famous father, the venerable Tejano pioneer **Roberto Pulido,** the younger Pulido patiently honed his vocal talents and wisely assembled a smart management team, which is key to the success of any group.

Pulido began playing with a local mariachi while he was in high school and soon after started playing in his father's band, Los Clásicos, filling in with sax and vocals. His break came when EMI released a compilation album *Branding Irons* in 1994, on which he was featured in a duet with his father called "Contigo." Then just twenty years old, Pulido dropped his business management studies a semester short of a degree at San Antonio's St. Mary's University to go into music full time.

Pulido debuted in September of 1995 with his CD *Desvelado,* which, according to EMI, sold more than 100,000 copies and included three songs written by Pulido. The singles "Desvelado" and "No Sé Por Qué" both broke into the Billboard Hot Latin Tracks chart. Pulido took time out of his career in July of 1996 to get married and then in September released his second CD, *Enséñame,* which included songs by Humberto Ramón and spun off the hits "Enséñame" and "Se Murió de Amor," which also landed on the Billboard Hot Latin Tracks chart.

Bobby Pulido
Courtesy of EMI Latin

In 1998 Pulido produced his next CD, *Llegaste a Mi Vida.* Later that year he won five of the twelve TMAs, including best male entertainer, best male vocalist, best Tejano crossover for "¿Dónde Estás?" and best album for *Llegaste a Mi Vida.*

Desvelado (EMI Latin)
Enséñame (EMI Latin)
Llegaste a Mi Vida (EMI Latin)

PULIDO, ROBERTO

Born March 1, 1950, Edinburg, Texas

Roberto "El Primo" (The Cousin) Pulido was recognized as the pioneer whose accordion and twin saxophone instrumentation helped bridge the traditional conjunto and the modern Tejano camps in the mid-1970s.

As a young boy, Pulido traveled with his migrant family, working the fields and picking crops. His first musical influence was his uncle and his band, Los Cardenales de Leonel Pulido. It was Leonel who took him under his wing, teaching Pulido music basics while working the fields. At the age of twelve, Pulido repaired his grandfather's old guitar and began playing and singing around the house. At the age of fifteen, then only a high school freshman, he joined Los Hermanos Layton of Elsa, Texas, and continued to play through his college years.

In the mid-1960s his father, José "Don Chuy" Pulido, purchased a saxophone for twenty dollars so that the younger Pulido could play in the high school band. As a senior in 1969, Pulido received several music scholarships and enrolled at Pan American University in Edinburgh, Texas, to study music. In 1970 he married Diana Montes, daughter of Mario Montes of **Los Donnenos,** and he began playing with Cecilio Garza y Los Kasinos of La Joya, Texas. In 1973 Pulido received his bachelor's degree in music and began teaching at the Pharr–San Juan–Alamo High School for a salary of $6,100 a year.

Music, however, was too big of a calling for Pulido, and after a short time he resigned from his teaching position. He established his own group—Roberto Pulido y Los Clásicos, which included uncle Leonel Pulido on accordion and brothers Roel and Joel on saxophones. A series of albums on indie labels produced only regional hits, including "Copa tras Copa," "Simplemente," "Señorita Cantinera," "No Nos Quieren, Corazón," and "La Flecha." Pulido won his first TMA for male vocalist in 1980. Pulido's band occasionally grew to ten members, including a *bajo sexto* player, but his recording output and touring strength were consistent through the late '80s.

In 1989 Pulido signed with the then-new player Capitol/EMI Latin, which bolstered his visibility and record sales. The following year Pulido joined **Vikki Carr** and a young **Emilio Navaira** at the first Go Tejano Day at the Astrodome for the Houston Rodeo.

In 1995 Pulido's son **Bobby Pulido** signed on with EMI after the two recorded a duet. In 1997 Pulido's daughter Alma also signed with EMI and she produced her own self-titled CD. In the '90s Pulido continued producing solid albums.

A Través de los Años (Capitol/EMI Latin)
Live (Capitol/EMI Latin)
Te Vi Partir (Capitol/EMI Latin)
Toro Prieto (Capitol/EMI Latin)
¿Qué Esperabas de Mí? (Freddie)

RAMÍREZ, AUGUSTIN

Born May 4, 1941, Lockhart, Texas

Augustin "El Guti" Ramírez learned to play the guitar as a teen after his family had moved to Austin from Lockhart because of financial difficulties.

In 1957, at the age of sixteen, he began his professional career, playing guitar and singing with Austin-based groups Dominoes, Cisco Rangel y Los Jesters, and the locally renowned Fred Salas y Los Latinos. Ramírez later noted that Salas, whom he considered to be one of his mentors, taught him the business of songwriting. In 1962 local orchestra leader Roy Montelongo "discovered" Ramírez and hired him as lead singer/guitarist, a union that produced the hit single "El Hijo de Sue."

In 1967 Ramírez struck out on his own, forming his own band and recording his first solo album, *Ojitos Traviesos,* on the indie Discos Grande label. His initial tour dates were packed affairs that generated a buzz in the industry. Eventually Johnny Gonzáles, president of El Zarape records, tracked him down and signed him to his label. From 1967 to 1971, Ramírez's popularity soared and he toured nationally on the strength of the hits "Tres Ramitas," "El Camaroncito," "Quiero Que Sepas," "Golpe Traidor," "Paloma, Déjame Ir," and—perhaps his biggest hit—the soulful ballad "Sangre de Indio." For several years Ramírez also featured two drummers in his band. Ramírez had hired a new drummer, but according to folklore he could not bring himself to fire the first drummer.

In late 1977 Ramírez also scored with "Qué Chulita Estás," on an album he recorded for Freddie Records. The next year he entered the nightclub business, opening his Dance Land Party House in Austin.

Augustin Ramírez
Courtesy of Freddie Records

Though his momentum had slowed considerably by the late '80s, Ramírez released albums periodically on his own indie label Guti Records, including *The Legendary Augustin Ramírez,* Vol. 1. In 1989 he signed with EMI Latin and released *The Legend is Back,* which produced the single "Lo Tengo Decidido."

In 1997 he was inducted into the TMA's Hall of Fame and the following year was recruited for the oldies project *Leyendas y Raices,* which featured other pioneers, including Carlos Guzmán, **Sunny Ozuna,** and **Freddie Martínez.**

Albur de Amor (Freddie)
Dámelo (Freddie)
Paloma, Déjame Ir (Freddie)
Para Mis Hijos (EMI)

RAMOS, RUBÉN

Born Rubén Pérez Ramos, February 9, 1940, Sugarland, Texas

A first-tier pioneer of modern Tejano music, Rubén Ramos developed a solid reputation as one of the smoothest singers and classiest bandleaders in the history of the genre. Like most Tejano artists, Ramos grew up listening to Mexican standards, blues, funk, and soul and, at his best, delivered a mesmerizing fusion that inevitably filled the dance floors. Like **David Marez, Jay Pérez,** and **Little Joe,** Ramos was at the top of his game when he was belting out the blues-drenched rancheras or riveting R&B tunes. And he also recognized that most Tejano fans also enjoy country, ranchera, pop-dance, salsa, and other forms as long as it is danceable—which has always been the essence of Tejano music.

Another distinction was Ramos's consistent use of a big band—a large group with a powerful horn section—sometimes with as many as four horn players. It was this element that elevated Ramos from the pack of clueless bands working the market. In Tejano history there have been few true big bands since the days of **Beto Villa** or **Isidro López. Latin Breed,** the **Royal Jesters,** and **Tierra Tejana** are among the few that followed this tradition.

Ramos came from a musical family. Although his father, Alfonso Ramos Sr., worked the cotton fields and the railroads, he also played the fiddle while his mother, Elvida Pérez, played the guitar at family gatherings. Ramos's older brother Alfonso Jr. (born 1936, Sugarland, Texas) joined their uncle's group, the Rubén Pérez Orchestra. Later Ramos dropped out of high school and joined as drummer. The band then became the Alfonso Ramos Orchestra. In his twenties Ramos went back to school for his GED and continued with the band on weekends, increasingly singing English cover R&B

tunes, even as he landed a "good job" with the state insurance department.

But in 1969 his brother Roy and other musicians left to form the Roy Montelongo Orchestra and the splintering faction asked him to help them form the Mexican Revolution. He did, leaving his brother Alfonso's group. But Ramos also faced a major crossroad in his career. It was time to either quit music or go into it full time. To do anything less would mean being relegated to the minor leagues forever. Fortunately for Ramos, and perhaps the industry, he jumped in full force and never looked back.

Rubén Ramos
Chris Borgman/Courtesy of Barb Wire

The name Mexican Revolution was picked, Ramos explained in later interviews, because, among other reasons, the '70s saw the emergence of the Chicano and civil rights movements. During that period, the band played the Chicano circuit that ran from Dallas–Fort Worth to the Rio Grande Valley, recording a number of albums on a series of independents. By 1981, though, Tejano had become the new term for the music and Ramos changed the band name to the Texas Revolution because he felt Tejanos were getting an identity in Texas.

In 1985 Alfonso and Rubén reunited for a series of albums that included *Back to Back, Again*. In 1987 Alfonso and Rubén were named best vocal duo at the 1987 TMAs. By this time Ramos had scored with the regional hit "El Gato Negro" (The Black Cat), which also became his nickname.

Through the '90s Ramos continued playing with a live horn section, eschewing the trend by many bands to substitute synthesizers and keyboards. In 1995 Ramos signed on with the Dallas-based indie Barb Wire and released one of his most popular CDs, *Nueve Vidas,* produced by noted keyboardist/arranger **Joel Guzmán,** which included the major hits "Paloma Negra," "Las Botellas," and "Voy Navegando." The video for the former won best video at the 1997 TMAs. Producer Bob Gallarza created additional magic on his 1996 *Visions* CD when he paired Alfonso, Rubén, and George Rivas for an inspired rendition of the **El Conjunto Bernal** classic "El Silencio de la Noche."

In 1998 Ramos teamed up with Guzmán again on the CD *El Gato Negro Smooth,* out of which came the singles "Un Suspiro" and "Tierras Planas del West."

Amor y Paz (Sony)
El Gato Negro y Paloma (Sony)
Nueve Vidas (Barb Wire)

RANCHERA

Sentimental, dramatic, and blues-drenched, the ranchera is the quintessential Mexican song form. Rancheras can be sung to a polka, bolero, or waltz beat. Polkas are most popular with Tejano/conjunto and norteño acts, and boleros and waltzes are preferred by mariachis and grupos.

During the Mexican Revolution, rancheras emerged as a popular song forms. Ranchera lyrics idealized rural life and celebrated unrequited love. During the golden age of Mexican cinema, **Jorge Negrete** and **Pedro Infante** personified the romantic singing cowboy of ranchera lore. The composer who best tapped into this sentiment was **José Alfredo Jiménez,** who had a knack for conveying the fears and frailties, hopes and dreams of everyday Mexicans. Many of his songs (he wrote more than 300) are considered classics, including "Ella," on accepting destiny, and "El Rey," about the ultimate macho spirit.

Both songs were interpreted definitively by Mexico's greatest ranchera singer since the 1960s, **Vicente Fernández,** who boasts an operatic voice and almost always sings with mariachi.

Tejano and norteño rancheras of the '90s featured romantic lyrics sung to a polka beat. However, mariachis and artists like **Los Temerarios** ("Mi Vida Eres Tú") and **Marco Antonio Solis** ("La Venia Bendita") continued recording smoky, emotional rancheras to a bolero or waltz beat.

RANCHERITOS DEL TOPO CHICO, LOS

Formed April 11, 1956, Monterrey, Nuevo León, México

First-tier norteño group Los Rancheritos del Topo Chico were founded by accordionist/songwriter Catarinos Leos Rodríguez with charter members Aurelio Pérez Rodríguez on bass; Ramiro Pérez on *bajo sexto;* Esteban Tirado on sax; and Francisco Villarreal on drums. In the '90s, Leos was the only remaining original member. Tirado was replaced by Roosvelt Delgado, father of former **Bronco** accordionist **Ramiro Delgado.** Ramiro González Garza, brother of the elder Delgado, replaced Pérez on *bajo sexto.*

In the course of forty-two years, Los Rancheritos have recorded more than seventy-four albums. Most of their biggest hits were written by Leos, including "Limosnas de un Hijo," "Chiquita Cariñosa," "Maldito Licor," "Me Tejaban," "¿Pa Qué y Por Qué?" "Imposible Olvidarte," "Mis Tres Grandes Amores," "Bodas de Plata," "Qué Quemadota," and "¿Dónde Estás, Juventud?" Although the band recorded on dozens of labels, its main output was produced on the Del Bravo label. Hits from the '80s included "Pero, ¿Cómo Voy a Olvidarte?" and "Sueño Bonito." By the '90s the group began to include more boleros and cumbias into its repertoire.

12 Éxitos Originales (EMI)
Árbol Torcido (EMI)
Boleros y Rancheras (CRP)
Cantan Boleros y Rancheras (CMI)

REHENES, LOS

Formed 1983, San José de Lourdes, Zacatecas, México

This keyboard-driven outfit was patterned on the **Los Bukis** mold, with lots of melodic cumbias and romantic ballads that focused on romantic discoveries and betrayals. The band was founded in 1983 in the small town of San José de Lourdes, some twenty kilometers outside of Fresnillo, Zacatecas, home of the famed **Los Temerarios** and Banda Toros. According to lead singer/songwriter, Javier Torres, the group took its name from the 1979 United States–Iran conflict when radical students took over the U.S. Embassy in Tehran.

The band produced four albums for Discos Rocillo in Durango, with limited success. In 1989 Los Rehenes released their fifth CD, which the band had decided would be its last, unless major success came along. Luckily, two singles hit big: "No Existe el Amor" and "Lágrimas de Coraje." In 1991 they scored again with *Corazones Rotos* and followed with "Limosnero de Cariño," from their debut DISA/FonoVisa CD, *Rehenes '92.*

Torres has written sixty percent of the band's material. The band includes two other founding members: Benajamin Torres on drums and Francisco Romo on keyboards. The others are: Jesús Ortega, guitar; Gerardo Torres, percussions; Robert Hernández, percussions/backing vocals; and Jesús Landeros, *bajo sexto.*

Verdades Que Duelen (DISA/FonoVisa)
16 Éxitos (DISA/FonoVisa)
Corazones Rotos (DISA/FonoVisa)
Todo Me Recuerda a Ti (DISA/FonoVisa)

RELÁMPAGOS DEL NORTE, LOS

Formed 1961, Reynosa, Tamaulipas, México; disbanded late 1971

Los Relámpagos del Norte were one of the most influential bands in the norteño genre. The seminal group was comprised of the legendary duo **Ramón Ayala** and **Cornelio Reyna.** Los Relámpagos were widely credited with bridging the rhythms of Mexican norteño and Texas conjunto music. The band has influenced countless artists—from **Los Traileros del Norte** to **Los Terribles del Norte, Intenso** to **Intocable.**

The fuse that would ignite Los Relámpagos first flickered in 1960 when accordionist Ayala, then fifteen years old, met songwriter/*bajo sexto* player Reyna, then twenty years old, at the Cadillac Bar in Reynosa's central square. Shortly afterward Ayala and Reyna formed a conjunto, playing on sidewalks, buses, cafes, and bars until accordionist Paulino Bernal discovered them and brought them to McAllen, Texas to record for his fledgling indie label, BEGO Records in 1963. The group settled on the name Los Relámpagos del Norte and recorded its first album, which produced the almost instant hits "Ya No Llores" and Bruno Villarreal's "Ingratos Ojos Míos." Reyna would later pen additional hits, including "Mi Tesoro," "Callejón sin Salida," "Hay Ojitos," "Mil Noches," and "Me Caí de las Nubes"—songs that would become part of the norteño canon.

During the mid-1960s, Los Relámpagos were huge on both sides of the U.S.-Mexico border, making it the first norteño duo to be successful in Texas.

In 1971 Los Relámpagos disbanded, reportedly amicably. Reyna wanted to persue acting in Mexico and sing with a mariachi. With the name Los Relámpagos "retired," Ayala quickly formed Los Bravos del Norte and kept on trucking. He signed with the then-expanding Freddie Records label, which Tejano superstar **Freddie Martínez** had just started, and remained in the norteño spotlight for the next three decades. Ayala and Reyna purchased homes one block apart in Hidalgo, Texas. The duo reunited for occasional concerts, most notably on May 15, 1991 at Expo Guadalupe in Monterrey, Nuevo León. They released *Juntos Para Siempre* on Freddie Records in 1995. Reyna died January 22, 1997, in Mexico City of complications from a ruptured ulcer.

20 Éxitos/En Concierto (Hacienda)
20 Éxitos Originales (SonoAmerica)
Popurrí de Éxitos, Vol. 3 (Hacienda)
Rey de Reyes (FonoVisa)

RENE Y RENE

Formed 1960, Laredo, Texas

Rene y Rene gained fame during the early '60s with saccharine bilingual hits "Lo Mucho Que Te Quiero" and "Angelito," which featured dulcet vocal harmonies. Singer/songwriter Rene Victor Ornelas (born 1936, Laredo, Texas) was born into a musical family. His father, Miguel Ornelas, conducted a Mexican American touring orchestra in which the younger Ornelas learned to play trumpet. The older Ornelas was inducted into the TMA's Hall of Fame in 1984.

Ornelas and high school friend Rene Herrera began as part of a harmony group known as the Quarter Notes in 1952. They enlisted in the U.S. Army in 1958 and continued to perform as a group at military events. After the service, Ornelas and Herrera auditioned for a small record company in San Antonio and soon recorded "Angelito," which reached No. 43 on the Billboard Top Pop Singles chart in 1964 and put them on the map.

In 1968 they followed up with the single "Lo Mucho Que Te Quiero," which reached No. 14 on the Billboard Top Pop Singles chart and was covered by over forty different artists. This hit led to the rerelease of "Angelito," which ended up on *Billboard*'s charts.

The duo could not repeat its success, though, and by 1974 it had split up. In 1979 Ornelas recorded "Cuando Vuelvo a México," a minor hit, and in the '80s produced several solo albums without chart success.

Época de Oro, Vol. 2 (Phonomaster)
Ganador (EMI)
El Perro (Joey International)
Quiero Pollo (Joey International)

REYES DEL CAMINO, LOS

Formed 1991, Monterrey, Nuevo León, México

The band, initially known as Los Arcangeles del Norte, transformed into Los Reyes del Camino when it signed with DISA/EMI Latin in 1994. Meaning "Kings of the Road," Los Reyes del Camino was a subtle reference to **Los Traileros del Norte** (Truck Drivers of the North), a group that was led by the father of Los Reyes del Camino's lead singer, Arnulfo López Jr. (born October 5, 1968, Monterrey, Nuevo León).

In 1994 the norteño band landed on the radio with the title track of its first album, *Ser Como Tú,* on DISA. López's fiery baritone bore an uncanny resemblance to his father's. The group later impacted with two title track "message" songs—"Muchacha Bonita" (1996), which warned that teenage sex led to single motherhood, and "Así Es la Vida" (1997), which warned that shacking up could lead to AIDS. Though the story-song format of these hits seemed to lend itself to a corrido rhythm, the songs were actually cumbias, a rhythm more popular with the female target audience. Both were sung by Gilberto Rodríguez Alanis, the group's tenor. In 1996 López was in an accident that left him blind in the right eye. Shortly after he had recovered enough to rejoin the group, López left to form his own outfit, Arnulfo Jr. Rey y As.

LOS REYES DEL CAMINO

Así Es la Vida (DISA/EMI Latin)
Muchacha Bonita (DISA/EMI Latin)
Ser Como Tú (DISA/EMI Latin)
Sólo Para Enamorados (DISA/EMI Latin)

ARNULFO JR. REY Y AS

Con la Ayuda de Dios (DISA/EMI Latin)
Para una Mujer (DISA/EMI Latin)

REYES LOCOS, LOS

Formed circa early 1970s, Nueva Rosita, Coahuila, México

These tropical cumbia merchants originally started out as a rock 'n' roll band known as the Crazy Kings. But after finding the road to be not lucrative, they translated the name and switched to tropical cumbias.

The original nine members met at Catholic church functions in their hometown of Nueva Rosita, where, according to band folklore, the priest, Padre Velez, helped the young musicians get sound equipment. With solid feverish cumbias—such as 1989's "Margarita" and 1992's "Suave Pa' Bailar,"—the band built a steady base and maintained an ever-increasing profile on radio.

Their 1994 novelty hit, "El Llorón," which was performed in a falsetto rap by vocalist Julián Tristán, helped Los Reyes become hot property. The song spawned exploitative remixes and parodies. Los Reyes Locos followed up with the similarly high-pitched "Mi Teta" in 1995. Longtime vocalist José Luis Benavides departed and the group's singles returned to more representative tropical output. Their 1997 CD, *Flores Para Mi Novia,* produced the radio faves "Apaga la Luz" and the title track.

El Ascensor (DISA)
Chones (DISA)
Flores Para Mi Novia (EMI)
Qué Susto (EMI)
Te Amaré a Escondidas (DISA)

REYES, LUCHA

Born María de la Luz Flores Aceves, May 23, 1906, Guadalajara, Jalisco, México; died June 25, 1944, Mexico City, México

With her powerful operatic voice and intense emotional delivery, Lucha Reyes became widely recognized as the first "Reina de los Mariachis" (Queen of the Mariachis). In 1920 her family moved to Mexico City, where Reyes, then only thirteen years old, sang corridos of the Mexican Revolution in vaudevillian shows at Plaza San Sebastián, alternating with Hermanos Acevedo and José Limón. She later traveled to Los Angeles, where she studied opera and became a lyrical soprano. Returning to Mexico, she was contracted to sing at the Teatro Esperanza Iris and Teatro Lirico and then joined Trio Reyes-Ascencio, where she formally took her stepfather's last name. Reyes's popularity peaked in 1930 when she performed at the famed radio station XEW and became the first female to sing in a mariachi. **Jorge Negrete,** who would later become Mexico's first *charro cantor* (singing cowboy), was said to have been influenced by Reyes. Like Reyes, Negrete was an operatic singer whose initial forays into the ranchero genre were not well received. Reyes toured the U.S. and Mexico. Among her biggest hits were "La Tequilera," "El Herredero," Chucho Monge's "La Feria de las Flores," and "Guadalajara," the signature patriotic song written by José "Pepe" Guizar in 1937. On June 25, 1944, Reyes died of an overdose of barbiturates.

12 Éxitos Rancheros (RCA)
15 Éxitos de Lucha Reyes (RCA)
Camden: Colección del Siglo (RCA)

REYNA, CORNELIO

Born September 16, 1940, Saltillo, Coahuila, México; died January 22, 1997, Mexico City, México

Cornelio Reyna was the songwriting half of the legendary norteño duo **Los Relámpagos del Norte,** which helped define the early '60s norteño music age.

Reyna was only sixteen years old when he began playing the *bajo sexto* (twelve-string guitar), singing and writing songs in Saltillo, Coahuila. Later he joined accordionist Juan Peña in Dueto Carta Blanca. But in 1960 Reyna ran across accordionist **Ramón Ayala,** then just fifteen years old, at the Cadillac Bar in Reynosa's central square. The duo soon christened itself Los Relámpagos del Norte and began an eight-year reign as a major force in norteño music. Los Relámpagos commercialized the elemental norteño sound, which featured the accordion and *bajo sexto* as the backing rhythms for melancholy corridos, punchy polkas, and fiery rancheras. The '60s belonged to Los Relámpagos, which emerged as a powerhouse, scoring consistently with such hits as "Te Traigo Estas Flores," "Un Día con Otro," and "Sufriendo Penas." Reyna gained a solid reputation as a formidable songwriter, penning such classics as "Mil Noches,"

"Callejón sin Salida," "Me Caí de las Nubes," and "Hay Ojitos."

In 1971 the group split up and Reyna began a prolific career singing with mariachis in Mexican films. He starred in over thirty movies, including *Me Caí de las Nubes* and *Lágrimas de Mi Barrio*. Reyna wrote **La Mafia**'s 1987 hit "Si Tú Supieras" and sang with La Mafia singer Oscar de la Rosa on the recorded version. Reyna went on to record more than two dozen albums, forming Los Reyes del Norte and reuniting with Ayala for the 1995 CD *Juntos Para Siempre*. Reyna died January 22, 1997, in Mexico City of complications from a bleeding ulcer. He was fifty-six years old. In early 1997 his son Cornelio Jr. was signed to Sony Discos and released an album *Ayer y Hoy*, which included unreleased songs written by his father.

CORNELIO REYNA

15 Éxitos Norteños (Freddie)
Del Cielo Cayó Una (Freddie)
Collar de Caracoles (Freddie)
Disco de Oro/25 Éxitos Gigantes (Freddie)
Eres Igual Que (Freddie)

CORNELIO REYNA JR.

Ayer y Hoy (Sony)

REYNA, CORNELIO, JR.

See Reyna, Cornelio

REYNOSO, JUAN

Born circa 1910, Santo Domingo, Guerrero, México

A virtuoso violinist, Juan Reynoso excelled at playing *sones* and *gustos*—folk rhythms still popular in the Tierra Caliente of western Mexico. Reynosa picked up his first violin at the age of five and, under the tutelage of poet/composer Isais Salmeron, learned the *gustos* and other local dance music. Often accompanied by harp, guitars, and percussion, Reynoso took his fellow musicians on a wild ride of improvisation and only played with the best. His work was captured on the 1993 Corason/Rounder CD *Paganini of the Tierra Caliente* (Paganini of the Mexican Hot Lands). On December 17, 1997, Reynoso received Mexico's prestigious National Arts and Sciences Award for his cultural contribution.

Paganini of the Tierra Caliente (Paganini of the Mexican Hot Lands) (Corason/Rounder)
Plays, Sones, & Gustos (Corason/Rounder)

RIELEROS DEL NORTE, LOS

Formed 1984, Hobbs, New Mexico

Los Rieleros del Norte peaked in the norteño genre in the late '80s when singer/bass player Leopoldo "Polo" Urías Ramírez, a native of Ojinaga, Chihuahua joined their ranks. The other members, musicians from the cities of Ojinaga and Chihuahua, had been playing with a singer named Milo Melendez, but in 1985, after the band's debut album on Joey International, Melendez was replaced by Urías.

With a solid bottom section and Daniel Esquivel's shimmering accordion runs, Los Rieleros hit their stride in 1990 with their big album *En Gira Internacional*, which featured the radio singles "Amor Prohibido" and "La Collección de Ester." The string of hits followed with "Me Contaron Ayer," "La Que Iba a Ser Mi Mujer," "¿Para Qué Quieres Que Vuelva?" and "¿Ya Para Qué?"

Urías left in 1995 to form **Polo Urías y Su Máquina Norteña** and Esquivel took over lead singer duties.

Éxitos del Siglo (FonoVisa)
El Invencible (FonoVisa)
El Maquinista (FonoVisa)
Tendré Que Compartir (FonoVisa)

ROBLES, ELISEO

Born November 19, 1958, Valle Hermoso, Tamaulipas, México

At the age of fourteen, singer/*bajo sexto* player Eliseo Robles joined Los Satelites, a group formed by Fidel Ayala, brother of **Ramón Ayala.** Robles first gained fame when he joined Ramón's group **Los Relámpagos del Norte** in the early '80s as the lead singer, replacing Tony Sauceda. Robles recorded on more than two dozen of Ayala's albums. He sang leads on such hits as "Mujer Paseada," "Chaparra de Mi Amor," "Juanita y Miguel," and the corrido "Gerardo González." By the mid-1980s, Robles left to form Los Bárbaros del Norte with brothers Noé, Ricardo, and César Hernández. Bárbaros's hits were "Cada Vez," "El Texano," and "Un Diez de Mayo." He also recorded an album with banda accompanied by Los Coyonquis.

Con los Bárbaros del Norte (Balboa)
Eliseo Robles (Balboa)
Necesito Olvidarla (Ramex)
Simplemente (Ramex)
Soberbia (PolyGram)

ROBLES, SALOMÓN, Y LOS LEGENDARIOS

Formed 1990, Monterrey, Nuevo León, México

Salomón Robles y Los Legendarios mined the norteño genre with solid rancheras and rhythmic cumbias. Salomón Robles launched his musical career in 1987 in his hometown of Villahermosa with Los Pirates del Norte. In 1990, though, the singer/songwriter split off on his own and moved to Monterrey to form Los Legendarios, eventually releasing thirteen LPs on the DISA label.

His 1998 CD, *Llegando Más Alto,* on DISA/EMI Latin produced the single "Todavía Duele" and included songs by Robles, Tirzo Paiz, Miguel Angel Alfaro, and Manuel Alejandro. Robles also played *bajo sexto* and his later hits included "Por Orgullo," "Niña Mia," "Mi Manera de Querer," and "Mujer de Dos Amigos."

Enamórate de Mí (DISA/EMI Latin)
La Hora de la Leyenda (DISA/EMI Latin)
La Ley del Corrido (DISA/EMI Latin)
Llegando Más Alto (DISA/EMI Latin)
Por Favor No Me Compares (DISA/EMI Latin)

RODARTE, LOS

Formed circa mid-1980s, Durango, Durango, México

Originally a group of brothers from Mexico, Los Rodarte launched their professional career in Chicago, Illinois in the mid-1980s. The group specialized in catchy, heartbroken ballads and cumbias sung in minor keys, most notably "No Soy un Cualquiera," "Guadalupe," "Hoy Tengo Ganas de Ti," and "Que Soy Pobre, Ya Lo Sé." Led by vocalist Eduardo Rodarte, Los Rodarte were regular players on *Billboard*'s singles and album charts in the early '90s. Original vocalist Adolfo Rodarte died in a car accident in January 1995. The group released its fifth album, *Silueta,* in 1997. It featured "Juntos," which was sung by Adolfo (before his death) and Eduardo and was included on the album as a tribute to Adolfo.

Devuelve Mi Cassette (FonoVisa)
Ellas (CBS)
Esta Vez (Sony)
Pensando En Ti (Sony)
Todo por el Todo (CBS)

RODRÍGUEZ, JOHNNY

Born Juan Raúl Davis Rodríguez, December 10, 1951, Sabinal, Texas

Although **Freddy Fender** may have made a bigger impact with his early 1975 country hit "Before the Next Teardrop Falls," Johnny Rodríguez was the first real Mexican

American country superstar. His single on Mercury Records, "You Always Come Back to Hurting Me," reached No. 1 on the Billboard Top Country Singles Sales chart in March 1973, almost two years before Fender's arrival.

But before he made it into the charts, Rodríguez made it into the local jail for goat rustling. Later on, he struggled with an admitted drug addiction.

As a young boy, Rodríguez (who was one of nine children) was influenced by Bob Seeger and the late Bob Willis. Rodríguez moved to Nashville in 1971 and through luck and opportunity soon fronted the Tom T. Halls Band. At this time he also began writing songs. Within a year, he recorded his first song, "Pass Me By," for Mercury. It reached No. 9 on the Billboard Top Country Singles Sales chart. Later in 1972 he released his debut CD, *Introducing Johnny Rodríguez,* which also made the country Top 10. Rodríguez recorded a bilingual Tejano album in 1989 for Capitol/EMI Latin titled *Coming Home,* which produced the singles "El Senderito" and "Las Penas." But he is better known for his country efforts. In the early '90s Rodríguez was playing gigs in Central Texas, mixing country, Mexican oldies, and Tejano.

Coming Home (Capitol/EMI Latin)

ROJAS, NYDIA

Born Nydia Myrna Rojas Verdin, March 28, 1981, Whittier, California

Nydia Rojas may be accurately described as the LeAnn Rimes of mariachi. Like Rimes, she was just a teen when she started her career, but she quickly impressed audiences with her vocal power, range, and control—especially on the passionate rancheras. At her 1996 debut at the South by Southwest music conference in Austin, Texas, Rojas proved that, though young, she could project more emotional intensity than singers twice her age.

Born in Whittier, California she grew up in Guadalajara, Jalisco. Rojas fell in love with Mexican music when, at the age of four, she saw the famous Mexican film *Nosotros los Pobres,* which starred the great ranchera singer **Pedro Infante.** According to family lore, Rojas was so moved she learned the lyrics to "Amorcito Corazón."

Although initially discouraged by her parents, Rojas persisted in making music her vocation. Her mother made her learn the *vihuela,* guitar, violin, and *guitarrón* before she finally relented, allowing her daughter to follow her passion. Rojas later studied with Heriberto Molina (who was an original member of **Mariachi Vargas de Tecalitlán**) and was soon enrolled in the Mariachi Heritage Society Program at the Los Angeles Music and Art School, where she was tutored by another master, founder José A. Hernández of **Mariachi Sol de México.** There Rojas learned how to read and write music.

Nydia Rojas
Courtesy of Olivia Rojas

In 1991 Rojas became the lead vocalist for the all-female **Mariachi Reyna de Los Angeles.** By 1995 she had recorded the Spanish theme song for *Don Juan de Marco,* a film starring Marlon Brando and Johnny Depp. The following year she signed with Arista/Latin and her self-titled debut CD included her inspired reading of the **José Alfredo Jiménez** classic "No Me Amenaces," as well as "La Número Uno," Rojas's Spanish rendition of Blondie's "The Tide Is High." The video for "La Número Uno" became the first all-Spanish video to air on MTV and MTV2. The CD also included "Hay Unos Ojos," a duet with Ricardo Castillon of **La Diferenzia,** and original compositions by Rojas.

Her second CD, *Florecer,* was produced by Carlos C. Junior (who also produced **Ana Gabriel**) and recorded at (ex-**Los Bukis**) **Marco Antonio Solis**'s studio in Mexico City. It had a pop/romantic ballad tilt and featured songs from **Juan Gabriel,** Aníbal Pastor, and Ana Gabriel. But despite her foray into the pop side, Rojas still delivered solid work on traditional songs such as "Mi Llanto Vale Más," a tune about the understanding that comes when love walks out the door.

Florecer (Arista)
Nydia Rojas (Arista)

RONSTADT, LINDA

Born July 15, 1946, Tuscon, Arizona

As a little girl, Linda Ronstadt grew up listening to the Mexican ranchera diva **Lola Beltrán.** Beltrán was her biggest influence and Ronstadt even admitted that her goal was to be the world's greatest Mexican singer.

Ronstadt was raised in a musically-inclined half-Mexican and half-German family. Her father, Gilbert Ronstadt, was a piano player and her paternal grandfather was a one-time mariachi orchestra leader in Tuscon. In addition, her aunt, an actress known as Luisa Espinel, was a singer and dancer.

In 1964, after her freshman year at the University of Arizona, Ronstadt moved to Los Angeles and helped form the rock group the Stone Poneys. She eventually went solo and produced a series of successful folk rock and country albums. In 1987 she released the critically acclaimed Spanish-language folk album *Canciones de Mi Padre,* which peaked at No. 42 on The Billboard 200 chart and eventually sold more than a million copies as well as won a Grammy in the best Mexican American performance category. The album included the classics "Por un Amor," "Hay Unos Ojos," and "Tú, Sólo Tú." Ronstadt said *Canciones* was inspired by her father, who used to sing the classic Mexican songs at home when she was a little girl. Produced by Peter Asher and Rubén Fuentes (who also arranged and conducted), the album included the world famous **Mariachi Vargas de Tecalitlán.**

Because Ronstadt was not fluent in Spanish, it took her fifteen to thirty hours to learn each song, practicing constantly until it came naturally. The subsequent Canciones tour was very successful. In 1991 she followed up with *Más Canciones,* which was produced by George Massenburg and Rubén Fuentes. The CD included the classics "El Toro Relajo," "Gritenme, Piedras del Campo," and "Siempre Hace Frío," but sales did not match the first one.

Canciones de Mi Padre (Asylum)
Más Canciones (Asylum)

ROYAL JESTERS, THE

Formed 1956, San Antonio, Texas; disbanded February 1977

The thread that led to the creation of the Royal Jesters began when Henry Hernández dropped out of the local band, the Five Angels, and teamed up with fellow Lanier High School students Oscar Lawson and Mike Pedraza. The new group was called the Young Ones and they were heavily influenced by both the *trío romántico* music and the doo-wop rhythms that were then popular on the airwaves.

The Royal Jesters; (from left to right) singer Oscar Lawson, singer Henry Hernández, and singer Dimas Garza
Courtesy of Manuel D. Castillo

The Young Ones played a mix of rock 'n' roll and Mexican traditional music at family gatherings and private parties. To reflect both their Mexican and Motown influences, they changed their name in 1958 to the Royal Jesters and later added a horn section. They followed with a series of singles that met with regional success, including "My Angel of Love," "Your Dreamy Eyes," and later on Cobra Records "Ask Me to Move a Mountain," "Let's Kiss and Make Up," and "I Want to Be Loved." They followed with additional singles on JOX records, including "Please Say You Want Me," "Wishing Ring," and "Muchachita."

Until that point success had been moderate and so in 1964 the Jesters decided to try their hand at hit-making, creating their own label, Jester Records, and releasing "Wisdom of a Fool," "We Go Together," "Lady Sunshine," "Manning Ave," and "That Girl."

In 1972 the group switched from Top 40 to Chicano music and released its first Tejano album, *Yo Soy Chicano,* which produced the hit "Soy Chicano." The album made *Billboard*'s Hot Latin LPs Special Survey charts in 1976. The follow-up albums, *Chicanita, Soy Feliz,* and *Latin Rhapsody* also landed on *Billboard*'s charts.

During the '70s, the band was a revolving door for a succession of singers: Joe Jama, **David Marez,** Dimas Garza, George Rivas, Joe Posada, and others. At the peak of their popularity, the Royal Jesters split up in February 1977. In 1995 they signed with BMG/U.S. Latin and released the tribute album, which featured a remix of the hit "Soy Chicano" as well as other classics by **Joe Bravo** ("Qué Casualidad"), **Jimmy Edward** ("Tú, Prieto"), **Sunny Ozuna** ("Reina de Mi Amor"), and **Rene y Rene** ("Angelito").

Tribute (RCA)

RUTH

Born Ruth Howard, February 11, 1973, Canton, Ohio

Green-eyed Ruth sang in school choirs, but she was chiefly influenced by the Monterrey, Nuevo León music scene while studying Spanish as an exchange student. She sang for local groups before getting signed by BMG/U.S. Latin stateside in 1996 and recording her debut CD, *Toquecito,* a harmonic work that included the radio faves "Toquecito," a pop-cumbia, and "Eres Mi Todo," a finger-snapping polka, and that was produced by rock guitarist Michael Morales. Ruth also impressed on the heartbreaking ranchera "No Quiero a Nadie."

Toquecito (BMG/U.S. Latin)

SALDIVAR, MINGO

Born Domingo Saldivar, May 29, 1936, Marion, Texas

Mingo Saldivar was only twelve years old when he began playing his guitar at home as his parents sang around the house. Back in the late '40s, music was his family's only source of entertainment. A year later he picked up his first accordion and began playing informally with Los Chavalitos.

Mingo Saldivar
Courtesy of Hacienda Records

Saldivar began his professional career in 1959 when he joined Los Guadalupanos, which during their short life (the band became **Los Aguilares**) included such players as Oscar Tellez, Toby Torres, and George y Mague. Saldivar had already started to write songs when he produced the band's first big hit, "Andan Diciendo," which also turned into a conjunto classic. Interestingly enough this hit song was on the flip side of the single release "Los Que Dios Recoge," which was supposed to be the hit. Two years later Saldivar joined **Los Caminantes,** replacing **Flaco Jiménez** (who had been drafted into the Army and shipped to Korea).

In 1964 Saldivar moved to Anchorage, Alaska to help his parents run a Mexican restaurant. There, a restless Saldivar formed Los Latinos, a group consisting of air force and army musicians. Saldivar liked to brag that Los Latinos became the first conjunto in Alaska. Saldivar developed a taste for country. He wrote original bilingual lyrics and new arrangements for country songs like "Marie" and Johnny Cash's "Rueda de Fuego" (Ring of Fire). Saldivar also became known for his energetic stage show. He would hang his accordion at waist level, while swinging, dancing, and singing. In 1970 Saldivar returned to San Antonio and later formed his own group, Mingo Saldivar y Sus Tremendos Cuatro Espadas. He has produced fourteen albums on Hacienda, TH-Rodven, Joey International, and his own label, Espada. In 1993 Saldivar was invited to perform for President Clinton's Inaugural Celebration in Washington, D.C.

El Chicano Alegre (Hacienda)
I Love My Freedom, I Love My Texas (Rounder)
Mírame (Hacienda)
Pájaro Negro (Hacienda)
Rueda de Fuego/20 Super Hits (Hacienda)

SALGADO, MICHAEL

Born Miguel Salgado, April 5, 1971, Big Spring, Texas

As a young boy, Michael Salgado was influenced by his father, Ernie Salgado, who played with Conjunto Alegría. In 1986, when the family lived in Rankin, Texas, the group became Los Salgados del Norte, a family group that included Michael, vocals/accordion; brother, Ernie Jr., *bajo sexto;* uncle James Salgado, drums; and cousin Joe Tanguma, bass.

Michael Salgado
Courtesy of Joey International

Los Salgados recorded four albums with Joey International in the early '90s but did not flourish until 1994 when Michael took the lead and recorded the CD that contained the title track, "Cruz de Madera," the old norteño classic. The single shot to No. 1 at Tejano and regional Mexican stations all over the Southwest and for good reason. The song, like the album, paid tribute to the glory days of early authentic norteño with thumping bass lines, floor-rattling percussions, and Salgado's weaving accordion runs. Salgado's fluid vocals carried echoes of a young **Ramón Ayala,** who incidentally was Salgado's biggest hero.

By the mid-1990s Salgado's Tejano/norteño fusion was producing consistent muscular cumbias and intense, accordion-fueled polkas that had him standing a head above the bland covers-for-inspiration game that was afflicting the Tejano industry.

Salgado's next release was *En Concierto,* which contained a tribute medley of **Los Relámpagos del Norte** hits called "Recordando Los Relámpagos." This album also included the hit "Sin Ella," written by Jorge Alejandro. The release of Salgado's next album, *De Buenas Raices,* included Salgado's bluesy-bolero take on **José Alfredo Jiménez**'s "La Media Vuelta" and the tense but rhythmic Valenzi-penned cumbia "Palomita Blanca." In the former, Salgado slowed the tempo and delivered new poignancy in this song about sacrificing ego for emotional deliverance. In 1998 Salgado won a TMA for conjunto traditional album of the year with *Un Recuerdo Especial.*

En Concierto (Joey International)
Cruz de Madera (Joey International)
De Buenas Raices (Joey International)
Mí Primer Amor (Joey International)
Un Recuerdo Especial (Joey International)

SAMURAY, GRUPO

Formed 1989, Rincón de Romos, Aguascalientes, México

Grupo Samuray rose quickly in the early '90s with its youthful energy and infectious ballads. Also key to the band's success was the angst-ridden vocals of singer/musical director Ignacio Romo. The self-proclaimed "Guerreros de Amor" (Warriors of Love), Samuray was a proficient merchant of syrupy romantic ballads, gaining radio play with the hot singles "Tiernas Mentiras," "Todo por Tu Amor," "Contigo o sin Ti," and "Nada Va a Cambiar Mi Amor por Ti," a cover of Glenn Medeiros's "Nothing's Gonna Change My Love for You." The group occasionally picked up the pace, displaying energetic enthusiasm on cumbias "Me Vale Chetos" and the novela-like "La Vuelta." The band's 1997 release, *Al Rojo Vivo,* featured songs by **Marco Antonio Solis, Joan Sebastián,** and Ciro

Paniagua, and included the hit single "Él Soy Yo."

15 Hits (EMI)
15 Para Ti (FonoVisa)
Al Rojo Vivo (EMI)
Cuando Amanezca (FonoVisa)
Todo México Lo Sabe (FonoVisa)

SÁNCHEZ, CHALINO

Born Marcelino Sánchez, August 30, 1960, Guayabo, Sinaloa, México; died May 16, 1992, Culiacan, Sinaloa, México

With his knack for writing descriptive and controversial narco-corridos (which are akin to gangsta-raps) in the early '90s, Chalino Sánchez rose quickly to become one of the most notorious and popular norteño singer/songwriters.

After sneaking into the United States in 1977, Sánchez found employment in the Los Angeles area as a farmworker, dishwasher, car salesman, and "coyote," or immigrant smuggler. An admirer of Mexican general Pancho Villa, Sánchez wrote his first corrido in 1984 about his brother who had been shot to death in Tijuana. Sánchez soon became known for writing corridos "on commission" for family, friends, or anyone who would pay. By 1987 Sánchez had talked several local bands into recording his songs.

He formed his own band, but because of his controversial narco-corridos, he was unable to get radio play. Unfazed, Sánchez began producing and distributing his own tapes at swap meets and car washes in Los Angeles, eventually attracting a bigger following. Interestingly, Sánchez did not fit the norteño star image. He had slurred speech and plain looks. According to folklore, Sánchez customarily wore a pistol onstage.

Despite the shutout by radio, Sánchez continued gaining popularity. In January 1992 Sánchez was shot onstage while performing in Coachella, twenty miles east of Palm Springs, California. According to police reports, Sánchez fired back. All told, there was one dead and several wounded. Sánchez's popularity exploded, and, after he recovered, his asking price per nightly performance reportedly rose from $1,500 to $10,000.

Sánchez recorded eighteen albums in his career, some of them for Musart, others for the Cintas Acuario label. His best-known hits were "Nieve de Enero," "Alma Enamorada," "El Pitallón," "El Navegante," "Una Tarde," and "El Pávido Navido."

On May 16, 1992, the day after a performance in Culiacan, Sinaloa, Sánchez was found dead beside a highway. He had been shot twice in the back of the head. Sánchez's death earned him even more notoriety and street credibility, eventually turning him into a folk legend. His CDs and tapes sold even faster. By 1995 officials with Cintas Acuario had inked a P&D deal with EMI Latin, a major label whose international marketing and promotional muscle meant Sánchez's recordings would reach a wider audience and generate even bigger sales.

Dos Grandes Sinaloenses (EMI Latin)
Un Homenaje al Mariachi (EMI Latin)
Mis Mejores Canciones (EMI Latin)
Monarca/Dos Grandes Sinalonenses (EMI Latin)
Nieves de Enero (Balboa)
Que Me Entierren Cantando (CIA)

SÁNCHEZ, CUCO

Born circa 1925, Altamira, Tamaulipas, México

Being in the Mexican military, Cuco Sánchez's father was transferred periodically. As a result, Sánchez traveled throughout Mexico as a child. Eventually, he moved to Mexico City.

Sánchez began writing in 1937 and ultimately proved to be a prolific songwriter. Among his best songs were "Qué Rechulo Es Querer" and "Mi Chata." His compositions were frequently tapped for Mexican movies, such as "Anillo de Compromiso," from the movie of the same name. His first hit as a singer was the now-standard "Grítenme, Piedras del Campo," which has been covered by hundreds of artists, including **Linda Ronstadt** in her 1987 Grammy-winning landmark CD, *Canciones de Mi Padre.* As an actor, Sánchez appeared in more than twenty soap operas, including 1997's *Esmeralda.* He has recorded twenty-five albums and over 200 singles.

Corridos Famosos (Sony)
Cuco Sánchez: La Voz de México (Sony)
Si Quieres Más (Sony)
Toda una Vida (Sony)
Voz de México (Sony)

SANDOVAL, CHRIS

Born Crisoforo Sandoval, December 17, 1924, Laredo, Texas

Singer/bandleader Chris Sandoval was a first-tier Tejano pioneer alongside **Beto Villa, Isidro López,** and Pedro Bugarin. These men helped lay the foundation for the Orquesta Tejana, a big-band genre that played accordion-spiced conjunto polkas, boleros, and big-band waltzes. Sandoval organized his ten-piece orchestra in the mid-1940s and reigned as a popular outfit from the mid-1950s through the early 1960s, playing a mix of big-band tunes, waltzes, boleros, and rancheras. His biggest hits were "Estando Yo Contigo," which was written by José Morantes, and "Porque Eres Tan Mala," which was written by Juan "Colorado" García. Famed accordionist Paulino Bernal, who would go on to form the seminal **El Conjunto Bernal,** also played with Sandoval. In 1983 Sandoval was inducted into the TMA's Hall of Fame. Performing at the ceremonies were then-new acts **Roberto Pulido** y Los Clásicos and a ten-year-old **Selena.**

Appears on:

Chris Sandoval (Arhoolie)
Pioneer of Tejano Music (Arhoolie)
Tejano Roots (Arhoolie)
Tejano Roots Orquestas Tejanas (Arhoolie)

SEBASTIÁN, JOAN

Born José Manuel Figueroa circa 1951, Juliantla, Guerrero, México

Joan Sebastián
Courtesy of Balboa/Discos Musart

Raised in a farming family, singer Joan Sebastián earned a reputation as a prolific songwriter, penning hits for **Vicente Fernández, Los Dinnos, Lucero, Rocío Durcal,** and others. Sebastián was also a talented producer, helming projects for Durcal, Mercedes Castro, and **Pepe Aguilar.** He started out as a ballad singer, but Sebastián also recorded cumbia, mariachi, and banda albums, scoring his biggest hit with the banda CD *Con Tambora,*

Vol. 1, on Musart. Like **Antonio Aguilar,** Sebastián also presented concerts in a Mexican rodeo setting. In 1995 he starred in the *telenovela* show *Tú y Yo* with Maribel Guardia, with whom he had a son, Julián, who was named after his pueblo.

In the mid-1990s, Sebastián's son from a previous marriage, José Manuel Figueroa (born 1975, Chicago, Illinois; he does not use Jr.) debuted with critically acclaimed ranchera CD, *Expulsado del Paraíso,* featuring the title track, a brassy cumbia, and the ballad "Quiero y Necesito." He released a self-titled CD in 1998. Sebastián produced both CDs and wrote most of the songs.

JOAN SEBASTIÁN

Con Mariachi (Balboa)
Gracias Por Tanto Amor (Musart)
Mariachi Disco de Oro (Musart)
Tatuajes (Musart)
Tú y Yo (Musart)

JOSÉ MANUEL FIGUEROA

Expulsado del Paraíso (FonoVisa)
José Manuel Figueroa (BMG/U.S. Latin)

SELENA

Born Selena Quintanilla, April 16, 1971, Freeport, Texas; died March 31, 1995, Corpus Christi, Texas

Selena's great talent was her ability to reinvent the basic Mexican cumbia, turning it into a keyboard-driven dance-party fever tune. Her pop hits crackled with catchy hooks, sing-along choruses, the celebratory improvisations of salsa, and even the sweaty jump fever of reggae.

Selena began her career at the age of eleven when her father encouraged her, her sister Suzette, and her brother A. B. to form a band—Selena y Los Dinos. Reluctant at first, they became a fledgling outfit on the Tejano circuit. Predictably, Selena y Los Dinos's first albums on indie labels suffered from unimaginative synth-driven rhythms that made little impact on the charts. But by 1989, just as they were signed by EMI, the outfit had matured into a solid group. From that point on, Selena was a multiple winner at the annual TMAs.

By 1991's Ven Conmigo, the group, which was then calling itself simply Selena, had evolved a rhythmic style that demonstrated its increasing prowess for catchy cumbias such as "Baila Esta Cumbia" and the title track. Selena began pouring more emotion and soul into her music. On the next album the band took a page from cumbia-meister Fito Olivares, producing the marvelous "La Carcacha," which was marked by what would prove to be its signature style—danceable tunes that moved the feet but also poked fun at life in the barrio. A. B. was improving as a songwriter, developing a penchant for power-pop, synth-driven cumbias.

Selena
Courtesy of Al Rendon

On April 2, 1992 Selena married band guitarist Chris Pérez in Corpus Christi, Texas. The following year, she won a Grammy for her *Selena Live* CD.

In the spring of 1994, the band was already riding the charts when *Amor Prohibido* was released. It was the band's crowning achievement, hinting at the pop potential of a band at its creative peak. "Fotos y Recuerdos" (a Spanish version of the Pretenders' "Back in the Chain Gang") was an inspired piece. That song—along with Selena's original "Bidi Bidi Bom Bom," a reggae-tinged tune—could just have easily worked (with French lyrics perhaps) in European clubs, as it was almost indistinguishable from the Euro-pop dance tunes on the radio. "No Me Queda Más" was another unforgettable work, a touching song about finding the strength to walk away from a romance. Selena fully conveyed the pain of love and the tone of redemption.

On March 31, 1995, Selena was shot and killed by Yolanda Saldivar, the former president of her fan club, in a Corpus Christi motel. In a scene reminiscent of Elvis's funeral at Graceland, more than 30,000 fans filed past Selena's casket at the Bayfront Plaza Convention Center. Attesting to her popularity, eight books, five videos, two CDs, and the motion picture *Selena,* were produced within two years of her death.

In April Selena had five CDs on The Billboard 200 chart, an accomplishment previously only achieved by superstars like Garth Brooks, Elvis Presley, and the Beatles.

Four months after Selena's death, and with much anticipation, EMI Records released the crossover album, *Dreaming of You,* which Selena had been working on before she was killed. The CD included three original English tracks and several previously released, but newly rearranged, hits. Her English material proved that she could handle pop songs as well as anyone, though perhaps the producers tried to dilute her "ethnic" sound a bit too much so as to not alienate the mainstream audience. Songs like "Bidi Bidi," "Como la Flor," and "Techno Cumbia," were remastered, injecting extra percussions to spice them up. *Dreaming of You* is the only CD with a bilingual version of "Wherever You Are" (Donde Quiera Que Estés), a wondrous, infectious tune that hinted at techno/hip-hop possibilities.

In the ensuing years EMI Latin released recompilations hyping "new" material, but in actuality these albums contained simply remastered or remixed material. On other occasions—such as *Siempre Selena* or the *Anthology* CD—Selena's vocal tracks were lifted and combined with different instrumental tracks. In 1998 Selena's widower, Chris Pérez, signed an English-language rock contract with Hollywood Records, whose roster included **Los Lobos** and **Nydia Rojas.**

Amor Prohibido (EMI)
Anthology (EMI)
Dreaming of You (EMI)
Entre a Mi Mundo (EMI)
Selena Live (EMI)
Selena y Los Dinos (EMI)
Ven Conmigo (EMI)

SILVA, CHELO

Born Consuelo Silva, August 25, 1922, Brownsville, Texas; died April 2, 1988, Corpus Christi, Texas

The oldest daughter in a family with seven children, Chelo Silva began singing as a teen at school and church. By her late teens she was singing regularly with the local Tito Crixell Orchestra.

In 1939, when her career was gaining momentum locally, she was invited to sing at a radio program hosted by the then-unknown poet and composer Américo Paredes, whom she later married and divorced. After a few idle years, Silva was back singing radio jingles and performing at the Continental Club in Corpus Christi. In 1952 she was signed by Discos Falcon in McAllen, Texas, where she recorded more than seventy titles. In 1955 she signed with Columbia Records and began scoring with a series of hits, including "Imploración," "Está Sellado," "Sabes de Qué Tengo Ganas," "Inolvidable," "Amor Aventurero," and "Soy Bohemia." A contemporary of **Lydia Mendoza,** Silva was considered the premier female interpreter of boleros, the slow ballad that originated from Cuba but that is an integral part of Mexican repertoire. Eventually Silva became known as "La Reina de los Boleros" (Queen of the Boleros) for her ability to interpret a torchy song and make it her own through stylized vocal phrasing and bent notes. Through the years she toured Mexico and the American Southwest, performing with such luminaries as **José Alfredo Jiménez, Javier Solis, Vicente Fernández,** and **Lola Beltrán.**

15 Éxitos (Sony)
Disco de Oro (Sony)
Fichas Negras (EMI)
La Reina Tejana del Bolero (Arhoolie)

SILVESTRE, FLOR

See Aguilar, Antonio

SOLDADOS DE LEVITA, LOS

Formed 1990, Houston, Texas

Originally formed by four Gamino brothers—Austeberto, Elias, Abelardo, and Amado—and friend Simeon Rodríguez, all of whom were from the state of Michoacán, Los Soldados de Levita have made a career out of military-themed songs from **Agustin Lara**'s "El Adiós de un Soldado" to "Corridos de la Revolución" from their 1990 debut album, *México de Mis Recuerdos.* Los Soldados experimented with rap on "Pancho López," a cut from the same album. The group, which signed with the indie Ramex Records, also got airplay during the '90s for songs like "La Casta," "El Ilegal," and "Arena Roja." They released their seventh album, *La Tercera Carta,* in 1998, with a new version of **Joan Sebastián**'s "Tatuajes." By then Austeberto (on *bajo sexto*) and Elias (on percussions) were the only original members remaining in the five-man group.

El Ilegal (Ramex)
México de Mis Recuerdos (Ramex)
Razón y Motivo (Ramex)
Qué Bonitas las Mujeres (Ramex)

SOLIS, JAVIER

Born Gabriel Siria Levario, September 1, 1931, Mexico City, México; died April 19, 1966, Mexico City, México

With his incredible smooth baritone and impeccable air of authority, Javier Solis became Mexico's quintessential bolero ranchero singer in the late '50s. His versatile vocals could inject a wealth of emotions into his music, but, perhaps more impressively, like the American pop singer Frank Sinatra, Solis could describe the hellish torture of love's addiction or the dark fear of being abandoned, while projecting a cool, exquisite detachment.

Solis was born to a modest family in the Tacubaya neighboorhood of Mexico City. He was raised by his uncle Valentine Levario and his wife, Angela, because Solis's father was reportedly a violent alcoholic.

Like many Mexicans of modest means, Solis worked as a child to help the family. He dropped out of school at the age of ten to work at a bakery and then at a mechanic's shop. In his free time he played soccer, baseball, and boxed. He practiced amateur boxing for six years, competing with the later-famous boxers Ratán Macías and José Medel. While still in his teens Solis entered an amateur singing contest at the Teatro Salón Obregón in Mexico City. The prize was a pair of shoes—and he won. Solis kept entering and winning the contest until the owners finally decided to hire him to sing at the place so he would not compete. Encouraged, Solis hooked up with longtime friend Pablo

Flores and formed Trio México, but with little success. When he turned sixteen years old Solis went to Puebla and sang with Mariachi Metepec for a year.

Returning to Mexico City, Solis debuted at the famed Centro Tipico Guadalajara in the two-block square that was Garibaldi Plaza, the world-renowned gathering place for mariachis. It was during a stint at the Azteca Bar in downtown Mexico City that Solis's luck turned. One fortuitous night, singers Julito Rodríguez and Alfredo Gil of the famed **Trío Los Panchos** heard Solis, who was then going by the name Javier Luquin. Sufficiently impressed, Rodríguez got Solis an audition with CBS México. In short order, Solis took his stage name of Javier Solis, signed a one-year contract with CBS, and cut his first record in 1950. Shortly after, he was hired to work at Teatro Lírico, where he met his future wife, the dancer Blanca Estela Sáenz.

After **Pedro Infante**'s death in 1957, Solis rose quickly as the undisputed ranchera king in Mexico. That Solis emerged after Infante had passed away is no devaluation of Solis's natural ability. Having recorded dozens of classics and appeared in fifty-odd movies, Infante was clearly a powerful force and a national icon. And, like **Jorge Negrete** before him, Infante died young—at the age of thirty-nine. It would seem only natural to expect some of the love, admiration, and national pride to be transferred from Infante to Solis. Solis was all of twenty-five years old at the time of Infante's death, but he was already on an upward trajectory.

The big hit for Solis came in 1958 with "Cenizas," which was followed by "Payaso." Both were bittersweet songs that impacted solidly on the market. The former described a great love that dies on the vine. The latter recounted the melancholy created by maintaining an outward smile while one's world is collapsing. In 1959 Solis began his film career by starring opposite leading women such as **María Victoria** and **Lola Beltrán.** He recorded thirty-six albums and appeared in twenty-three movies, including his last film in 1965, *Juan Pistolas.* In 1956 Solis scored another massive national hit with Rafael Ramírez's bolero "Llorarás, Llorarás," a you'll-be-sorry-when-I'm-gone treatise. Solis's signature hit came later that year with "Sombras," a dark song propelled by ominous tones about having romantic aspirations that cross social class. An international hit, "Sombras" sold millions in South and Central America. That same year he also recorded Luis Demetrio's classic "Si Dios Me Quita la Vida," a haunting song about love transcending the temporal plane.

Ultimately Solis's best works were gripping torch songs wrapped in lush mariachi symphonic arrangements. As a strong but tender singer, Solis conveyed the full range of emotion, from the sense of desolation ("Payaso") and macho pride ("Llorarás") to joyful nostalgia ("Mi Viejo San Juan"). His vocals were powerful and versatile. He could go from soft whispers of anguish ("Gema" and "Entrega Total") to full-throttle macho yells ("Sombras").

Amigo Organillero (Sony)
Boleros del Alma (Sony)
Leyendas (Sony)
Payaso (Sony)
Sombras (Sony)
Valses (Sony)

SOLIS, JOSÉ JAVIER

Born circa 1970, Ario de Rosales, Michoacán, México

The younger brother of famed producer/songwriter **Marco Antonio Solis,** José Javier Solis struck out on his own in 1989 after spending seven years with **Los Bukis** during their heyday as Mexico's top romantic pop outfit. Solis's last album with Los Bukis was the 1988 *Si Me Recuerdas,* which went on to be nominated for a Grammy for best Mexican performance in 1989. Solis was also nominated in the same category with his debut solo CD, *No Me Olvidarás*. The band and Solis lost to **Linda Ronstadt**'s Mexican folk roots CD, *Canciones de Mi Padre*. On Solis's 1995 CD, *Se Remata el Jacalito,* and his 1997 CD, *Tú Otra Vez,* he reunited with his brother Marco Antonio who wrote three songs on each CD.

No Me Olvides (FonoVisa)
Que Hable (FonoVisa)
Sentimental (FonoVisa)
Se Remata el Jacalito (FonoVisa)
Tú Otra Vez (FonoVisa)

SOLIS, MARCO ANTONIO

Born December 29, circa late 1960s, Ario de Rosales, Michoacán, México

When **Los Bukis** were at the top of their game, there was no question that singer/songwriter/producer Marco Antonio Solis was the main driving force. Beyond Bukis though, Solis also wrote for and produced a myriad of artists, including Estela Núñez, María Sorte, **Los Freddy's**, Mojado, and Marisela. Along the way Solis, who had his own Marco Musical recording studios in Mexico City, collected a shelfload of awards and honors.

Solis's interest in music came early. Solis was only twelve years old when he formed Los Hermanitos (also called Los Hermanos) with his brother Joel. They eventually became Los Bukis in 1975 and enjoyed a twenty-year run with innumerable hits and sales records that all came to an end in late 1995. Solis launched his solo career with his FonoVisa debut CD, *En Pleno Vuelo,* which was nominated for a Grammy for best Latin pop performance. It produced the hits "Recuerdos, Tristeza y Soledad," "Qué Penas Me Das," and "Así Como Te Conocí"—all of which reached No. 1 on the Billboard Hot Latin Tracks chart. In *Billboard*'s year-end special in 1996, Solis was named top producer and composer. His string of chart hits continued with his sophomore CD, *Marco Antonio Solis,* producing the single "Ya Aprenderás."

But like **Juan Gabriel,** another of Mexico's most prolific singer/songwriters, Solis was also in constant demand for his songwriting and producing skills. He produced two albums for Spanish pop singer **Rocío Durcal,** including the critically acclaimed *Como Tu Mujer* CD, which produced the hits "Falso" and the title track. In the '90s, Solis also produced **Ezequiel Peña**'s *Orgullo Ranchero,* Laura Flores's *Me Queda Vacía,* and his brother José Javier Solis's *Se Remata el Jacalito* CD.

En Pleno Vuelo (FonoVisa)
Marco Antonio Solis (FonoVisa)

SOMBRA, LA

Formed 1972, Chicago, Illinois

During Tejano's major expansion in the early '90s La Sombra, **La Fiebre,** and **La Mafia** were among the leading showbands, demonstrating that in the age of MTV, just standing onstage and playing was not entertaining enough—at least if you wanted to attract the youth. The group included a brass section, incorporated arena rock lights and sound, dressed in ragged jeans and leather jackets, and added light choreography to its stage shows.

All of the band members except singer Gavino (born August 9, 1967, Chicago, Illinois) were born in Texas. In 1984 the group was signed to the Corpus Christ–based Freddie Records and its debut CD, *Mi Güerita Coca-Cola,* generated the hit single title track, which was written by María Luisa G. Ramírez. By the late '80s La Sombra had built a loyal following on the strengths of follow-up hits "Botoncito de Cariño," "El Sapo," and "La del Moño Colorado," two cumbia remakes of Tejano classics. In 1990 Sombra left Freddie and signed with FonoVisa and, within a month, its label debut CD produced the smash single "El Sancho."

By the mid-1990s, La Sombra was well established as a top show band with a signature sound that featured a thunderous rap-cumbia fusion. But by follow-up hits "El Sancho" and

"¿Por Qué No Te He de Querer?" the novelty of their rap-cumbias wore off. In 1994 lead singer Gavino struck out on a solo career that saw limited success with his CD, *Soy el Único,* before he returned to the fold. Gavino married Gina Esparza (singer of Inocencia) on January 9, 1993. The couple had a daughter, Gianna Gabriella Guerrero, on March 24, 1995. In 1996 La Sombra signed on with EMI Latin and released *Alborotados,* but failed to reach any significant chart success.

Botoncito de Cariño (Freddie)
Chicago's Wild Side (Freddie)
Chi-Town Boys (Freddie)
Las Mejores Cumbias (Freddie)
Our Very Best/El Sapo (Freddie)

SONORA DINAMITA

Formed 1960, Medellín, Colombia

Widely credited with spreading the cumbia's popularity in the '60s and '70s, Sonora Dinamita was formed by salsa great Julio Estrada "Fruko" Rincón and composer Lucho Argain. The group achieved great popularity in Mexico and Latin America with its brassy, innuendo-soaked cumbias such as "A Mover la Colita" and "Mi Cucu." The group relocated to southern California in 1988.

The original Sonora Dinamita continued into the '90s, changing its name to La Internacional Sonora Show, led by Kiko Vargas with singers Susana Velasquez and Vilma Díaz. The name change was caused by a legal dispute with its ex-label Discos Fuentes. After Sonora Dinamita split with the Fuentes, the label formed another group called La Sonora Dinamita. And yet a third version of Sonora Dinamita was authorized to perform throughout Mexico.

Con Sonido Banda (Vedisco)
Explotando con la... (Sonotone Latin)
Pegaditas de Oro, Vol. 1 (Vedisco)
Picante y Caliente (Sonotone Latin)
El Show de... (Discos Fuentes)
Sonora Dinamita, Vol. 3 (Sonotone Latin)
Sonora Dinamita y Sigue la Fiesta (Vedisco)
La Vibrante (Sonotone Latin)
Vuela Vuela (Sonotone Latin)

SONORA SANTANERA, LA

Formed 1956, Barra de Santa Ana, Tabasco, México

As a youth, founder Carlos Colorado belonged to a local *orquesta.* But he realized his dream when he moved to Mexico City and hooked up with several musicians to form Tropical Santanera. In the band's early days of playing private parties, they attracted the attention of promoter Jesús "Palillo" (Toothpick) Martínez, who contracted them at the Follies Bergere Theater. There the group became La Sonora Santanera and began playing a mix of mambo, cha-cha, *danzón,* bolero, and tango. After signing with CBS México in 1960, Sonora Santanera scored its first hits, "La Boa" and "Los Aretes de la Luna." The band quickly drew a reputation as a brassy, percussion-driven big band that played Afro-Caribbean cumbias. Additional hits included "El Orangután," "Mi Adiós," "El Barbarazo," "El Mudo," and "Luces de Nueva York." During the '60s, the group's moniker changed once again, to La Internacional Sonora Santanera de Carlos Colorado.

After Colorado died in a car accident in 1986, the group disappeared for a few years. The 1996 Sony Discos release *Nuestro Aniversario* was a tribute album that featured the group's hits sung by stars such as **Vicente Fernández,** Celia Cruz, and Yuri. Its 1997 release *Como en los Buenos Tiempos,* produced by **Armando Manzanero** and arranged by Antonio Méndez, maintained the group's tropical vein.

Nuestro Aniversario (Sony Discos)
Personalidad (Sony Discos)
La Sonora Santanera (Sony Discos)

SONORA TROPICANA

Formed 1989, Medellín, Colombia

Founder Rey Carreño wanted a tropical/cumbia band fronted by female singers when he organized Sonora Tropicana in Medellín. He quickly recruited singer Benetia Vassilladi, and later Ledy Patricia and Elvis Botero. The band's first album had minimal impact, but its second produced their signature Colombian cumbias—"El Chuponcito," which cracked the Billboard Hot Latin Tracks chart, and "El Golf." But just when the band was picking up substantial momentum, especially in Mexico, the group met with tragedy in June of 1992. Bass player Juan De Diós Lescano was killed in an auto accident outside Montemorelos, Nuevo León that also injured other band members. After recovering, the band produced several more albums, generating the hit singles "Déjame Llorar," "De Colombia con Amor," and "Me Regale Contigo." In 1994 the group was named the best tropical/cumbia group of the year at the Furia Musical Awards in Mexico City.

Acaríciame (Luna)
Desayuno de Besos (Luna)
Éxitos, Éxitos, Éxitos (Luna)
Loca Enamorada (FonoVisa)
Me Gusta (FonoVisa)

STEFANI

Born Stefani Melissa Sullivan, December 23, 1972, Albuquerque, New Mexico

The self-proclaimed "All-American Sweetheart," Stefani was one of the new faces that helped reinvigorate the Tejano genre in the early '90s. Although her repertoire covered the standard cumbia/polka/ranchera, Stefani injected a pop sheen into her act with minor choreography and the occasional dance pop ballad.

Stefani
Courtesy of Sony Discos

In late 1990, through the help of her then-promoter Dale García, Stefani released two singles with EMI Latin, "Primer Beso" and "Tú y Nadie Más," as a marketing test by talent scout Bob Grever. The singles had massive impact, but a contractual disagreement with EMI eventually led, after much legal wrangling, to her signing a multi-year contract with Sony Discos. In 1994, under the direction of **La Mafia** manager Henry Gonzáles, Stefani produced her debut CD, *Te Voy a Enamorar,* which included songs by Humberto Ramón and E. J. Ledesma as well as a cover of Daniela Romo's "Celos," which was released as the first single. Stefani impressed with her vocals on the standard polkas, but she shined best on the torchy ballads. Carrying her all-American theme further, Stefani posed wrapped in an American flag on the CD's inside cover art. Subsequent regional hits included the title track and "Baila Conmigo" from the CD *Porque Soy Mujer.* Stefani's patriotic stance as the all-American girl drew minor controversy in August 1996 when she gave birth to her daughter, Ileah Cristiana, out of wedlock. García downplayed the controversy, saying

Stefani "has the love and support of her family and her fans."

Te Voy a Enamorar (Sony Discos)
Todo Mi Amor (Sony Discos)
Porque Soy Mujer (Sony Discos)

STEPHANIE LYNN

Born Stephanie Lynn Rivera, January 26, 1973, San Antonio, Texas

With a pop-cumbia approach and minor stage choreography, Stephanie Lynn debuted in the burgeoning Tejano market in the early '90s and scored a series of similarly titled hits: "Amarradita," "Cuidadita," and "Pegadita."

At the outset, Stephanie Lynn's band included her three brothers—Bobby, Rick, and Karlos. They were originally known as Stephanie Lynn and Hi Energy, playing a mix of pop, dance, and Tejano covers. The group's first single—the title track from its debut LP, *Sólo Ojos para Ti*—reached No. 32 on the Billboard Hot Latin Tracks chart in late 1994. In 1996 Stephanie Lynn's career stalled when she separated from her brothers, due to undisclosed reasons, and subsequently left EMI Latin. In 1997 she was signed by FonoVisa and quickly released her label debut CD, *¿Qué Debo Hacer?* but it failed to generate any chart activity.

Bésame (EMI)
Sólo Ojos para Ti (EMI)
Stephanie Lynn (EMI)
¿Qué Debo Hacer? (FonoVisa)

SUPER SEVEN, LOS

Formed 1998, Austin, Texas

The brainchild of artist manager Dan Goodman, Los Super Seven came together initially as an all-star Mexican American studio band with **Texas Tornados**'s **Flaco Jiménez,** Freddie Fender, **Los Lobos**'s César Rosas and David Hidalgo, country singer Rick Treviño, Tejano **Rubén Ramos,** and Texas country-rocker Joe Ely. The idea for the group was seeded when Goodman presented a Tex-Mex showcase using the same artists at the massive 1997 South by Southwest (SXSW) music and media conference in Austin. After a repeat showcase in 1998's SXSW, the group recorded a self-titled CD, which was produced by Steve Berlin (who produces for Los Lobos), and later that year played selected U.S. dates. The CD featured classic Mexican and folk tunes, including **Agustin Lara**'s "Piensa en Mí," Felipe Valdéz Leal's "El Ausente," and Woody Guthrie's "Deportee." Guest musicians included mariachi **Campanas de América,** *bajo sexto* player Max Baca, and accordionist **Joel Guzmán.**

Treviño said he rediscovered his roots when he sang leads on the evergreens "Mi Ranchito" and "El Ausente." Like many Mexican Americans, Treviño had lost his Spanish language and even his accent growing up in the suburbia of Houston, and later Austin. But while working with legends like Fender, Jiménez, and Ramos during the recording, Treviño said he reconnected with his cultural past, and enjoyed the Tejano and ranchera music that his father, Rick Sr., had loved when he played in the Neto Pérez Tejano band. Jiménez teamed up with smooth, soulful singer Rubén Ramos to recharge the classic polka "Margarita," which was first made a hit in the 1950s by Jiménez's father, **Don Santiago Jiménez.**

For Fender, the project was a way of reliving the past. He sang leads on "Piensa en Mí," a late '40s bolero sung by **Lydia Mendoza.** As a young boy, Fender heard the tune on the radio and his mother used to sing it. "For me, this was reliving a simpler time in my life, of kind of bringing my mother back from the grave. That's why this music is so powerful."

Los Super Seven won a Grammy in the best Mexican American category for their self-titled CD in February of 1999, edging out veterans such as **Ramón Ayala, Vicente Fernández, La Mafia,** and **Los Terribles del Norte.**

Los Super Seven (RCA)

TAM Y TEX, LOS

Formed 1979, Sabinas Hidalgo, Nuevo León, México

In this small town just thirty miles south of Nuevo Laredo, founder/keyboardist/singer Argelio Cantú organized Tam y Tex, a group that included future cumbia king **Fito Olivares** among its graduates. The seven-member outfit, which featured Juventino Cantú on accordion, was named for the border states of Tamaulipas and Texas, where several of the group's members got their first break as musicians.

The band's early hits included "Noches de Santa Martha" and "La Musiquera," which was written by a young Olivares as he was just honing in on the mechanics of songwriting. The song was the basis of the ensuing movie *La Musiquera,* produced by cinematographer Arnulfo "Gordo" (Fatso) Delgado. Other big hits for the group were "La Suavecita," "La Tra-ca-ca," and 1988's "El Tikita."

Chuya de Monterrey (Ramex)
Lagarton (PolyGram)
La Morralera (Ramex)
La Musiquera (Ramex)
Mi Tamaulipeca (Ramex)

TECOLINES, TRÍO LOS

Formed 1951, Mexico City, México

Established during the golden age of the bolero, this trio debuted at famed radio station XEQ in 1951. Like **Trío Los Dandys,** the trio was in fact a quartet, consisting of Sergio Flores M., *requinto;* Jorge Flores M., vocals/guitar; Jesús "Chucho" García López, lead vocals; and Lazaro Galindo, vocals/guitar.

Signed to the Peerless record label in 1952, Trío Los Tecolines became best known for their inspired take on Alfredo Carrasco's song "Adiós," which was also called "El Adiós de Carrasco" and for which the group won the Guitarra de Oro Award. Trío Los Tecolines also won the Disco de Oro Award for their *Cerezo Rosa.* Other hits included "Ahora y Siempre," "Flores Negras," "Lágrimas del Alma," "Cosas del Ayer," and "Sé Muy Bien Que Vendrás."

Boleros de la Época de Oro, Vol. 1 (Sony)
Boleros de Oro (Peerless)
Homenaje a P. Flores (Peerless)
Melodías de Siempre (Peerless)
Serenata con... (Peerless)

TEJANO

Tejano, which is Spanish for "Texan," is a roots-based hybrid of traditional Mexican rancheras, polkas, and cumbias that have been updated with blues, pop, and country strains. It is a uniquely American-made music that was forged by working-class Mexican Americans in Texas during the late '50s. Since it is a hybrid, there is no definition of genuine Tejano. Classic Tejano, however, used a big horn section, taking its cues from its precursor, the Orquesta Tejana, a genre that peaked in the '50s with such bandleaders as **Beto Villa** and **Chris Sandoval,** who were themselves influenced by the waltzes and foxtrots of Glenn Miller and Tommy Dorsey.

In 1954 bandleader **Isidro López** became the father of modern Tejano music when he added conjunto elements—like accordions, polkas, and rancheras—and his lead vocals to his *orquesta.* Tejano anthems include "El Tejano Enamorado" and "Las Nubes." Through the years the music was known by various terms—including Mexican Music, *la Onda Chicana, Onda Tejana,* Tex-Mex, funk, and brown soul—until Tejano became the widely accepted term.

In the '90s Tejano continued to borrow from various genres. The modern age splintered Tejano into the subgenres of Tejano/norteño (**Intocable, Michael Salgado**); Tejano/R&B (**Jay Pérez, David Marez**); Tejano/country (**Emilio,** Joel Nava); Tejano/pop (**Selena, Amber Rose**).

Like the heroes of American rock 'n' roll, Tejano's top stars—such as Selena, Emilio, and **La Tropa F**—borrowed from the past and injected original melodies, reinventing the music for a younger, wider audience.

TEMERARIOS, LOS

Formed 1982, Fresnillo, Zacatecas, México

When Los Temerarios first began to emerge with their original pop/ballad tunes they were often compared to **Los Bukis.** However, after a few years the band equaled and then surpassed the mix of romantic themes and melodic hooks that were the signature sound of the highly successful Bukis bandleader **Marco Antonio Solis.** By the mid-1990s Los Temerarios were one of Mexico's hottest groups, enjoying a thrilling run of No. 1 singles, including "Tu Infame Engaño," "Creo Que Voy a Llorar," and "Cuando Fuiste Mía."

Brothers Adolfo (born 1963, Fresnillo, Zacatecas) and Gustavo (born 1968, Fresnillo, Zacatecas) Ángel realized they wanted to go into music in the late 1970s when their father rented a rehearsal room to local musicians. They would sneak in the room to play music after the musicians had left. Encouraged by their parents, the brothers formed their first band—La Brisa—in 1977 and played local weddings. By 1982 they renamed themselves Los Temerarios and recruited cousin Fernando Angel on bass and friend Mario Ortiz on drums. Gustavo was the lead singer/guitarist while Adolfo handled the keyboards and became the group's main songwriter.

Los Temerarios produced a number of independent albums, none of which had any major chart success. In 1988 they signed onto the Monterrey, Nuevo León–based DISA label and began charting a series of hits, including "Tu Infame Engaño," "Ven Porque Te Necesito," "Si Quiero Volver," "Creo Que Voy a Llorar," "Sólo Te Quiero a Ti," and "Como Ayer."

Los Temerarios; with keyboardist/songwriter Adolfo Ángel (third from left) and lead singer/guitarist Gustavo Ángel (fourth from left)
Courtesy of FonoVisa

In 1990 they won a Univision Premio Lo Nuestro Award for best new group. And in 1991 their LP *Lo Nuevo y lo Mejor* peaked in the Top 10 of The Billboard Latin 50 chart, where it enjoyed an unprecedented (for the group) fifty-nine week run. Los Temerarios reached a creative peak on the 1991 album, *Mi Vida Eres Tú,* whose title track was a mariachi-tinged tune. The CD was solid though, producing the hit singles "Yo Te Amo," "Perdóname," and "Esa Mujer." The following year the band was the only Mexican group invited to perform at Acapulco '92.

In June of 1993 Los Temerarios created a modern studio in Monterrey and announced plans to record their next LP on their own AFG Sigma label. This led to a contractual dispute with DISA, but the matter was eventually resolved out of court. The parties agreed that a final Temerarios CD would be released under DISA. Meanwhile Los Temerarios began releasing their own material as well as recently signed up bands (Zeus, **Mr. Chivo**) on its AFG (initials for Adolfo, Fernando, Gustavo) Sigma label.

Despite the distractions, Los Temerarios continued on their ascent in the market, building on the combined strengths of ever-improving band songwriting, youthful good looks, sharp coat-and-tie outfits, and melodic pop sound. In July of 1994 they became the first grupo to play El Palacio de Deportes in Mexico City. Additional hits included "Ven Porque Te Necesito," "Si Quiero Volver," "Creo Que Voy a Llorar" and "Sólo Te Quiero a Tí." In 1996 the band signed on with FonoVisa releasing the album *Como Te Recuerdo,* which included the **Cornelio Reyna**–penned song "Botella Envenenada."

Edición de Oro (FonoVisa)
En Concierto (FonoVisa)
Mi Vida Eres Tú (FonoVisa)
Te Quiero (FonoVisa)
Tu Última Canción (FonoVisa)

TENTACIÓN, GRUPO

Formed circa 1991, Irapuato, Guanajuato, México

Slickly coifed with matching pastel suits, Tentación carved a niche in Mexico's emerging grupo scene in the early '90s with a decidedly pop-oriented fusion of syrupy ballads and weepy romantic laments. The band—especially the delicate vocals of singer Noé Martin—recalled the bubblegum sound of early **Los Temerarios.**

The band's debut album, *Amándote,* sold more than 100,000 copies, according to FonoVisa, and produced the successful single "El Seis." Consecutive albums followed the same pop-ballad approach and generated the radio faves "Vida," "Sólo un Sueño," "Mi

Última Canción," "Como Olvidarte," "Aroma de Mujer," and "Anillo de Compromiso," which was written by **Cuco Sánchez.** All of these hits made the Billboard Hot Latin Tracks chart. The band also tried its hand at the Mexican folkloric genre with the album *No Canta Mal las Rancheras* in 1997.

Aroma de Mujer (FonoVisa)
La Huerfanita (FonoVisa)
Mi Última Canción (FonoVisa)
No Canta Mal las Rancheras (FonoVisa)

TERRIBLES DEL NORTE, LOS

Formed 1983, San Luis Potosí, San Luis Potosí, México

Los Terribles del Norte were an energetic four-man unit that emerged as a force in norteño, playing a workman-like blend of earthy corridos and bluesy boleros.

The band members were originally from San Luis Potosí, but they made Belton, Texas their home base. Signed by Freddie Records in the late '80s, they began making inroads with the album *Ya Me Voy a California,* which made the Top 40 on The Billboard Latin 50 chart. In 1995 the band was nominated for a Grammy in the best Mexican American performance category for its *El Bronco* CD.

During live performances the band was spunky and keen on keeping the dance floor packed with slow-trotting but solid cumbias and percussive polkas. The group was fronted by energetic singer/*bajo sexto* player Juan Acuña, who twirled and skipped across the stage while singing. The band's biggest impact singles have been "Carga Blanca" and a revamped cumbia version of the ranchera classic "Hay Unos Ojos."

14 Cumbiazos (Freddie)
El Bronco (Freddie)
Carrera de Muerte (Freddie)
Disco de Oro/20 Grandes Éxitos (Freddie)

TEXAS TORNADOS, THE

Formed 1989, San Francisco, California

With their mix of rock and country oldies, norteño classics, and Tex-Mex soul, the Texas Tornados emerged as music industry media darlings in the early '90s.

Band members were **Flaco Jiménez,** accordion; **Freddy Fender,** guitar; Augie Meyers, vox organ/keyboards/accordion, *bajo sexto;* and Doug Sahm, guitar. All four had been working individually until Sahm brought them together for a gig in San Francisco at Slim's, the rock and blues club owned by Boz Scaggs. Manager Cameron Randle, then with Refugee Management, got the group signed to Warner Brothers.

In 1965 Sahm and Meyers founded the Sir Douglas Quintet, whose hits included "Mendocino" and "She's about a Mover." Fender and Jiménez also had separate solo careers. The Tornados' spicy blend of oldies, Mexican standards, and Tex-Mex originals appealed to a broad range of generations and cultures. This led to their being tagged as "The Tex-Mex Grateful Dead."

In 1990 the band's first LP, *Texas Tornados,* was released in English and in Spanish, produced the single hits "Who Were You Thinking Of?" "A Man Can Cry," and a conjunto classic, "Soy de San Luis," which was written by Jiménez's father, **Don Santiago Jiménez,** and which won them a Grammy for best Mexican American performance. The Tornados' 1996 release, *4 Aces,* produced the hit single "Little Bit Is Better Than Nada," which was featured on the soundtrack for the movie *Tin Cup,* featuring Kevin Costner and Cheech Marín. The Tornados were regulars on VH1 and the Country Cable channel. Another notable hit was "Hey, Baby, ¿Qué Paso?"

4 Aces (Warner Bros.)
Hangin' On by a Thread (Warner Bros.)
Texas Tornados (Warner Bros.)
Zone of Your Own (Warner Bros.)

TIERRA TEJANA

Formed 1977, Seguin, Texas

Tierra Tejana was one of the finest horn-driven units that played an energetic, soulful mix of Tejano polkas, party funk tunes, and R&B numbers. The band's moment in the sun came on the hit single "Las Hijas de Don Simon," an infectious rap/cumbia.

The group was originally founded in 1962 as the Miracles by brothers Frank, Joe, Jesse, Lupe, and Mike Gonzáles. Jesse and Lupe are twins. When their father, Frank B. Gonzáles, a farmer, was stricken with an illness and unable to work, the brothers started performing at an early age out of sheer necessity. Gonzáles senior and his wife, Gregoria, had fifteen children—ten sons and five daughters. When, at the age of four, brother Pete joined the band, it became Little Pete and the Miracles.

By 1977 the civil rights and Chicano movements had been steadily growing and making news across the country. The band changed its name to Tierra Tejana and signed with the Venezuelan-based label TH-Rodven and made an impact with its first single "Puro Party Polka," which was written by Lupe. Through the years, the band recorded more than twenty LPs and sixty singles. The brothers always had an appreciation for the classic Tejano sound, the days of the Orquesta Tejana, or big band, and they worked diligently to give that sound a contemporary freshness.

The group produced a series of regional hits, including "Pensé Rogarte," "Parranda de Oso Negro," and the **Isidro López** classic "Nuevo Contrato." But it was not until 1991, when the band recorded the catchy rap-cumbia "Las Hijas de Don Simon," that it jumped up to top concert draw status. Produced on their *Where's the Party, Dude?* CD, the single thrilled with an infectious cumbia beat, winsome vocal harmonies, and sing-along choruses. In 1992 the band followed up with a similar sounding hit single "Yo Quiero Bailar" from the LP *Time to Celebrate,* but lack of chart success proved that the party was over.

Nos Corrieron por Borrachos (TH-Rodven)
Puro Party Raza (TH-Rodven)
Where's the Party, Dude? (TH-Rodven)
Zapatéale con Tierra Tejana (TH-Rodven)

TIGRES DEL NORTE, LOS

Formed 1968, Rosa Morada, Sinaloa, México

Along with accordionist **Ramón Ayala,** Los Tigres del Norte are the longest running, and perhaps the greatest, norteño band in the history of the genre. Despite their larger-than-life status as superstars in Latin America, they are still universally acknowledged as "Los Ídolos del Pueblo" (The Idols of the Town). Their nickname is partially due to their constantly humble comportment; but it is also, and perhaps more importantly, due to the band's deliberate decision in the late '70s to tackle (within their music) the controversial issues that affected the millions of Mexicans who were migrating into the U.S. yearly—especially anti-immigration politics and the disillusionment that is caused by living in a hostile country.

Los Tigres were founded by the four Hernández brothers—Jorge, Raúl, Eduardo, and Hernan—plus cousin Oscar Olivos. All came from working-class families in the rural town of Rosa Morada, where their earliest influences include the then-popular groups like **Los Alegres de Terán, Los Tremendos Gavilanes,** and **Los Cadetes de Linares.**

Only Jorge finished junior high school and received some type of music training. The others learned to play by ear. At the outset they played at local weddings and private parties, but they soon moved to the border city of Mexicali to try to find work as musicians in the mid-1960s.

In 1968 the brothers, who were then teenagers, moved to San Jose, California, where they were hired by a local promoter to play a *Diez y Seis de Septiembre* gig (September 16 is the Mexican independence holiday). According to Tigres folklore, the band took their name because an immigration official kept calling them "the little tigers." The Mexican population in San Jose was small but growing and Los Tigres soon found steady work.

But it was not until their 1971 megahit corrido, "Contrabando y Traición," that Los Tigres became known in the U.S. and Mexico. The song's central characters, Emilio Varela and Camelia La Tejana, became as well known among Mexican Americans as Lorne Green's "Ringo" or Charlie Daniels's "The Devil Went Down to Georgia" ballads. Mexican corridos are story ballads and the tradition dates back to the turn of the century when the principal subjects were Mexican revolutionary heroes and border bandits. Utilizing that tradition, Los Tigres substituted modern heroes and villains. The success of the second megahit, "La Banda del Carro Rojo," revealed a market for this type of song and established them as the premier norteño corrido group. In essence, these corridos were the precursors to today's controversial narco-corridos—modern corridos about drug cartels by such groups as **Los Tucanes de Tijuana** and Los Invasores del Norte.

In the ensuing years, Los Tigres maintained a steady pace, producing forty-three albums in the space of some thirty years and also appeared in more than two dozen films. Perhaps their biggest seller was the 1989 *Corridos Prohibidos,* an entire album about drug smuggling. But by the end of the decade, Los Tigres, sensing the shifting politics on the street, changed their subject matter and began focusing on the life and struggles of Mexican immigrants. The band teamed up with noted songwriter Enrique Franco and produced corridos like "La Jaula de Oro," which dealt with the 1986 Immigration Reform and Control Act in a story about an undocumented Mexican immigrant who struggled to bring his family north only to become disillusioned.

In 1988 Los Tigres won a Grammy for their *Gracias! América sin Fronteras* CD.

Los Tigres del Norte; (from left to right) accordionist/guitarist Eduardo Hernández, drummer Oscar Lara, lead singer/accordionist Jorge Hernández, guitarist Luis Hernández, bass player Hernan Hernández, and saxophonist Guadalupe Olivo
Courtesy of FonoVisa

The band also overcame personal tragedy in April 1993 when Freddie Hernández, the youngest member, died at the age of twenty-five of unknown causes in a Los Angeles hotel room after a concert. Six months prior, Isabela—the wife of Jorge Hernández who recorded under the name **Chavela**—died after falling from a horse during a photo session for an LP cover.

Other major hits for the group included "Dos Plebes," "Tumba del Mojado," "Puerta Negra," "El Tahúr," "Jefe de Jefes," and "El Cellular." In 1996 they won a Billboard Latin Music Award and a Univision Premio Lo Nuestro Award for *Unidos Para Siempre.* Later that year, after recording his last album with the group, *El Ejemplo,* **Raúl Hernández** left the band. In 1997 Los Tigres became the first norteño band allowed into the Alcatraz Prison island to film a video for their first double (all corridos) CD *Jefe de Jefes,* which was nominated for a Grammy for best Mexican American performance that year.

Throughout their career, but especially in the '90s, Los Tigres have been the most emulated and copied band in the norteño genre, influencing countless bands through their own major success. Los Tigres's album, *Así Como Tú,* has spun off the single "La Baraja Bendita," which was sung by Jorge Hernández and was written by Luis Torres Canez.

Así Como Tú (FonoVisa)
La Banda del Carro Rojo (FonoVisa)
Corridos Prohibidos (FonoVisa)
La Garra de... (FonoVisa)
Gracias! América sin Fronteras (FonoVisa)
Ídolos del Pueblo (FonoVisa)
Incansables! (FonoVisa)
Jefe de Jefes (FonoVisa)

TIRANOS DEL NORTE, LOS

Formed March 1990, Mexicali, Baja California Norte, México

This six-man outfit burst on the scene with a youthful sound and pop-leaning norteño music exemplified by the early hits "Hasta la Miel Amarga" and "Para Morir Iguales." The band came together in early 1990 when singer/*bajo sexto* player Gustavo Cota teamed up with bassist José Luis Montaño and accordionist Omar Velasco in their hometown of Mexicali. They were all of fifteen years old at the time, but they shared their mutual admiration of norteño pioneers such as **Los Alegres de Terán** and **Los Tremendos Gavilanes,** and their idols—**Los Tigres del Norte.** They quickly recruited Daniel Morales on percussions, Ricardo Carrasco on drums, and Luis "Memo" Bernal as MC.

From the beginning, the founding members agreed not to record any controversial narco-corridos, story ballads about drug-traffickers that had become trendy among many norteño outfits in the '90s. In 1996 the band was nominated for best new group at the Univision Premio Lo Nuestro Awards in Miami. That was the year of their biggest hits—"Hasta la Miel Amarga" and "Charola de Plata."

Musically, Los Tiranos combined the traditional accordion/*bajo sexto* grooves with lighter norteño/pop stylings. Their **Ramón Ayala**–influenced smooth rhythmic hooks were topped by vocal harmonies that recalled **Los Palominos**—especially tunes like "No Oro, ni Plata" from their *Sol* CD, which was about coming to terms with a bad love. The band also flexed its chops on torchy boleros.

Like their idols, the Tiranos focused on themes familiar to struggling immigrants, including wayward romances, ambitions beyond the U.S. border, and a longing for home. Most of the band's original material was either written by Cota or by outside songwriters Eva Torres and Enrique Franco, who have produced CDs and written a lot of material for Los Tigres. Manager Javier Martínez and all the Tiranos handled producer duties.

Con Sangre Norteña (FonoVisa)
Hermosa Tirana (FonoVisa)
Inolvidables (FonoVisa)
Sol (Sony)

TORRES, EDUARDO "LALO"

See Pavos Reales, Los

TORRES, PATSY

Born Patricia Donita Torres, November 30, 1957, San Antonio, Texas

Patsy Torres played in local bands in high school before she formed her own band in 1979. Her first regional hit single was "Mi Casa Está Vacía." In the '80s Torres was mostly playing locally as a Top 40 cover band. A series of albums on independent labels produced only regional hits, but Torres had enough fan support to win her first and only TMA in 1987 for best female entertainer. She was signed by WEA Latina in 1990 and later by Joey International, but subsequent albums produced mostly local chart singles.

Bien Cuidada (Joey International)
Romántica (Peerless)
Te Juro (Balboa)

TORTILLA FACTORY

See Little Joe y La Familia

TOVAR, RIGO, Y COSTA AZUL

Formed 1972, Houston, Texas

The mid-1970s were the heyday for singer/songwriter Rigo Tovar (born Rigoberto Tovar García, circa 1950, Matamoros, Tamaulipas). Tovar's name is synonymous with the tropical cumbia genre that solidified after his creative peak. Like **Mike Laure y Sus Cometas,** which preceded him in the mid-1960s, Tovar specialized in the percolating, rhythmic Afro-Caribbean cumbias for which later heroes like **Fito Olivares, Aniceto Molina,** and **Mr. Chivo** were known.

After forming his band, Costa Azul, Tovar began turning out his trademark keyboard-driven cumbias, with his first single "Rosa Valencia." With that group, he recorded signature songs and biggest hits "Mi Matamoros Querido" and "Lamento de Amor." Later on he pursued a solo career, reportedly breaking the attendance record at Río Santa Catarina in Monterrey with a crowd of more than 40,000. Tovar disappeared during the '80s due to an illness, and re-emerged with 1989's *La Fiera* and 1991's *El Sirenito,* CDs on the BMG/U.S. Latin label.

Con Mariachi (FonoVisa)
Noche de Cumbia (FonoVisa)
Ranchero (FonoVisa)
El Sirenito (BMG/U.S. Latin)
Tropicalísimo (FonoVisa)

TRAILEROS DEL NORTE, LOS

Formed 1983, Monterrey, Nuevo León, México

Los Traileros del Norte
Courtesy of FonoVisa

Los Traileros del Norte really were truck drivers, or *traileros,* as the name implies. The band was founded by lead singer Arnulfo Sánchez López. Band members self-produced and distributed their tapes and continued their day jobs during the early years, but positive reception from their coworkers spurred them to seek a label deal. Then known as Los Caballeros del Estilo Diferente, the group signed with DISA in 1983.

The group's trademark was Sánchez López's fiery vocals, which were sung over accordion-propelled polkas, cumbias, and corridos. López occasionally wrote and guitarist Juan García has written more than fifteen songs, including the group's hits "Mi Mal Amor" and "El Conejito." Los Traileros continued racking up hits, including 1991's "El Canto de un Mexicano,"a *huapango* about immigration, "Veneno y Lodo," and 1994's "Atrás del Escenario." Sánchez López's son Arnulfo Jr. formed Arnulfo Jr. Rey y As; another son, Eduardo López Gallegos, became a percussionist for **Los Cardenales de Nuevo León.**

15 Grandes Éxitos (EMI)
16 Auténticos Éxitos (EMI)
Amor de los Dos (FonoVisa)
Atrás del Escenario (FonoVisa)
Quisiera Ser una Lágrima (EMI)
Te Sigo Amando (FonoVisa)
Tres por Una (FonoVisa)

TREMENDOS GAVILANES, LOS

Formed circa 1962, Monterrey, Nuevo León, México

Los Tremendos Gavilanes were part of the dawn of the modern norteño age. Alongside **Los Alegres de Terán, Los Relámpagos del Norte,** and **Los Cadetes de Linares,** Los Tremendos Gavilanes established the sound (two- and sometimes three-part harmonies, with accordion runs woven in) and the basic template (accordion and *bajo sexto*) of norteño groups.

During their heyday, Los Gavilanes produced songs that became part of the norteño canon—classics such as "Quiero Que Sepas," "Cuando Paso por Tu Casa," "Paloma Loca," "Dos Gotas de Agua," and "La Chiva Colgada."

Los Tremendos Gavilanes were formed when accordionist Juan Torres and guitarist Salomón Prado joined forces in Monterrey at the behest of Del Valle Records executive Cristóbal García. Both men had already been touring and recording separately. Prado (born May 13, 1932) was from General Terán, Nuevo León and he learned to play guitar when he was nineteen years old. In 1954 he played with his cousins Anselmo and Guadalupe in Los Hermanos Prado. He recorded three albums with them, including the songs "Esos Alegres de Terán" and "Paloma Loca," before leaving to go solo in 1960.

Torres (born December 27, 1938) was from Cadereyta, Nuevo León, and, unlike Prado, he came from a musical family. He learned to play the *bajo sexto* at the age of ten from his father and later learned the violin. When he was twelve years old he learned the accordion and played at family gatherings with his brothers. By 1954 he left for Monterrey and played with Conjunto del Fraile and later formed Los Gavilanes. In 1962 Los Gavilanes became Los Tremendos Gavilanes, over time recording more than 105 albums on various indie labels. In 1988 the duo was inducted into the Tejano Conjunto Hall of Fame.

15 Hits (Hacienda)
Corridos (FonoVisa)
La Mafia No Perdona (Freddie)

TRES ASES, LOS

Formed 1953, Mexico City, México

Los Tres Ases came together when smooth singer Marco Antonio Muñiz met guitar players Juan Neri and Hector González and started the trio as the house musicians for La Bandida bordello in Mexico City. They chose their name after band members and others submitted suggestions in an urn. Los Tres Ases was the first slip of paper pulled out.

Muñiz was the first voice while Neri, who was also music director, handled first guitar. They were signed to RCA by Mariano Rivera Conde and, although they did not write or compose, they impacted with the early hits "Mi Último Fracaso," "Deliro," "Estoy Perdido," "La Puerta," and "Contigo a la Distancia." They were named the best trio in Mexico in 1955 and in 1956 and began touring Cuba and the rest of Latin America, including Venezuela, Puerto Rico, the Dominican Republic, Colombia, and Peru. In 1959 Muñiz left to pursue a solo singing career while Neri tried his hand as a solo guitarist. González kept the Los Tres Ases's name, running through a series of replacements without much luck.

La Bamba y Más Éxitos (RCA)
Boleros Inolvidables (Sony)
Siluetas en Trío (RCA)
Los Tres Ases (RCA)

TRES CABALLEROS, LOS

Formed 1952, Mexico City, México

Guitarist/songwriter Roberto Cantoral (born July 7, 1930) founded Los Tres Caballeros when he teamed up with famed *requinto* player Benjamin "Chamin" Correa Pérez de León and lead singer Leonel Gálvez Polanco. The men debuted on July 1, 1952 on radio station XEW and followed quickly with numerous shows around Mexico City.

After a tour of the United States in 1956, they were signed by Musart and released their debut self-titled album late that year, which included the monster hits "La Barca" and "El Reloj," both originals by Cantoral. Both songs would enter the bolero canon. Other hits followed, including "El Teléfono," "Me Odio," "Te Perdono," and "Déjame Solo."

The trio dissolved in the late '60s with Cantoral continuing a prolific songwriting career. His hits included "Yo Lo Comprendo" and "El Triste." Correa went on to perform as the house band at the Crowne Plaza Hotel in Mexico City and later began producing records, working with Aida and Carlos Cuevas and Francisco Javier.

Barca (Sony)
Inimitables Tres Caballeros (Musart)
Tres Palabras (Vedisco)
Volumen 2 (Sony)

TRES DIAMANTES, LOS

Formed October 1948, Mexico City, México

Los Tres Diamantes were considered to be the longest-running group in the history of trios, which is saying a lot considering the average life span of any trio is somewhere in the neighborhood of ten years. After **Trío Los Panchos,** Los Tres Diamantes had the widest recognition outside of Mexico. But their style was markedly different—their voices were softer and their guitar playing gentler. Their first hit came with famed songwriter María Grever's "Cuanda Me Vaya," and later with Grever's "Te Quiero, Dijiste." Their next signature hits were "Usted," "Reina Mia," and "Condición." By the late '50s the group was established as a major force.

Los Diamantes were formed in 1948 when guitarists Enrique Quezada Reyes (born July 15, 1920) and Gustavo Prado Gutiérrez (born March 25, 1923) teamed up with lead singer Saulo Sedano Chavira (born July 25, 1925). Signed by RCA in 1949, they began a series of hits that soon led to international tours—including Europe and Japan. Los Diamantes were still together in the early '90s.

Boleros Clásicos (Sony)
Enlace (RCA)
En Serenata (BMG/U.S. Latin)
Los Tres Diamantes y las Canciones de... (RCA)

TRES REYES, LOS

Formed October 1958, Nuevo Laredo, Tamaulipas, México

Requinto player Gilberto Puente's (born November 29, 1936, Ciudad Anáhuac, Nuevo León) speed and exquisite control and lead singer Hernando Aviles's **Trío Los Panchos** lineage ensured that Los Tres Reyes emerged as a top player in the late '50s with the hits "Gema," "Un Consejo," and "Déjame Solo." But the group lasted only until 1966, playing only on special occasions thereafter.

The Puente brothers, Gilberto and Raúl, were fraternal twins born in Nuevo Laredo, Tamaulipas. While in their late teens, they moved to Mexico City, on the pretext, they told their parents, of studying at a business school. In actuality, the brothers were looking to start music careers and they enrolled at the José F. Vasquez Music School. The only job they could find, though, was playing for customers in a small restaurant called Polancos. As fate would have it, Hernando Aviles happened to walk in one day. He was sufficiently impressed to discuss working with them and so trio Los Tres Reyes was born.

Initial hits included "Fueron Tres Años," "Novia Mía," "Como un Duende," "Engañada," and "El Almanaque." But their moment in the sun was short. After five albums Aviles left, reason unknown.

In the late '80s Gilberto Puente played his *requinto* on **Linda Ronstadt**'s remarkable heritage CDs, *Canciones de Mi Padre* and *Más Canciones,* and toured with her Fiesta Méxicana tour. Puente also appeared on Ronstadt's Cuban roots CD *Frenesí* and on *The Mambo Kings* film soundtrack.

In 1991 Puente reformed Los Tres Reyes with lead singer Luis Villa and second guitarist Niño Placios and began regular tours of Mexico and the U.S. Later that year they played with the Albuquerque Orchestra and, in 1993, they backed **Vikki Carr** during a performance at the Greek Theater in Los Angeles. In the '90s Puente was still considered the world's best *requinto* player.

LOS TRES REYES

20 Éxitos Original (Sony)
Boleros, Vol. 2 (Sony)
Éxitos, Vol. 1 (Sony)

GILBERTO PUENTE

Estrellas del Fonógrafo (RCA)
La Guitarra y el Sonido (RCA)
El Mejor Guitarrista de México (RCA)

TRIO

Driven by soft vocal harmonies and acoustic guitar, trio music provided the romantic soundtrack to Mexico's golden age of cinema—during the 1940s and 1950s. Typically, a trio consisted of three guitar players who also sang in harmony. The most widely known trio, **Trío Los Panchos,** formed in 1944 in New York City, where another harmonizing style, doo-wop, would take root ten years later. Founded by two Mexicans and a Puerto Rican, Los Panchos was responsible for the genre's unique contribution to music, a guitar called the *requinto.*

Los Panchos member Alfredo Gil, who was looking for a way to play faster song introductions, developed the *requinto,* a small guitar tuned two-and-one-half steps higher than a conventional guitar. The *requinto*'s sound and size proved indispensable to the trios. But it was Gilberto Puente of the trio **Los Tres Reyes** (founded 1958) who perfected the technique and became known as the world's best *requinto* player.

Trios played a variety of styles, including rancheras, *sones, huapangos, huastecos,* and *valses.* But trio will forever be associated with the bolero, a type of slow, romantic ballad. Trío Los Panchos was credited with turning boleros into works of art. Other successful trios from the golden era were **Los Tres Ases, Los Tres Diamantes,** and **Los Tres Caballeros.** Signature boleros from the trio era were "Reloj," "Somos Novios," and "Sin Ti."

TRÍO CALAVERAS

Formed 1936, Mexico City, México

While the mariachi tradition has seen wider recognition beyond Mexico, the romantic trio genre has remained vibrant since its initial development in the late '40s.

Among the oldest of the trios, Trío Calaveras featured guitarists Raúl Prado and Miguel Bermejo, and *requinto* player José "Pepe" Zaldivar Pacheco, who replaced the Bermejo brothers' original member, Guillermo Bermejo. In 1935 Prado married a young María Felix, who would become one of Mexico's biggest actresses and who later married **Jorge Negrete** a year before he died in 1953. Like most trios, the Calaveras took traditional folk styles from different states in Mexico—such as the *huapango,* the *redowa* and the *son*—and gave them romantic form. Los Calaveras peaked in popularity during the '40s and '50s, coinciding with Mexico's golden age of cinema. Los Calaveras appeared in eighteen films, mostly backing ranchera great Jorge Negrete. In 1986 the band released its fiftieth anniversary album and in the early '90s the trio was still performing weekly in Mexico City.

25 Aniversario (RCA)
Rancheras en Trío (Orfeon)
Trío Calaveras (RCA)

TRIO LOS MÉXICANOS

Formed 1947, Mexico City, México

One of the few trios that has lasted more than fifty years, Trio Los Méxicanos was comprised of the Rocha brothers—Salvador, Juan, and Victor—who performed in about ninety percent of Luis Aguilar's movies. With only eight albums to their credit, but some 250 films, it was chiefly their cinematic work that made this trio famous.

The group appeared in landmark films such as **Pedro Infante**'s *El Mil Amores* and *Tal para Cual* with **Jorge Negrete** and Luis Aguilar. Los Méxicanos's repertoire included songs by **José Alfredo Jiménez, Cuco Sánchez,** and Manuel Esperón. Interestingly, the trio found itself popular behind the former Iron Curtain and toured the Eastern Bloc, the former USSR, China, Turkey, Iran, and Pakistan in 1957. In 1981 the former USSR awarded the group a medal of merit and invited the trio to stay—an offer the group declined.

1994 Éxitos de Oro de Chava Flores (Sony)

TRÍO TARIÁCURI

Founded 1930, Mexico City, México

The Mendoza brothers—Norberto, Jerónimo, and Juan—were a Mexican folk music guitar-strumming trio that peaked in the 1930s and 1940s. A 1939 award for best folkloric group of Mexico landed them an appearance on the classic 1936 Mexican film *Allá en el Rancho Grande,* which starred **Tito Guizar.**

In 1942 Jerónimo died in an auto accident and was replaced by younger brother Eligio. In 1960, after twenty-nine years with the trio, Juan (born June 17, 1917, Huetamo, Michoacán; died August 22, 1978, Mexico City) went solo, recording boleros, rancheros, and corridos. Among his best known hits were his version of the Chucho Monge–penned "Creí" plus his originals "Cielo de Sonora" and "Dos Hermanos," a corrido. Mendoza also wrote a narrative series of songs about the Tariácuri family and occasionally sang duets with his younger sister, the ranchera great Amalia (born circa 1920, Huetamo, Michoacán).

Amalia, who was known as "La Tariácuri," gained a reputation as a fiery singer who could inject a rush of emotions in her rancheras. Along with **Lucha Villa** and the late **Lola Beltrán,** she sang on the **Juan Gabriel**–produced 1996 album *Las Tres Señoras,* which also featured guest singer **Vicente Fernández.** For her contributions in promoting and conserving the Mexican folkloric tradition, she was awarded the inaugural Lucha Reyes Award in 1998 as part of the Golden Eagle Awards.

AMALIA "LA TARIÁCURI" MENDOZA

Boleros y Rancheras de Oro (Sony)
Canta la Tariácuri (RCA)
Grandes de la Música Ranchera (RCA)
La Tariácuri, Vol. 2 (Sony)
La Tariácuri, Vol. 3 (Sony)

TRÍO TARIÁCURI

Éxitos de Oro (Sony)
Historia Musical de Trío Tariácuri (Orfeon)
Lo Nuevo del Trío Tariácuri (Antilla)

JUAN MENDOZA

Al Estilo Norteño (Musart)
Aquí Llegó Juan Mendoza (Musart)
Me Aconseja el Corazón (Peerless)
El Tariácuri (Peerless)

TROPA F, LA

Formed 1970, San Antonio, Texas

La Tropa F became a dominant player in Tejano in the mid-1990s with its combination of jaunty conjunto polkas, original rhythmic cumbias, and vocal harmonies.

In the early '60s, Joe Farías Jr. (born November 25, 1955), the oldest of the five brothers, learned to play the accordion from his uncle Jesse Hernández who was in the band Los Compadres Alegres. By the late '60s Joe and brother Juan (born February 8, 1958, San Antonio, Texas) joined their father and uncle in Los Compadres Alegres. By 1970 Joe and Juan left Los Compadres to form Los Hermanos Farías, which included their younger brothers: David (born May 10, 1963, San Antonio, Texas), lead vocals/accordion; Jaime (born November 7, 1967, San Antonio, Texas), songwriter/keyboards; and Jesse (born March 25, 1961, San Antonio, Texas), bass guitar. In 1975 the young outfit scored its first single, "Ando Perdido," and through the '80s recorded on a series of independent record labels.

In 1990 local TV personality Plácido Salazar nicknamed the band "La Tropa F" and the name stuck. Later that year the group signed with the indie label Manny Music and produced its first hit single, "Mil Noches." In 1993 the band won its first TMA for conjunto traditional album (for *Right on Track*). However, it was not until the band signed on with a major—EMI Latin—in 1995 that it was poised to make a run for the top. Bolstered by wider distribution and increased label promotion, the group began to gel as a unit. Brothers Joe and Jaime became increasingly inventive in their songwriting, combining infectious vocal harmonies and tight musicianship for a mix that yielded hits on the next four albums, including "Lágrimas," "Quiero Yo Saber," "¿Qué Más Has Hecho Tú?" "El Arco Iris," "Chaparrita," "Otro Día," and "Juan Sabor." Most of their hits were written by songwriter Jaime Farías, who was presented in 1996 with two BMI Awards.

By the mid-1990s the band was also including original country tunes on its albums such as *It's Over* and *Just When I Needed You Most.* In 1997 it won a TMA for best show band and received a Billboard Latin Music Award in the regional Mexican category for the video *Juan Sabor.* That same year the band performed with **La Mafia** as coheadliners at the 10,000-capacity Freeman Coliseum for the San Antonio Livestock Show and Rodeo. The following year,

La Tropa F returned, this time teamed up with pop-norteño sensation **Grupo Límite.**

A un Nuevo Nivel (EMI)
Desde el Corazón de Texas (EMI)
Música Sin Frontera (EMI)
Otro Día (EMI)

TROPA VALLENATA, LA

Formed circa 1995, Monterrey, Nuevo León, México

In 1995 La Tropa Vallenata impacted on the charts with the monster hit, the heartbroken tropical cumbia "Los Caminos de la Vida." The tune became the theme song for the novela of the same name. Led by trombonist Alfonso Ríos, the ten-man outfit followed up in 1997 with the solid song "Corazón Contento" from the album *Cumbias de Mi Tierra.* Later hits included the accordion-driven cumbias "Sonríeme" and "Mi Cafetal."

Los Caminos de la Vida (EMI)
Cumbia de los Pobres (EMI)
Cumbias de Mi Tierra (EMI)
Mi Cafetal (EMI)

TROPICAL/CUMBIA

Although tropical/cumbia is a genre that has received less fanfare than, say, norteño or ranchera, it is a solid, widely popular form that dates back to the 1960s.

The best of Mexico's tropical cumbieros whip out boisterous, good-time cumbias peppered with humerous lyrics (often with double-entendres) to packed dance floors with couples dancing with almost reggae fever. Aggressively syncopated percussion is a must, and most ensembles include layered keyboards and sax, with cumbias that tend to be faster than those of the balladeers, sometimes approaching *charanga* speed. Not to be confused with music on *Billboard*'s tropical/salsa chart category (a subcategory of the Billboard Hot Latin Tracks chart), most tropical/cumbia output originates in Mexico, emphasizes cumbia over salsa, features the *soneo (*the call-and-response exchange between a lead singer and the backing vocalists), and is played on regional Mexican stations. Though many regional labels and Mexican record stores differentiate among tropical, norteño, banda, and pop performers, most regional Mexican stations play all styles in varying degrees.

The basic template for modern tropical/cumbieros or *grupos tropicaleros* was forged when the distinct genres of *balada romántica,* salsa/cumbia, and Mexican rock 'n' roll coalesced in the form of **Mike Laure y Sus Cometas** in the mid-1960s. Formerly a rocker who idolized Bill Haley and the Comets (hence the name Cometas), Laure became the father of the tropical/cumbiero genre and an *onda grupera* pioneer by incorporating cumbia into his rock-tinged rhythms, creating a new sound called *chunchaca,* which featured the *güiro.* Cuban mambo and cha-cha-cha from the '40s and '50s (Pérez Prado, Orquesta Aragón) and Colombian tropical music from the '60s (which **Sonora Dinamita** is known for) both influenced the first wave of tropical cumbieros.

By the early '70s Matamoros-based **Rigo Tovar y Costa Azul** had emerged as another major player in the evolution of *tropicalero* groups with the seminal hit "Mi Matamoros Querido." Other big names in the '70s were Colombian accordionist **Aniceto Molina** and Renacimiento '74, whose musical director, Pollo Estevan, went on to become part of **Grupo Pegasso.** Major figures who peaked in the '80s included **Fito Olivares** ("Juana La Cubana"), **Mr. Chivo** ("Ron con Coca-Cola"), and Grupo Pegasso ("Tambalea"). In the '90s Coahuila-based **Yahari** carried the torch, turning Quad City DJ's "C'mon Ride the Train" into a frenetic tropical/cumbia for the next generation of rug-cutters. Yahari also paid tribute to tropical/cumbia founder Mike Laure with a medley of his hits, including "Tiburón" and "0.39" on the band's 1998 CD *La Pura Sabrosura.*

TROPICAL PANAMA

Formed 1980, San Nicolás de los Garza, Nuevo León, México

This tropical/cumbia rig, which was formed in a suburb of Monterrey, Nuevo León, rapidly gained audiences with rhythmic, keyboard-driven, vallenato-tinged tunes. Signature hits included "Me Duele la Boca" and "I Don't Speak Spanish." In 1992 the group appeared in the movie *Bronco.* Early in the band's career, lead singer Francisco Javier González's W.C. Fields–like vocals were criticized for sounding like a knockoff of Renacimiento '74. González was known for abusing his throat by drinking ice water during performances. Best-selling albums included *¿Cuándo Volverás, Amor?* and *La Chica Que Soñé.*

El Carita (DISA)
La Chica Que Soñé (DISA)
I Don't Speak Spanish (FonoVisa)
I Now Speak English (FonoVisa)
Me Engañó la Bruja (DISA)
Nomas Tantito (FonoVisa)
Pollera Colora (DISA)

TUCANES DE TIJUANA, LOS

Formed 1986, Tijuana, Baja California Norte, México

With their tight musicianship, original material, and clean youthful looks, Los Tucanes de Tijuana shot to the crème de la crème in norteño circles in the mid-1990s. The band's rise was sparked by singer/bandleader Mario Quintero Lara's creative corridos and ballads and by its timely acquisition by the major record label EMI Latin.

The band members were born in Guamuchil, Sinaloa, an agricultural valley adjacent to marijuana- and poppy-growing regions. They were cousins whose fathers made up the group **Los Incomparables de Tijuana.** With just a junior high education, Quintero (born circa 1968, Guamuchil, Sinaloa) and his cousins moved to Tijuana and found work at a *maquiladora,* an American factory, and later in a sandpaper factory before they decided to form Los Tucanes de Tijuana. Quintero said he named the band after the toucan, a brilliantly colored bird.

The band signed with the indie Alacran records in 1989 and early albums began attracting a small following. They later starred in the movie *Clave Privada,* a story about their success. When the band's popularity surged, they began receiving an abundance of fan mail, including anonymous correspondence from people detailing successful drug smuggling techniques. Quintero incorporated some of those tales into his corridos like "La Piñata" and "El Güero Palma," which rarely received radio play. By late 1995 Alacran signed a distribution agreement with EMI Latin. It was a strategic and fortuitous move, since it gave the rising Los Tucanes substantially increased distribution and, more importantly, national promotion. The move worked. By November 1995 Los Tucanes got on *Billboard*'s charts for the first time. In May of 1997 Los Tucanes had six albums on The Billboard Latin 50 chart, the biggest chart impact by any group since August 26, 1995, when label-mate **Selena** had accomplished the same chart feat. The group's mainstream releases quickly became radio fixtures that heated up dance floors—such as the norteño *quebraditas* "La Chona," "Tucanazo," and "Ando Bien Arreglado." Meanwhile the ballads "Mundo de Amor" and "Desde Que Te Amo" showed the group's romantic side.

Quintero and Los Tucanes stirred up increasing controversy by portraying drug smugglers as the good guys and describing the trade more explicitly than their contemporaries

Los Tigres del Norte. Quintero's standard media reply was that as long as the public requested it, he would continue to write and record it.

Ajuste de Cuentas (EMI)
Mundo de Amor (EMI)
El Pachangón (EMI)
Tucanes de Oro (EMI)
Tucanes de Plata (EMI)

URÍAS, POLO, Y SU MÁQUINA NORTEÑA

Formed 1995, Ojinaga, Chihuahua, México

Máquina Norteña came to life when its leader Leopoldo "Polo" Urías Ramírez (born 1956, Ojinaga, Chihuahua) left **Los Rieleros del Norte** and rounded up his sons Aaron and Erick, as well as Jody Vasquez, bass; Keith Nieto, sax; and Jimmy Torres, accordion. The band played traditional norteño, but with sax-infused tropical flavorings. The group's biggest hits came with "Cuando Lloran los Hombres" and "Amor sin Esperanzas."

Urías began his career in his early twenties when he formed Los Jilgueros del Arroyo with his brothers Israel, Alberto, Jesús, and Raúl in his hometown of Ojinaga. Eight albums and ten years later, in 1985 Urías joined Los Rieleros del Norte, replacing lead singer Milo Melendez. His tenure there took him into 1995 and into Hobbs, New Mexico where La Máquina Norteña came together.

A Todo Vapor (FonoVisa)
Campeón de Campeones (FonoVisa)
Corridos (FonoVisa)
Sigue la Aventura (FonoVisa)

VALLENATO

Like the ubiquitous cumbia, the vallenato was another Colombian folk rhythm that influenced Mexican music. Traditional vallenato generally featured plaintive vocals, warm, reedy three-row button accordions, *guacharacas* (cane scrapers), and *caja vallenatas* (bongo-like drums) in its basic cumbia repertoire. Despite the different tone, vallenato accordion has sentimental riffs that are similar to those found in Tex-Mex. According to folklore, the word vallenato either means valley-born, or it relates to Valledupar, Colombia, on the Atlantic coast.

Colombian accordionist **Aniceto Molina** helped popularize the genre in Mexico in the 1970s. Vallenato got a shot in the arm in the early '90s with Colombian singer Carlos Vives's pop-vallenato album *Clásicos de la Provincia,* which brought the once-obscure regional style to a new generation, selling 1.5 million copies in Colombia alone. Mexican groups **Los Angeles Azules** and **Los Vallenatos** used vallenato instrumentation in their cumbias. Molina himself staged a comeback in the late '90s.

VALLENATOS, LOS

Formed 1992, Monterrey, Nuevo León, México

This Monterrey-based quintet traded in vallenato-styled cumbias. Typically, the band's cumbia-vallenatas are brassy and feature sweeping accordion tones.

By 1993 Los Vallenatos included eight members when they turned heads with the popular single "Sal y Agua." In 1997 they hit big again with the title track from their CD *Volver.* In 1998 Los Vallenatos released *Como No Pensar en Ti.*

Como No Pensar en Ti (EMI)
Lucero Ojos de Miel (DISA)
Playa, Brisa, y Mar (DISA)
Volver (EMI)

VARGAS, CHAVELA

Born Isabel Vargas Lizano, April 17, 1919, Guerrero, México

Chavela Vargas started her career in the mid-1930s and she peaked as a well-known ranchera singer during the '50s, eventually touring with the famous singer/songwriter **José Alfredo Jiménez.** Her first recordings appeared in the early '60s and at this time she also wrote the songs "Macorina," "María la Tepozteca," and "Adiós Paloma." Vargas's music was rediscovered by Spanish director Pedro Almodóvar, who used it in some of his movies. Vargas lived in Tepoztlán, Morelos in the '90s. Ironically, her favorite song was "La Última Copa" (The Last Drink), which was written by José Alfredo Jiménez, whom she often said was her favorite composer and who was a longtime friend. It was ironic because Vargas often and freely admitted her alcoholic problem, noting that other artists, including the late **Lola Beltrán,** often tried to help her. Vargas retired in 1979. In 1990, though, Vargas appeared in the Werner Herzog film *A Cry of Stone.* She also sang on the soundtrack of *Tacones Lejanos.*

Chavela Vargas (Tropical)
Chavela Vargas (WEA Latina)
De México y del Mundo (Sony)

VARGAS, PEDRO

Born Pedro Vargas Mata, April 29, 1904, San Miguel de Allende, Guanajuato, México; died October 30, 1989, Mexico City, México

In the pre-TV era Pedro Vargas rose to prominence as Mexico's premiere balladeer and first top radio star. This was during the '30s and '40s, a time that was widely considered to be Mexico's golden age of popular music. His international appeal helped cross the cultural bridge between American and Mexican pop music. Together with famed songwriter **Agustin Lara,** Vargas helped popularize the bolero, the slow romantic song, and the *paso doble,* the fast-paced Spanish double-footstep dance.

Vargas began singing in the church choir, making his local debut singing Schubert's "Ave María." His family had wanted him to become a priest, but Vargas later tried his hand at bullfighting and even studied medicine for a while before he began his singing career. His strong, rich tenor earned him admission into the Conservatorio Nacional in Mexico City and later earned him the title of "El Tenor de las Americas" (America's Tenor).

In 1928 Vargas sang opera in Mexico City's Esperanza-Iris Theater and made his first tour of the U.S. That same year he recorded his first single, "Mi Primer Amor," and was signed to RCA. Eventually he recorded some 3,000 songs with the label. In 1930 Vargas won a singing contest with the waltz "Ann Harding," a performance that impressed Agustin Lara enough to name Vargas as the official interpreter of his songs. By then an established singer/songwriter, Lara took Vargas and singer Ana María Fernández with him on his first international tours, which included Spain, France, and Italy.

Vargas's career lasted more than sixty years and through innumerable world tours, including performances at the celebrated venues Carnegie Hall and Madison Square Garden. He hosted his own TV show, *El Estudio de Pedro Vargas,* for twelve years and appeared in twenty films, including *Los Chicos de la Prensa,* opposite other golden age stars such as **Jorge Negrete,** María Felix, and Tona La Negra. Vargas also sang for U.S. and Mexican presidents. His signature songs were "Bésame Mucho" and "Solamente una Vez." In the 1970s the United Nations honored Vargas by naming him as the leading exponent of Latin American Music.

In 1985 Vargas was part of the historic *Cantaré, Cantarás,* the We-Are-the-World-type song/video project by Latin music artists to help ease world hunger. In his later years Vargas performed in a wheelchair, but he never lost the clarity of his voice. Among the last projects Vargas recorded was a duet with **Julio Iglesias.**

Con Sus Amigos (RCA)
Pedro Vargas (RCA)
Serie Platino (RCA)
El Tenor de las Américas, Vol. 2 (RCA)

VELA, RUBÉN

Born May 10, 1937, San Antonio, Texas

Rubén Vela
Courtesy of Hacienda Records

Rubén Vela spent most of his life in the Rio Grande Valley in Texas and he remembered when he was a young boy that his father played drums when they were strung *de un árbol* (from a tree). Vela began playing in '50s and eventually became a marquee figure in South Texas conjunto music. Vela's contemporaries included such notables as **Don Santiago Jiménez, Valerio Longoria,** Paulino Bernal, and **Tony De La Rosa.** Like De La Rosa, Vela was one of the first to incorporate electric bass and drums into his conjunto in the late '50s.

Vela recorded for numerous indie labels and his early hits included "Adolorido," "El Pajuelazo," "Vencido," "El Regalo de Corazón," "Mi Amigo," "Ángel de Mis Anhelos," and "Genoveva." In 1983 Vela was inducted into the Tejano Conjunto Hall of Fame. In the mid-1990s, Vela's career got a major boost thanks to his invigorating cumbia "El Coco Rayado" on Hacienda Records. Fueled by Vela's percolating accordion and a galloping percussion, the cumbia was infectious and easily danceable. The life of the hit single was extended further when label producers created club and radio remixes of the tune.

¿Dónde Estás, Mujer? (Freddie)
El Maestro (Hacienda)
Piquetes de Hormiga (Freddie)
Polkas Redowas (Freddie)

VERDUZCO, ROBERTO

See Industria del Amor

VILLA, BETO

Born Alberto Villa Jr., October 26, 1915, Falfurrias, Texas; died November 1, 1986, Corpus Christi, Texas

Beto Villa became known as the father of Orquesta Tejana, or big-band, music because in the mid-1950s he was the most successful and prolific Mexican American bandleader in the American Southwest.

With its big horn section, the Orquesta Tejana was part of the basic template that would form the essence of modern Tejano music. Although he was a successful bandleader and talented saxophonist, Villa did not sing. In the late '50s, Villa's compatriot **Isidro López** completed the foundation of future Tejano when he added accordions, the conjunto repertoire of polkas and rancheras, and lead vocals to his *orquesta* mix.

Beto Villa
Courtesy of Arhoolie

Villa's father, Alberto Sr., a prosperous tailor who learned to play music by ear, encouraged Beto to learn to read music and take lessons. In 1932, while he was still in high school, Villa formed his first band, the Sonny Boys, which included his uncle Arturo Villa on drums. The group performed at school dances and other gatherings and played American big-band and other popular music.

In 1936 Villa got his first full-time contract to play at the Barn, a dance hall in Freer, Texas. Four years later, Villa dropped out of music and decided to pursue business with his father-in-law, using the money he had saved from his gigs to open a meat market. During World War II, Villa served in the U.S. Navy, where he joined a band that played for enlisted personnel. Upon discharge, he and his family opened the Pan American and La Plaza dance halls in Falfurrias, Texas. From his experiences in the navy Villa had the idea to merge American and Mexican music. He quickly discovered that he could earn more money playing music on the weekends than working all week as a butcher.

In 1946 Villa's friend Armando Marroquín, producer for Discos Ideal, allowed him to record some tunes with his *orquesta*. They recorded two sides, "Las Delicias" and "¿Por Qué Te Ríes?" In 1948 Villa recorded "Rosita," which became his first hit. Later hits included "Monterrey," "Las Gaviotas," "La Picona," and "Tamaulipas." From that point on, Villa's popularity grew and he began touring all over Texas and the U.S.

For almost twelve years, Villa's Orquesta toured as a popular group throughout the Southwest, recording over one hundred 78s and many LPs for Discos Ideal. Villa insisted that his band members be able to read music and he worked in the recording studio with such luminaries as conjunto accordionist **Narciso Martínez,** ranchera singer **Lydia Mendoza,** and the duo Carmen y Laura. Villa and Martínez teamed up to record two polkas, "Madre Mía" and "Monterrey," as well as two waltzes, "Rosita" and "Morir Soñando."

In 1960 health problems forced him to stop touring, but his *orquesta* continued to record and tour occasionally. His music mixed the sound of the traditional Mexican *orquesta típica* with the regionally evolving norteño accordion music. In 1983 Villa was inducted into the TMA's Hall of Fame.

Al Compás de las Polleras (DISA)
Beto Villa: Father of Orquesta Tejana (Arhoolie)
Cabellos Largos (DISA)
Maldita Pobreza (DISA)
No Gozas ni Dejas Gozar (DISA)

VILLA, LUCHA

Born Luz Elena Ruíz Bejarano, November 30, circa 1934, Ciudad Camargo, Chihuahua, México

Lucha Villa
Courtesy of Balboa/Discos Musart

Since the early 1960s Lucha Villa has been a constant presence in ranchera music and Mexican films. As a youth, she competed in talent and beauty contests. Later, she came to the attention of TV producer Luis G. Dillon, who christened her Lucha Villa—after Pancho Villa, and Lucha, Chihuahua, the general's military stomping grounds. Early hits included "Viva Quien Quiera Saber," "La Cruz del Cielo," and "Media Vuelta," written by **José Alfredo Jiménez.** She rose to stardom when tapped by writers Gabriel García Marquez and Juan Rulfo to star in *El Gallo de Oro.* Villa went on to record more than fifty albums and appear in more than fifty films, including *Mecánica Nacional,* which won the Ariel, the Mexican equivalent of an Oscar. She also appeared in the sentimental *Lagunilla Mi Barrio* and *Lagunilla Mi Barrio II* with Manolo Fabregas, Hector Suárez, and Leticia Perdigon.

Villa—along with fellow ranchera greats Amalia "La Tariácuri" Mendoza of **Trío Tariácuri** and the late **Lola Beltrán**—was feted with a 1996 **Juan Gabriel**-directed tribute CD *Disco del Siglo: Las Tres Señoras*. Villa fell into a four-day coma in August 1997 after suffering cardiac arrest during a liposuction operation in Monterrey, Nuevo León, but recovered after a lengthy hospital stay.

12 Éxitos Rancheros (RCA)
15 Éxitos (Musart)
Interpreta a Juan Gabriel (RCA)
Una Mujer, una Banda (WEA Latina)
Puro Norte (Musart)

VILLARREAL, NICK

Born Nicolás Zimmerle Villarreal III, March 5, 1951, San Antonio, Texas

Nick Villarreal was part of a talented musical family that goes back to his maternal grandfather, Jimmy Zimmerle. His uncles were the late **Fred Zimmerle** and Henry Zimmerle Sr. Villarreal's father, Nicolás Jr., also sang in local groups.

Villarreal started playing the accordion when he was five years old and by the age of twelve he was sitting in with El Conjunto de Joe Ramírez. He played with various groups through high school, including his own conjunto with his brothers Roger and David. Later he played upright bass with **Los Tres Reyes** and by 1969 also played the *bajo sexto*.

In 1975 he formed Nick Villarreal y Su Conjunto. But after a serious car accident that injured his back, Villarreal devoted more time to songwriting and produced a number of regional hits. His biggest hits included "Brincando Cercas," "Las Gallinas del Pasado," "La-I-Gotta-Go," and "El Mayor," a humorous song about former San Antonio Mayor Henry Cisneros's well-publicized extramarital affair in 1995. In 1994 his body of work helped garner him a Pura Vida Award for songwriter. His band was named best conjunto/traditional the same year.

El Enamorado (Joey International)
Mis Hermanos Los Soldados (Joey International)

XELENCIA

Formed 1988, Houston, Texas

Like **La Fiebre,** Xelencia carved a niche for itself by fusing the basic Tejano repertoire of rancheras, polkas, and cumbias with edgy wailing guitar intros and hard rock theatrics—lights, fog, leather outfits, and big hair.

Alto/tenor saxophone player Jesse Perales (born January 8, 1955)—whose resumé included stints with area bands Los Flamingos and **La Mafia** for twelve years (he was a founding member)—teamed up with bass/vocalist Israel "Speedy" Villanueva (born July 26, 1962), another ex-La Mafia member. Villanueva wanted to combine an **El Conjunto Bernal**-type traditional outfit with the youthful energy of Los Chavalos. The synergy gelled when Perales and Villanueva met with ex-**Jaime y Los Chamacos** guitarist/vocalist David de Anda (born February 23, 1962) to form Xelencia. Keyboardist Randy Caballero and ex-La Mafia drummer Adam Mosqueda rounded out the band.

Xelencia debuted in October of 1988 in Houston at a Halloween dance. The band's initial hits included "Un Ángel No Debe Llorar," "Por Tus Celos," and "Aquí Me Encuentro." The group's 1989 CD, *Ni por Mil Puñados de Oro,* reached No. 10 on Billboard's Hot Latin LPs chart and remained on the chart for weeks. Villanueva wrote about sixty percent of the band's material. De Anda had an uncanny resemblance to bassist/singer Gene Simmons of the rock band Kiss.

12 Éxitos (EMI)
Un Ángel No Debe Llorar (EMI)
Por Tus Celos (EMI)
Puro Oro (EMI)

YAHARI

Formed 1990, Nueva Rosita, Coahuila, México

Led by drummer Jordano Alonzo Borjon, Yahari was named after the Japanese word for "unexpected." Alonzo and guitarist Juan Antonio de la Cruz y Trejo wrote some of the group's material. The band members met in high school and reportedly used the school's equipment to rehearse.

Yahari emerged in 1993 with the power ballads "Mensaje en la Luna" and "Primera Cosa Bella," but quickly shifted to the Afro-Caribbean tropical/cumbia style of their idol **Fito Olivares.** Soon, Yahari enjoyed regular rotations on regional Mexican airwaves with sax-driven tropical/cumbias and occasional double entendres in the songs' lyrics. Yahari settled into its tropical/cumbia band form and began collecting radio hits, including "Me Pica El Ojo," "Ahí Va," and "El Tren," which was a cover of Quad City DJ's "C'mon Ride the Train." The band also paid tribute to tropical/cumbia originator **Mike Laure** on its *La Pura Sabrosura* CD.

Lo Inesperado (DISA)
Más Sabrosura (EMI)
La Pura Sabrosura (EMI)

YBARRA, EVA

Born circa 1958, San Antonio, Texas

One of the few female accordionists in the male-dominated conjunto gene, Eva Ybarra was considered a master of the instrument.

She was born into a musical family—her mother sang, and her father and brothers played various instruments. Ybarra began playing the accordion at the age of four when her parents bought her a two-row button accordion. She learned by listening to the radio and watching her brother Pedro and others play. She briefly played in her brothers' conjunto and after the conjunto broke up she joined a mariachi. She later played with a series of local conjuntos, eventually forming her own Eva Ybarra y Sistema.

Most recently playing as Eva Ybarra y Su Conjunto, Ybarra impressed with her throaty vocals on traditional polkas, rancheras, ballads, corridos, *Schottishes,* and waltzes. Ybarra, whose nephew Pete Ybarra was **Emilio**'s accordionist, was also an instructor at the Guadalupe Cultural Arts Center.

A Bailar con Eva (Hacienda)
A Mi San Antonio (Rounder)
Romance Inolvidable (Rounder)

YNDIO

Formed 1972, Sonora, México

When Yndio came together, the group had hoped to name itself Yaqui after the Indian tribe that lives in Sonora. The name was already taken, so the group settled on Yndio. With only sixteen albums in twenty-six years, the band's output has been slow but steady, beginning with the first hit in the mid-1970s, "Sin Tu Amor." Additional chart singles included "Eres Mi Mundo," "Herida de Amor," and "Dame un Beso y Dime Adiós." The band occasionally recorded Spanish covers of English ballads by Barry Gibbs, Diane Warren, and others. Their "Melodía Desencadenada" was a cover of the Righteous Brothers' "Unchained Melody." The 1998 CD *El León Despierto* included guest musicians—famed *requinto* player Chamin Correa Pérez de León and mariachi Arriba Juárez.

Aniversario (PolyGram)
El León Despierto (FonoVisa)
Nuestras Mejores Canciones (EMI)
Reencuentro (PolyGram)
Romanticamente (EMI)

YONICS, LOS

Formed 1977, San Luis San Pedro, Guerrero, México

Los Yonics started out as a tropical/cumbia band in the late '70s after they won a local contest sponsored by the Televisa network. But in 1988 the band switched direction under the guidance of keyboardist/producer Johnny Ayvar, plunging headlong into the fledgling grupo movement.

Los Yonics's first hit came in 1979 with "Soy Yo." They followed with "Palabras Tristes" and "Rosas Blancas." Lead singer José Manuel Zamacona had emotional depth in his singing, injecting plaintive tones in his romantic tales. A disciplined outfit, group members practiced sports in their free time and did not permit drugs or alcohol in the band. In 1992 a chance visit to the recording studio by former **Los Bukis** band member **Marco Antonio Solis** led to the duet by Zamacona and Solis on "Pero Te Vas a Arrepentir," which was written by Solis. The song landed on the Billboard Hot Latin Tracks chart. Los Yonics later scored with "Frente a Frente" and "¿Por Qué Volví Contigo?" The group continued its soft ballad output throughout the 1990s, though its popularity began to fade after '95.

Le Falta un Clavo a Mi Cruz (EMI)
Romántico, Vol. 1 (FonoVisa)
Sólo Baladas (EMI)
Tu Recuerdo (FonoVisa)

ZIMMERLE, FRED, Y SU TRÍO SAN ANTONIO

Formed circa early '50s, San Antonio, Texas

Fred Zimmerle (born February 2, 1931, San Antonio, Texas) was a pioneer accordionist who, at the age of only fifteen, recorded his first sides for RCA in 1945. He hailed from a musical family that included his grandfather Fritze Zimmerle, who was a native of Germany, brother Henry Zimmerle Sr., nephew **Nick Villarreal,** and son Larry.

Fred Zimmerle picked up his first guitar at the age of six and learned to play the harmonica and accordion at the age of ten. His first gig was with his uncle Jimmy Zimmerle. At the age of fifteen, he began recording for RCA and eventually Zimmerle and his conjunto Trío San Antonio recorded for several labels and produced the hits "Dos Corazones," "Mira Luisa," "Concha Perdida," and "Monterrey Polka." The conjunto produced more than 250 songs, forty of them Zimmerle's own compositions. In 1989 he was inducted into the Tejano Conjunto Hall of Fame. In the '90s, Zimmerle also taught accordion classes at the Guadalupe Cultural Arts Center. Zimmerle passed away on March 5, 1998 from a heart attack.

Conjuntos Norteños (Arhoolie)

ZIMMERLE, HENRY, Y CONJUNTO SAN ANTONIO

Formed 1961, San Antonio, Texas

Henry Zimmerle Jr. (born June 16, 1940, San Antonio, Texas), a noted *bajo sexto* player/singer, was also part of the Zimmerle musical heritage. His father was the late Henry Zimmerle Sr., a conjunto musician/songwriter, and his late uncle was the accordionist **Fred Zimmerle** of the well-known Trío San Antonio. Zimmerle was also a cousin of singer/songwriter **Nick Villarreal.**

At the age of twelve, Zimmerle began to sit in with the likes of local heroes **Flaco Jiménez** y Los Caporales and later with Salvador García y **Los Pavos Reales.** He was also inspired by watching the guitar duo of Pedro Rocha and Lupe Martínez in San Antonio's downtown plaza in the late 1940s. In 1952 he received his first guitar from the famous *bajo sexto* maker Martin Macías. After forming his Conjunto San Antonio, he produced more than 100 recordings and scored with a song his father had written, "El Señor de los Milagros." Zimmerle also wrote the hits "Mis Penas," "Borracho Me Han de Amar," and "Mi Negro Traición."

Alma Olvidada (Hacienda)

Tex-Mex Chronology

1897 Famed singer and bolero songwriter **Agustin Lara** is born in Mexico City, México; **Mariachi Vargas de Tecalitlán** forms in Tacalitlán, Jalisco, México

1904 Mexican tenor balladeer **Pedro Vargas** is born in San Miguel de Allende, Guanajuato, México

1908 **Mariachi Cuarteto Coculense** is the first mariachi ever recorded in 1908; **Tito Guizar** is born in Guadalajara, Jalisco, México

1911 Mexican actor/ranchera singer **Jorge "El Charro Cantor" Negrete** is born in Guanajuato, Guanajuato, México; Father of Tejano/conjunto, **Narciso "El Huracán del Valle" Martínez,** is born in Reynosa, Tamaulipas, México; **Pedro Ayala** is born in General Terán, Nuevo León, México

1913 Accordionist/conjunto pioneer **Don Santiago Jiménez** is born in San Antonio, Texas

1915 Father of Orquesta Tejana, **Beto Villa,** is born in Falfurrias, Texas

1916 Mambo king Pérez Prado is born in Mantanzas, Cuba; **Lydia Mendoza** is born in Houston, Texas

1917 Actor/singer **Pedro Infante** is born in Guamuchil, Sinaloa, México; Ranchera singer **Miguel "The Golden Falsetto" Aceves Mejía** is born in Chihuahua, Chihuahua, México

1919 Ranchera singer **Antonio Aguilar** is born in Villanueva, Zacatecas, México

1926 Singer/songwriter **José Alfredo Jiménez** is born in Dolores Hidalgo, Guanajuato, México

1929 **Isidro "El Indio" López,** father of modern Tejano, is born in Bishop, Texas

1931 Bolero ranchero singer **Javier Solis** is born in Mexico City, México; Tejano/conjunto accordionist **Tony De La Rosa** is born in Sarita, Texas;

1932 Ranchera singer **Lola "La Grande" Beltrán** is born in Rosario, Sinaloa, México; **Agustin Lara** composes **"Granada"**

1933 During a tour of Brazil **Agustin Lara** composes **"Solamente una Vez"**

1934 **Lydia Mendoza** records **"Mal Hombre"**

1935 Singer/songwriter **Armando Manzanero** is born in Mérida, Yucatán, México

1936 Among the oldest *trío románticos* in history forms when guitarists Raúl Prado and Miguel Bermejo form **Trío Calaveras** in Mexico City, México

1937 Famed composer José "Pepe" Guizar writes the mariachi standard **"Guadalajara,"** which **Lucha "La Reina de los Mariachis" Reyes** later records

1938 Seminal group **Banda El Recodo de Cruz Lizárraga** forms in Mazatlán, Sinaloa, México; **Tito Guizar** appears in and sings title track in Mexican film *Allá en el Rancho Grande*

1939 Alberto Dominguez writes the first widely popular boleros **"Pérfida"** and **"Frenesí";** Tejano/conjunto accordionist **Flaco Jiménez** is born in San Antonio, Texas; **Mike "El Rey del Trópico" Laure,** founder of tropical/cumbia genre, is born in El Salto, Jalisco, México

1940 Ranchera singer **Vicente Fernández** is born in Huentitán el Alto, Jalisco, México; Norteño singer/songwriter **Cornelio Reyna** is born in Saltillo, Coahuila, México; Tejano singer **Rubén "El Gato Negro" Ramos** is born in Sugarland, Texas; Tejano singer **Little Joe** is born in Temple, Texas

1941 Boleros enter a golden age with the newly written classics **"Solamente una Vez"** (Agustin Lara) and **"Bésame Mucho"** (Consuelo Velásquez)

1943 Months before he dies of tuberculosis in April, songwriter Pedro Junco Jr. composes **"Nosotros"** as a farewell letter to his girlfriend; this lovely ballad was later made famous by **Eydie Gorme** and **Trío Los Panchos**

1944 **Trio Los Panchos** forms in New York, New York; **Rocío Durcal** is born in Madrid, Spain

1945 Norteño singer/accordionist **Ramón Ayala** is born in Monterrey, Nuevo León, México

1946 **Agustin Lara** marries the actress María Felix; they divorce the following year and Lara writes **"María Bonita"** as a tribute

1947 Tropical/cumbiero and songwriter **Fito Olivares** is born in Ciudad Miguel Alemán, Tamaulipas, México

1948 José "Pepe" Guizar writes bolero evergreen **"Sin Ti";** Accordionist Eugenio Abrego and *bajo sexto* player Tomas Ortiz form **Los Alegres de Terán** in General Terán, Nuevo León, México, laying the seeds of the original norteño sound

1950 Singer/songwriter **Juan Gabriel** is born in Paracuaro, Michoacán, México; Tropical/cumbiero singer/songwriter **Rigo Tovar** is born in Matamoros, Tamaulipas, México; **Orquesta Tejana** genre enjoys its golden age as bandleaders **Beto Villa, Chris Sandoval, Isidro López,** Balde González, and others enjoy massive popularity in big record sales and packed concerts

1952 **Pedro Infante** and **Jorge Negrete** are in a rare joint appearance in Mexican film *Dos Tipos de Cuidado*; in October, **Jorge Negrete** weds actress María Felix in a celebrity marriage billed in Mexico as "the wedding of the century;" Brothers Paulino and Eloy Bernal form **El Conjunto Bernal** in Raymondville, Texas

1953 **Jorge Negrete** dies at the age of forty-two in December from cirrhosis of the liver at the Cedars of Lebanon Hospital in Los Angeles

1954 **Isidro "El Indio" López,** at the age of twenty-five, creates modern Tejano music when he combines conjunto's accordion with the *orquesta*'s horn section

1955 Pérez Prado enjoys ten-week run at No. 1 on *Billboard*'s pop single chart with **"Cherry Pink and Apple Blossom White"** and launches a mambo craze in North America

1956 Composer Roberto Cantoral writes and, together with his trio **Los Tres Caballeros,** records the classic boleros **"El Reloj"** and **"La Barca";** Carlos Colorado forms **La Sonora Santanera,** in Santa Ana, Tabasco, México; Catarinos Leos Rodríguez forms **Los Rancheritos del Topo Chico** in Monterrey, Nuevo León, México; Oscar Lawson,Mike Pedraza, and Henry Hernández form the **Royal Jesters** in San Antonio, Texas

1957 **Pedro Infante,** at the age of thirty-nine, dies on April 15 after the converted WWII B-24 bomber he was copiloting crashes in Mérida, Yucatán, México

1958 Pop/folkloric singer/songwriter **Ana Gabriel** is born in Guamuchil, Sinaloa, México; Famed *requinto* player Gilberto Puente, his brother Raúl, and ex-Trío Los Panchos singer Hernando Aviles form **Los Tres Reyes** in Mexico City, México

1959 Little Joe and the Latinaires (which eventually became **Little Joe y La Familia**) form in Temple, Texas

1960 **Sonora Dinamita,** one of the most influential tropical/cumbia outfits in Latin America, forms in Medellín, Colombia

1961 **Little Joe** emerges with his first hits **"El Corrido del West"** and **"Cuando Salgo a los Campos"**

1962 **Sunny Ozuna** and the Sunglows score with **"Talk to Me,"** which lands on *Dick Clark's American Bandstand;* Ozuna leaves the band to form Sunny and the Sunliners; Ozuna is replaced by **Joe Bravo; Rocío Durcal** appears in her first movie *Canción de Juventud;* Accordionist Juan Torres and guitarist Salomón Prado join to form **Los Tremendos Gavilanes** in Monterrey, Nuevo León, México; Emilio Navaira is born in San Antonio, Texas, and as **Emilio** he would become one of the most popular Tejano artists in the 1990s.

1963 **Cornelio Reyna** and **Ramón Ayala** team up to form **Los Relámpagos del Norte** in Reynosa, Tamaulipas, México; a car accident outside of San Luis Potosí, San Luis Potosí, México, kills bolero singer/songwriter **Luis Arcaraz** on June 1

1966 Bolero singer **Javier Solis** dies on April 19 at the age of thirty-five from complications from a gallbladder operation in Mexico City, México; after several record label rejections, **Vicente Fernández** is signed to CBS México

1968 Jorge Hernández and brothers form **Los Tigres del Norte** in Rosa Morada, Sinaloa, México

1969 Rudy Guerra, Charlie McBurney, and Pete Garza form **Latin Breed** in San Antonio, Texas; **Rubén Ramos** leaves his brother Alfonso Jr.'s orchestra to form the nucleus of **Rubén Ramos** and the Mexican Revolution

1970 **Marco Antonio Solis** and brothers form **Los Bukis** first as Los Hermanos Solis in Ario de Rosales, Michoacán, México; Composer and singer **Agustin Lara** dies at the age of seventy-three in Mexico City, México; brothers Miguel "El Gorrión" Luna and Cirilo "El Palomo" Luna form **El Palomo y El Gorrión** in Aramberri, Nuevo León, México; Tejano enters its golden age with hits including **Freddie Martínez's "Te Traigo Estas Flores," Joe Bravo's "La Patita de Conejo," Latin Breed's "Tejano Enamorado,"** and **Augustin Ramirez's "Sangre de Indio"**

1971 Influential group **Los Relámpagos del Norte** disband after eight years together, and Ayala and Reyna launch solo careers; Pioneer grupo **Los Angeles Negros** dominates Mexican radio with the singles **"Y Volveré"** and **"Murió la Flor"; Los Tigres del Norte** deliver megahit in corrido cannon, **"Contrabando y Traición"; Juan Gabriel** debuts with first hit smash **"No Tengo Dinero"; Alejandro Fernández** is born in Mexico City, México; Selena Quintanilla is born in Freeport, Texas, and as **Selena** she would reinvent the Mexican cumbia and become a major pop star of the early 1990s

1973 **José Alfredo Jiménez,** the most prolific and successful folkloric songwriter in Mexico, dies at the age of forty-seven in Mexico City, México; **Bobby Pulido** is born in Edinburg, Texas; Mexican American singer **Johnny Rodríguez** lands No. 1 hit with **"You Always Come Back to Hurting Me"**

1974 Homero Guerrero Sr. and Lupe Tijerina form influential norteño group **Los Cadetes de Linares** in Linares, Nuevo León, México

1975 **Freddy Fender** becomes Mexican American crossover success with No. 1 chart hit **"Wasted Days and Wasted Nights"**; Singer **Jimmy Edward** departs Latin Breed and launches solo career

1976 **Vicente Fernández** becomes undisputed genre leader with his ranchera megahit **"Volver, Volver"**

1977 Keyboardist/producer Johnny Ayvar forms **Los Yonics** in San Luis San Pedro, Guerrero, México; **Mazz** forms as Brown Express in Brownsville, Texas, and later that year signs with Bob Grever's Cara Records; the **Royal Jesters** disband

1978 **Bronco** forms in Monterrey, Nuevo León, México; Henry Gonzáles Jr. and younger brothers Oscar and Leonard form **La Mafia** in Houston, Texas

1980 **Rocío Durcal** releases her first ranchera album, which includes the **Juan Gabriel**–penned **"Amor Eterno"; Fito Olivares** leaves Los Tam y Tex to form La Pura Sabrosura

1981 MTV Network launched; Tejano Music Awards and Tejano Music Hall of Fame are established in San Antonio, Texas, and the first inductee is **Mariachi Sol de México; Nydia Rojas** is born in Whittier, California

1982 Tejano Conjunto Festival and Tejano Conjunto Hall of Fame are established in San Antonio, Texas, and the first inductee is **Los Temerarios;** the Grammys expand the one best Latin recording field to three: Latin pop, Tropical Latin, and Mexican/American

1984 Spanish crooner **Julio Iglesias** begins his American conquest with English-language pop CD *1100 Bel Air Place,* which features the hit single, a duet with Willie Nelson on **"To All the Girls I've Loved Before"**; Conjunto patriarch **Don Santiago Jiménez** dies on December 2, in San Antonio, Texas

1985 Little Joe records benchmark CD ***25th Silver Anniversary*** at Fiesta Plaza, San Antonio, Texas; **Mazz** releases ***No. 16***

1986 **Los Tucanes de Tijuana** form in Tijuana, Baja California Norte, México; **Beto Villa,** the "Father of Orquesta Tejana" dies at the age of seventy-one, in Corpus Christi, Texas; **Flaco Jiménez** wins his first Grammy in the newly formed best Mexican American category for ***Ay Te Dejo en San Antonio;* Fito Olivares** writes monster cumbia hit **"Juana La Cubana"; Little Joe** becomes first Tejano signed by CBS Discos; Puerto Rican Hernando Aviles of **Trío Los Panchos** dies; *Billboard* expands its Latin sales surveys to three charts: pop, tropical/salsa, and regional Mexican

1987 **Los Lobos** scores big with summer biopic about Ritchie Valens ***La Bamba;*** the title track from the soundtrack reaches No. 1 on the Billboard Hot 100 Singles Sales chart, while the soundtrack goes to No. 1 on The Billboard 200 chart; **Linda Ronstadt** releases landmark roots ranchera CD ***Canciones de Mi Padre***

1988 **Linda Ronstadt** wins Grammy for ***Canciones de Mi Padre;* Los Tigres del Norte** wins Grammy for ***"Gracias! América sin Fronteras*** CD

1989 **Los Bukis** dominate the grupo scene with hit single **"Como Fui Enamorarme de Ti"** from the top-selling CD ***Y Para Siempre;*** **Pedro "El Tenor de las Américas" Vargas** dies at the age of eighty-five in Mexico City, México; New Latin imprint Capitol/EMI Latin launches with José Behar and Manolo González signing **Mazz, Emilio,** and **Selena; Los Lobos** win Grammy for the folk acoustic CD ***La Pistola y el Corazón;*** **Texas Tornados** (Flaco Jiménez, Doug Sahm, Augie Meyers, and Freddie Fender) form in San Francisco, California; **Emilio Navaira** leaves David Lee Garza y Los Musicales to launch a solo career

1990 **Banda Machos** form in Villa Corona, Jalisco, México; **Emilio, Roberto Pulido,** and **Vikki Carr** perform at first Go Tejano Day at the Astrodome for the Houston Rodeo in front of 51,000 fans; Capitol/EMI buys Bob Grever's San Antonio–based indie Cara Records, at the time distributed by CBS Discos

1991 **Texas Tornados' "Soy de San Luis"** from their self-titled CD wins Grammy for best Mexican American performance; **Juan Gabriel** receives Lifetime Achievement Award at the Billboard/Univision Latin Music Awards; **Banda Maguey** forms in Villa Corona, Jalisco, México

1992 Father of Tejano conjunto, **Narciso Martínez,** dies at the age of eighty in San Benito, Texas; **Little Joe** is first Tejano to win Grammy for best Mexican American performance for ***Diez y Seis de Septiembre;*** **Los Temerarios** reach No. 6 on the Billboard Hot Latin Tracks chart with the smash Adolfo Angel–written ballad **"Mi Vida Eres Tú";** On April 2, **Selena** marries guitarist **Chris Pérez** in Corpus Christi, Texas; Sony Discos, Freddie, TH-Rodven, and FonoVisa labels rock the industry when they pull out from the Tejano Music Awards; Tejano station KXTN reaches No. 1 general market in San Antonio, Texas

1993 In February KLAX-FM reaches No.1 spot in Los Angeles, California, the country's largest radio market, playing a mix of bandas and rancheras; **Selena** wins Grammy for ***Selena Live;*** Mexican Jesús "Chucho" Navarro Moreno of **Trío Los Panchos** dies in Mexico City

1994 **Flaco Jiménez** is inducted into the Tejano Conjunto Hall of Fame; singer/songwriter Alicia "La Güera" Villarreal teams up with accordionist Gerardo Padilla and *bajo sexto* player Jesús Cantu to form **Grupo Límite** in Monterrey, Nuevo León, México

1995 **Marco Antonio Solis** goes solo, leaving Los Bukis, who re-emerge as **Los Mismos; Selena** and **Emilio** break attendance record at the Astrodome for the Houston Rodeo with 61,041; On March 31, **Selena,** at the age of twenty-three, is killed by ex-fan club president in motel shooting in Corpus Christi, Texas; In April **Selena** has five CDs on The Billboard 200 chart, an accomplishment previously only achieved by superstars like Garth Brooks, Elvis Presley, and the Beatles

1996 **Lola Beltrán** dies of a stroke in Mexico City, México; In December, norteño superstar **Bronco** stuns music world by announcing retirement, scheduling year-long farewell tour

1997 **Mariachi Vargas de Tecalitlán** launches year-long celebration of 100th anniversary; Singer/songwriter **Cornelio Reyna,** one half of the famed **Los Relámpagos del Norte,** dies at the age of fifty-six of complications of a bleeding ulcer in Mexico City, México; ***Selena,*** the biopic depicting the life of the late singer, is released; **Bronco** performs its last show on December 21 at 115,000-capacity Estadio Azteca in Mexico City, México; **Los Tigres del Norte** film *Jefe de Jefes* video at Alcatraz Prison; **La Mafia** wins Grammy for *Un Millón de Rosas*

1998 *Bajo sexto* player Eloy Bernal, co-founder of **El Conjunto Bernal,** dies at the age of sixty-one in a bus accident outside of Corpus Christi, Texas; **Vicente Fernández** is inducted into the Billboard Latin Music Hall of Fame; **La Mafia** wins Grammy for *En Tus Manos;* conjunto accordionist Rúben Naranjo dies on October 12 at the age of fifty-three of heart failure in Alice, Texas; **Mazz** splits into two groups (lead singer Joe López plays under the name Joe López y Nuevo Imagen Mazz while guitarist Jimmy González tours under the name Original Grupo Mazz); two-time Grammy winner **La Mafia** announces retirement on December 2

1999 Two members of the Tejano band **Intocable** (onstage MC José Ángel Farías and bass player Silvestre Rodríguez Jr.) are killed in a car crash outside Monterrey, Nuevo León on January 31; Tejano music finally gets its own category at the Grammy Awards; Flaco Jiménez wins first Grammy for best Tejano category with *Said and Done;* Los Super Seven win Grammy for best Mexican American category with their self-titled CD.

Ramiro Burr's Top 10 Lists

Picking and debating Top 10 lists in the world of music is an enduring source of ardent argument and debate. Fans debate comparative values of heroes and songs, picking and choosing the music that moves them the most. The exercise—especially among knowledgeable folks—can elicit fond memories, inspiration, revelation, and understanding.

The following is a list of the all-time greatest albums and influential hit songs in the five major regional Mexican subgenres from Tejano to trio. The final picks were determined by me, but they were arrived at as a result of endless hours of incessant, abundant, and highly persuasive input from an army of veteran industry officials, critical experts, and music lovers. Among the many subjective and qualitative factors we used in our criteria were performance, execution, lyrics, continuity, production, impact, and influence.

The last—but perhaps the most important—factor in determining these selections, was availability of the works. In other words, we did not want to list albums that are no longer in print or available anywhere.

Given the opinionated nature of the music's fervent fans, we are sure that the Top 10 lists will generate spirited feedback and a little heated controversy. So in the spirit of D-I-Y, we have graciously included a blank page so that those instant sidewalk critics and armchair analysts will have the opportunity to submit their own Top 10 picks.

Tejano

TOP 10 TEJANO ALBUMS

1. *Timeless,* Little Joe
2. *Breaking the Rules,* Latin Breed
3. *Con el Tiempo,* David Lee Garza with Jay Pérez
4. *25th Silver Anniversary,* Little Joe
5. *El Disgusto,* Eddie González
6. *Forever,* Bob Gallarza
7. *No. 16,* Mazz
8. *Live,* Emilio Navaira
9. *Bachata Rosa,* Ramiro Herrera
10. *Tejano Goldies,* Various Artists

Honorable Mentions:
1392, David Lee Garza; *Para la Gente,* Little Joe

TOP 10 TEJANO SONGS

1. "Las Nubes," Little Joe
2. "Don Luis el Tejano" Latin Breed
3. "Ay Mujer," Jay Pérez
4. "El Tejano Enamorado," Latin Breed
5. "Qué Tristeza," David Lee Garza with Jay Pérez
6. "El Disgusto," Eddie González
7. "Cuando Salgo a los Campos," Little Joe
8. "Soy Como Soy," Mazz
9. "No Me Queda Más," Selena
10. "Paloma Negra," Rubén Ramos

Honorable Mentions:
"Amor Prohibido" and "Bidi Bidi Bom Bom," Selena; "Mi Nena," Little Joe

Conjunto

TOP 10 CONJUNTO ALBUMS

1. *Mi Único Camino,* El Conjunto Bernal
2. *Así Se Baila en Tejas,* Tony De La Rosa
3. *El Mero Mero Sí Señor,* Rubén Naranjo
4. *El Coco Rayado,* Rubén Vela
5. *I Love My Freedom, I Love My Texas,* Mingo Saldivar
6. *Buena Suerte, Señorita,* Flaco Jiménez
7. *Caballo Viejo,* Valerio Longoria
8. *A Través de los Años,* Roberto Pulido
9. *Said and Done,* Flaco Jiménez
10. *Amor y Lágrimas,* Joe Ramos y Ellos

Honorable Mention:
Conjunto! Tex-Mex Border Music, Vol. 1, Various Artists

TOP 10 CONJUNTO SONGS

1. "Mi Único Camino," El Conjunto Bernal
2. "Sucedió en la Baranca," Tony De La Rosa
3. "Ojos Querendones," Rubén Naranjo
4. "La Flecha," Roberto Pulido
5. "El Silencio de la Noche," El Conjunto Bernal
6. "Preso sin Delito," Rubén Naranjo
7. "Margarita," Don Santiago Jiménez
8. "Mire Amigo," The Hometown Boys
9. "Atotonilco," Tony De La Rosa
10. "La Chicarronera," Narciso Martínez

Norteño

TOP 10 NORTEÑO ALBUMS

1. *Callejón sin Salida,* Los Relámpagos del Norte
2. *Casas de Madera,* Ramón de Ayala
3. *Jefe de Jefes,* Los Tigres del Norte
4. *Tucanazo,* Los Tucanes de Tijuana
5. *Para Mi Pueblo,* Michael Salgado
6. *Intocable,* Intocable
7. *Partiéndome el Alma,* Grupo Límite
8. *Vuelven,* Los Alegres de Terán
9. *Ingratos Ojos Míos,* El Palomo y El Gorrión
10. *Amigo,* Bronco

TOP 10 NORTEÑO SONGS

1. "La Banda del Carro Rojo," Los Tigres del Norte
2. "Juguete," Grupo Límite
3. "Un Rinconcito en el Cielo," Ramón Ayala
4. "Si Tú Supieras," Cornelio Reyna
5. "Me Caí de las Nubes," Cornelio Reyna
6. "Prenda Querida," Los Cadetes de Linares
7. "Qué No Quede Huella," Bronco
8. "Cruz de Madera," Michael Salgado
9. "El Güero Estrada," Los Alegres de Terán
10. "Solo Contigo," Grupo Límite

Mariachi/Ranchera

TOP 10 MARIACHI/RANCHERA ALBUMS

1. *La Historia de Javier Solis,* Javier Solis
2. *Las Clásicas de José Alfredo Jiménez,* Vicente Fernández
3. *Recordando,* José Alfredo Jiménez
4. *Fiesta Mexicana,* Jorge Negrete
5. *Las Románticas,* Pedro Infante
6. *Mis Canciones,* Vicente Fernández
7. *Muy Dentro de Mi Corazón,* Alejandro Fernández
8. *Viva el Mariachi,* Mariachi Vargas de Tecalitlán
9. *Sólo Vine a Cantar,* Angeles Ochoa
10. *Canciones de Mi Padre,* Linda Ronstadt

TOP 10 MARIACHI/RANCHERA SONGS

1. "Ella," José Alfredo Jiménez
2. "El Rey," Vicente Fernández
3. "Cien Años," Pedro Infante
4. "Sombras," Javier Solis
5. "Camino de Guanajuato," Vicente Fernández
6. "Los Laureles," Linda Ronstadt
7. "Yo," José Alfredo Jiménez
8. "Alma de Acero," Vicente Fernández
9. "Si Dios Me Quita la Vida," Javier Solis
10. "Si Nos Dejan," José Alfredo Jiménez

Honorable Mentions:
"Te Propongo," Ana Gabriel; "Cuatro Milpas," Antonio Aguilar; "Dos Arbolitos" and "Hay Unos Ojos," Linda Ronstadt; "Vámonos," Vicente Fernández

Trio/Bolero

TOP 10 TRIO/BOLERO SONGS

1. "Reloj," Trío Los Panchos
2. "Novia Mía," Los Tres Reyes
3. "Contigo a la Distancia," Los Tres Ases
4. "Usted," Los Tres Diamantes
5. "La Barca," Los Tres Caballeros
6. "Sin Ti," Trío Los Panchos
7. "Gema," Trío Los Dandys
8. "Contigo Aprendí," Trío Los Panchos
9. "Sabor a Mí," Eydie Gorme and Trío Los Panchos
10. "Nosotros," Eydie Gorme

Glossary

This is a list of simple definitions for a variety of words, song styles, genres, and other terms that are referred to in the encyclopedia and history sections. In some cases, such as the genres and unique song forms, there are references to detailed essays within the encyclopedia section that provide additional description or history.

Accordion (squeeze box) The button accordion is indispensable to Tejano and norteño music. Accordionists play the melody with their right hand and the bass with their left hand. Most accordions have buttons, though some have a keyboard for the right hand. The more rows of buttons an accordion has, the more notes it can play. Chromatic accordions play all the notes in the scale, the equivalent to the white and black keys on a piano. Diatonic accordions, which were common in the early days of conjunto, typically had just two rows of buttons and could only play the do-re-mi-fa-so-la-ti-do scales. (*See A–Z entry:* Accordion)

ANDA Asociación Nacional de Actores (National Association of Actors). The Mexican counterpart to the Screen Actors' Guild in the U.S.

ASCAP American Society of Composers, Authors, and Publishers. A New York–based songwriters' licensing and royalty collecting agency.

Aztlan The mythical homeland of Aztec Indians. The name was appropriated in the 1970s by leftist Chicano activists to describe the portion of the southwestern U.S. that was purchased from Mexico in the nineteenth century. It is also the general area where conjunto acts toured on the *carpa* circuit and where Tejano and regional Mexican music is most popular. Some activists claim Aztlan should be an independent country and should eventually be reunited with Mexico.

Baile de plataforma (bi-lay day plahta-formah) Outdoor, rural conjunto dances that are held on wooden platforms. *Bailes de plataforma* were most common in the 1930s and 1940s before conjunto music moved to the dance halls and ballrooms.

Baile grande (bi-lay grand-eh) A "big" dance held in a large ballroom; also an all-night mini–Woodstock-style outdoor concert.

Bajo sexto (ba-ho sex-toe) A heavy twelve-string Spanish bass guitar that is used to provide rhythm and bass in conjunto music. (*See A–Z entry:* Bajo Sexto)

Banda (bahn-dah) A horn-driven Mexican musical genre especially popular in western Mexico and California. Electro-banda or techno-banda are bandas that use keyboards and/or electric bass and retain smaller horn sections. (*See A–Z entry:* Banda)

Billboard An authoritative music industry trade publication. *Billboard* publishes music news and charts that represent a wide variety of genres, including Latin. The Billboard Hot Latin Tracks chart, which monitors current hits, has forty positions and is compiled from a national sample of airplay supplied by Broadcast Data Systems' (BDS) Radio Track Service. The Billboard Latin 50 chart, which tracks album sales, is compiled from a national sample of retail store and rack sales reports that are collected, compiled, and provided by SoundScan. Both charts also list the top fifteen entries by format: pop, tropical/salsa, and regional Mexican.

Billboard Latin Music Awards Annual music awards sponsored by *Billboard* that are based on year-end survey of airplay (tabulated by BDS) and CD sales (tabulated by SoundScan).

BMI Broadcast Music Inc. A New York–based music performing rights organization and songwriters' and publishers' royalty collecting agency.

Bolero A sentimental ballad song form whose modern incarnation originated in Cuba but was widely popularized by Mexican trios. (*See A–Z entries:* Bolero and Trio)

Caja vallenata (ka-ha va-yeh-nah-tah) A box-shaped, bongo-like drum used in vallenato music. (See A–Z entry: *Vallenato)*

Campesino (camp-eh-see-no) Spanish for "country dweller."

Canción (can-see-on) Spanish for "song."

Carpas, Las (las car-pahs) Spanish for "the tents." *Carpas* were traveling tent shows that toured the Tejano migrant worker circuit in the southwestern U.S. during the 1930s, 1940s, and 1950s and brought entertainment to the workers.

Charanga (cha-rahn-gah) A fast, bouncy rhythm similar to *la quebradita.* (*See glossary entry:* Quebradita) Also an ensemble that originated in the early twentieth century and that included, but was not limited to, the wooden Creole flute, piano, bass, violin, *güiro,* and timbal.

Charreada (cha-ria-da) A Mexican rodeo.

Charro (cha-ro) A Mexican horseman or cowboy. A *traje de charro* or *traje de gala* is an exquisite, close-fitting outfit worn by mariachi musicians. (*See A–Z entry:* Mariachi)

Chicano Movement A civil rights and leftist movement of the 1960s and 1970s that influenced Tejano artists such as the Royal Jesters and Little Joe. Some Mexican Americans, especially those with liberal leanings, call themselves Chicanos. (*See A–Z entries:* Joe Bravo and Little Joe)

Chunchaca (shun-cha-kah) A rock/cumbia fusion developed by *onda grupera* pioneer Mike Laure. (*See A–Z entry:* Tropical/cumbia)

Cinco de Mayo (seen-co day my-oh) Spanish for "the fifth of May." A celebration of the anniversary of the Battle of Puebla, May 5, 1862, when heavily outmanned Mexican forces, led by Texan General Ignacio Zaragoza, defeated French forces. The French eventually conquered the country, but their reign was short-lived (1864–1867). The event is celebrated in the U.S. and Mexico with parties, parades, and concerts.

Compas (cohm-pahs) Spanish for "rhythm." *El compas* colloquially refers to a good atmosphere.

Conjunto (cohn-hoon-toe) Spanish for "ensemble." In a musical context, conjunto refers to accordion- and *bajo sexto*–fueled music from Texas. Norteño is conjunto's Mexican counterpart. (*See A–Z entry:* Conjunto)

Conjunto de arpa (cohn-hoon-toe day ar-pah) Precursor to mariachi, a four-man ensemble that includes the harp. (*See A–Z entry:* Mariachi)

Corrido (coh-ree-doh) A narrative ballad or story-song usually sung in norteño music to a waltz or polka beat. Narco-corridos are corridos that deal with drug smuggling. (*See A–Z entry:* Corrido)

Cover A song an artist performs that is associated with (and was first performed by) another artist; also known as a take or an interpretation.

Coyote A slang term for a smuggler of illegal immigrants. Often referred to in corridos. (*See A–Z entry:* Corrido)

Cumbia (coom-bee-ya) A simple dance rhythm that originated in Colombia. Also a song performed in this rhythm. Cumbia is one of the most popular rhythms in Tejano and norteño music, and is ubiquitous in Mexican *musica tropical.* Cumbieros are musicians who specialize in cumbias. (*See A–Z entries:* Cumbia and Tropical/cumbia)

Danzón (dahn-zone) A ballroom dance popularized in Cuba in the 1870s; also a rhythm that was used by the Orquesta Tejana.

Diez y Seis de Septiembre (dee-ez ee say-zz day sep-tee-em-brey) Spanish for "the sixteenth of September." On September 16, 1810, Mexico declared its independence from Spain. Like *Cinco de Mayo,* the event is celebrated in the U.S. and Mexico with parties, parades, and concerts.

Dueto (doo-eh-toe) Spanish for "duet." *Dueto* is used to refer to the male or female conjunto duets of the 1950s such as Las Hermanas Mendoza.

Frontera, La (la fron-teh-rah) Spanish for "the border." In norteño music *la frontera* usually refers to the U.S.-Mexican border.

Grammy Music awards given annually by the National Academy of Recording Arts and Sciences. Grammy winners are selected by the 7,000-plus members of the academy, which gives awards in more than ninety categories. It is considered the most prestigious music award in the world. In Latin music, there are categories for: Latin pop, tropical/salsa, Mexican American, Tejano, Latin jazz, and rock *en Español.* (*See glossary entry:* NARAS)

Grupera (*See glossary entry:* Onda grupera)

Grupo (gru-po) A term for bands that tour and record together as a cohesive unit. Grupo music refers to romantic, pop-leaning regional Mexican groups such as Los Temerarios, Los Bukis, and Los Fugitivos. (*See A–Z entry:* Grupo)

Guacharaca (gooah-cha-rah-kah) A cane scraper used in vallenato music. (*See A–Z entry:* Vallenato)

Guapachosa (gooah-pa-cho-sah) Colloquial Spanish for "catchy" or "contagious." Many tropical/cumbieros use the word *guapachosa* to describe their music. (*See A–Z entry:* Fito Olivares)

Güiro (goo-we-row) A round, wooden, serrated, hand-held percussion instrument that is played with a wooden scraper and is common in tropical/cumbia music. (*See A–Z entry:* Tropical/cumbia)

Guitarra de golpe (gee-ta-rah day goal-pay) A five-string guitar used in mariachi music. (*See A–Z entry:* Mariachi Vargas de Tecalitlán)

Guitarrón (gee-ta-rohn) A fat, four- or five-string acoustic Mexican bass guitar that is frequently used in mariachis. (*See A–Z entry:* Mariachi)

Huapango (gua-pahn-go) A fast-paced folk dance, popular in the northeast of Mexico, sometimes also called the Mexican Hat Dance.

Hispanic The most frequently used term in the U.S. to describe people of Latin American or Spanish descent.

Ice house A contemporary slang term for "neighborhood bar." In actuality, ice houses were neighborhood stores that sold ice. Later they began selling other products common to convenience stores, including beer.

Independent/indie label A record company that has at least one of the following characteristics: specializes in just one type of music, has limited distribution, has operations that are limited to one country, and makes the national charts rarely (if ever). Successful indies are often able to arrange distribution deals with major labels, and the most successful indies are often bought by major record labels.

Jaripeo (ha-ree-payo) A Mexican rodeo.

Juke joint A term that originated in the southeastern U.S. to describe a roadhouse or bar with a jukebox. South Texas juke joints sprung up in the 1940s and featured the latest hits on the jukeboxes.

Latino/a A synonym for Hispanic, commonly used among Spanish speakers.

Major record label A record label that records artists in a variety of formats, operates in many countries, has a constant chart presence, and has a national distribution network and major promotion/ marketing budgets. Major record labels that publish in Tejano music include Sony and EMI Latin.

Mambo A rhythm developed by Afro-Cuban religious cults. Mambo was largely popularized and developed in the U.S. during the 1940s and 1950s, after mambo king Pérez Prado introduced it in Cuba. It was known for its alternating brass and sax riffs. Mambo rhythm was favored by the Orquesta Tejana.

Mariachi A trumpet-, violin-, and guitar-based sentimental Mexican music; also a band that plays such music. (*See A–Z entry:* Mariachi)

Mazurka A Polish dance step similar to a polka.

Merequetengue (meh-reh-kay-ten-gey) A frenetic rhythm similar to the *huapango* that often incorporates horns. Notable examples of *merequetengue* include "El Sheriff de Chocolate" by Bronco and "Virgencita de Guadalupe" by Okiroqui. Banda standout Ezequiel Peña and norteño stars Los Tucanes de Tijuana are also known to use *merequetengue* rhythm during concerts.

Mexican American An American citizen of Mexican descent.

NARAS National Academy of Recording Arts and Sciences. The organization that awards the Grammys. (*See glossary entry:* Grammy)

Norteño (nor-tane-yo) Spanish for "northern." Norteño music originated in northern Mexico and uses accordion and *bajo sexto* instrumentation. The similarly styled conjunto is norteño's Texan counterpart. (*See A–Z entry:* Norteño)

Onda grupera (on-dah groo-pey-rah) *Onda* is Spanish for "wave," but when it is used with *grupera* it usually means "grupo music." (For example, "¿Qué hay de nuevo en la onda grupera?" means "What's new in grupo music?")

Onda Tejana (ohn-da tey-ha-na) Refers to Tejano genre.

Orquesta Tejana (or-kay-stah tey-ha-na) A big-band music performed by Mexican Americans. Orquesta Tejana peaked in the early 1950s. Bandleader Beto Villa is considered the father of the movement. (*See A–Z entry:* Orquesta Tejana)

Pachanga (pa-chan-ga) Spanish for "party" or "festival."

Paisano (pie-sa-no) Spanish for "countryman" or "compatriot."

Palenque (pa-len-kay) The Mexican equivalent of county fairs. Also refers to places where cockfights are held. *Palenques* are frequent venues for Mexican roots-music acts.

Parranda (pah-rahn-da) A partying binge often accompanied by drinking.

Plaza Garibaldi A two-block-long central square in Mexico City that is considered the traditional capital of live mariachi music.

Polka A fast rhythm that developed in Europe during the nineteenth century and that became the basis for most Tejano and norteño music. (*See A–Z entry:* Polka)

Premio Lo Nuestro (pray-me-oh lo nway-stro) An annual Latin music award sponsored by the U.S.-based Spanish TV network Univision. Awards are presented for categories (best album, song, group, artist, etc.) within three subgenres: Latin pop, tropical/salsa, and regional Mexican.

Quebradita (kay-bra-dee-tah) A dance that combines *lambada,* country-western, and flamenco elements; also a fast rhythm used by many bands. (*See A–Z entry:* Banda)

Ranchera (ran-che-rah) A sentimental Mexican song form with romanticized lyrics about love or pastoral life. (*See A–Z entry:* Ranchera)

Redowa (ray-dow-vah) A Bohemian dance that has a meter that is similar to the polka.

Requinto (re-keen-toe) A small guitar invented by Trío Los Panchos member Alfredo Gil in 1947. The *requinto* soon became a standard trio instrument as its size allowed guitarists to play faster and reach higher tones. (*See A–Z entry:* Trio)

RIAA Recording Industry Association of America. The trade association that certifies U.S. record sales. The RIAA awards a gold record for 500,000 sales, platinum for one million. U.S. Latin record labels award gold records for 50,000 sales and platinum for 100,000, though these do not represent official RIAA certifications.

Schottische (sho-tish) German for "Scottish." A slow polka; also known as German polka.

SESAC Inc. A New York–based performing rights agency.

SGAE Sociedad General de Autores y Editores (Society of Spanish Composers, Authors, and Publishers). A New York–

based songwriters' licensing and royalty collection agency.

Side Before cassette and CD singles of the '90s, record companies released single cuts on eight-inch 45 rpm vinyl discs. Rpm stands for revolutions per minute, which is the speed the disc was played on turntables. Full length CDs, introduced in the late '80s, replaced the twelve-inch 33⅓ rpm albums that came into vogue around the early '60s. Albums had replaced 78 rpm discs, which were thick and heavy and made out of acetate, and which also played on primitive turntables during the dawn of recorded music in the 1930s.

Sol a sol (soul-ah-soul) Spanish for "sun to sun." *Sol a sol* can mean sunup to sundown, as in agricultural work, or sundown to sunup, as in outdoor conjunto dances of yore and Mexican norteño and grupo dances of today.

Son (sohn) An all-encompassing term for various Mexican folk styles that are often performed by mariachi. The *son* originated in Cuba as a precursor to salsa. (*See A–Z entry:* Mariachi)

Soneo (son-knee-oh) A call-and-response exchange between a lead singer and the backing vocalists used in salsa music and also incorporated by some tropical/cumbia groups. (*See A–Z entry:* Tropical/cumbia)

Tacuachito (ta-qua-chee-toe) Spanish for "little possum." *Tacuachito* describes a shuffling possum-like step made by dancers. The dance caught on with Tejano audiences in the 1950s as the polka tempo slowed a bit. (*See A–Z entries:* Tony De La Rosa and Polka)

Tambora de rancho (tam-boh-ra de ran-show) Spanish for "ranch drum." The *tambora de rancho* is a homemade drum made from goat skin. It was used by working-class musical groups along the Texas-Mexico border in the late nineteenth and early twentieth centuries. (*See A–Z entry:* Conjunto)

Tejano (tay-ha-noe) Spanish for "Texan." Tejano is a roots-based hybrid of traditional Mexican rancheras, polkas, and cumbias updated with blues, pop, and country strains. Some Mexican Americans from Texas refer to themselves as Tejanos. (*See A–Z entry: Tejano*)

Tejano Conjunto Festival An annual week-long live music festival organized in 1982 by San Antonio's Guadalupe Cultural Arts Center, a Latino community center that provides arts programming. The festival annually features conjunto pioneers and contemporary performers and also inducts influential artists into its hall of fame.

Tejano Music Awards/TMAs Tejano's version of the People's Choice Awards. The TMAs are held annually in the Alamodome, in San Antonio, Texas, and the awards are sponsored by the Texas Talent Musicians' Association, which started the event in 1981. Most winners are selected through a survey of some 50,000 Texas households with Hispanic surnames. Within the encyclopedia entries, these awards are referred to as the TMAs. Music industry professionals vote on separate Industry Awards for best musician categories. Tejano's best musicians are annually inducted into the TMA's Hall of Fame.

Texachi A Tex-Mex take on mariachi music invented by Tejano music pioneer Isidro Lopez.

Tex-Mex A hybrid umbrella term that encompasses all the musical subgenres featured in this book—cumbia, conjunto, mariachi, norteño, ranchera, Tejano, trio, and tropical/cumbia. However, Tex-Mex is often used as a synonym for Tejano, or any of the music along the Texas-Mexican border. The term was interchangeably used with Chicano, brown soul, and Tex-Mex funk to refer to what is widely considered modern Tejano music.

Tololoche (toe-low-low-che) A contrabass, double bass, or upright bass. The *tololoche* was commonly used in conjunto music until the electric bass pushed it aside in the 1950s.

Trio A three-guitar group that specializes in vocal harmonies and boleros. Trios are associated with the golden age of Mexican film during the 1940s and 1950s. (*See A–Z entries:* Trio and Bolero)

Tropical/Cumbia (tro-pee-cahl coom-bee-ah) A Mexican style of cumbia that uses sax, keyboards, syncopated percussion, and often humorous lyrics. Cumbias are fast songs and cumbieros are musicians who specialize in cumbias. (*See A–Z entry:* Tropical/Cumbia)

Vallenato (val-yeh-na-toe) A Colombian folk rhythm that has influenced Mexican music. (*See A–Z entry:* Vallenato)

Vaquero (vah-kay-row) A Mexican cowboy.

Vihuela (vee-way-la) A small guitar-like instrument that was invented in Spain in the thirteenth century. *Vihuelas* are common among mariachis.

Zapatéale! (za-pa-tay-ah-lay) Spanish for "Kick up your heels and dance!" *Zapatéale* is a yell that is often invoked by conjunto musicians. Another common shout is "*Anda a bailar el taconazo,*" which means "Dance the *taconazo.*"

Index

B

D

E

N

S